California Northern District

COURT AND CHAMBERS PRACTICE MANUAL

DISTRICT COURT
Standing Orders
Selected General Orders

INDIVIDUAL JUDGES
Procedures and Practices
Standing Orders
Case Management Orders and Forms
Scheduling Information
Chambers and Biographical Information

Mid-2012 Edition

Compiled by Practicing Attorneys
Meliora Law

Printed and bound in the United States of America.
ISBN: 978-0-9838302-3-8

Comments and corrections may be sent to comments@melioralaw.com. Although the publisher has made every effort to ensure the accuracy of information contained in this publication, it cannot assume liability for inadvertent errors.

Meliora Law LLC
19250 Stevens Creek Boulevard, Suite 100
Cupertino, CA 94015
www.melioralaw.com

PUBLISHER'S PREFACE

The information contained herein are current as received through March 2012.

THE PUBLISHER

March 2012

TABLE OF CONTENTS

PART II. INDIVIDUAL JUDGES – PROCEDURES AND PRACTICES, STANDING ORDERS, CASE MANAGEMENT ORDERS, AND FORMS; CHAMBERS, SCHEDULING, AND BIOGRAPHICAL INFORMATION

PART I

District Court

Standing Orders

Selected General Orders

I. Standing Orders

A. *Standing Order for All Judges of the Northern District of California – Contents of Joint Case Management Statement*

STANDING ORDER FOR ALL JUDGES OF THE NORTHERN DISTRICT OF CALIFORNIA

CONTENTS OF JOINT CASE MANAGEMENT STATEMENT

Commencing July 1, 2011, all judges of the Northern District of California will require the identical information in Joint Case Management Statements filed pursuant to Civil Local Rule 16-9. The parties must include the following information in their statement which, except in unusually complex cases, should not exceed ten pages:

1. Jurisdiction and Service: The basis for the court's subject matter jurisdiction over plaintiff's claims and defendant's counterclaims, whether any issues exist regarding personal jurisdiction or venue, whether any parties remain to be served, and, if any parties remain to be served, a proposed deadline for service.
2. Facts: A brief chronology of the facts and a statement of the principal factual issues in dispute.
3. Legal Issues: A brief statement, without extended legal argument, of the disputed points of law, including reference to specific statutes and decisions.
4. Motions: All prior and pending motions, their current status, and any anticipated motions.
5. Amendment of Pleadings: The extent to which parties, claims, or defenses are expected to be added or dismissed and a proposed deadline for amending the pleadings.
6. Evidence Preservation: Steps taken to preserve evidence relevant to the issue reasonably evident in this action, including interdiction of any document-destruction program and any ongoing erasures of e-mails, voice mails, and other electronically recorded material.
7. Disclosures: Whether there has been full and timely compliance with the initial disclosure requirements of Fed. R. Civ. P. 26 and a description of the disclosures made.
8. Discovery: Discovery taken to date, if any, the scope of anticipated discovery, any proposed limitations or modifications of the discovery rules, and a proposed discovery plan pursuant to Fed. R. Civ. P. 26(f).
9. Class Actions: If a class action, a proposal for how and when the class will be certified.
10. Related Cases: Any related cases or proceedings pending before another judge of this court, or before another court or administrative body.
11. Relief: All relief sought through complaint or counterclaim, including the amount of any damages sought and a description of the bases on which damages are calculated. In addition, any party from whom damages are sought must describe the bases on

which it contends damages should be calculated if liability is established.

12. Settlement and ADR: Prospects for settlement, ADR efforts to date, and a specific ADR plan for the case, including compliance with ADR L.R. 3-5 and a description of key discovery or motions necessary to position the parties to negotiate a resolution.

13. Consent to Magistrate Judge For All Purposes: Whether all parties will consent to have a magistrate judge conduct all further proceedings including trial and entry of judgment.

14. Other References: Whether the case is suitable for reference to binding arbitration, a special master, or the Judicial Panel on Multidistrict Litigation.

15. Narrowing of Issues: Issues that can be narrowed by agreement or by motion, suggestions to expedite the presentation of evidence at trial (e.g., through summaries or stipulated facts), and any request to bifurcate issues, claims, or defenses.

16. Expedited Trial Procedure: Whether this is the type of case that can be handled under the Expedited Trial Procedure of General Order No. 64 Attachment A. If all parties agree, they shall instead of this Statement, file an executed Agreement for Expedited Trial and a Joint Expedited Case Management Statement, in accordance with General Order No. 64 Attachments B and D.

17. Scheduling: Proposed dates for designation of experts, discovery cutoff, hearing of dispositive motions, pretrial conference and trial.

18. Trial: Whether the case will be tried to a jury or to the court and the expected length of the trial.

19. Disclosure of Non-party Interested Entities or Persons: Whether each party has filed the "Certification of Interested Entities or Persons" required by Civil Local Rule 3-16. In addition, each party must restate in the case management statement the contents of its certification by identifying any persons, firms, partnerships, corporations (including parent corporations) or other entities known by the party to have either: (i) a financial interest in the subject matter in controversy or in a party to the proceeding; or (ii) any other kind of interest that could be substantially affected by the outcome of the proceeding.

20. Such other matters as may facilitate the just, speedy and inexpensive disposition of this matter.

B. *Standing Order Regarding Case Management in Civil Cases – San Jose Division*

STANDING ORDER REGARDING CASE MANAGEMENT IN CIVIL CASES

This order sets forth requirements for initial case management in all civil matters assigned to District Judges Ronald M. Whyte, Jeremy Fogel, Lucy H. Koh, and Edward J. Davila, and Magistrate Judges Howard R. Lloyd and Paul S. Grewal. All papers filed must include the case number of the action followed by the initials of the assigned district judge or magistrate judge and, if applicable, the initials of the magistrate judge to whom the action is referred for discovery or other pretrial activity.

Plaintiff shall serve a copy of this Standing Order on all parties to this action and on all parties subsequently joined, in accordance with Fed.R.Civ.P. 4 and 5. Following service, plaintiff shall file a certificate of service in accordance with Civil L.R. 5-6(a).

All disclosure or discovery disputes in cases assigned to district judges are referred to the assigned magistrate judge for determination pursuant to Fed.R.Civ.P. 72(a). Magistrate judges themselves handle disclosure and discovery disputes in the cases assigned to them.

Before selecting a hearing date for a motion before any of the judges of the San Jose Division, counsel must confer with opposing counsel to determine that the proposed hearing date will not cause undue prejudice.

Civil motions under Civil L.R. 7-2 in cases assigned to Judge Whyte may be noticed for hearing on any Friday at 9:00 a.m.

Civil motions under Civil L.R. 7-2 in cases assigned to Judge Fogel may be noticed for hearing only after contacting Judge Fogel's administrative law clerk, Christian Delaney, at 408-535-5426 and obtaining an available date.

Civil motions under Civil L.R. 7-2 in cases assigned to Judge Koh may be noticed for hearing only after contacting Judge Koh's Courtroom Deputy, Martha Parker Brown, at 408-535-5346 and obtaining an available date.

Civil motions under Civil L.R. 7-2 in cases assigned to Judge Davila may be noticed for hearing only after contacting Judge Davila's Courtroom Deputy, Elizabeth Garcia, at 408-535-5356.

Civil motions under Civil L.R. 7-2 in cases assigned to Magistrate Judge Lloyd may be noticed for hearing on any Tuesday at 10:00 a.m.

Civil motions under Civil L.R. 7-2 in cases assigned to Magistrate Judge Grewal may be noticed for hearing on any Tuesday at 10:00 a.m.

Pursuant to Fed.R.Civ.P. 16 and 26 and Civil L.R. 16-10(a), a Case Management Conference will be held on ____________________ at ______________, at the United States Courthouse, 280 South First Street, San Jose, California. This conference may be continued only by court order pursuant to Civil L.R. 16-2(e). Parties may not stipulate to continue a Case Management Conference without court approval.

Pursuant to Civil L.R. 16-3, in advance of the Case Management Conference, counsel shall confer with their respective clients and opposing counsel for the purposes specified in Fed.R.Civ.P. 26(f), Civil L.R. 16-8 and 16-9, and in patent cases, Patent L.R. 3-1 through 3-6. A meaningful meet and confer process prior to the Case Management Conference and good faith compliance with the requirements of this Order are essential elements of effective case management. Failure to meet and confer, to be prepared for the Case Management Conference or to file a Joint Case Management Conference Statement may result in sanctions. Parties may, but are not required, to attend the Case Management Conference.

In all "E-Filing" cases when filing papers in connection with any motion for determination by a judge, the parties shall, in addition filing papers electronically, lodge with chambers a printed copy of the papers by the close of the next court day following the day the papers are filed electronically. These printed copies shall be marked "Chambers Copy" and shall be submitted to the Clerk's Office, in an envelope clearly marked with the Judge's name, case number and "E-Filing Chambers Copy." Parties shall not file a paper copy of any document with the Clerk's Office that has already been filed electronically.

IT IS SO ORDERED.

Dated: April 25, 2011

RONALD M. WHYTE
United States District Judge

JEREMY FOGEL
United States District Judge

LUCY H. KOH
United States District Judge

EDWARD J. DAVILA
United States District Judge

HOWARD R. LLOYD
United States Magistrate Judge

PAUL S. GREWAL
United States Magistrate Judge

II. General Orders

A. *General Order No. 68 – Policy on Court Refunds of Fee Over-payments*

GENERAL ORDER NO. 68

POLICY ON COURT REFUNDS OF FEE OVERPAYMENTS

The Judicial Conference of the United States has a long-standing policy that generally prohibits the refunding of fees, subject to the following narrow exceptions: duplicate payments or other erroneous overpayments of fees, special assessments, fines or restitution may be refunded. The court hereby delegates its authority to the Clerk of Court to administer refunds in such limited circumstances. Records of all fee refunds shall be maintained for a minimum of seven years.

I. The following refund procedures apply to fees not paid electronically via Pay .gov:

A. If a party discovers an overpayment, the party may request a refund by writing to the Clerk of Court. The letter should explain the circumstances leading to the request and specify the amount of the requested refund.

B. Upon receipt of a request for a refund or, in the event that court staff discover an overpayment, a Clerk's Office supervisor will review the information and, if appropriate, approve the refund.

C. If approved by a supervisor, the request or court-initiated overpayment information will be transmitted to the Financial Administrator for review and data entry, and thereafter to the Chief Deputy of Administration for final processing of the refund. If for any reason the request is denied, the requesting party shall be promptly notified of the reason for the denial.

II. The following procedures apply to fees paid electronically via Pay .gov:

A. The Clerk of Court may refund only duplicate payments in which the payor has inadvertently paid the filing fee more than once in the same case, resulting in two or more identical credit card charges and erroneous payments in which the payor has inadvertently made a fee payment when no fee was due.

B. To request a refund after making a duplicate or erroneous overpayment, the payor should, complete an Application for Refund form, which is available under the Forms section of the court's website. The Application for Refund should then be submitted to the Clerk of Court via the court's CM/ECF system by selecting "Application for Refund" from the CM/ ECF events menu.

C. Upon receipt of the Application for Refund, the Financial Administrator may approve or deny an application for refund.

D. The approval or denial of the application for refund will be entered on the case docket.

E. If the Financial Administrator denies an application for refund, the payor may make written request to the Clerk of Court to review the basis for the denial, if the Clerk of Court upholds the denial, the payor may, within ten business days of the Clerk's denial, file a motion making a request that the assigned judge or the Chief Judge if it is not case specific review the denial.

F. All authorized refunds shall be processed through the electronic credit card system, Pay.gov. If the payor's credit card is no longer valid, the Clerk of Court may cause a check to be issued through the United States Treasury. In no event shall the Clerk of Court make a cash refund.

G. In the event that an attorney or law firm repeatedly requests refunds for mistakes made when paying filing fees online, the Clerk of Court may request that the Chief Judge issue an order to show cause why additional requests for refunds by that attorney or law firm should not be denied. The order to show cause will be filed under a miscellaneous case.

IT IS SO ORDERED.

ADOPTED: November 21,2011

FOR THE COURT:

____

JAMES WARE
Chief Judge

B. *General Order No. 65 – Cameras in the Courtroom (Pilot Program)*

GENERAL ORDER NO. 65

CAMERAS IN THE COURTROOM
PILOT PROGRAM

The Northern District of California having been selected as a pilot site for the Cameras in the Courtroom Project of the Judicial Conference of the United States, any judge who elects to record a particular proceeding, shall adhere to the guidelines promulgated by the Judicial Conference Committee on Court Administration and Case Management, which are attached hereto as Appendix A.

Adopted: September 1, 2011

For the Court:

____
JAMES WARE
Chief Judge

APPENDIX A

Judicial Conference Committee on Court Administration and Case Management Guidelines for the Cameras Pilot Project in the District Courts

In September 2010, the Judicial Conference authorized a three-year pilot project to evaluate the effect of cameras in district court courtrooms, video recordings of proceedings therein, and publication of such video recordings by making them available through www.uscourts.gov, as well as participating courts' websites, if so desired. (JCUS-SEP 10, pp. 3-4). The pilot is national in scope, consisting of up to 150 individual judges from districts chosen to participate by the Federal Judicial Center (FJC), in consultation with the Court Administration and Case Management Committee (CACM).

At the Conference's direction, the CACM Committee promulgated these guidelines under which the pilot program must proceed. The Conference also authorized this Committee to periodically amend the guidelines, as necessary, to assist the pilot participants.

The Conference also directed the CACM Committee to request that the FJC conduct a study of the pilot, and the FJC will prepare interim reports after the first and second years of the pilot.

1. General Provisions

a. Participating courts must abide by these guidelines as a condition for participating in this pilot program. These guidelines will remain in effect for the duration of the pilot, unless changed by the Conference or the CACM Committee acting on its behalf.

b. Only courts participating in the pilot program may record court proceedings for the purpose of public release.

c. The pilot is limited to civil proceedings in which the parties have consented to recording.

d. Courts participating in the pilot must amend their local rules (providing adequate public notice and opportunity to comment) to provide an exception to the Judicial Conference ban on recording for judges participating in the pilot consistent with the guidelines. (A sample model local rule is included at Attachment 1.)

e. It is not intended that a grant or denial of a request to record a proceeding be subject to appellate review insofar as it pertains to and arises under these guidelines, except as otherwise provided by law.

f. Courts participating in the pilot will record or control the recording of proceedings. Recordings by other entities or persons, unless hired by or under the control of the court, are not allowed.

g. Courts participating in the pilot program will be expected to cooperate with the FJC and the CACM Committee in collecting study-specific data needed by the FJC to evaluate the pilot project on behalf of the CACM Committee.

2. Selection of Cases for Video Recording

a. The presiding judge will select cases for participation in the pilot, although parties to a case or the media may request video recording of the proceedings. Participating judges should consider recording different types of proceedings (e.g., trial and non-trial proceedings; a variety of case types; proceedings of varying sizes such as hearings, large cases, and multidistrict litigation; and proceedings with varying levels of expressed public interest).

b. Under any circumstances, proceedings may not be recorded without the approval of the presiding judge.

c. Parties must provide consent to the recording of each proceeding in a case. Consent to the recording of one proceeding in a case will not be construed as consent to any other proceeding in a case.

d. The court may

(1) establish a procedure for obtaining party consent to the recording of a proceeding selected for the pilot, including a time frame by which consent must be given; and

(2) in its discretion, hold a hearing to address objections by parties, witnesses, or others to the recording or posting of a recording for public access. Such hearings should not be recorded.

e. Using forms provided by the FJC, courts should gather data on and report to the FJC on the consent process, including which parties did not provide consent and the reasons why they did not consent.

3. Cameras and Equipment

a. Judges participating in the pilot should use the following equipment configuration for recording proceedings:

(1) Optimally, there should be at least three but no more than four cameras with microphones to record the proceedings in the courtroom. The cameras should be inconspicuous and fixed on the judge, the witness, the lawyers' podium, and/or counsel tables.

(2) The security cameras in the courtroom should not be used to record the proceedings for the pilot.

(3) There should also be a feed from the electronic evidence presentation system.

(4) The recording equipment should transmit the camera inputs to a switcher that incorporates them onto one screen. The recording equipment also should include an encoder to record the file for posting.

(5) The presiding judge should have a switch or be able to direct staff to stop a recording if the judge deems it necessary. The pilot recordings are not simulcast; thus, the judge can choose not to post the video for public view.

b. The Administrative Office will develop technical guidelines for the digital video recording equipment and will provide those guidelines to the courts selected to participate in the pilot.

c. The Administrative Office is authorized to provide limited funding for equipment as well as technical support to courts participating in the pilot. Participating courts are discouraged from purchasing new equipment. A participating court is encouraged to use its existing recording equipment so long as the equipment meets the requirements of the pilot. The court should contact the Administrative Office's Court Administration Policy Staff to request assistance and/or online/distance training for court personnel to use new or pre-existing equipment.

4. Managing the Recording

a. A presiding judge may refuse, limit, or terminate the recording of an entire case, portions thereof, or testimony of particular witnesses: in the interests of justice; to protect the rights of the parties, and witnesses, and the dignity of the court; to assure the orderly conduct of proceedings; or for any reason considered necessary or appropriate by the presiding judge.

b. The following must not be recorded:

(1) Privileged communications between the parties and their attorneys, non-public discussions between attorneys, and sidebar conversations between attorneys and the presiding judge, without the express permission of the judge.

(2) Jurors or alternate jurors while in the jury box, the courtroom, the jury deliberation room, or during recess, or while going to or from the deliberation room at any time. Coverage of the prospective jury during *voir dire* is also prohibited.

c. The court should remind all persons present in the courtroom that a recording is taking place, so as to limit noise, side conversation, and other disturbances.

d. Nothing in these guidelines will prevent a court from placing additional restrictions, or prohibiting recording or broadcasting in designated areas of the courthouse.

e. The court should help ensure that personal information covered by Fed. R. Civ. P. 5.2 and the Judicial Conference privacy policy not be uploaded for public view, including providing warnings to attorneys, parties, witnesses, and jurors about disclosing confidential and personal information.

f. If security concerns arise, the judge might consider consulting with the United States Marshals Service regarding the video recording of the judge.

5. Operating the Equipment

a. A court employee, such as a courtroom deputy, or a private contractor controlled by the court, must control the recording equipment. The Administrative Office will provide online/distance training to existing court personnel on operating the recording equipment and handling the digital files. Courts are also encouraged to seek the assistance of court personnel from other districts who have experience with the recording equipment.

b. In order to control the costs of the cameras pilot program, courts are discouraged from contracting with a private vendor for purchasing, installing, and operating the necessary equipment. If a court finds it necessary to contract with a private vendor, such a vendor must be under the authority and control of the court, including any recording activity, any files created, and the posting of recordings for public access. Moreover, the court should contact the Administrative Office's Court Administration Policy Staff for assistance in locating and contracting with the vendor.

c. The media or its representatives will **not** be permitted to create recordings of courtroom proceedings.

6. Storage and Access to Recordings

a. It is preferable that recordings of proceedings should be broken down into one- to four-hour increments (shorter time-frames are preferable due to the size of these digital files), but only as resources and equipment permit. Unless the presiding judge deems otherwise, recordings of court proceedings should be made publicly available within a few hours. Recordings should be made according to the following procedures:

(1) Recordings of court proceedings will be stored on a national server (www.uscourts.gov) to prevent burdening the operations of local court automation systems and to provide data to the FJC for the required study. Courts may also maintain a link to their recordings on their public website. Regardless of how the link is accessed, all access will be tracked on the judiciary's video hosting service.

(2) The judiciary's video hosting service will provide a unique, stable URL for use on www.uscourts.gov and on a court's own website.

b. The Administrative Office will prepare an educational instructional video to assist the courtroom deputy and court staff regarding publishing the file.

c. The court should be mindful of protecting sensitive and private information and of Judicial Conference requirements regarding transcripts in civil proceedings. (A copy of that policy is included at Attachment 2.) The court may wish to consider creating a procedure by which the parties may request that the recording, or a portion thereof, not be made publicly accessible due to privacy concerns.

d. In the event that the presiding judge decides not to make the recording publicly available, the judge must document, using the forms provided by the FJC, the reasons for the decision and send that information to the FJC.

e. The decision to upload the recording is final, and the recording will automatically be made available to the public through a national server (www.uscourts.gov) and, at the court's discretion, through a link on its public website.

f. The digital recordings emanating from the pilot (as well as any transcripts made from the recordings) are not the official record of the proceedings, and should not be used as exhibits or part of any court filing.

g. The court may wish to designate certain court personnel to coordinate media questions, and confer with the Administrative Office's Office of Public Affairs in handling those requests.

C. *General Order No. 64 – Expedited Trial Procedure*

GENERAL ORDER NO. 64
EXPEDITED TRIAL PROCEDURE

An Expedited Trial offers an abbreviated, efficient and cost effective litigation and trial process. The Northern District of California adopts the following Expedited Trial Procedure as a General Order of the Court:

Attachment A:	Procedure for Expedited Trials
Attachment B:	(Form) Agreement for Expedited Trial and Request for Approval
Attachment C:	(Form) Standing Order for All Judges of the Northern District of California – Contents of Joint Case Management Statement
Attachment D:	(Form) Standing Order for All Judges of the Northern District of California – Joint Expedited Case Management Statement

Adopted: June 21, 2011

For the Court:

____

JAMES WARE
Chief Judge

GENERAL ORDER NO. 64 – ATTACHMENT A PROCEDURE FOR EXPEDITED TRIALS

1. **Expedited Trial Procedure.**
The court encourages parties to agree to an expedited trial. The Expedited Trial Procedure is meant to offer an abbreviated, efficient and cost-effective litigation and trial alternative. Subject to the approval of the assigned judge, the following procedures shall govern. "Expedited Trial" means a consensual, binding trial before a jury or before a judge with limited discovery and limited rights to appeal.
2. **Effective Date.**
The parties shall file a written agreement, using the court form titled "Agreement for Expedited Trial and Request for Approval." Neither the agreement nor its existence shall be disclosed to the jury. The time schedule for expedited procedures and trial shall begin on the date the agreement is approved by the court.
3. **Termination of Agreement.**
The agreement may be terminated by the court upon a showing that one or more parties have not participated in good faith with the provisions of this General Order or that previously undisclosed facts have been discovered that make it inappropriate to proceed pursuant to the agreement.
4. **Applicable Rules.**
The provisions of the Expedited Trial Agreement, as approved by the court, shall supersede and govern over any inconsistencies or conflicts that arise between it and the Federal Rules of Civil Procedure or the Local Rules of this Court. Otherwise, all Federal Rules of Civil Procedure, Rules of Evidence, and Local Rules of this Court shall apply.
5. **Initial Disclosures.**
If initial disclosures have not been exchanged, or if they are not yet due, the disclosures required by Rule 26(a) (1) (A) shall be exchanged within seven (7) days after the agreement is approved by the court.
6. **Expedited Trial Conference.**
Immediately upon the filing of the agreement, plaintiff shall contact the courtroom deputy for the assigned judge and request an initial expedited trial conference. The conference shall occur no later than thirty (30) days after the filing of the agreement. Upon request of any party, the court shall permit counsel to appear by telephone. A Joint Expedited Trial Statement shall be filed seven (7) days before the conference addressing all of the topics set forth in the Standing Order for All Judges of the Northern District of California – Joint Expedited Case Management Statement, found on the Court's website: www.cand.uscourts.gov.
A case management order shall be issued following the conference. Unless otherwise ordered by the court, the order shall require the parties to exchange the documents described in Rule 26(a) (3) of the Federal Rules of Civil Procedure no later than fifteen (15) days before the pretrial conference and shall require the parties to complete all discovery no later than ninety 90 days after the expedited trial conference. All Rule 12 and pleading issues shall be resolved by the court at the expedited trial conference, except as provided in section 10 of this General Order. The court may determine the extent, if any, that previous case management orders on

matters subject to the expedited rules shall supersede or be combined with any previous orders.

7. **Pretrial Conference.**
The pretrial conference shall be held no later than one hundred fifty (150) days after the agreement is approved by the court.

8. **Discovery.**
Unless otherwise ordered by the court or by agreement of the parties, discovery shall be limited to ten (10) interrogatories per side, ten (10) document requests, ten (10) requests for admission, and fifteen (15) hours of depositions, per side. The parties may agree or the court may order, that the time for response to written discovery be shortened. Deposition time limits are inclusive of fact witnesses and expert witnesses.

9. **Expert Witnesses.**
No party shall call more than one expert witness to testify, unless permitted by the court or by agreement of the parties.

10. **Pretrial Motions.**
No pretrial motion shall be filed without leave of court, which shall be sought by a letter not to exceed one page. If leave is granted, the motion shall be in letter form, filed with the clerk, unless otherwise ordered. The response to the motion shall be by letter filed with the clerk not later than seven calendar days after receipt of the motion.
Unless otherwise permitted, no letter shall exceed three pages. A letter reply, not to exceed one page may be filed within three days after receipt of opposition. The court may decide the motion without a hearing. If the court finds that a hearing is necessary, it may establish a briefing schedule and order further briefing. Pendency of a dispositive motion shall not stay any other proceedings.

11. **Trial Date.**
Unless otherwise ordered, trial shall be held no later than six months after the agreement is approved by the court.

12. **Trial.**
Jury trial will be before six jurors and may proceed before a five-person jury if a juror is unable to serve through conclusion of trial and deliberations. The court shall conduct all voir dire and shall determine time limits for opening statements and closing argument. Each side shall have three hours to present evidence, not including time for opening statement and time for closing argument. There shall be no findings of fact or conclusions of law in non-jury trials. In multi-party trials, plaintiffs shall divide the three hours among themselves, and defendants shall divide the three hours among themselves. If the parties cannot agree to a division of trial time, the judge shall order a division.

13. **Post-trial Motions**
   (a) Post-trial motions shall be limited to determination of costs and attorney's fees, correcting a judgment for clerical error, conforming the verdict to the agreement, enforcement of judgment and motions for a new trial.
   (b) Within ten (10) court days after notice of entry of a jury verdict, a party may file with the clerk and serve on each adverse party a notice of intention to move for a new trial on any of the grounds specified in section 13(c) of these procedures. The notice shall be deemed to be a motion for a new trial.

(c) Grounds for motions for a new trial shall be limited to: (1) judicial misconduct that materially affected the substantial rights of a party; (2) misconduct of the jury; (3) corruption, fraud, or other undue means employed in the proceedings of the court or jury.

14. Judgment.
Judgment shall be entered within 30 days after a bench trial, except as ordered by the court for good cause.

15. Appeal.
Before filing an appeal, a party shall make a motion for a new trial pursuant to paragraph 13 of these procedures. If the motion for a new trial is denied, the party may appeal the judgment and seek a new trial only on grounds specified in subsection 13(c). All other grounds for appeal shall be waived and are not permitted, unless the parties agree otherwise.

GENERAL ORDER NO. 64 – ATTACHMENT B

IN THE UNITED STATES DISTRICT COURT
FOR THE NORTHERN DISTRICT OF CALIFORNIA

Case Number: C 11-xxxx

Plaintiff(s),

v.

AGREEMENT FOR EXPEDITED TRIAL AND REQUEST FOR APPROVAL

Defendant(s).
_______________________________________/

The parties agree that all litigation in the above captioned matter shall be governed by General Order No. 64, Procedure for Expedited Trials of the United States District Court for the Northern District of California ("the Expedited Trial Procedure"). This Agreement, when approved by the court, shall be binding on the parties and on the court, subject to the Termination of Agreement provision set forth in paragraph 3 of Attachment A to General Order No. 64.

In addition to the terms set forth in General Order No. 64, the parties elect and agree to the following:

□ 1. That regardless of the ultimate decision of the jury or the court, plaintiff will receive no less than $__________ in damages from defendant(s), and defendant will pay no more than $_______in damages to plaintiff. (The floor/ceiling amounts may be kept under seal by filing this document in accordance with General Order 62.)

□ 2. That plaintiff will receive no less than $__________ in attorney fees and defendant will pay no more than $ __________ in attorney fees. The judge shall determine attorney fees within the range agreed by the parties. (The floor/ceiling amounts may be kept under seal by filing this document in accordance with General Order 62.)

□ 3. That the judge may order equitable relief consistent with and within the options agreed to by the parties, e.g., injunctive relief, promises to implement policies or practices, etc.

□ 4. That the following trade-offs to reduce the scope of the litigation and the trial be adopted (e.g., to forego pretrial motions, such as motions to dismiss, motions for summary judgments, etc., in exchange for limitations on damages, including waiver of punitive damages): ___________.

□ 5. That the following limitations on Pre-Trial Conference obligations to the extent permitted by the court be adopted:____.

□ 6. That the number of peremptory challenges will be reduced to ______ per side.

□ 7. That limits on evidentiary matters (e.g., allow hearsay, limit objections in deposition to form and reserving all others) will be altered as follows: ___________________________.

□ 8. Other:____.

The parties agree that any and all rights to appeal from the judgment are waived by all parties, except as provided in section 15 of Attachment A to General Order No. 64.

Dated: ____________________ ________________________
Counsel for plaintiff

Dated: ____________________ ________________________
Counsel for defendant

IT IS ORDERED that the forgoing Agreement is approved. The parties shall request an Initial Expedited Trial Proceeding and file a Joint Expedited Trial Statement.

Dated: ____________________ ________________________
United States District Judge

GENERAL ORDER NO. 64 – ATTACHMENT C

STANDING ORDER FOR ALL JUDGES OF THE NORTHERN DISTRICT OF CALIFORNIA

CONTENTS OF JOINT CASE MANAGEMENT STATEMENT

Commencing July 1, 2011, all judges of the Northern District of California will require the identical information in Joint Case Management Statements filed pursuant to Civil Local Rule 16-9. The parties must include the following information in their statement which, except in unusually complex cases, should not exceed ten pages:

1. Jurisdiction and Service: The basis for the court's subject matter jurisdiction over plaintiff's claims and defendant's counterclaims, whether any issues exist regarding personal jurisdiction or venue, whether any parties remain to be served, and, if any parties remain to be served, a proposed deadline for service.
2. Facts: A brief chronology of the facts and a statement of the principal factual issues in dispute.
3. Legal Issues: A brief statement, without extended legal argument, of the disputed points of law, including reference to specific statutes and decisions.
4. Motions: All prior and pending motions, their current status, and any anticipated motions.
5. Amendment of Pleadings: The extent to which parties, claims, or defenses are expected to be added or dismissed and a proposed deadline for amending the pleadings.
6. Evidence Preservation: Steps taken to preserve evidence relevant to the issue reasonably evident in this action, including interdiction of any document-destruction program and any ongoing erasures of e-mails, voice mails, and other electronically recorded material.
7. Disclosures: Whether there has been full and timely compliance with the initial disclosure requirements of Fed. R. Civ. P. 26 and a description of the disclosures made.
8. Discovery: Discovery taken to date, if any, the scope of anticipated discovery, any proposed limitations or modifications of the discovery rules, and a proposed discovery plan pursuant to Fed. R. Civ. P. 26(f).
9. Class Actions: If a class action, a proposal for how and when the class will be certified.
10. Related Cases: Any related cases or proceedings pending before another judge of this court, or before another court or administrative body.
11. Relief: All relief sought through complaint or counterclaim, including the amount of any damages sought and a description of the bases on which damages are calculated. In addition, any party from whom damages are sought must describe the bases on which it contends damages should be calculated if liability is established.

12. Settlement and ADR: Prospects for settlement, ADR efforts to date, and a specific ADR plan for the case, including compliance with ADR L.R. 3-5 and a description of key discovery or motions necessary to position the parties to negotiate a resolution.

13. Consent to Magistrate Judge For All Purposes: Whether all parties will consent to have a magistrate judge conduct all further proceedings including trial and entry of judgment.

14. Other References: Whether the case is suitable for reference to binding arbitration, a special master, or the Judicial Panel on Multidistrict Litigation.

15. Narrowing of Issues: Issues that can be narrowed by agreement or by motion, suggestions to expedite the presentation of evidence at trial (e.g., through summaries or stipulated facts), and any request to bifurcate issues, claims, or defenses.

16. Expedited Trial Procedure: Whether this is the type of case that can be handled under the Expedited Trial Procedure of General Order No. 64 Attachment A. If all parties agree, they shall instead of this Statement, file an executed Agreement for Expedited Trial and a Joint Expedited Case Management Statement, in accordance with General Order No. 64 Attachments B and D.

17. Scheduling: Proposed dates for designation of experts, discovery cutoff, hearing of dispositive motions, pretrial conference and trial.

18. Trial: Whether the case will be tried to a jury or to the court and the expected length of the trial.

19. Disclosure of Non-party Interested Entities or Persons: Whether each party has filed the "Certification of Interested Entities or Persons" required by Civil Local Rule 3-16. In addition, each party must restate in the case management statement the contents of its certification by identifying any persons, firms, partnerships, corporations (including parent corporations) or other entities known by the party to have either: (i) a financial interest in the subject matter in controversy or in a party to the proceeding; or (ii) any other kind of interest that could be substantially affected by the outcome of the proceeding.

20. Such other matters as may facilitate the just, speedy and inexpensive disposition of this matter.

GENERAL ORDER NO. 64 – ATTACHMENT D

STANDING ORDER FOR ALL JUDGES OF THE NORTHERN DISTRICT OF CALIFORNIA

CONTENTS OF JOINT EXPEDITED CASE MANAGEMENT STATEMENT

Commencing July 1, 2011, all judges of the Northern District of California will require the following information in Joint Expedited Case Management Statements filed pursuant to General Order No. 64, which should not exceed five pages:

1. Expedited Trial Approval: Date Expedited Trial Agreement approved by the Court.
2. Motions: All prior and pending motions, their current status, and any anticipated motions.
3. Disclosures: Whether there has been full and timely compliance with the initial disclosure requirements of Fed. R. Civ. P. 26 and General Order No. 64 Attachment A, ¶ 5.
4. Discovery: Discovery taken to date, if any, the scope of anticipated discovery, any proposed limitations or modifications of the discovery rules, and a proposed discovery plan pursuant to Fed. R. Civ. P. 26(f) and General Order No. 64, Attachment A, ¶ 8.
5. Settlement and ADR: Whether the parties wish a settlement conference before a magistrate judge or some other form of ADR.
6. Consent to Magistrate Judge For All Purposes: Whether all parties will consent to have a magistrate judge conduct all further proceedings including trial and entry of judgment.
7. Narrowing of Issues: Issues that can be narrowed by agreement or by motion, suggestions to expedite the presentation of evidence at trial (e.g., through summaries or stipulated facts), and any request to bifurcate issues, claims, or defenses.
8. Scheduling: Proposed dates for designation of experts, discovery cutoff, hearing of motions permitted by General Order No. 64, Attachment A, ¶ 10, pretrial conference, and trial.
9. Trial: Whether the case will be tried to a jury or to the court.
10. Such other matters as may facilitate the just, speedy and inexpensive disposition of this matter.

D. General Order No. 62 – Electronic Filing of Documents Under Seal

GENERAL ORDER NO. 62

ELECTRONIC FILING OF DOCUMENTS UNDER SEAL

Pending consideration of a revision to Civil Local Rule 79-5, **IT IS HEREBY ORDERED** that effective May 10, 2010, the following procedures shall apply to the filing of sealed documents in civil cases:

1) Motions to file documents under seal shall be made electronically.

2) In order to move to electronically file [e-file] an entire document under seal pursuant to Civil Local Rule 79-5(b), or a portion of a document under seal pursuant to Civil Local Rule 79-5(c), (1) e-file an Administrative Motion to File Under Seal, in conformance with Civil Local Rule 7-11, (2) e-file under seal and serve manually one or more Declarations (instructions on how to e-file under seal are available on the ECF website under FAQs), (3) e file the Proposed Order (filed unsealed) and e-mail the Proposed Order to the Judge's proposed order e-mail address and (4) serve manually, but do not e-file, the documents to be filed under seal.

3) Lodge with the Clerk for delivery to the Judge's chambers a copy of the entire filing including the documents to be filed under seal, contained in an 8 ½- inch by 11- inch sealed envelope or other suitable sealed container, with a cover sheet affixed to the envelope or container, setting out the information required by Civil Local Rule 3-4(a) and (b) prominently displaying the notation: "DOCUMENT SUBMITTED UNDER SEAL AND CHAMBERS COPY" no later than noon on the business day following the day that the Administrative Motion is filed electronically.

4) If the Court orders that the motion to file under seal is denied in part or in full, neither the document nor any proposed redacted version may be e-filed under seal. If the motion is denied in full, the submitting party may retain the document and not make it part of the record in the case, or, within 4 days, e-file the document unsealed. If the motion is denied in part and granted in part, the party may within 4 days resubmit the document in a manner that conforms to the Court's order and this rule.

5) If a motion to file under seal is granted in part or full, the requesting party will e-file the document under seal according to the procedures outlined in the FAQs on the ECF website.

6) Unless otherwise ordered by the Court, any document filed under seal shall be kept from public inspection, including inspection by attorneys and parties to the action, during the pendency of the case. The chambers copy of sealed documents will be disposed of in accordance with the assigned Judge's discretion. Ordinarily these copies will be recycled, not shredded, unless special arrangements are made.

7) Any document filed under seal in a civil case shall be open to public inspection without further action by the Court 10 years from the date the case is closed. However, a party that submitted documents that the Court placed under seal in a case may, upon showing good

cause at the conclusion of the case, seek an order that would continue the seal until a specific date beyond the 10 years provided by this rule. Nothing in this rule is intended to affect the normal records destruction policy of the United States Courts.

ADOPTED: April 27, 2010

FOR THE COURT:

VAUGHN R WALKER
United States District Chief Judge

E. General Order No. 61 – Immigration Mandamus Cases

GENERAL ORDER NO. 61

IMMIGRATION MANDAMUS CASES

In any civil action seeking a writ of mandamus regarding immigration benefits, filed pursuant to the mandamus statute, 28 USC § 1361, and/or the Administrative Procedure Act, 5 USC §§ 701 *et seq*, the court **ORDERS**, pursuant to Federal Rule of Civil Procedure 16, that the following shall apply:

1. Plaintiff shall identify each such action as an "IMMIGRATION MANDAMUS CASE" in the case caption on the first page of the complaint.

2. The clerk's office shall file in each such action a procedural order which specifies that (a) the defendant shall serve and file an answer within 60 days of receipt of service of the summons and complaint; (b) subject to sub-paragraph (c), the plaintiff may file a motion for summary judgment at any time permitted by the Federal Rules of Civil Procedure and this court's local rules, in which event defendant may respond as permitted by the Federal Rules of Civil Procedure and this court's local rules; (c) if the plaintiff has not filed a motion for summary judgment within 90 days of filing the complaint, the defendant shall be the party who shall first file a motion for summary judgment, and the defendant must serve and file that motion within 120 days of service of the complaint; (d) unless a motion pursuant to Federal Rule of Civil Procedure 56(f) is filed, the plaintiff shall serve and file any opposition and/or counter-motion within 30 days of service of defendant's motion;(e) defendant may serve and file a reply and/or opposition within 14 days of service of plaintiff's opposition or counter-motion; and (f) if plaintiff filed a counter-motion, plaintiff may serve and file a reply within 14 days of service of defendant's opposition.

3. For scheduling purposes, motions shall be noticed in accordance with Civil Local Rule 7-2. If a party wishes to have the court decide the matter on the briefs and without oral argument, a party may make that request pursuant to Civil Local Rule 7-1(b).

4. Unless the court orders otherwise, no case management conference will be held, and no ADR process is required.

5. Any party who wishes to have a case management conference, pursuant to Civil Local Rule 16-10, may request that the court set a case management conference, consistent with the time frame set forth in Civil Local Rule 16-2. The rules set forth under Federal Rule of Civil Procedure 26 and Civil Local Rules 16-9 and 16-10 shall apply.

6. The court on its own motion or on the joint request of the parties may waive any requirement of this order.

ADOPTED: June 17, 2008

FOR THE COURT:

VAUGHN R. WALKER
United States District Chief Judge

F. *General Order No. 59 – Electronic Availability of Transcripts of Court Proceedings*

GENERAL ORDER NO. 59

ELECTRONIC AVAILABILITY OF TRANSCRIPTS OF COURT PROCEEDINGS

Pursuant to the requirements of the E-Government Act of 2002 and in accordance with the policy adopted by the Judicial Conference of the United States (the "Conference") in September 2007, transcripts of proceedings before United States District Judges and Magistrate Judges in the Northern District of California that are filed with the Court shall also be filed in electronic format. The Court will follow Conference policy as to when such transcripts will be electronically available to the public as delineated below. The Court will also follow the requirements of the E-Government Act relating to the redaction of personal identification information from transcripts before they are made electronically available to the general public as further delineated below. That policy, as delineated below, establishes a procedure for counsel to request the redaction from the transcript of specific personal data identifiers before the transcript is made electronically available to the general public. The personal identifiers that must be redacted are as follows: social security numbers; financial account numbers; names of minor children; dates of birth; and, home addresses of individuals.

1. Any transcript of a proceeding filed on or after May 15, 2008 shall be electronically filed through the Court's Case Management/Electronic Case Files (CM/ECF) system. Any transcript of a sealed proceeding shall be filed in accordance with whatever procedure is in effect for the filing of sealed documents at the time of filing.

2. For the first 90 days after the transcript is electronically filed, access to the transcript in CM/ECF will be restricted to (a) court staff; (b) public terminal users; (c) attorneys of record or parties who have purchased the transcript from the court reporter or transcriber; and (d) other persons as directed by the court.

3. The Clerk shall provide to all parties electronic notice of the filing and of the redaction requirements. Redaction is limited to the following personal identifiers which must be redacted: (a) Social Security numbers; (b) financial account numbers; (c) names of minor children; (d) dates of birth; and, (e) home addresses of individuals. Within five business days of the filing of an official transcript, a party must file electronically a Notice of Intent to Request Redaction for any transcript in need of such redaction on the court-approved form, which shall be available on the forms page of the Court's Internet site: http://www.cand.uscourts.gov. The Clerk shall provide the court reporter with a copy of the filed form. If no such notice is filed, the Court will assume no redaction of personal identifiers from the transcript is necessary.

4. If a party files a Notice of Intent to Request Redaction, within 21 calendar days from the filing of the transcript with the Clerk, or longer if ordered by the Court, the party must submit directly to the court reporter a statement indicating where the personal identifiers appear in the transcript by page and line and how they are to be redacted. The format of redactions shall comply with Civil Local Rule 3-17. For example, if a party wanted to redact

the Social Security number 123-45-6789 appearing on page 12, line 9 of the transcript, the statement would read: "Redact the Social Security number on page 12, line 9 to read xxx-xx-6789." A party is only responsible for reviewing and indicating the redactions in the testimony of the witnesses it called and its own statements (*e.g.*, opening statements and closing arguments). Only the personal identifiers listed above may be redacted by the court reporter on a party's request. Within 31 calendar days of the original transcript filing date, the court reporter or transcriber shall perform the redactions and electronically file a redacted version of the transcript. If a party wants other information redacted from the transcript, that party must move the Court for further redaction by noticed motion served on all parties and the court reporter. The transcript will not be electronically available to the general public until the Court has ruled on any such motion. Counsel appointed pursuant to the Criminal Justice Act may claim compensation, at the applicable rate, for the time spent reviewing the transcript and preparing the request for redaction, as well as for costs associated with obtaining a copy of the transcript.

5. If a transcript is redacted by the court reporter pursuant to this General Order, the following certification shall be used: "I certify that the foregoing is a correct transcript from the record of the proceedings in the above-entitled matter, as amended by the redaction of certain personal identifiers at the request of the parties [and by the Court]."

6. To minimize the need for redaction of a transcript, counsel are admonished to minimize their use of unnecessary personal identifiers at any proceeding at which a record is being taken.

7. Nothing in this order or Conference policy is intended to create a private right of action against a court reporter for any failure to redact the required information or for any errors associated with such redaction. This order and Conference policy do not affect in any way the obligation of the court reporter to file promptly with the Clerk of Court the court reporter's original records of a proceeding or the inclusion of a filed transcript with the records of the court pursuant to Title 28 USC § 753, nor do they affect the obligation of the Clerk to make the official transcript included in the court file available for copying by the public without further compensation to the court reporter.

ADOPTED: April 25, 2008

FOR THE COURT:

____

VAUGHN R. WALKER
United States District Chief Judge

G. *General Order No. 58 – Regulating Possession and Use of Electronic Devices in the Courthouse*

GENERAL ORDER NO. 58

REGULATING POSSESSION AND USE OF ELECTRONIC DEVICES IN THE COURTHOUSE

The purposes of this General Order are to promote security for all persons who enter federal courthouses (or the portions of federal buildings occupied by the District Court), to protect the integrity of judicial proceedings, to facilitate legitimate use of electronic devices for communication or for the storage, retrieval, or presentation of information, and to comply with the mandates of the Federal Rules of Criminal Procedure and the policies of the Judicial Conference of the United States.

I. Definition: "Electronic Device"

As used in this General Order, the phrase "electronic device" embraces all equipment (regardless of how it is powered or operated) that can be used for

A. wireless communication; or

B. receiving, creating, capturing, storing, retrieving, sending, or broadcasting any signals or any text, sound, or images; or

C. accessing the internet or any other network or off-site system or equipment for communicating or for storing or retrieving information.

II. Federal Rule of Criminal Procedure 53 prohibits "the taking of photographs in the courtroom during judicial proceedings or the broadcasting of judicial proceedings from the courtroom."

III. Policy of the Judicial Conference of the United States prohibits, in both civil and criminal cases in all district courts, broadcasting, televising, recording, or photographing courtroom proceedings for the purpose of public dissemination.

IV. Additional Rules in this District

Except as may be otherwise ordered by a judge of this court, possession and use of electronic devices and cameras in federal courthouses in this district, and in the portions of buildings in which judicial proceedings are held, shall be governed by the following rules and policies:

A. Court security personnel will screen all electronic devices and cameras before permitting them to be brought into the courthouse or into any facility or portion of any facility in which a judicial proceeding is held. The purpose of this screening is to make sure that the items do not contain weapons, dangerous devices or materials, or contraband.

1. Court security personnel may bar from the courthouse, or from portions of a building in which judicial proceedings are held, any item that appears to pose a threat to security or safety.

2. In response to a violation of any provision of this General Order, or of any court order addressing matters covered by this General Order, court security personnel may order immediate compliance, direct the offender to leave the courtroom or the building, temporarily confiscate the device(s) used in violation of these rules, and/or report the violation to the presiding judge, the Chief Judge, and/or the United States Attorney.

B. Subject to the screening described in the preceding paragraph and to other provisions of this General Order, electronic devices may be brought into the courthouse and may be used in a nondisruptive manner in the common areas of the building.

C. Photographs may not be taken and images may not be captured by any means in the courthouse or in the courthouse portions of the building (this prohibition does not apply to sketch artists).

D. Except as may be permitted pursuant to paragraph E, below, or as authorized for the taking of the official record of judicial proceedings or grand jury deliberations by a court reporter or court recording operator, or as necessary to facilitate necessary language translations, no part of any judicial proceedings or of any deliberations by a petit jury or a grand jury may be recorded, or transmitted.

E. With the exception of court personnel and court reporters, and with the further exception of laptops, PDAs or their equivalent used by counsel during and in connection with judicial proceedings, no electronic device may be used in any courtroom without express permission, in advance, from the presiding judge.

1. Counsel who wish to use electronic devices other than laptops, PDAs or their equivalent during and in connection with judicial proceedings must secure permission, in advance, from the judge presiding over those proceedings.

2. Cell phones, pagers, and other electronic communication devices may be activated only in the 'vibration' mode inside courtrooms or jury rooms. Such devices may not be activated in courtrooms or jury rooms in any mode that uses any sound to alert the user to incoming communication.

F. Jurors may not use any electronic device in a courtroom during judicial proceedings or in a jury room during or in connection with deliberations.

Grand jurors may not use any electronic device during or in connection with any proceedings before or deliberations by the grand jury. Cell phones, pagers, and their equivalent may be activated in courtrooms or jury rooms only in the 'vibration' mode.

ADOPTED: October 20, 2005 FOR THE COURT:

VAUGHN R. WALKER
United States District Chief Judge

H. General Order No. 56 – Americans with Disabilities Act Access Litigation

GENERAL ORDER NO. 56

AMERICANS WITH DISABILITIES ACT ACCESS LITIGATION

In any action which asserts denial of a right of access protected by Titles II or III of the Americans with Disabilities Act, 42 USC §§ 12131-89, the Court **ORDERS**, pursuant to Federal Rule of Civil Procedure 16, that the following shall apply:

1. Plaintiff shall, pursuant to Federal Rule of Civil Procedure 4(m), forthwith complete service on all necessary defendants. A plaintiff who is unable to complete service on all necessary defendants within 60 days may, prior to the expiration of that period, file a Motion For Administrative Relief pursuant to Civil Local Rule 7-11 requesting an extension of the schedule required by this Order.

2. Initial disclosures required by Federal Rule of Civil Procedure 26(a) shall be completed no later than seven days prior to the joint inspection and review required by ¶3. For example, in a Title III action, if defendant intends to dispute liability based on the construction or alteration history of the subject premises, defendant shall disclose all information in defendant's possession or control regarding the construction or alteration history of the subject premises. In a Title II action, if defendant intends to dispute liability based on overall programmatic compliance, a transition plan, or a self-evaluation plan, defendant shall disclose all information in defendant's possession or control regarding such programmatic compliance, transition plan, or self-evaluation plan. If plaintiff claims damages under California law, plaintiff shall include in the initial disclosures the damages computation required by Rule 26(a)(1)(A)(iii), but need not include attorney's fees. All other discovery and proceedings are STAYED unless the assigned judge orders otherwise. Notwithstanding any other provision of this General Order, any dispute concerning the adequacy of the Rule 26(a) disclosures may be submitted to the court under Civil Local Rule 7.

3. No later than 100 days after filing the complaint, the parties and their counsel, accompanied by their experts if the parties so elect, shall meet in person at the subject premises. If plaintiff alleges only programmatic or policy violations, the parties and their counsel may meet in person at any mutually agreeable location. They shall jointly inspect the portions of the subject premises, and shall review any programmatic or policy issues, which are claimed to violate the Americans with Disabilities Act.

4. At the joint inspection and review required under ¶3, or within ten (10) business days thereafter, the parties, and their experts if the parties so elect, shall meet in person and confer regarding settlement of the action. The meet and confer obligation cannot be satisfied by telephone or by exchanging letters. At the conference, the parties shall discuss all claimed access violations. Plaintiff shall specify all claimed access violations and the corrective actions requested of defendant. With respect to each claimed violation, defendant shall specify whether defendant is willing to undertake the requested corrective actions or has an alternate proposal. If defendant claims any proposed corrective action is not readily achievable under Title III or otherwise required by law, defendant shall specify the factual basis for this claim.

5. If the parties reach a tentative agreement on injunctive relief, plaintiff shall forthwith provide defendant with a statement of costs and attorney's fees incurred to date, and make a demand for settlement of the case in its entirety (including any additional damages not included in the Rule 26(a) disclosures).

6. If within 45 days from the joint site inspection and review, the parties cannot reach an agreement on injunctive review, or cannot settle the damages and fees claims, plaintiff shall file a "Notice of Need for Mediation" in the form set forth on the Court's ADR Internet site www.adr.cand.uscourts.gov and on the ECF Website www.ecf.cand.uscourts.gov. The matter will then be automatically referred to mediation and the ADR Program will schedule a mediation as soon as possible. The mediator shall have the authority to preside over settlement negotiations that address all issues presented by this matter, including requests for injunctive relief, damages and attorney's fees. Should a settlement be reached, the mediator shall ensure that the parties make a written or audio record of the essential terms of the settlement sufficient to permit any party to move to enforce the settlement should it not be consummated according to its terms. Should any settlement be conditioned upon future conduct such as remediation, the assigned judge will retain jurisdiction to enforce that component of the settlement.

7. If the case does not resolve at mediation, plaintiff shall within seven calendar days of the mediator's filing of a Certification of ADR Session reporting that the mediation process is concluded, file a Motion For Administrative Relief pursuant to Civil Local Rule 7-11 requesting a Case Management Conference.

8. Any party who wishes to be relieved of any requirement of this order may file a Motion for Administrative Relief pursuant to Civil Local Rule 7-11.

ADOPTED: June 21, 2005
AMENDED: February 17, 2009
November 5, 2009

FOR THE COURT:

____

VAUGHN R. WALKER
United States District Chief Judge

I. *General Order No. 54 – Submission of Sentencing Materials to the United States Sentencing Commission*

GENERAL ORDER NO. 54

SUBMISSION OF SENTENCING MATERIALS TO THE UNITED STATES SENTENCING COMMISSION

This General Order of the Northern District of California is intended to constitute compliance with Section 994(w)(1) of Title 28 as amended effective May 1, 2003.

The United States Probation Department of this District shall submit to the United States Sentencing Commission ("Sentencing Commission" or "Commission") within 30 days of the entry of judgment in every criminal case the following materials:

A) the judgment and commitment order;

B) the statement of reasons for the sentence imposed (which shall include the reason for any departure from the otherwise applicable guideline range);

C) all plea agreements including agreements filed under seal which shall be accompanied by the court order sealing the agreement;

D) all indictments, superseding indictments, informations and superseding informations filed in the action from the inception of the action; and

E) the presentence report which shall be accompanied by the court's sealing order.

It is the practice in this District that the presentence reports include the offense or offenses upon which the sentence is imposed, the age, race, and sex of the offender and all information regarding factors made relevant by the guidelines. The reports shall continue to include this information.

The court finds that the above materials contain all of the information required by Section 994(w)(1) sufficient to constitute the written report until such time as the Commission instructs otherwise.

Any sealed materials required to be submitted to the Commission shall be accompanied by the issuing court's sealing order.

This order is intended to meet the continuing requirement that the Chief Judge of this District ensure compliance with Section 994(w)(1) of Title 28 as amended effective May 1, 2003, until further instruction by the Sentencing Commission.

ADOPTED: May 20, 2003

FOR THE COURT:

MARILYN HALL PATEL
Chief Judge

Sample Sealing Order

IN THE UNITED STATES DISTRICT COURT
FOR THE NORTHERN DISTRICT OF CALIFORNIA

No. CR_________

Plaintiff,

SEALING ORDER

v.

Defendant.
____________________________________/

The following documents in this action are placed under seal and shall not be opened except by the United States Sentencing Commission for its eyes only and shall not be transmitted or otherwise opened except by order of this court upon application:

□ Presentence Report _____________
□ Plea Agreement ________________
□ _______________________(Other)

IT IS SO ORDERED.

Dated: _________________

____
United States District Judge

J. *General Order No. 50 – Amended Criminal Justice Act Procedures for Voucher Payment and Funding Requests*

GENERAL ORDER NO. 50

AMENDED CRIMINAL JUSTICE ACT PROCEDURES FOR VOUCHER PAYMENT AND FUNDING REQUESTS

I. VOUCHER SUBMISSIONS AND APPROVAL

A. Introduction

Payment of fees and expenses to counsel appointed under the Criminal Justice Act (CJA) Plan of the United States District Court for the Northern District of California (General Order 2, referred to herein as the "Plan"), and payment for investigative, expert and other services shall be made in accordance with the provisions as set forth herein, Volume 7 of the Guide to Judiciary Policy, the fiscal policies of the Administrative Office of the United States Courts and the CJA Panel Attorney Manual for the Northern District of California.

B. Approval Authority

Claims for compensation of private attorneys and others furnishing services under the Act shall be submitted to the Clerk's Office CJA Unit on the appropriate CJA voucher with supporting documentation. Authority under the Criminal Justice Act to approve vouchers claiming reimbursement is delegated to the CJA Supervising Attorney, who will authorize payment for the following after reviewing for reasonableness and mathematical accuracy:

1. Vouchers for attorneys;
2. Vouchers for service providers requesting payment under $800 or that are within funding limits pre-authorized by a District or Magistrate Judge in felony, misdemeanor, non-capital habeas and other criminal proceedings;
3. Vouchers for attorneys and service providers in capital habeas cases in which the expenditures were previously authorized in a budget that was approved by a District Judge;
4. Vouchers for transcript services, interpreter services and routine travel.

C. Voucher Reductions

1. Judicial Approval. The CJA Supervising Attorney shall obtain the approval of the assigned Judge with respect to a proposed voucher reduction which exceeds $450.
2. Attorney Notification. If the CJA Supervising Attorney determines that an appointed counsel's claim should be reduced, the attorney will be provided prior notice of the proposed reduction, a brief statement of the reason(s) for it, and a reasonable opportunity to address the matter.

D. Statutory Maximums

When compensation exceeds, or is expected to exceed, the statutory maximums permitted pursuant to 18 U.S.C. § 3006A(d)(3), counsel must submit a supporting declaration or memorandum justifying excess payment before payment will be authorized. Counsel may also use the CJA Form 26 for this purpose, which may be downloaded from the Court's website. All vouchers claiming amounts in excess of the statutory maximums will be forwarded by the CJA Supervising Attorney to the Court of Appeals as required by Vol. 7 of the Guide to Judiciary Policy.

E. Authorization to Submit Interim Vouchers
Appointed counsel may request to submit interim vouchers for cases that are extended or complex in nature. In all cases where an interim payment order has been filed, including those where withholding has previously been ordered, the Clerk's Office shall discontinue withholding funds from interim payments, effective March 21, 2000.

F. CJA Forms 20 and 30 (Attorneys)

1. Billing Worksheets. When submitting CJA Forms 20 and 30, Counsel must also submit: a) one or more worksheets in the same format as the worksheets provided on the Court's website (cand.uscourts.gov/cja/forms); or b) an invoice generated by the attorney's timekeeper system in a format that provides itemization of tasks in chronological order and sorted by voucher category. When the Court implements an electronic voucher system, counsel will be required to submit worksheets according to the requirements of that system. The CJA Unit will reject worksheets and billing documentation that are not in the proper format.

2. Worksheet Detail. If the level of detail is insufficient for auditing purposes, vouchers will be returned to counsel for resubmission with adequate detail. Worksheets and timekeeper invoices must include the following:

   a. Time billed must be in tenths of an hour;

   b. Each entry must reflect discreet tasks;

   c. Attorneys may not "bundle" separate unrelated tasks in one entry;

   d. Attorneys may not list multiple tasks performed in a specific block of time;

   e. Without violating the Canons of Ethics or disclosure of attorney work product, entries must include specific detail to permit meaningful review including, but not limited to: specifying identifying information for witness interviews;[1]

   f. Identification of participants in telephone conversations or conferences and topic discussed;[2]

   g. Specific topics researched and identification, by ECF docket number, of pleadings filed as a result of the research;

   h. Identification of documents reviewed, including the number of pages;

   i. Identification of documents prepared, including the number of pages

---

1 In lieu of identifying witnesses by name, counsel may identify witnesses by type (i.e., "guilt-phase witness #1") in sufficient detail to enable the Court to distinguish between individuals interviewed.

2 A simple description of the general topic of discussion is sufficient.

and ECF docket number, if filed; for documents not filed, an explanation sufficient to explain their relevance to the case.

G. CJA Forms 21 and 31 (Service Providers)
Appointed experts and other service providers shall submit supporting documentation for services rendered in a format that provides adequate detail. Interpreters must use the invoice that is available on the Court's website (cand.uscourts.gov/cja/forms).

H. Compensation
No claim for compensation or reimbursement will be honored unless filed within sixty (60) days of the termination of the representation; for good cause shown, this deadline may be extended by counsel contacting the CJA Supervising Attorney and requesting additional time.

II. REQUESTS FOR INVESTIGATIVE, EXPERT AND OTHER SERVICES

A. Authority to Approve Funding Requests

1. CJA Supervising Attorney. The CJA Supervising Attorney is authorized to approve and authorize requests for transcripts, routine travel and interpreter services. In addition, District and Magistrate Judges may delegate to the CJA Supervising Attorney authority to approve requests for associates, paralegals and investigators.

2. District and Magistrate Judges. All funding requests that exceed $800, except those indicated in Part II A)(1), must be approved and authorized by the assigned District or Magistrate Judge, if the services are required in connection with a matter over which the Magistrate Judge has jurisdiction (or if a District Judge has otherwise referred such application to a Magistrate Judge).

B. Procedures for Obtaining Funding

1. Counsel appointed under the Act may obtain investigative, expert or other services. Counsel not appointed under the Act may also obtain such services for a person who is financially unable. Requests for services rendered in cases handled by the Federal Public Defender Organization do not require court approval if they are paid from the Federal Public Defender Office budget.

2. Quality of Services. The Court, in all cases, will hold counsel accountable to obtain only qualified service providers and to carefully review the providers' bills to assure that the charges are accurate and reasonable.

3. Upon Request. To request services, counsel appointed under the Act must either (1) submit an ex parte sworn application and declaration to the District or Magistrate Judge assigned to the matter or (2) through an *in camera* ex parte proceeding, if permitted by the assigned District or Magistrate Judge. All ex parte applications must be submitted to the CJA Unit. The assigned District or Magistrate Judge, or the CJA Supervising Attorney to whom this responsibility has been delegated, will decide whether (1) the services are necessary and the person is financially unable to obtain them, and (2) will establish the limitations of such services including number of hours, hourly

rate and dollar maximum.

4. Without Prior Request. Counsel appointed under the Act may obtain, subject to later review, investigative, expert or other services without prior authorization if necessary for adequate representation under the following circumstances:

   a. the total cost of services obtained without prior authorization does not exceed $800 plus the cost of expenses reasonably incurred; counsel must submit a detailed invoice with CJA Form 21 or 31, as appropriate.

   b. the services exceed $800 and prior authorization could not have reasonably been obtained. Counsel must submit an ex parte application and declaration as soon as possible justifying the services, a request for *nunc pro tunc* authorization to the date services were first rendered, and a thorough explanation of why prior authorization could not have reasonably been obtained. If the Court denies the request in whole or in part, the Court will not be liable for refusal to pay for services rendered in excess of authorized funds.

III. CJA DOCUMENTATION

A. Confidentiality

All CJA documents shall be filed in the confidential CJA financial files maintained by the Clerk's Office. Documents maintained in the CJA financial files shall not be disclosed to the public except as provided by statute, by the Guide to Judiciary Policy or by order of the Court. Accordingly, it is not necessary for counsel to request sealing of CJA documents.

B. Standardized Forms

Where standard forms have been approved by the Judicial Conference of the United States or an appropriate committee thereof and have been distributed by the Administrative Office, such forms shall be used in connection with all actions taken under the Plan and the provisions set forth herein.

C. All questions not addressed herein should be directed to the CJA Unit.

This General Order becomes effective on December 20, 2011.

IT IS SO ORDERED.

ADOPTED: JUNE 30, 2000
AMENDED: OCTOBER 16, 2000
APRIL 24, 2001
JUNE 18, 2002
MARCH 15,2005
DECEMBER 20, 2011

FOR THE COURT:

____

CHIEF JUDGE
United States District Court
Northern District of California

K. General Order No. 45 – Electronic Case Filing Guidelines

GENERAL ORDER NO. 45
ELECTRONIC CASE FILING

I. Rules and Orders.

A. Authorization. Local Rule 5-4 authorizes electronic filing in conjunction with Federal Rule of Civil Procedure 5(e) and Federal Rule of Criminal Procedure 49(b) and (d). The following policies shall govern electronic filing in this district.

B. Modification by the court. In extraordinary circumstances in a particular case, a judge may modify these policies in the interest of justice.

C. Applicability of Other Rules and Orders. Unless modified by approved stipulation or order of the court or a judge, all Federal Rules of Civil and Criminal Procedure, Local Rules, and orders of the court shall continue to apply to cases which are subject to electronic filing.

II. Definitions and Instructions.

The following definitions and instructions shall apply to these policies regarding electronic filing:

A. The term "ECF" refers to the court's Electronic Case File program.

B. The term "ECF web site" refers to the official Electronic Case File Internet site of the Northern District of California at http://ecf.cand.uscourts.gov.

C. "Electronic Filing" refers to the process of logging in to the court web site and completing a transaction which includes the uploading of the document(s) comprising the filing to the court's system. Sending a document by email does not constitute an electronic filing.

D. The term "party" shall include counsel of record.

E. An "ECF User," as set forth in Section 4 below, is a person who is registered to use the ECF site. An ECF login is an attorney's individual electronic signature equivalent.

F. The "E-Mail Address of Record" is the e-mail address of each party to the case as maintained by the Clerk.

G. A "Notice of Electronic Filing" is generated automatically by the ECF system upon completion of an electronic filing. The Notice of Electronic Filing when e-mailed to the email addresses of record in the case acts as the proof of service.

H. All hours stated shall be Pacific time.

I. All days are calculated according to the provisions of Federal Rule of Civil Procedure 6(a).

J. "PACER" is the Federal Judiciary's system for Public Access to Court Electronic Records. A PACER account is required for retrieving documents from the ECF system as it is for most Judiciary online systems. A firm may register for a PACER account by visiting the PACER Service Center's web site at http://pacer.psc.uscourts.gov.

K. Procedures and instructions for using the Court's ECF system consistent with these policies may be found on the ECF web site. The ECF web site, as well as providing access to filing and retrieval of documents, also contains instructions, a user manual, tutorials, an extensive posting concerned with Frequently Asked Questions ("FAQs"), bulletins of changes in the program, including its software, etc.

L. The term "PDF" refers to Portable Document Format, a specific computer file format which is the only format in which a document may be electronically filed. Information about PDF can be found on the ECF web site. (*See also* Sec. VI.B.)

III. Selection of Cases.

Except for certain types of cases, all cases shall be presumptively designated for participation in the court's ECF program. A list of the types of cases exempt from e-filing may be found on the ECF web site. In the event that a *pro se* party obtains counsel in a case which had been excluded from e-filing because of *pro se* party status, the case will be automatically designated for the e-filing program.

IV. Registration, Appearance and Access.

A. Obligation to Register. Each attorney of record is obligated to become an ECF User and be assigned a user ID and password for access to the system upon notification that the action is subject to ECF. Registration shall be on a form prescribed by the Clerk. Attorneys of record who fail to register timely shall be subject to such sanctions as may be imposed by the Court.

B. Obligation to Keep Account Information Current. An e-filer login account is a permanent, individual electronic signature equivalent for a particular attorney. Registered attorneys are required to keep their account information current. Account information may be updated online at the ECF web site.

C. Notification of Appearance. Because the ECF system's e-mailed Notices of Electronic Filing (*see* Sec. II.G) will only be delivered to the original addressee, it is important to keep the list of counsel current. Counsel shall follow these instructions:

1.) A Notice of Appearance should be filed whenever counsel joins a case.

2.) In the event that counsel from the same firm replace one another as representatives of a client, a Notice of Substitution of Counsel shall be filed.

3.) In the event that a particular counsel ceases to be involved with a case when the party is still represented by other counsel, a Notice of Change in Counsel shall be filed.

4.) The withdrawal of a party's sole remaining counsel is governed by Civil Local Rule 11-5 and requires an order of the court.

5.) The replacement of one firm by another as counsel for a party also requires an order of the court.

Upon receipt of the preceding notifications, the Clerk of Court will update the record of appearances of counsel.

D. Authorizing Use of User ID and Password by Others. An ECF User may authorize another person to file a document using the User ID and Password of the ECF User, and the ECF User shall retain full responsibility for any document so filed.

E. Access.

1.) Filing: Only an ECF user as defined in Section IV.A may file documents.

2.) Retrieval: Any person may review at the clerk's office all filings, electronic or paper, that have not been sealed by the court. Any person also may access the Electronic Filing System at the court's ECF web site by obtaining a PACER log-in and password. Any person who has PACER access may retrieve online docket sheets in civil and criminal cases which are not sealed, and may retrieve online documents which are not sealed with the following exceptions:

a.) Exceptions in Civil Cases: Any person who has PACER access may retrieve online electronically filed documents in civil cases other than Social Security appeals. Only counsel for a party to the case may retrieve online documents in a Social Security appeal.

b.) Exceptions in Criminal Cases (**Limited Access** filings): Any person who has PACER access may retrieve online electronically filed documents in criminal cases, except that counsel in criminal cases may designate particular filings as **"Limited Access"** if they contain sensitive personal information. Any document, filed in response to a Limited Access filing, that also refers to the personal information shall also be designated as Limited Access. The words **LIMITED ACCESS** shall be prominently displayed on any such documents so designated. Such documents can be retrieved at the clerk's office but may not be retrieved online.

V. Filing and Service of Documents.

A. Initiating Documents. Complaints, indictments and informations, including superseding indictments and informations, and other case-initiating documents shall be filed, any fees paid, and summons issued and served in the traditional manner on paper rather than electronically. For cases subject to ECF pursuant to Section III. above, all previously filed documents shall be submitted in electronic form (PDF format only) within ten days. Submission of initiating documents must be made by email rather than by efiling. A list of email addresses for the submission of PDF documents may be found at the ECF web site. In Bankruptcy appeal and Social Security appeal cases, the record from the court or agency below shall not be submitted electronically, but shall be submitted on paper only. Failure to email PDF copies of initiating documents timely shall be subject to such sanctions as may be imposed by the Court.

B. Documents Filed on Paper in Cases Designated for ECF. Whenever a paper filing is made of any document in a case designated for e-filing, the document shall be submitted in electronic form (PDF format only) within ten days via email to the appropriate email address. A list of email addresses for the submission of PDF documents may be found at the ECF web site.

C. Documents E-Filed in Cases Not Designated for ECF. Filings in cases not designated for electronic filing should be made on paper only. In the event a document is e-filed in a case not designated for electronic filing, the document must be submitted to the court for the purpose of completing the paper file; the document should not be filed again. The filer of the document should mark the paper copy clearly with "E-filed on [date]. Copy for paper file."

D. Service and Answer. Upon the filing of a complaint in an action which is subject to ECF, the plaintiff(s) shall serve notice upon the defendant(s) that the action is subject to ECF, and shall serve the ECF handout, received by the filer at the time of opening the case which contains information necessary for registration, together with the complaint. The defendant shall register to become an ECF User following the procedures outlined at the ECF web site if not already registered. If the defendant is a registered ECF User pursuant to Section II.D above, the answer shall be filed electronically. If the defendant is unable to electronically file the answer or other responsive document, it may be filed nonelectronically, and the defendant shall within ten days submit the answer or other responsive documents in electronic form (PDF format only), to an e-mail address for that purpose which may be found on the ECF web site, for attachment to docket entries previously made by the Clerk's Office.

VI. Electronic Filing.

A. Generally. In any case subject to electronic filing, all documents required to be filed with the Clerk shall be filed electronically on the ECF web site, except as provided otherwise in Section VII or authorized otherwise by the court.

B. Format. Documents filed electronically must be submitted in the PDF format. Documents which the filer has in an electronic format must be converted to PDF from the word processing original, not scanned, to permit text searches and to facilitate transmission and retrieval. Only documents of which the filer possesses only a paper copy may be scanned to convert them to PDF format. (*See* Section X. for rules governing the filing of documents with signatures not those of the e-filer.)

C. Completion of Filing. Electronic transmission of a document consistent with the procedures adopted by the court shall, upon the complete receipt of the same by the Clerk and together with the receipt of a Notice of Electronic Filing from the court, constitute filing of the document for all purposes of the Federal Rules of Civil and Criminal Procedure and the Local Rules of this Court, and shall constitute entry of that document onto the docket maintained by the Clerk pursuant to Federal Rules of Civil Procedure 58 and 79, and to Federal Rules of Criminal Procedure 49 and 55.

D. Deadlines. Filing documents electronically does not alter any filing deadlines. All electronic transmissions of documents must be completed (*i.e.*, received completely by the Clerk's Office) prior to midnight in order to be considered timely filed that day. Where a specific time of day deadline is set by Court order or stipulation, the electronic filing shall be completed by that time. Although parties can file documents electronically 24 hours a day, attorneys and parties are strongly encouraged to file all documents during normal working hours of the Clerk's Office when assistance is available.

E. Technical Failures. The Clerk shall deem the ECF web site to be subject to a technical failure on a given day if the site is unable to accept filings continuously or intermittently over the course of any period of time greater than one hour after 12:00 noon that day, in which case filings due that day which were not filed due solely to such technical failures shall become due the next business day. Such delayed filings shall be accompanied by a declaration or affidavit attesting to the filing person's failed attempts to file electronically at least two times after 12:00 noon separated by at least one hour on each day of delay due to such technical failure. The initial point of contact for any practitioner experiencing difficulty filing a document into the ECF system shall be the toll-free number posted on the ECF web site.

F. Docket. The record of filings and entries created by the ECF system for each case shall constitute the docket.

G. Courtesy Copies. In all cases subject to ECF, in addition to filing papers electronically, the parties are required to lodge for chambers no later than noon on the business day following the day that the papers are filed electronically, one paper copy of each document that is filed electronically. These printed copies shall be marked "Chambers Copy" and shall be clearly marked with the judge's name, case number, and "Chambers Copy-Do Not File." The printed copies shall be delivered to the Clerk's Office. Parties shall not file a paper copy of any document with the Clerk's Office that has already been filed electronically.

VII. Manual Filing.

A. Generally. Parties otherwise participating in ECF may be excused from filing a particular component electronically if it is not available in electronic format and it is not feasible for the filer to convert it to electronic format by scanning it. Such component shall not be filed electronically, but instead shall be manually filed with the Clerk of Court and served upon the parties in accordance with the applicable Federal Rules of Civil and Criminal Procedure and the Local Rules for filing and service of non-electronic documents. Parties manually filing a component shall file electronically a Manual Filing notification setting forth the reason(s) why the component cannot be filed electronically. Further information regarding the notification of the manual filing of a document can be found on the ECF web site.

1. Exhibits. Exhibits whose electronic original is not available to the filer and must therefore be scanned to PDF should be filed electronically only when the size of the document does not exceed the limit specified on the ECF web site. Scanning documents often produces files which are too large to be readily usable. Exhibits which are filed on paper because they are too large to scan should be represented in the electronic filing by a Notice of Manual Filing attached in place of the actual document.

B. Exclusions. Some types of documents shall only be filed conventionally and not electronically unless specifically authorized by the court. A list of documents to be filed manually may be found on the ECF web site.

VIII. Proposed Orders.

A. Generally. In addition to being filed, proposed orders in cases designated for e-filing shall be lodged with the court by being transmitted by electronic mail to the specific addresses for that purpose which may be found on the ECF web site.

B. Format. Documents transmitted pursuant to this section shall be submitted in an approved format, a list of which can be found on the ECF web site. When a proposed order accompanies a filing, a copy of the proposed order in PDF format should also be attached to its electronically filed document (*e.g.*, stipulations and motions.)

IX. Service of Electronically Filed Documents.

A. Generally. Parties in cases subject to ECF shall make available electronic mail addresses for service. Upon the filing of a document by a party, an e-mail message will be automatically generated by the electronic filing system and sent to all parties in the case. Receipt of this message shall constitute service on the receiving party. In addition to receiving e-mail notifications of filing activity, the parties are strongly encouraged to check the docket in their case on the electronic filing system at regular intervals. A PACER account will be necessary to check the electronic docket.

B. Parties in Cases Subject to ECF. The automatic e-mail message generated by the ECF system and sent to all parties whose e-mail addresses have been registered in the case, as described in Section A. above, shall constitute service on the attorney or other persons in a case subject to ECF.

C. Parties Who Have Not Registered as ECF Users.

1. Third Party Defendants. Upon the filing of a third-party complaint in an action which is subject to ECF, the third-party plaintiff(s) shall serve notice upon the third-party defendant that the action is subject to ECF, and shall serve the ECF handout, received by the filer at the time of opening the case which contains information necessary for registration, together with the third-party complaint. The third-party defendant shall register to become an ECF User following the procedures outlined at the ECF web site if not already registered. If the third-party defendant is a registered ECF User pursuant to Section II.D above, the third-party answer shall be filed electronically. If the third-party defendant is unable to electronically file the answer or other responsive document, it may be filed nonelectronically, and the defendant shall within ten days submit the answer or other responsive documents in electronic form (PDF format only), to an e-mail address for that purpose which may be found on the ECF web site, for attachment to docket entries previously made by the Clerk's Office.

2. Others. In an action subject to ECF, when service of a document other than a third-party complaint is required to be made upon a person who is not a registered ECF User, a paper copy of the document shall be served on the person (as otherwise required by the Federal Rules of Civil and Criminal Procedure or the Local Rules), along with a copy of the ECF handout received by the filer at the time of opening the case which contains information necessary for registration. If the person so served is permitted or required to respond to the document, such time to respond shall be computed without regard to ECF. The person shall register to become an ECF User following the procedures outlined at the ECF web site if not already registered. If the person is a registered ECF User pursuant to Section II.D above, the responsive document shall be filed electronically. If the

defendant is unable to electronically file the responsive document, it may be filed nonelectronically, and the defendant shall within ten days submit the responsive document in electronic form (PDF format only), to an e-mail address for that purpose which may be found on the ECF web site, for attachment to docket entries previously made by the Clerk's Office.

D. Service of the Court's Orders. Orders filed by the court in cases designated for electronic filing will be served only via the email Notice of Electronic Filing. No paper service will be made by the court.

X. Signatures.

A document filed with the court electronically shall be deemed to be signed by a person (the "Signatory") when the document identifies the person as a Signatory and the filing complies with either subparagraph A or B. Any filing in accordance with any of these methods shall bind the Signatory as if the document were physically signed and filed, and shall function as the Signatory's signature, whether for purposes of Rule 11 of the Federal Rules of Civil Procedure, to attest to the truthfulness of an affidavit or declaration, or for any other purpose.

All orders, decrees, judgments, and proceedings of the court will be filed in accordance with these rules which will constitute entry on the docket kept by the clerk under Federal Rules of Civil Procedure 58 and 79 and Federal Rules of Criminal Procedure 49 and 55. All signed orders will be filed electronically by the court or court personnel. Any order filed electronically without the original signature of a judge has the same force and effect as if the judge had affixed the judge's signature to a paper copy of the order and it had been entered on the docket in a conventional manner.

A. ECF Users. In the case of a Signatory who is an ECF User, such document shall be deemed signed, regardless of the existence of a physical signature on the document, provided that such document is filed using the User ID and Password of the Signatory.

B. Others. In the case of a Signatory who is not an ECF User, or who is an ECF User but whose User ID and Password will not be utilized in the electronic filing of the document, as in the case of documents requiring multiple signatures, the filer of the document shall list thereon all the names of any other signatory or signatories. The filer shall attest that concurrence in the filing of the document has been obtained from each of the other signatories, or from the single signatory (in the case, *e.g.*, of a declaration) which shall serve in lieu of their signature(s) on the document. The filer's attestation may be incorporated in the document itself, or take the form of a declaration to be attached to the document. The filer shall maintain records to support this concurrence for subsequent production for the court if so ordered or for inspection upon request by a party until one year after final resolution of the action (including appeal, if any). The filer may attach a scanned image of the signature page(s) of the document being electronically filed in lieu of maintaining the paper record for subsequent production if required.

C. Criminal Cases. Any document signed by a criminal defendant shall be scanned in its entirety to insure that an image of the defendant's signature is visible in the filing, notwithstanding the provisions of Section VI.B. Any document with multiple signatories in a criminal case shall be scanned in its entirety. Certain documents which may be used by other agencies shall be scanned in their entirety to include images of the signatures; a list of such documents will be found on the ECF web site.

XI. Record on Appeal.

Until such time as the United States Courts of Appeals for the Ninth Circuit and the Federal Circuit institute rules and procedures to accommodate Electronic Case Filing, notices of appeal to those courts shall be filed, and fees paid, in the traditional manner on paper rather than electronically. All further documents relating to the appeal shall be filed and served in the traditional manner as well. Appellant's counsel shall provide paper copies of the documents that constitute the record on appeal to the District Court Clerk's Office.

XII. Access to Rules.

These policies, as well as operational guidelines and instructions, shall be posted on the ECF web site and may be published in official legal newspapers in this district. Any amendments to ECF procedures shall be similarly published.

ADOPTED: 12/15/98
AMENDED: 1/16/01
AMENDED: 2/12/02
AMENDED: 4/8/03
AMENDED: 11/18/04

FOR THE COURT:

____
VAUGHN R. WALKER
United States District Chief Judge

L. *General Order No. 43 – Procedures Regarding Execution Scheduled Within Seven Days*

GENERAL ORDER NO. 43

PROCEDURES – EXECUTION SCHEDULED WITHIN SEVEN DAYS

I. PURPOSE

The purpose of this General Order is to ensure prompt, orderly processing of death penalty-related cases and requests for stays filed when an execution is imminent. To this end, it allocates and centralizes responsibility for making the initial decisions required for proper filing and assignment of these cases. It also provides that these decisions shall conform to existing local rules, general orders and the Assignment Plan, except as specifically otherwise noted in this order.

II. PROCEDURES

A. Application

The procedures set forth in this General Order shall be in effect during the seven days preceding a scheduled execution of any California state inmate under sentence of death. While they are in effect, the procedures apply to filings by or on behalf of that inmate.

B. Duties of the Clerk of Court

1. The Clerk shall at all times maintain a record of all filings in this Court by California inmates sentenced to death that seek *habeas corpus* or civil rights relief from the execution of the sentence of death, showing the name of the petitioner, the date of each filing and the Judge to whom the cases are assigned.

2. When an execution is scheduled, the Clerk shall determine whether the condemned inmate has previously filed an action that seeks *habeas corpus* or civil rights relief from the execution of the sentence of death in this or any other district court in California. If so, the Clerk shall assist the San Francisco General Duty Judge ("the General Duty Judge") in making arrangements so that the Judge assigned the prior case will be immediately available to decide any emergency stay requests based on any new filing that may be assigned or transferred to that Judge pursuant to this General Order.

3. The San Francisco Office of the Clerk of Court shall remain open for telephone and filing access, on an emergency basis, after the close of normal business hours on the last court day before a scheduled execution, until notice is received that: the execution has gone forward; or, the execution is stayed and all applications to vacate the stay have been denied; or, the execution warrant has expired.

4. During the time described in B.3. above, the Clerk shall designate a person or persons to receive the filings on an emergency basis and make the required telephone calls, and a person or persons to serve as messenger to deliver papers to and from the General Duty Judge, the assigned Judge, and the Court of Appeals. The Clerk shall maintain 24-hour telephone and facsimile numbers for: the Judge assigned to any previous action that seeks *habeas corpus* or civil rights relief from the execution of the sentence of death filed by the inmate whose execution is scheduled, the Office of the Clerk and Motions Panel of the Ninth

Circuit Court of Appeals, the Warden of San Quentin Prison and the United States Supreme Court staff attorney responsible for coordinating emergency applications in capital cases.

5. Immediately upon receipt of papers presented for filing that request a stay of execution the Clerk shall deliver the papers to the General Duty Judge, and shall notify the Judge assigned to that inmate's previous related filings, if any.

6. If the General Duty Judge is unavailable within one hour after the Clerk attempts to contact him or her, or not available immediately if the execution is scheduled within the hour, the Clerk shall contact the Chief Judge immediately for designation of a Duty Judge. If the Chief Judge is not available, the Clerk shall call each active judge of the court in order of seniority, and then each senior judge, until an available Judge is located. That Judge will act as General Duty Judge for the purposes of this order.

C. Duties of the General Duty Judge

1. During the seven days preceding a scheduled execution, the General Duty Judge shall be immediately available during normal business hours. After the close of normal business hours on the last court day before a scheduled execution, the General Duty Judge shall be in the Bay Area and immediately available by telephone until notice is received that: the execution has gone forward; or, the execution is stayed and all applications to vacate the stay have been denied; or, the execution warrant has expired. The Clerk shall provide a cellular telephone and facsimile machine, if needed, to the General Duty Judge.

2. The General Duty Judge shall act as the decision-maker in applying the rules and procedures of the court. Before the inmate's papers requesting a stay of execution are filed, the General Duty Judge shall decide, among other things, whether the inmate has previously filed in this court an action that seeks *habeas corpus* or civil rights relief from the execution of the sentence of death, and whether the inmate has previously sought *habeas* relief in another district court. The General Duty Judge shall then instruct the Clerk how the case shall be assigned, in accordance with subsection C.3. below.

3. Local court rules and the Assignment Plan shall apply to the assignment of all cases where an emergency stay of execution is requested, except as set forth in this order.

a. If the inmate has previously filed in this court an action that seeks *habeas corpus* relief from the conviction and sentence of death, the new filing shall be assigned to the Judge assigned to the prior petition. If the inmate has not previously filed in this court a *habeas corpus* petition seeking relief from the conviction and sentence of death but has previously filed an action that seeks civil rights relief from the execution of the sentence of death, the case shall be assigned to the Judge assigned to the prior civil rights proceeding.

b. If the inmate has previously sought *habeas corpus* relief from the conviction and sentence of death in another district court, the General Duty Judge shall transfer any new *habeas* filing seeking such relief to that district court. The Clerk shall assign any such case a miscellaneous case number and immediately transmit a copy of the transfer order by facsimile to the other district.

c. If the case is not assigned or transferred pursuant to C.3.a. or b. above, or if the Judge of this Court who had the prior case or petition is no longer sitting or has taken senior status and elected not to hear death-penalty-related cases, the Clerk shall assign the case randomly either from the Capital *Habeas Corpus* category if it falls within that category (*see* footnote 1 to General Order 44) or from the Prisoner Petitions case category. Consistent with General Order 44, Sec. O.2.c., cases assigned pursuant to this subparagraph may not be assigned to a newly-appointed judge until after that judge has received his or her first capital *habeas corpus* assignment.

d. If an inmate files a Notice of Related Case seeking to relate the newly filed case to another case not filed by that inmate, the procedures of Local Rule 3-12(e) shall be followed, except that the Notice of Related Case shall be submitted immediately to the Judge assigned to the earliest filed case, without waiting for support or opposition. If the Clerk cannot contact that Judge to obtain an immediate ruling on the related case request within one hour of the filing of the Notice of Related Case, or immediately if the execution is scheduled within the hour, the request to relate the cases shall be deemed denied without prejudice.

e. Notwithstanding the above, the General Duty Judge shall have the power to assign any patently frivolous execution-related filing by or on behalf of the prisoner to himself or herself as a miscellaneous filing, and to dismiss such filing summarily as provided by law.

4. The Clerk shall attempt to reach the Judge to whom the case should be assigned pursuant to C.3. a., c. or d. above. If the Clerk cannot contact that Judge within one hour of the filing of the request for the stay of execution, or immediately if the execution is scheduled within the hour, the General Duty Judge shall decide the request for the stay.

5. The regularly assigned General Duty Judge and Chief Judge may transfer the duties of the General Duty Judge to another Judge of the Court.

ADOPTED BY THE COURT: February 20, 1996
AMENDED: July 18, 2000

FOR THE COURT:

____

MARILYN HALL PATEL
Chief Judge

M. General Order No. 42 – Limitations on Referrals of Matters to Magistrate Judges

GENERAL ORDER NO. 42

LIMITATIONS ON REFERRALS OF MATTERS TO MAGISTRATE JUDGES

It is the policy of the court to promote the efficient utilization of magistrate judges and to avoid the unnecessary duplication of judicial action. Good cause appearing,

IT IS HEREBY ORDERED that the following matters shall not be referred to a magistrate judge:

1. Civil pretrial matters that are dispositive of a claim or defense and require a *de novo* review by a district judge under Rule 72(b), F.R.Civ.P. unless: (a) the parties consent to final disposition of the matter by a magistrate judge pursuant to Rule 73, F.R.Civ.P.; or (b) the matter requires an evidentiary hearing which can be conducted by a magistrate judge without being repeated before a district judge. Case dispositive matters include motions for summary judgment, for judgment on the pleadings, for injunctive relief, to dismiss for failure to state a claim upon which relief can be granted, to dismiss or permit maintenance of a class action, and to involuntarily dismiss an action. *See* 28 U.S.C. § 636(b)(1)(A);

2. Prisoner petitions and *habeas corpus* cases unless: (a) the parties consent to final disposition of the matter by a magistrate judge pursuant to Rule 73, F.R.Civ.P.; or (b) the matter is not a capital *habeas* case and requires an evidentiary hearing which can be conducted by a magistrate judge without being repeated before a district judge;

3. Case dispositive matters in criminal felony cases including motions to dismiss an indictment or information made by a defendant or to suppress evidence;

4. Acceptance of guilty pleas of a defendant in a criminal felony case pursuant to Rule 11, F.R.Crim.P. unless there are exceptional circumstances that warrant referral; and

5. Claim Construction hearings and determinations in patent infringement cases pursuant to Patent Local Rule 4-6, unless the parties consent to disposition by a magistrate judge pursuant to Rule 73, F.R.Civ.P. Exceptions to this Order in individual cases or in emergency circumstances may be granted by the Executive Committee.

ADOPTED: January 23, 1996
AMENDED: January 16, 2001

FOR THE COURT:

____

MARILYN HALL PATEL
Chief Judge

N. General Order No. 40 – Prohibition of Bias

GENERAL ORDER NO. 40
PROHIBITION OF BIAS

Prologue

The Court is committed to ensuring that all forms of bias and prejudice are eliminated from the practice of law in our district. Accordingly, the Court enacts the following General Order and shall amend its local rules to implement the policy set forth herein. It should be noted that the General Order is intended to govern the conduct of attorneys and litigants since existing law already places a duty of fair treatment on judges and court employees. While the enforcement procedures set forth in paragraphs (2) through (6) apply only to attorneys, paragraph (1) calls upon all participants involved in court business to treat all individuals with respect and courtesy.

Duties and Procedures

(1) The practice of law before the United States District Court for the Northern District of California must be free from prejudice and bias in any form. Treatment free of bias must be accorded all other attorneys, litigants, judicial officers, courtroom jurors or support personnel. The duty to exercise nonbiased behavior includes the responsibility to avoid comment or behavior manifesting prejudice or bias toward another. This duty is owed by all attorneys, judges, judicial officers and court personnel in connection with cases pending before the district court.

(2) The purpose of the facilitation process set forth herein shall be principally to promote understanding and education through voluntary peer review of biased behavior. To implement the policy set forth in paragraph (1), the Court shall appoint a committee of attorneys practicing in the Northern District to constitute the Advisory Committee on Professional Conduct ("the Committee"). The roster of the Committee shall remain on file with the Clerk of the Court. It shall be the responsibility of the Committee, serving at the discretion of the Court as an advisory adjunct, to hear complaints of biased behavior and to provide a forum for the voluntary resolution of conflicts of this nature.

(3) Upon being directly notified of an alleged violation of paragraph (1) or upon referral from the Court, the chair of the Committee shall, after consultation with the complaining party, appoint a member of the Committee or other appropriate, neutral facilitator who shall provide the parties a copy of this rule, and then attempt to facilitate a resolution of the matter. When deemed necessary in a particular case by the Committee, the chair of the Committee may appoint a facilitator who is not on the roster. Participation by the parties shall be voluntary, but the Court, by this rule, encourages participation. All matters that are the subject of facilitation, including the names of the parties, shall remain absolutely confidential.

(4) Attorneys are encouraged to resolve alleged violations of paragraph (1) informally, without resort to the processes set forth herein. If attempts at informal resolution fail or would be inappropriate, an alleged violation of paragraph (1) may be raised through: a) referral to the Committee; or b) formal presentation to the Court. When the matter has been

presented to the Court, the Court has discretion to send the matter to the Committee for facilitation. However, nothing in this rule shall affect the Court's inherent power to use its processes to ensure that the practice of law before the Court is free from bias. Where a Judge or Magistrate Judge is alleged to have engaged in biased behavior, enforcement of paragraph (1) shall be made with reference to Title 28 U.S.C. §372(c) and to the Rules of the Judicial Council of the Ninth Circuit Governing Complaints of Judicial Misconduct or Disability.

(5) All communications by the parties and witnesses pursuant to an investigation under this rule shall be deemed confidential. Unless required by law, the Committee shall not retain written records of the facilitation processes. However, the Committee may collect data on types of alleged violations or underlying anecdotes that might be useful in educational programs, provided that the identities of participants shall not be disclosed.

(6) Notwithstanding the foregoing, any violation of paragraph (1) committed in the presence of the Court should be addressed promptly by the Court. Any violation, whether or not committed in the presence of the Court (such as misconduct in the presence of witnesses or jurors), that affects the integrity of the judicial process should be promptly raised with the Court.

ADOPTED: January 10, 1995

O. *General Order No. 32 – Modification of Probation/Supervised Release Conditions for Placement in a Community Treatment Center*

GENERAL ORDER NO. 32

MODIFICATION OF PROBATION/SUPERVISED RELEASE CONDITIONS FOR PLACEMENT IN A COMMUNITY TREATMENT CENTER

The United States Probation Office for the U.S. Courts often finds that, for the protection of society or the rehabilitation of the offender, it must place probationers/supervised releasees or parolees in community treatment centers. A similar need arises when a probationer is arrested, taken before a Magistrate and it is ordered that, pending a final disposition, the probationer is temporarily housed in a halfway house. On those occasions, when the need arises to place a probationer/supervised releasee in such a facility, the probation officer finds it difficult to arrange placement through the Bureau of Prisons, who is given the responsibility for payment of all Public Law placements.

Therefore, it appears that the orderly operation of the court and the United States Probation Office would be improved by allowing the United States Probation Officer of this court the authority to place probationers and supervised releasees in community treatment centers on an emergency basis and for a limited time, of not more than five (5) working days or until modified by the court, whichever is sooner.

It is hereby ordered that the United States Probation Officer of this court has the authority to place a probationer or supervised releasee in a community treatment center for a limited term, not to exceed five (5) court working days, or until further order of the court.

IT IS SO ORDERED.

DATED: September 28, 1990 FOR THE COURT:

____

CHIEF JUDGE

P. *General Order No. 25 – Appointment and Reimbursement of Pro Bono Counsel*

GENERAL ORDER NO. 25

APPOINTMENT AND REIMBURSEMENT OF PRO BONO COUNSEL

In civil cases in which one or more parties is not represented, the Court may appoint pro bono counsel pursuant to: (1) the Federal Pro Bono Project of this Court (if the pro se litigant is not a prisoner), (2) the Federal Pro Bono Prisoner Litigation Project (if the pro se litigant is a prisoner), and (3) other order or directive of the Court. The Court may appoint counsel for all purposes or for limited purposes such as representation on a dispositive motion, conduct of a deposition, representation in ADR processes, etc.

The Court may stay the case pending appointment of pro bono counsel. As soon as possible after the expiration of any such stay, the Court shall conduct a status conference with all parties represented to consider, among other things, whether expedited discovery and/or other proceedings are appropriate to facilitate efficient resolution of the case.

Pro bono counsel appointed by the Court may seek reimbursement for reasonable costs. The Court may order reimbursement for all out of pocket costs to any appointed attorney accepting clients through the Project under the following conditions:

a. The trial judge shall determine whether the expenses claimed are reasonable and necessary and may authorize reimbursement of costs up to a maximum of $15,000. Any single expense in excess of $1,000 must be approved by the trial judge prior to its incurrence of expenditure.

b. If appropriate, pro bono counsel should seek reimbursement for deposition expenses from the State of California's Transcript Reimbursement Fund, Cal. Bus. & Prof. Code § 8008 *et seq.*, before applying for reimbursement of such expenses from court funds.

c. Reimbursable costs shall include, but shall not be limited to, amounts reasonably and necessarily spent on:

- **i.** Deposition costs, except to the extent reimbursed under the California State Transcript Reimbursement Fund
- **ii.** Serving of process and delivery service
- **iii.** Filing fees, if any
- **iv.** Expert consultant and witness fees, if any
- **v.** Reasonable travel expenses for attorney
- **vi.** Reasonable investigation expenses
- **vii.** Long-distance telephone

It is the policy of the Court that reimbursement requests for this Project be liberally considered.

d. Cost reimbursement requests may be submitted by letter directly to the referring trial judge at:

United States District Court
450 Golden Gate Avenue, 16th Floor
San Francisco, CA 94102

Letters shall *not* be served on opposing parties.

e. Any expenses paid pursuant to paragraphs (a) and (b) (*see* above) must be repaid to the Court and/or to the State of California's Transcript Reimbursement Fund upon recovery of judgment or monetary settlement up to the amount of such recovery subject to allocation by the trial judge.

f. In compelling cases (for example, where pro bono representation causes a severe financial hardship on the pro bono counsel), a trial judge, with the approval of the Non-Appropriated Fund Committee, may authorize reimbursement of attorney's fees at rates commensurate with Criminal Justice Act rates up to a maximum amount of $25,000.

g. Any attorney appointed to provide legal representation without compensation through the Federal Pro Bono Project shall be exempt from paying the pro hac vice filing fee.

ADOPTED: October 13, 1982
AMENDED: November 28, 2007
September 15, 2009
January 17, 2012

FOR THE COURT:

____
JAMES WARE
United States District Chief Judge

This page intentionally left blank.

PART II

INDIVIDUAL JUDGES

PROCEDURES AND PRACTICES

STANDING ORDERS

CASE MANAGEMENT ORDERS AND FORMS

SCHEDULING INFORMATION

CHAMBERS AND BIOGRAPHICAL INFORMATION

District Judges

Hon. William H. Alsup

District Judge

Chambers Information

U.S. District Court, Northern District of California
Courtroom 8, 19th Floor
450 Golden Gate Avenue
San Francisco, CA 94102

Scheduling Information

Courtroom Deputy: (415) 522-2020

Civil Law and Motion	Thursdays at 8:00 a.m.
Criminal Law and Motion	Tuesdays at 2:00 p.m.
Case Management Conferences	Thursdays at 11:00 a.m.
Pretrial Conferences	Mondays at 2:00 p.m.

Judge's Biography

Born 1945 in Jackson, MS

Federal Judicial Service:

-Judge, U. S. District Court, Northern District of California
-Nominated by William J. Clinton on March 24, 1999, to a seat vacated by Thelton Eugene Henderson; Confirmed by the Senate on July 30, 1999, and received commission on August 17, 1999.

Education:

-Mississippi State University, B.S., 1967
-Harvard University, J.D., 1971
-Harvard University, John F. Kennedy School of Government, M.P.P., 1971

Professional Career:

-Law Clerk, Justice William O. Douglas, U.S. Supreme Court, 1971-1972
-Private Practice, San Francisco, CA, 1972-1978
-Assistant to U.S. Solicitor General, U.S. Department of Justice, 1978-1980
-Private Practice, San Francisco, CA, 1980-1998
-Special Counsel, Antitrust Division, U.S. Department of Justice, 1998
-Private Practice, San Francisco, CA, 1998-1999

I. Judge Alsup's Procedures and Practices

A. *Guidelines for Trial and Final Pretrial Conference in Civil Bench Cases*

GUIDELINES FOR TRIAL AND FINAL PRETRIAL CONFERENCE IN CIVIL BENCH CASES BEFORE THE HONORABLE WILLIAM ALSUP

FRCP 26(a)(3) Disclosures

1. All parties are reminded of their disclosure duties under FRCP 26(a)(3), which begin **THIRTY CALENDAR DAYS** before trial. The FRCP 26(a)(3)(A)(ii) requirement for designating deposition transcripts, however, need not be done until later, as set forth below, although the name of each trial witness to appear by deposition must be so designated at least **THIRTY CALENDAR DAYS** before trial.

Final Pretrial Conference

2. At least **SEVEN CALENDAR DAYS** in advance of the final pretrial conference, please file the following:

(a) A joint proposed final pretrial order, signed and vetted by all counsel, that contains: (i) a brief description of the substance of claims and defenses which remain to be decided, (ii) a statement of all relief sought, (iii) all stipulated facts, (iv) a list of all factual issues which remain to be tried, (v) a joint exhibit list in numerical order, including a brief description of the exhibit and Bates numbers, a column for when it is offered in evidence, a column for when it is received in evidence, and a column for any limitations on its use, and (vi) each party's separate witness list for its case-in-chief witnesses (including those appearing by deposition) providing, for all such witnesses other than an individual plaintiff and an individual defendant, a short statement of the substance of his/her testimony and, separately, what, if any, non-cumulative testimony the witness will give (to be used to set time limits). Items (v) and (vi) should be appendices to the proposed order.

(b) Any motion *in limine*, with the opposition, filed as follows:

At least **TWENTY CALENDAR DAYS** before the conference, serve, but do not yet file, the moving papers. At least **TEN CALENDAR DAYS** before the conference, serve the oppositions. When the oppositions are received, the moving party should collate the motion and the opposition together, back to back, and then file the paired sets at least **SEVEN CALENDAR DAYS** before the conference.

Each motion should be presented in a separate memo and numbered as in, for example, "Plaintiff's Motion in Limine No. 1 to Exclude . . . ." Please limit motions *in limine* to circumstances that really need a ruling in advance. In bench trials, usually three or fewer motions per side is sufficient at the conference stage (without prejudice to raising matters *in limine* as the trial progresses).

Each motion should address a single topic, be separate, and contain no more than seven pages of briefing per side.

(c) Copies of the Rule 26(a)(3) disclosures.

(d) Each side's proposed findings of fact and conclusions of law.

(e) Trial briefs are optional.

3. The above shall be submitted in *Word Perfect X3 or 10 format* to whapo@cand.uscourts.gov and in hard copies. *All hard-copy submissions should be three-hole punched on the left, so the judge's copy can be put in binders. Please provide them at least seven calendar days prior to the pretrial conference for the judge's study and review — THIS IS IMPORTANT.*

4. At the final pretrial conference, counsel must take notes on rulings and promptly submit a joint summary of all rulings in proposed-order format.

Pretrial Arrangements

5. Should a daily transcript and/or real-time reporting be desired, the parties shall make arrangements with Deb Campbell, Court Services Coordinator, at debra_campbell@cand.uscourts.gov.

6. Counsel are encouraged to use overhead projectors, laser-disk/computer graphics, poster blow-ups, models or specimens. The United States Marshal requires a court order to allow equipment into the courthouse. For electronic equipment, either know how to fix it or have a technician handy. For overhead projectors, have a spare bulb. Tape extension cords to the carpet for safety. Please take down and store the equipment (in the courtroom) at the end of each court day. Please work with Dawn Toland (415-522-2020) on courtroom-layout issues and contact her to learn how to use the electronic presentation system.

Scheduling

7. The normal trial schedule will be 8:00 a.m. to 1:00 p.m. (or slightly longer to finish a witness) with two fifteen-minute breaks and ending before lunch. Counsel must arrive by 7:30 a.m. The trial week is usually Monday through Friday.

Opening Statements

8. Each side will have a time limit for its opening statement (to be determined at the final pretrial conference). Counsel must cooperate and meet and confer to exchange any visuals, graphics or exhibits to be used in the opening statements.

Witnesses

9. Except for good cause, all counsel are entitled to written firm notice of the order of witnesses for the next court day and the exhibits (including merely illustrative exhibits) to be used on direct examination (other than for true impeachment of a witness). The Court encourages two days notice, *i.e.*, written notice by 2:00 p.m. on the *second* calendar day before the witnesses testify or the exhibit is used. At a minimum, notice must be no later than 2:00 p.m. on the calendar day *immediately* preceding. If two days written notice is given or two days notice is given that no documents will be used, then all other counsel must give written notice of all other exhibits to be used on cross-examination (except for true impeachment) by 2:00 p.m. on the calendar day immediately preceding the testimony; otherwise, other responding counsel need not give notice of exhibits they may use. Any exhibit timely noticed by anyone for the witness is usable as if timely noticed by everyone, subject to substantive objections. Similarly, if reference is made to an exhibit during an examination (even if not offered in

evidence and even if not noticed for use with the witness), then in any follow-up examination by others, the exhibit may be used to the same extent as if it had been timely noticed, subject to substantive objections. All notices shall be sent by fax or electronically and be time-and-date verifiable. If counsel decides not to call a noticed witness, then prompt written notice of the cancellation must be given. Impeachment exhibits are ordinarily limited to statements signed by or adopted by the witness. Compliance with a two-day notice period, of course, will not satisfy compliance with FRCP 26 or any other disclosure rule.

10. The official tagged exhibit should be shown to witnesses — not supposed copies or notebooks of supposed copies. Before the examination begins, retrieve the official tagged exhibits to be used and have them at the ready. Using copies leads to discrepancies between the exhibit actually introduced into the record (*always* the official tagged exhibit) versus the stray before the witness. The required procedure also helps find any glitches in the official tagged exhibits.

11. Always have your next witness ready and in the courthouse. Failure to have the next witness ready or to be prepared to proceed with the evidence will usually constitute resting. If counsel plans to read in a transcript of a deposition anyway, it is advisable to have a deposition prepared and vetted early on to read "just in case."

12. When there are multiple parties, counsel are responsible for coordination of the cross-examination to avoid duplication. Stand at or near the microphone to ask questions, straying only to point out material on charts or overheads. Please request permission to approach the witness or the bench.

Experts

13. A recurring problem in trials is the problem of expert witnesses trying to go beyond the scope of their expert reports on direct examination. FRCP 26(a)(2) and FRCP 37(c) limit experts to the opinions and bases contained in their timely reports (absent substantial justification or harmlessness). The Court regularly enforces these rules. FRCP 26(a) also requires that any "exhibits to be used as a summary of or support for the opinions" be included in the report. Accordingly, at trial, the direct testimony of experts will be limited to the matters disclosed in their reports. New matter may not ordinarily be added on direct examination. This means the reports must be complete and sufficiently detailed. Illustrative animations, diagrams, charts and models may be used on direct examination only if they were part of the expert's report, with the exception of simple drawings and tabulations that plainly illustrate what is already in the report, which can be drawn by the witness at trial or otherwise shown to the jury. If cross-examination fairly opens the door, however, an expert may go beyond the written report on cross-examination and/or re-direct examination. By written stipulation, of course, all sides may relax these requirements. Material in a "reply" report must ordinarily be presented in a party's rebuttal (or sur-rebuttal) case *after* the other side's expert has appeared and testified.

14. Another recurring problem is the retained expert who seeks to vouch for the credibility of fact witnesses and/or to vouch for one side's fact scenario. Qualified experts, of course, are always welcome to testify concerning relevant scientific principles, professional

standards, specialized facts known within a trade or discipline and the like (so long as it is in the report). They are also welcome to apply those principles and standards to various assumed fact scenarios. This is so even if an opinion is given on the "ultimate issue." But they should not try to vouch for one side's *fact* scenario, *i.e.*, witness believability.

15. There is an important exception. Experts and doctors who perform scientific tests, site visits or treat victims, among other possibilities, may testify to their findings within the scope of their firsthand knowledge. This is because they have made personal observations and have reached professional judgments based thereon. Carrying this one step further, even a retained expert may read a financial statement in evidence, watch a video in evidence, listen to a recording in evidence and so on, and offer opinions based on the contents. This is because the contents themselves are clearly defined.

16. As to damages studies, the cut-off date for *past damages* will be as of the expert report (or such earlier date as the expert may select). In addition, the experts may try to project *future damages* (*i.e.*, after the cut-off date) if the substantive standards for future damages can be met. With timely leave of Court or by written stipulation, the experts may update their reports (with supplemental reports) to a date closer to the time of trial.

Use of Depositions to Impeach and Short Read-Ins

17. Depositions can be used at trial to impeach a witness testifying at trial or, in the case of a party deponent, "for any purpose." Please follow the following procedure:

(a) On the first day of trial, be sure to bring the original and clean copies of any deposition(s) for which you are responsible. Any corrections must be readily available. If you are likely to need to use the deposition during a witness examination, then give the Court a copy with any witness corrections at the outset of your examination. This will minimize delay between the original question and the read-ins of the impeaching material. Opposing counsel should have their copy immediately available.

(b) When you wish to read in a passage, simply say, for example: "I wish to read in page 210, lines 1 to 10, from the witness' deposition." A brief pause will be allowed for any objection.

(c) When reading in the passage, state "question" and then read the question exactly. Then state "answer" and then read the answer exactly. Stating "question" and "answer" is necessary so that the judge and court reporter can follow who was talking at the deposition.

(d) The first time a deposition is read, state the deponent's name, the date of the deposition, the name of the lawyer asking the question, and if it was FRCP 30(b)(6) deposition, please say so.

(e) Please do NOT ask, "Didn't you say XYZ in your deposition?" The problem with such a question is that the "XYZ" rarely turns out to be exactly what the deponent said and is part spin. Instead, ask for permission to read in a passage, as above, and read it in exactly, without spin.

(f) Subject to FRE 403, party depositions may be read in whether or not they contradict (and regardless of who the witness is on the stand). For example, a short party deposition excerpt may be used as foundation for questions for a different witness on the stand.

(g) Rather than reading the passage, counsel are free to play an audiovisual digitized version of the passage but counsel must have a system for immediate display of the precise passage.

DEPOSITION DESIGNATION

18. The following procedure applies only to witnesses who appear by deposition. It does not apply to live witnesses whose depositions are read in while they are on the stand. To save time and avoid unnecessary work, it is not necessary to make all deposition designations before trial (as normally required by FRCP 26(a)(3)(A)(ii)). In the Court's experience, by the time the read-in occurs, the proponent has usually reduced substantially the proposed read-ins. Instead, the following steps should be followed.

(a) To designate deposition testimony, photocopy the cover page, the page where the witness is sworn, and then each page from which any testimony is proffered. Line through or x-out any portions of such pages not proffered. Also, line through objections or colloquy unless they are needed to understand the question. Please make sure any corrections are interlineated and that references to exhibit numbers are conformed to the trial numbers. Such interlineations should be done by hand. The finished packet should then be the actual script and should smoothly present the identification and swearing of the witness and testimony desired. The packet should be provided to all other parties at least **FIVE CALENDAR DAYS** before it will be used in court. For the rare case of voluminous designations, more lead time will be required. Please be reasonable.

(b) All other parties must then promptly review the packet and highlight in yellow any passages objected to and write in the margin the legal basis for the objections. If any completeness objection is made, the objecting party must insert into the packet the additional passages as needed to cure the completeness objection. A completeness objection should normally be made only if a few extra lines will cure the problem. Such additions shall be highlighted in blue and an explanation for the inclusion shall be legibly handwritten in the margin. Please line out or x-out any irrelevant portions of the additional pages.

(c) The packets, as adjusted, must then be returned to the proffering party, who must then decide the extent to which to accept the adjustments. The parties must meet and confer as reasonable. Counsel for the proffering party must collate and assemble a final packet that covers the proffer and all remaining issues. At least **TWO CALENDAR DAYS** before the proffer will be used, the proponent must provide the Court with the final packet, with any objected-to portions highlighted and annotated as described above. If exhibits are needed to resolve the objections, include copies and highlight and tag the relevant passages. Alert the Court on the record that the packet is being provided and whether any rulings are needed. *Tag all passages that require a ruling*. The Court will then read the packet and indicate its rulings. Ordinarily, argument will not be needed.

(d) Counter designations must be made by providing a packet with the counter-designated passages to the proponent at the same time any objections to the original proffer are returned to the first proffering party, who must then supply its objections in the same manner.

(e) When the packet is read in court, the examiner reads the questions (and any relevant colloquy) from the lectern and a colleague sits in the witness stand and reads the answers. When a video-taped deposition is to be played instead, the packets must still be prepared, as above, in order to facilitate rulings on objections. The video should omit any dead time, long pauses, and objections/colloquy not necessary to understand the answers.

REQUESTS FOR ADMISSIONS AND INTERROGATORIES

19. Please designate responses to requests for admissions and interrogatory answers in the same manner and under the same timetable as depositions.

EXHIBITS

20. As stated, FRCP 26(a)(3) disclosures regarding proposed exhibits must be made at least **THIRTY CALENDAR DAYS** before trial and any objections thereto must be made within **FOURTEEN CALENDAR DAYS** thereafter (or waived unless excused for good cause). The joint list must be filed **SEVEN CALENDAR DAYS** in advance of the final pretrial conference (as per paragraph 2 above). By designating an exhibit, a party waives any objection to authenticity and any reciprocal objection, meaning any objection mutually available to both the designating party and the opposing party if and when offered by one against the other. Therefore, the non-designating party may offer the exhibit subject only to non-reciprocal objections. For example, if P designates a record from a non-party, such as a telephone company, then D can equally offer the same exhibit save for any objection that would be unique against D. To take a contra example, if P designates D's internal email, it will usually not be admissible at the instance of D, there being a non-reciprocal hearsay hurdle when offered by D. If the designating party states that the exhibit is only for a limited purpose, then the waiver extends only to the same limited purpose. Notwithstanding the foregoing, FRE 403 objections are never waived. And, any party may always attempt to lay full foundation to admit any exhibit designated by itself or by any other party without regard to any waiver.

21. Prior to the final pretrial conference, counsel will please meet and confer in person over all exhibit numbers and objections and to weed out duplicate exhibits and confusion over the precise exhibit. Use numbers only, not letters, for exhibits, preferably the same numbers as were used in depositions. Blocks of numbers should be assigned to fit the need of the case (*e.g.*, Plaintiff has 1 to 100, Defendant A has 101 to 200, Defendant B has 201 to 300, etc.). A single exhibit should be marked only once, just as it should have been marked only once in discovery (if this Court's guidelines were followed). If the plaintiff has marked an exhibit, then the defendant should not re-mark the exact document with another number. Different *versions* of the same document, *e.g.*, a copy with additional handwriting, must be treated as different exhibits with different numbers. To avoid any party claiming "ownership" of an exhibit, all exhibits shall be marked and referred to as "Trial Exhibit No.____," not as "Plaintiff's Exhibit" or "Defendant's Exhibit." If an exhibit number differs from that used in a deposition transcript, then the latter transcript must be conformed to the new trial number if and when the deposition testimony is read to the jury (so as to avoid confusion over exhibit numbers).

22. The exhibit tag shall be in the following form:

UNITED STATES DISTRICT COURT
NORTHERN DISTRICT OF
CALIFORNIA

TRIAL EXHIBIT 100

CASE NO. ____________________
DATE ENTERED______________
BY ___________________________
DEPUTY CLERK

Place the tag on or near the lower right-hand corner or, if a photograph, on the back. Counsel should fill in the tag but leave the last two spaces blank. The parties must jointly prepare a *single* set of all trial exhibits that will be the official record set to be used with the witnesses and on appeal. Each exhibit must be tagged and in a separate folder (not in notebooks). Deposit the exhibits with the deputy clerk (Dawn Toland) on the first day of trial.

23. Please move exhibits into evidence as soon as the foundation is laid and it is fresh in the judge's mind. Do not postpone motions and expect the judge to remember the foundation. Counsel must consult with each other and with the deputy clerk at the end of each trial day and compare notes as to which exhibits are in evidence and any limitations thereon. If there are any differences, counsel should bring them promptly to the Court's attention.

24. Any objections ordinarily must have been preserved under FRCP 26(a)(3). However, evidence that is cumulative or excludable under Rules 402-403 may possibly be excluded even if no objection has been preserved under FRCP 26(a)(3).

25. In addition to the official record exhibits, a *single joint* set of bench binders containing a copy of the exhibits only (usually the combined top twenty will do) should be provided to the Court on the first day of trial. Each exhibit must be separated with a label divider (an exhibit tag is unnecessary for the bench set). In large letters, the labels should say the exhibit number on the binders. Please use binders thin enough to lift with one arm and with locking rings.

Objections During Examination

26. Counsel shall stand when making objections and shall not make speaking objections. The one-lawyer-per-side rule is usually followed but will be relaxed to allow young lawyers a chance to perform.

Time Limits

27. Ordinarily, the Court shall set fixed time limits at the final pretrial conference. All of your examination time (whether direct, cross, re-direct or re-cross) for all witnesses must fit within your time limit and you may allocate it as you wish. Opening and closing time limits shall be *in addition* to your examination allocation.

Settlements and Continuances

28. Shortly before trial or a final pretrial conference, counsel occasionally wish jointly to advise the clerk that a settlement has been reached and seek to take the setting off calendar (but it turns out later that there was only a settlement "in principle" and disputes remain). Cases, however, cannot be taken off calendar in this manner. Unless and until a stipulated dismissal or judgment is filed or placed on the record, all parties must be prepared to proceed with the final pretrial conference as scheduled and to proceed to trial on the trial date, on pain of dismissal of the case for lack of prosecution or entry of default judgment. Only an advance continuance expressly approved by the Court will release counsel and the parties from their obligation to proceed. If counsel expect that a settlement will be final by the time of trial or the final pretrial conference, they should notify the Court immediately in writing or, if it occurs over the weekend before the trial or conference, by voice mail to the deputy courtroom clerk. The Court will attempt to confer with counsel as promptly as circumstances permit to determine if a continuance will be in order. Pending such a conference, however, counsel must prepare and make all filings and be prepared to proceed with the trial.

29. The Court strongly encourages law firms to permit young lawyers to examine witnesses at trial and to have an important role. It is the way one generation will teach the next to try cases and to maintain our district's reputation for excellence in trial practice.

IT IS SO ORDERED.

Dated: March 5, 2012.

WILLIAM ALSUP
United States District Judge

B. *Guidelines for Trial and Final Pretrial Conference in Civil Jury Cases*

GUIDELINES FOR TRIAL AND FINAL PRETRIAL CONFERENCE IN CIVIL JURY CASES BEFORE THE HONORABLE WILLIAM ALSUP

FRCP 26(a)(3) Disclosures

1. All parties are reminded of their disclosure duties under FRCP 26(a)(3), which begin **THIRTY CALENDAR DAYS** before trial. The FRCP 26(a)(3)(A)(ii) requirement for designating deposition transcripts, however, need not be done until later, as set forth below, although the name of each trial witness to appear by deposition must be so designated at least **THIRTY CALENDAR DAYS** before trial.

Final Pretrial Conference

2. At least **SEVEN CALENDAR DAYS** in advance of the final pretrial conference, please file the following:

(a) A joint proposed final pretrial order, signed and vetted by all counsel, that contains: (i) a brief description of the substance of claims and defenses which remain to be decided, (ii) a statement of all relief sought, (iii) all stipulated facts, (iv) a list of all factual issues which remain to be tried, stating the issues with the same generality/specificity as any contested elements in the relevant jury instructions, all organized by counts, (v) a joint exhibit list in numerical order, including a brief description of the exhibit and Bates numbers, a column for when it is offered in evidence, a column for when it is received in evidence, and a column for any limitations on its use, and (vi) each party's separate witness list for its case-in-chief witnesses (including those appearing by deposition) providing, for all such witnesses other than an individual plaintiff and an individual defendant, a statement of the substance of his/her testimony and, separately, what, if any, non-cumulative testimony the witness will give (to be used to set time limits). Items (v) and (vi) should be appendices to the proposed order. Please state which issues, if any, are for the Court to decide, rather than the jury.

(b) A joint set of proposed instructions on *substantive* issues of law arranged in a logical sequence. If undisputed, an instruction shall be identified as "Stipulated Instruction No. ___ Re ________" with the blanks filled in as appropriate. If disputed, each version of the instruction shall be inserted together, back to back, in their logical place in the overall sequence. Each such disputed instruction shall be identified as, for example, "Disputed Instruction No. ___ Re ________ Offered by ____________," with the blanks filled in as appropriate. All disputed versions of the same basic topic shall bear the same number. Citations with pin cites are required, even if the instruction is by stipulation. Any modifications to a form instruction must be plainly identified. If a party does not have a counter-version and simply contends no such instruction in any version should be given, then that party should so state (and explain why) on a separate page inserted in lieu of an alternate version. You need not provide any preliminary instructions, general instruction or concluding instructions, all of which the Court will do on its own in a draft for comment.

(c) A separate memorandum of law in support of each party's disputed instruction, organized by instruction number. *Please quote exactly (without ellipses) controlling passages from the authorities and give pin cites.*

(d) A joint special verdict form with the questions (as few as possible) arranged in a logical sequence.

(e) A joint set of proposed voir dire questions supplemented as necessary by separate requests.

(f) Any motion *in limine*, with the opposition, filed as follows:

At least **TWENTY CALENDAR DAYS** before the conference, serve, but do not yet file, the moving papers. At least **TEN CALENDAR DAYS** before the conference, serve the oppositions. When the oppositions are received, the moving party should collate the motion and the opposition together, back to back, and then file the paired sets at least **SEVEN CALENDAR DAYS** before the conference.

Each motion should be presented in a separate memo and numbered as in, for example, "Plaintiff's Motion in Limine No. 1 to Exclude . . . ." Please limit motions *in limine* to circumstances that really need a ruling in advance. Usually five or fewer motions per side is sufficient at the conference stage (without prejudice to raising matters *in limine* as the trial progresses).

Each motion should address a single topic, be separate, and contain no more than seven pages of briefing per side.

(g) Copies of the Rule 26(a)(3) disclosures.

(h) Trial briefs are optional.

3. The above shall be submitted in *Word Perfect X3 or 10* format to whapo@cand.uscourts.gov, as well as in hard copies. *All hard-copy submissions should be three-hole punched on the left, so the judge's copy can be put in binders. Please provide them at least seven calendar days prior to the pretrial conference for the judge's study and review — THIS IS IMPORTANT.*

4. At the final pretrial conference, counsel must take notes on rulings and later submit a joint summary of all rulings in proposed-order format.

PRETRIAL ARRANGEMENTS

5. Should a daily transcript and/or real-time reporting be desired, the parties shall make timely arrangements with Deb Campbell, Court Services Coordinator, at debra_campbell@cand.uscourts.gov.

6. So that the jury may follow the evidence, counsel are strongly encouraged to use overhead projectors, laser-disk/computer graphics, poster blow-ups, models or specimens. The United States Marshal requires a court order to allow equipment into the courthouse. For electronic equipment, either know how to fix it or have a technician handy. For overhead projectors, have a spare bulb. Tape extension cords to the carpet for safety. Please take down and store the equipment (in the courtroom) at the end of each court day. Please work with Dawn Toland (415-522-2020) on courtroom-layout issues and contact her to learn how to use the electronic presentation system.

Scheduling

7. The normal trial schedule will be 7:30 a.m. to 1:00 p.m. (or slightly longer to finish a witness) with two fifteen-minute breaks and ending before lunch. Counsel must arrive by 7:30 a.m., or earlier as needed for any matters to be heard out of the presence of the jury. The jury will be on-site by 7:45 a.m. Counsel should be prepared to begin jury proceedings as soon as the morning's *in limine* proceedings end, which will normally be by 8:00 a.m. at the latest. Once the jury begins deliberations, it usually stays past 1:00 p.m. The trial week is usually Monday through Friday.

Jury Selection

8. On the first day of trial, counsel shall please submit a joint statement of the case to be read to the jury during voir dire. This statement should normally be one page. The Court will usually conduct the voir dire with supplemental questions by counsel at the end. Counsel should not use voir dire to indoctrinate the jury.

9. In civil cases, there are no alternate jurors. To end up with a final jury of eight jurors, we will do the following: Fourteen prospective jurors will be called to fill the jury box and given seat numbers (1 through 14). Others will remain on the public benches. For those in the jury box, hardship excuses will be considered first and then voir dire will proceed. Some will usually be excused for cause or hardship during voir dire and their seats will be filled as excusals are made. After the panel is passed for cause (or all cause motions are denied), each side may exercise its allotment of peremptory challenges against the fourteen in the jury box. Blind challenges are made simultaneously. Each side writes down the names and seat numbers of those to be stricken. The eight surviving the challenge process become the final jury. For example, if the plaintiff strikes 1, 5 and 7 and the defendant strikes 2, 4 and 9, then 3, 6, 8, 10, 11, 12 13 and 14 become the final jury. If both sides strike one or more of the *same* candidates, then the eight unstruck jurors with the *lowest* seat numbers will be sworn. Once the jury selection is completed, they will be re-seated in the jury box and sworn. The Court may alter the procedure in its discretion. If more than eight jurors (or less) are to be seated, then the starting number will be adjusted. So too if more than a total of six peremptories are allowed.

Opening Statements

10. Each side will have a time limit for its opening statement (to be determined at the final pretrial conference). Counsel must cooperate and meet and confer to exchange any visuals, graphics or exhibits to be used in the opening statements, allowing for time to work out objections and any reasonable revisions. Be prepared for opening statements as soon as the jury is sworn.

Witnesses

11. Except for good cause, all counsel are entitled to written firm notice of the order of witnesses for the next court day and the exhibits (including merely illustrative exhibits) to be used on direct examination (other than for true impeachment of a witness). The Court encourages two days notice, *i.e.*, written notice by 2:00 p.m. on the *second* calendar day before the witnesses testify or the exhibit is used. At a minimum, notice must be no later than 2:00

p.m. on the calendar day *immediately* preceding. If two days written notice is given or two days notice is given that no documents will be used, then all other counsel must give written notice of all other exhibits to be used on cross-examination (except for true impeachment) by 2:00 p.m. On the calendar day immediately preceding the testimony; otherwise, other responding counsel need not give notice of exhibits they may use. Any exhibit timely noticed by anyone for the witness is usable as if timely noticed by everyone, subject to substantive objections. Similarly, if reference is made to an exhibit during an examination (even if not offered in evidence and even if not noticed for use with the witness), then in any follow-up examination by others, the exhibit may be used to the same extent as if it had been timely noticed, subject to substantive objections. All notices shall be sent by fax or electronically and be time-and-date verifiable. If counsel decides not to call a noticed witness, then prompt written notice of the cancellation must be given. Impeachment exhibits are ordinarily limited to statements signed by or adopted by the witness. Compliance with a two-day notice period, of course, will not satisfy compliance with FRCP 26 or any other disclosure rule.

12. The official tagged exhibit should be shown to witnesses — not supposed copies or notebooks of supposed copies. Before the examination begins, retrieve the official tagged exhibits to be used and have them at the ready. Using copies leads to discrepancies between the exhibit actually introduced into the record (*always* the official tagged exhibit) versus the stray before the witness. The required procedure also helps find any glitches in the official tagged exhibits.

13. Always have your next witness ready and in the courthouse. Failure to have the next witness ready or to be prepared to proceed with the evidence will usually constitute resting. If counsel plans to read in a transcript of a deposition anyway, it is advisable to have a deposition prepared and vetted early on to read "just in case."

14. When there are multiple parties, counsel are responsible for coordination of the cross-examination to avoid duplication. Stand at or near the microphone to ask questions, straying only to point out material on charts or overheads. Please request permission to approach the witness or the bench.

Experts

15. A recurring problem in trials is the problem of expert witnesses trying to go beyond the scope of their expert reports on direct examination. FRCP 26(a)(2) and FRCP 37(c) limit experts to the opinions and bases contained in their timely reports (absent substantial justification or harmlessness). The Court regularly enforces these rules. FRCP 26(a) also requires that any "exhibits to be used as a summary of or support for the opinions" be included in the report. Accordingly, at trial, the direct testimony of experts will be limited to the matters disclosed in their reports. New matters may not ordinarily be added on direct examination. This means the reports must be complete and sufficiently detailed. Illustrative animations, diagrams, charts and models may be used on direct examination only if they were part of the expert's report, with the exception of simple drawings and tabulations that plainly illustrate what is already in the report, which can be drawn by the witness at trial or otherwise shown to the jury. If cross-examination fairly opens the door, however, an expert may go beyond the written report on cross-examination and/or re-direct examination. By written

stipulation, of course, all sides may relax these requirements. Material in a "reply" report must ordinarily be presented in a party's rebuttal (or sur-rebuttal) case *after* the other side's expert has appeared and testified.

16. Another recurring problem is the retained expert who seeks to vouch for the credibility of fact witnesses and/or to vouch for one side's fact scenario. Qualified experts, of course, are always welcome to testify concerning relevant scientific principles, professional standards, specialized facts known within a trade or discipline and the like (so long as it is in the report). They are also welcome to apply those principles and standards to various assumed fact scenarios. This is so even if an opinion is given on the "ultimate issue." But they should not try to vouch for one side's *fact* scenario, *i.e.*, witness believability. It is the jury's responsibility to sort out whose fact scenario is correct, including issues of credibility. An expert, therefore, should give opinions based only on one or more *assumed* fact scenarios.

17. There is an important exception. Experts and doctors who perform scientific tests, site visits, or treat victims, among other possibilities, may testify to their findings within the scope of their firsthand knowledge. This is because they have made personal observations and have reached professional judgments based thereon. Carrying this one step further, even a retained expert may read a financial statement in evidence, watch a video in evidence, listen to a recording in evidence, and so on and offer opinions based on the contents. This is because the contents themselves are clearly defined.

18. As to damages studies, the cut-off date for *past damages* will be as of the expert report (or such earlier date as the expert may select). In addition, the experts may try to project *future damages* (*i.e.*, after the cut-off date) if the substantive standards for future damages can be met. With timely leave of Court or by written stipulation, the experts may update their reports (with supplemental reports) to a date closer to the time of trial.

Use of Depositions to Impeach and Short Read-Ins

19. Depositions can be used at trial to impeach a witness testifying at trial or, in the case of a party deponent, "for any purpose." Please follow the following procedure:

(a) On the first day of trial, be sure to bring the original and clean copies of any deposition(s) for which you are responsible. Any corrections must be readily available. If you are likely to need to use the deposition during a witness examination, then give the Court a copy with any witness corrections at the outset of your examination. This will minimize delay between the original question and the read-ins of the impeaching material. Opposing counsel should have their copy immediately available.

(b) When you wish to read in a passage, simply say, for example: "I wish to read in page 210, lines 1 to 10 from the witness' deposition." A brief pause will be allowed for any objection.

(c) When reading in the passage, state "question" and then read the question exactly. Then state "answer" and then read the answer exactly. Stating "question" and "answer" is necessary so the jury and the court reporter can follow who was talking at the deposition.

(d) The first time a deposition is read, state the deponent's name, the date of the deposition, the name of the lawyer asking the question, and if it was FRCP 30(b)(6) deposition, please say so. The first time a deposition is read, the Court will give an appropriate explanation to the jury about depositions. Please do not embellish on this with follow-on questions.

(e) Please do **NOT** ask, "Didn't you say XYZ in your deposition?" The problem with such a question is that the "XYZ" rarely turns out to be exactly what the deponent said and is part spin. Instead, ask for permission to read in a passage, as above, and read it in exactly, without spin, so that the jury can hear what was actually testified to.

(f) Subject to Rule 403, party depositions may be read in whether or not they contradict (and regardless of who the witness is on the stand). For example, a short party deposition excerpt may be used as foundation for questions for a different witness on the stand.

(g) Rather than reading the passage, counsel are free to play an audiovisual digitized version of the passage but counsel must have a system for immediate display of the precise passage.

Deposition Designation

20. The following procedure applies only to witnesses who appear by deposition. It does not apply to live witnesses whose depositions are read in while they are on the stand. To save time and avoid unnecessary work, it is not necessary to make all deposition designations before trial (as normally required by FRCP 26(3)(A)(ii)). In the Court's experience, by the time the read-in occurs, the proponent has usually reduced substantially the proposed read-ins. Instead, the following steps should be followed:

(a) To designate deposition testimony, photocopy the cover page, the page where the witness is sworn, and then each page from which any testimony is proffered. Line through or x-out any portions of such pages not proffered. Also, line through objections or colloquy unless they are needed to understand the question. Please make sure any corrections are interlineated and that references to exhibit numbers are conformed to the trial numbers. Such interlineations should be done by hand. The finished packet should then be the actual script and should smoothly present the identification and swearing of the witness and testimony desired. The packet should be provided to all other parties at least FIVE CALENDAR DAYS before it will be used in court. For the rare case of voluminous designations, more lead time will be required. Please be reasonable.

(b) All other parties must then promptly review the packet and highlight in yellow any passages objected to and write in the margin the legal basis for the objections. If any completeness objection is made, the objecting party must insert into the packet the additional passages as needed to cure the completeness objection. A completeness objection should normally be made only if a few extra lines will cure the problem. Such additions shall be highlighted in blue and an explanation for the inclusion shall be legibly handwritten in the margin. Please line out or x-out any irrelevant portions of the additional pages.

(c) The packets, as adjusted, must then be returned to the proffering party, who must then decide the extent to which to accept the adjustments. The parties must meet and confer as reasonable. Counsel for the proffering party must collate and assemble a final packet that covers the proffer and all remaining issues. At least TWO CALENDAR DAYS before the proffer will be used, the proponent must provide the Court with the final packet, with any objected-to portions highlighted and annotated as described above. If exhibits are needed to resolve the objections, include copies and highlight and tag the relevant passages. Alert the Court on the record that the packet is being provided and whether any rulings are needed. *Tag all passages that require a ruling.* The Court will then read the packet and indicate its rulings. Ordinarily, argument will not be needed.

(d) Counter designations must be made by providing a packet with the counter-designated passages to the proponent at the same time any objections to the original proffer are returned to the first proffering party, who must then supply its objections in the same manner.

(e) When a witness appears by deposition rather than live, counsel may present it by reading or by video. When reading, it is best — for jury comprehension — to use a "witness" (usually co-counsel, a legal assistant or opposing counsel) to read the answers from the witness stand while counsel reads the questions from the lectern. If the read-in is short, a single attorney can read it all, being careful to say "question" and "answer," as appropriate, so that everyone including the court reporter, will follow exactly who said what. The exhibits, if admitted, may be projected onto the screen during the read-in as they are referenced. In the Court's judgment, this is an effective procedure and avoids the problems of paper-shuffling, background noise, long pauses, difficult accents, and video-quality problems. When showing a videotaped deposition, it is best to scroll the question and answer in text near the bottom of the screen and to show any exhibits on a split screen. The entire length of all designations should never be longer than one hour without prior court clearance. Anything longer is usually counterproductive to jury comprehension. Remember that court reporters do *not* transcribe video excerpts, so counsel must file with the deputy clerk an exact record of what was shown and identify it for the record.

Requests for Admissions and Interrogatories

21. Please designate responses to requests for admissions and interrogatory answers in the same manner and under the same timetable as depositions.

Exhibits

22. As stated, FRCP 26(a)(3) disclosures regarding proposed exhibits must be made at least **THIRTY CALENDAR DAYS** before trial and any objections thereto must be made within **FOURTEEN CALENDAR DAYS** thereafter (or waived unless excused for good cause). The joint list must be filed **SEVEN CALENDAR DAYS** in advance of the final pretrial conference (as per paragraph 2 above). By designating an exhibit, a party waives any objection to authenticity and any reciprocal objection, meaning any objection mutually available to both the designating party and the opposing party if and when offered by one against the other. Therefore, the non-designating party may offer the exhibit subject only to non-reciprocal objections. For example, if P designates a record from a non-party, such as a telephone company, then D can equally offer the same exhibit save for any objection that would be unique against D. To take a contra example, if P designates D's internal email, it will usually not be admissible at the instance of D, there being a non-reciprocal hearsay hurdle when offered by D. If the designating party states that the exhibit is only for a limited purpose, then the waiver extends only to the same limited purpose. Notwithstanding the foregoing, FRE 403 objections are

never waived. And, any party may always attempt to lay full foundation to admit any exhibit designated by itself or by any other party without regard to any waiver.

23. Prior to the final pretrial conference, counsel will please meet and confer in person over all exhibit numbers and objections and to weed out duplicate exhibits and confusion over the precise exhibit. Use numbers only, not letters, for exhibits, preferably the same numbers as were used in depositions. Blocks of numbers should be assigned to fit the need of the case (*e.g.*, Plaintiff has 1 to 100, Defendant A has 101 to 200, Defendant B has 201 to 300, *etc.*). A single exhibit should be marked only once, just as it should have been marked only once in discovery (if this Court's guidelines were followed). If the plaintiff has marked an exhibit, then the defendant should not re-mark the exact document with another number. Different *versions* of the same document, *e.g.*, a copy with additional handwriting, must be treated as different exhibits with different numbers. To avoid any party claiming "ownership" of an exhibit, all exhibits shall be marked and referred to as "Trial Exhibit No. ___," not as "Plaintiff's Exhibit" or "Defendant's Exhibit." If an exhibit number differs from that used in a deposition transcript, then the latter transcript must be conformed to the new trial number if and when the deposition testimony is read to the jury (so as to avoid confusion over exhibit numbers). The jury should always hear any given exhibit referred to by its trial number.

24. The exhibit tag shall be in the following form:

UNITED STATES DISTRICT COURT
NORTHERN DISTRICT OF
CALIFORNIA

TRIAL EXHIBIT 100

CASE NO. ____________________
DATE ENTERED________________
BY ____________________________
DEPUTY CLERK

Place the tag on or near the lower right-hand corner or, if a photograph, on the back. Counsel should fill in the tag but leave the last two spaces blank. The parties must jointly prepare a *single* set of all trial exhibits that will be the official record set to be used with the witnesses, in the jury room, and on appeal. Each exhibit must be tagged and in a separate folder (not in notebooks). Deposit the exhibits with the deputy clerk (Dawn Toland) on the first day of trial.

25. Please move exhibits into evidence as soon as the foundation is laid and it is fresh in the judge's mind. Do not postpone motions and expect the judge to remember the foundation. Counsel must consult with each other and with the deputy clerk at the end of each trial day and compare notes as to which exhibits are in evidence and any limitations thereon. If there are any differences, counsel should bring them promptly to the Court's attention.

26. Any objections ordinarily must have been preserved under FRCP 26(a)(3). However, evidence that is cumulative or excludable under Rules 402-403 may possibly be excluded even if no objection has been preserved under FRCP 26(a)(3).

27. In addition to the official record exhibits, a *single, joint* set of bench binders containing copies of the key exhibits only (usually the combined top twenty will do) should be provided to the Court on the first day of trial. Each exhibit must be separated with a label divider (an exhibit tag is unnecessary for the bench set). In large letters, the labels should say the exhibit number on the binders. Please use binders thin enough to lift with one arm and with locking rings.

28. Before the closings, counsel must confer with the clerk to make sure the exhibits in evidence are in good order. Counsel should, but are not required to, jointly provide a revised list of all exhibits actually in evidence (and no others) stating the exhibit number and a brief, non-argumentative description (*e.g.*, letter from A. B. Case to D. E. Frank, dated August 17, 1999). This joint list shall go into the jury room to help the jury sort through exhibits in evidence.

Objections During Examination

29. Counsel shall stand when making objections and shall not make speaking objections. The one-lawyer-per-witness rule is usually followed but will be relaxed to allow young lawyers a chance to perform. Side bar conferences are discouraged.

30. To maximize jury time, counsel must alert the Court in advance of any problems that will require discussion outside the presence of the jury, so that the conference can be held before court begins or after the jury leaves for the day.

Stipulations

31. You must read all stipulations to the jury (slowly) in order for them to become a part of the jury record. They do not automatically go into the jury room.

32. To improve jury comprehension of the evidence, counsel should agree on a non-argumentative posterboard timeline to be ever-present in the courtroom for ready reference by the jury as the evidence comes in. It will provide an undisputed fixed frame of reference about which the jury can organize the disputed issues. It should be large enough to view from across the courtroom, about four by eight feet, and in timeline format. Counsel should also stipulate to the maximum feasible extent as to all facts that in good faith cannot be disputed, so that the jury can concentrate on assessing the issues in play. Some evidence can still be presented on any stipulated point as it is often necessary to do so to tell the story but stipulations allow the jury and counsel to concentrate their time on the points in controversy (and for the jury to appreciate *which* points are in controversy). In a further effort to improve jury comprehension, the Court will sua sponte invite counsel at various points during the evidence to make short statements to alert the jury to the upcoming items of interest. The Court welcomes other ideas for improving jury comprehension.

Time Limits

33. Ordinarily, the Court shall set fixed time limits at the final pretrial conference. All of your examination time (whether direct, cross, re-direct or re-cross) for all witnesses must fit within your time limit and you may allocate it as you wish. Opening and closing time limits shall be *in addition to* your examination allocation.

Punitive Damages

34. For punitive damages, the jury will ordinarily be asked in their main deliberations only to determine whether a defendant acted with fraud, malice or oppression. If the jury answers "yes," then (after a fifteen-minute recess) a short supplemental jury proceeding shall be held. The parties may then present evidence of that defendant's financial condition, followed by brief argument by each side. The Court will then give the jury a supplemental instruction on punitives and a special verdict form. For this proceeding, counsel typically stipulate to the financial condition of the defendant. Failing a stipulation, the parties must put on proof in the traditional way. It is the responsibility of counsel to make whatever motions are necessary, in a timely way, to obtain any relevant financial information.

Charging Conference

35. As the trial progresses and the evidence is heard, the Court will fashion a comprehensive set of jury instructions to cover all issues actually being tried. A few days before the close of the evidence the Court will provide a draft final charge to the parties. After a reasonable period for review, one or more charging conferences will be held at which each party may object to any passage, ask for modifications, or ask for additions. Any instruction request must be renewed specifically at the conference or it will be deemed waived, whether or not it was requested prior to trial. One reason for this ground rule is that, before trial, parties usually submit numerous instruction requests that fall away as the evidence is received. The draft charge will omit points of law that appear irrelevant to the Court. If, however, a party still wishes to request an omitted instruction after reviewing the Court's draft, then it must affirmatively re-request it at the charging conference in order to give the Court a fair opportunity to correct any error. Otherwise, as stated, the request will be deemed abandoned or waived.

Settlements and Continuances

36. Shortly before trial or a final pretrial conference, counsel occasionally wish jointly to advise the clerk that a settlement has been reached and seek to take the setting off calendar (but it turns out later that there was only a settlement "in principle" and disputes remain). Cases, however, cannot be taken off calendar in this manner. Unless and until a stipulated dismissal or judgment is filed or placed on the record, all parties must be prepared to proceed with the final pretrial conference as scheduled and to proceed to trial on the trial date, on pain of dismissal of the case for lack of prosecution or entry of default judgment. Only an advance continuance expressly approved by the Court will release counsel and the parties from their obligation to proceed. If counsel expect that a settlement will be final by the time of trial or the final pretrial conference, they should notify the Court immediately in writing or, if it occurs over the weekend before the trial or conference, by voice mail to the deputy courtroom clerk. The Court will attempt to confer with counsel as promptly as circumstances permit to determine if a continuance will be in order. Pending such a conference, however, counsel must prepare and make all filings and be prepared to proceed with the trial.

37. Local Rule 40-1 provides that jury costs may be assessed as sanctions for failure to provide the Court with timely written notice of a settlement. Please be aware that any settlement reached on the day of trial, during trial, or at any time after the jury or potential jurors have been summoned without sufficient time to cancel, will normally require the parties to pay juror costs.

38. The Court strongly encourages lead counsel to permit young lawyers to examine witnesses at trial and to have an important role. It is the way one generation will teach the next to try cases and to maintain our district's reputation for excellence in trial practice.

IT IS SO ORDERED.

Dated: March 5, 2012.

WILLIAM ALSUP
United States District Judge

C. Supplemental Order to Order Setting Initial CMC in Civil Cases

SUPPLEMENTAL ORDER TO ORDER SETTING INITIAL CASE MANAGEMENT CONFERENCE IN CIVIL CASES BEFORE JUDGE WILLIAM ALSUP

INTRODUCTION

The purpose of this supplemental order is to guide the parties on recurring practical questions that arise prior to trial and to impose certain requirements for the conduct of the case. Counsel must please read this order and follow it.

SERVICE OF THIS ORDER

1. For cases originating in this Court, plaintiff(s) must serve this order and the order setting the initial case management conference (along with any other required pleadings) on each defendant. For cases removed from state court, the removing defendant(s) must serve this order and the order setting the initial case management conference (along with any other required pleadings) immediately on each and every party that has previously appeared or that appears within thirty days after removal. Thereafter, any existing party to the action that brings a new party into the action must immediately serve a copy of this order and the order setting the initial case management conference (along with any other required pleadings) on the new party.

CASE MANAGEMENT CONFERENCE

2. The parties will please address the standardized items in the court-wide format for the joint case management statement. This is available at the Standing Order For all Judges of the Northern District of California — Contents of Joint Case Management Statements. Please file (electronically or manually depending on your case) at least **SEVEN CALENDAR DAYS** prior to the case management conference.

3. Each party shall be represented at the case management conference by counsel prepared to address all such matters and with authority to enter stipulations and to make admissions.

4. Pursuant to FRCP 26(d), no formal discovery shall be initiated by any party until after the meet-and-confer session required by FRCP 26(f), except by stipulation or prior court order. As soon as a party has notice of this order, however, the party shall take such affirmative steps as are necessary to preserve evidence related to the issues presented by the action, including, without limitation, interdiction of any document-destruction programs and any ongoing erasures of e-mails, voice mails, and other electronically-recorded material.

ELECTRONIC CASE FILING — LODGING HARD COPIES WITH CHAMBERS

5. In all "E-Filing" cases, in addition to filing papers electronically, the parties are required to lodge for chambers one paper copy of each document that is filed electronically. These printed copies shall be marked "Chambers Copy — Do Not File" and shall be in an envelop clearly marked with the judge's name and case number. It shall be delivered to the Clerk's office no later than noon on the day following the day that the papers were filed electronically. Parties shall *not file* a paper copy of any document with the Clerk's Office that has already been filed electronically. For the final pretrial conference, please follow

Guidelines for Trial and Final Pretrial Conference In Civil Jury Cases Before the Honorable William Alsup.

SETTING MOTIONS FOR HEARING

6. Counsel need not request a motion hearing date and may notice non-discovery motions for any Thursday (excepting holidays) at 8:00 a.m. The Court sometimes rules on the papers, issuing a written order and vacating the hearing. If a written request for oral argument is filed before a ruling, stating that a lawyer of four or fewer years out of law school will conduct the oral argument or at least the lion's share, then the Court will hear oral argument, believing that young lawyers need more opportunities for appearances than they usually receive.

FORM OF SUBMISSIONS

7. On summary judgment motions, joint statements of undisputed facts are not required but are helpful if completely agreed upon. Please do *not* file separate statements of "undisputed facts."

8. Reply declarations are disfavored. Opening declarations should set forth all facts on points foreseeably relevant to the relief sought. Reply papers should not raise new points that could have been addressed in the opening.

9. The title of the submission must be sufficient to alert the Court to the relief sought; for example, please do not bury a request for continuance in the body of a memorandum.

10. All submissions filed with the Court shall include on the cover sheet the date and time of the hearing or conference. Counsel should include their facsimile transmission numbers along with their telephone numbers on their papers.

DISCOVERY

11. The following paragraphs on discovery provide counsel and the parties with views and guidelines of Judge Alsup so that they can plan accordingly. For good cause, the parties are invited to propose any modifications in their joint case management conference statement. Unless and until modified, however, the following provisions shall supplement the requirements of the Federal Rules of Civil Procedure and the local rules.

12. In responding to requests for documents and materials under FRCP 34, all parties shall *affirmatively state* in a written response the full extent to which they will produce materials and shall, promptly after the production, confirm in writing that they have produced *all* such materials so described that are locatable after a diligent search of *all* locations at which such materials might plausibly exist. It is not sufficient to state that "responsive" materials will be or have been produced. Such a response leaves open the distinct possibility that other responsive materials have not been produced.

13. In searching for responsive materials in connection with FRCP 34 requests or for materials required to be disclosed under FRCP 26(a)(1), parties must search computerized files, e-mails, voice mails, work files, desk files, calendars and diaries, and any other locations and sources if materials of the type to be produced might plausibly be expected to be found there. The Court has found that certain basic information normally learned by counsel anyway should be made available to the other side at the time of production, as if it were a response to a standing interrogatory, as follows. At the time of the production, the responding party should provide a written list to the requesting party setting forth in detail each specific source

and location searched. The list must also identify, by name and position, all persons conducting the search and their areas of search responsibility. The producing party shall also provide a list describing the specific source for each produced item as well as for each item withheld on a ground of privilege, using the unique identifying numbers to specify documents or ranges. Materials produced in discovery should bear unique identifying control numbers on each page.

14. To the maximum extent feasible, all party files and records should be retained and produced in their original form and sequence including file folders, and the originals should remain available for inspection by any counsel on reasonable notice.

15. Except for good cause, no item shall be received as case-in-chief evidence if the proponent has failed to produce it in response to a reasonable and proper discovery request covering the item, regardless of whether any discovery motion was made. A burden or overbreadth or similar objection shall not be a valid reason for withholding requested materials actually known to counsel or a party representative responsible for the conduct of the litigation.

16. Privilege logs shall be promptly provided and must be sufficiently detailed and informative to justify the privilege. *See* FRCP 26(b)(5). No generalized claims of privilege or work-product protection shall be permitted. With respect to each communication for which a claim of privilege or work product is made, the asserting party must at the time of assertion identify:

(a) all persons making or receiving the privileged or protected communication;

(b) the steps taken to ensure the confidentiality of the communication, including affirmation that no unauthorized persons have received the communication;

(c) the date of the communication; and

(d) the subject matter of the communication.

Failure to furnish this information at the time of the assertion will be deemed a waiver of the privilege or protection. The log should also indicate, as stated above, the location where the document was found.

17. Absent extraordinary circumstances, counsel shall consult in advance with opposing counsel and unrepresented proposed deponents to schedule depositions at mutually-convenient times and places. That some counsel may be unavailable shall not, however, be grounds for deferring or postponing a deposition if another attorney from the same firm or who represents a party with similar interests to that witness is able to attend. Ordinarily, if one side desires a prompt deposition, the other side is expected to agree to dates falling within *thirty days* of the request. On the other hand, rarely should one side expect the other side to agree to a deposition sooner than *seven days* of the request.

18. If any objection to a request for materials is overruled, and if the disputed request was due and pending at the time of a deposition, the withholding party or counsel must, at the request of any other party, re-produce all deponents under its control or represented by them for further deposition examination as to any new materials produced in response that are germane to that deponent and must bear the expense of doing so. A party

objecting to producing requested materials may not use the existence of its own objections as a basis for postponing any deposition unless such party promptly meets and confers and then, if failing to reach an agreement, seeks to bring a prompt motion for a protective order.

19. Counsel and parties shall comply with FRCP 30(d)(1). Deposition objections must be as to privilege or form only. Speaking objections are prohibited. Under no circumstances should any counsel interject, "if you know," or otherwise coach a deponent. When a privilege is claimed, the witness should nevertheless answer questions relevant to the existence, extent or waiver of the privilege, such as the date of a communication, who made the statement, to whom and in whose presence the statement was made, other persons to whom the contents of the statement have been disclosed, and the general subject matter of the statement. Private conferences between deponents and attorneys in the course of examination, including a line of related questions, are improper and prohibited except for the sole purpose of determining whether a privilege should be asserted.

20. Deponents and their counsel must make a good-faith effort to prepare for depositions and to refresh witness memories on important matters in the suit about which the witness reasonably should be expected to have knowledge. Deponents who claim to lack recollection during their deposition but who later claim at trial to have had their memories refreshed in the interim, may be, among other things, impeached with their previous failures of recollection during their depositions or be subject to preclusion. In preparing deponents, defending counsel shall segregate and retain all materials used to refresh their memories and shall provide them to examining counsel at the outset of the deposition.

21. To the maximum extent feasible, deposition exhibits shall be numbered in a simple manner that will allow the same numbering at trial. In discovery, counsel shall agree on blocks of exhibit numbers to be used by the respective parties. Identical exhibits should not be re-marked, but various versions of the same document, such as copies with hand notes added, should be separately marked if used. *See* Local Rule 30-2(b)(3).

22. FRCP 26(a)(2)(B) requires disclosure of all opinions, bases, reasons and other information considered by an expert. Counsel shall preserve all drafts of expert reports (partial or complete) and notes and other evidence of communications with experts (or with any intermediaries between counsel and the experts) on the subject of this actual or potential testimony, and shall instruct their experts and any intermediaries to do likewise. These materials, however, need not be produced absent the showing required by FRCP 26(b)(3) and (4).

23. With respect to depositions under FRCP 30(b)(6), the fundamental purpose is to allow a party to notice a deposition by subject matter, thereby requiring the respondent to designate and to produce one or more organization witnesses knowledgeable on the designated topic, a useful procedure when the roles of percipient witnesses controlled by an adverse party are unknown. In some cases, however, counsel routinely appear to notice Rule 30(b)(6) depositions on numerous and wide-ranging topics, including even the basis for "contentions" made by adverse parties. To obviate disputes and to give guidance, these guidelines will be observed:

(a) Without a prior order increasing the limit, a party may seek Rule 30(b)(6) depositions from another party on up to a total of ten subject matters (for the entire case) described with "reasonable particularity." In framing the subjects, it is normally improper to ask for Rule 30(b)(6) deponents to testify concerning the entire basis of a claim or defense. On the other hand, examples of proper subjects, which would require the respondent to find and to produce knowledgeable deponents, include "the time line of research and development leading to the invention in question" or "the efforts undertaken by defendant to locate documents responsive to plaintiff's document request." The notice should be directed at discovering percipient facts in the possession of the adverse party, not at forcing a supposed "fact witness" to appear and defend the entire thesis of a claim or defense. If a notice includes an overbroad topic, the overbroad topic shall be unenforceable and may not be later replaced with a proper topic.

(b) Each witness-designee deposed for one half-day or more in a Rule 30(b)(6) deposition shall count as a single deposition for purposes of the deposition limit under FRCP 26 or under any case management order setting a limit on the number of depositions. A corporate designee may, immediately after being deposed on the stated subject, be deposed in his or her individual capacity. Both such sessions shall count together as a single deposition (although they should be separately transcribed). If two designees, to take another example, are interrogated, each for one half-day or more, then they count as two depositions.

(c) If an organization cannot reasonably locate a witness to testify based on personal knowledge, there is no requirement under Rule 30(b)(6) for the organization to "woodshed" or to "educate" an individual to testify on the subject. If the organization does not produce any such deponent, however, the organization may not present case-in-chief evidence at trial or on summary judgment on that topic from any witness it could have so designated.

(d) Rule 30(b)(6) testimony never constitutes an irrebuttable judicial admission. It will normally, however, be evidence admissible against the organization producing the witness. The jury may, upon request, be instructed on the significance of the testimony under Rule 30(b)(6).

24. If a dispute arises during a deposition and involves either a persistent obstruction of the deposition or a refusal to answer a material question on a ground other than privilege, counsel may attempt to arrange a telephone conference with the Court through the courtroom deputy, Dawn Toland, at 415-522-2020. Any such conference should be attended by the same court reporter recording the deposition.

25. All other requests for discovery relief must first be summarized in a letter no longer than three pages from the party seeking relief after having met and conferred. Up to twelve pages of attachments may be added. In the letter, counsel should identify themselves in the signature block as "counsel for ___________." *The letter should be electronically-filed in the official file along with the discovery-dispute requests and responses, as well as any timely letter cancelling the hearing if settlement is reached.* (Please note that with all communications with the Court by e-filing, *a hard copy must be lodged* in the Court's mail box in the Clerk's Office on the sixteenth floor no later than noon of the following day.) The Court will then advise the parties whether a response, written motion or a telephone conference or court hearing will be required. After

the telephone conference or hearing, counsel should submit their proposed order (agreed as to form) by e-filing it. This paragraph applies only to cases wherein discovery is being supervised by the district judge rather than by a magistrate judge or special master.

DISCLOSURES

26. Apart from discovery, Rule 26 requires certain automatic disclosures and requires them to be made in a timely manner. Under Rule 37(c), untimely-disclosed materials may not be used at trial or on summary judgment unless the delay in disclosure is "harmless" or unless "substantial justification" for the delay is shown.

COMMUNICATIONS WITH CHAMBERS

27. Please do not send any letters to the Court (except for requests for discovery conferences, short cover letters for dismissals, orders agreed-upon as to form, or chambers copies of electronically-filed documents). When corresponding with the Court by letter, always identify whom you represent. Please do not fax or messenger anything to chambers without advance permission specific to the item. Please e-file all submissions to the Court and make sure a hard copy is lodged in the Court's mail box in the Clerk's Office on the sixteenth floor no later than noon of the following day.

28. You may contact the courtroom deputy, Dawn Toland (on the sixteenth floor in the Clerk's Office), at 415-522-2020 with appropriate inquiries. Except for the letters described above, please do not attempt to make contact by telephone or any other *ex parte* means with chambers staff.

CROSS REFERENCE TO OTHER STANDING ORDERS AND GUIDELINES

29. The Court has separate standing guidelines for preparation for the final pretrial conference and trial. In securities cases, the Court has a standing order concerning early notice to class members. They are always available for review at the website for the United States District Court for the Northern District of California at www.cand.uscourts.gov.

Dated: July 6, 2011.

WILLIAM ALSUP
United States District Judge

II. Judge Alsup's Forms

A. *Application for Permission to Enter Plea of Guilty and Order Accepting Plea*

IN THE UNITED STATES DISTRICT COURT
FOR THE NORTHERN DISTRICT OF CALIFORNIA

UNITED STATES OF AMERICA,

Plaintiff,

v.

Defendant.

_______________________________________/

No. CR_________ WHA

APPLICATION FOR PERMISSION TO ENTER PLEA OF GUILTY AND ORDER ACCEPTING PLEA

(Fed. R. Crim. P., Rules 10 and 11)

The defendant represents to the Court:

1. My full true name is ________________. I am _____ years of age. I have gone to school up to and including ________________________________. My most recent occupation has been________________________________. I request that all proceedings against me be in my true name.

2. I am represented by a lawyer. His/her name is______________________.

3. I received and read a copy of the indictment/information. *If applicable:* An interpretator who speaks__________________ read it to me in _______________, and I have discussed it with my lawyer.

I fully understand every charge made against me. I understand these charges to be as follows:____________________________.

4. I have told my lawyer all the facts and circumstances known to me about the charges made against me in the indictment/information. I believe that my lawyer is fully informed on all such matters.

5. I know that the Court must be satisfied that there is a factual basis for a plea of "GUILTY" before my plea can be accepted. I represent to the Court that I took the following actions in connection with the charges made against me in Count[s] __________ and that these facts are true and correct: ____________________.

6. My lawyer has counseled and advised me on the nature of each charge, all lesser included charges, all penalties and consequences of each charge, all possible defenses that I may have in this case and constitutional rights I am waiving.

7. I understand that my constitutional rights are as follows:

(a) the right to plead not guilty or, having already so pleaded, to persist in that plea;

(b) the right to a jury trial;

(c) the right to represented by counsel – and if necessary have the Court appoint counsel – at trial and at every other stage of the proceeding; and

(d) the right at trial to confront and cross-examine adverse witnesses, to testify and present evidence, to compel the attendance of witnesses, to be protected from compelled self-incrimination, and to remain silent, such that if I do not take the witness stand, no inference of guilt may be drawn from such failure and the jury must be so advised.

8. I know that I may plead "NOT GUILTY" to any offense charged against me and exercise all of my rights as listed above.

9. I know that if I plead "GUILTY," I am giving up all of the trial rights enumerated in paragraph 7 and that there will be no trial either before a court or jury.

10. I know that if I plead "GUILTY," the result of my plea is more than just an admission or confession of guilt. I understand that it will result in my conviction, and the Court may impose the same punishment as if I had pleaded "NOT GUILTY," stood trial and been convicted by a jury.

11. My lawyer has informed me that the maximum and minimum, if any, punishments which the law provides for the offense charged in Count(s) __________ are as follows:

(For multiple counts, include the following information for each count)

(a) Maximum prison sentence: _______ years

(b) Mandatory minimum prison sentence (if applicable): _______ years

(c) Maximum supervised release term: _______ years

(d) Minimum supervised release term (if applicable): _______ years

(e) Mandatory special assessment: $__________

(f) Restitution: $__________ (or determined by the Court)

(g) Maximum fine equal to the greater of the following:

(1) $_____________ (generally $250,000 for a felony, $100,000 for a Class A misdemeanor, or $5,000 for a Class B misdemeanor or lower; <u>see</u> 18 U.S.C. § 3571)); or

(2) $_______________ (twice the gross pecuniary gain I derived from the offense); or

(3) $_____________ (twice the gross pecuniary loss caused by the offense to another person or persons).

If applicable: I understand that, because I am pleading guilty to more than one count, the Court may order the sentences on those counts to run consecutively.

I understand that if I violate any condition of supervised release, the release may be revoked, and I may be sentenced to all or part of the term of supervised release imposed in addition to any other term of imprisonment which I have received. I understand that if I violate any term of probation, the probation may be revoked, and I may be sentenced up to the maximum statutory term of imprisonment for the offense.

I understand that I may be assessed the costs of confinement and/or supervision. I understand I may be ordered to pay restitution in an amount determined by the Court.

12. I know that the sentence I will receive will be decided solely by the Judge. I understand that the Judge will make no decision regarding my sentence until the Judge has read and considered the pre-sentence investigation report prepared and submitted to the Court by the Probation Department. I also understand that the Court and counsel cannot promise me now what sentence will be imposed. I understand that in deciding what sentence it will impose, the Court will calculate my sentencing range under the Sentencing Guidelines. I understand that while the Court is not bound to apply the Guidelines, it must take them into consideration when sentencing me, together with the factors set forth in 18 U.S.C. § 3553(a).

13. I understand that under provisions of certain criminal statutes, certain property of mine may be forfeited to the United States. I have been advised by my lawyer whether, and to what extent, my property may be subject to forfeiture.

14. If I am on probation, supervised release or parole in this or any other Court, I know that by pleading guilty here, my probation, release or parole may be revoked, and I may be required to serve time in that case, which may be consecutive (that is, in addition to) any sentence imposed upon me in this case.

15. I declare that no officer or agent of any branch of government (federal, state or local) has promised or suggested that I will receive a lighter sentence, or probation, or any other form of leniency, nor have any other promises been made if I plead "GUILTY" except as follows: ______________________________.

(In the space above, insert any promises or concessions made to the defendant or to his/her attorney).

If anyone else made such a promise or suggestion, except as noted in the previous sentence, I know that it was entirely without authority or effect.

16. I believe that my lawyer has done all that a lawyer could do to counsel and assist me, and I am satisfied with the advice and help he/she has given me.

17. I know that the Court will not permit anyone to plead "GUILTY" who maintains he/she is innocent and, with that in mind and because I am "GUILTY," I respectfully request the Court to accept my plea of "GUILTY" and to have the clerk enter my plea of "GUILTY" as follows:________.

18. My mind is clear. I am not under the influence of alcohol or drugs, and I am not under a doctor's care. The only drugs, medicines, or pills that I have taken within the past seven days are:_____________________________________. (*If none, so state.*)

19. I confirm that my decision to plead guilty is made voluntarily, and no one coerced or threatened me to enter into this Agreement. I offer my plea of "GUILTY" freely and voluntarily and of my own accord, and with full understanding of all the matters set forth in the indictment/information, in this application, and in the certificate of my lawyer which is attached to this application. In offering my plea of "GUILTY," I freely and voluntarily waive (that is, give up) the constitutional rights guaranteed to me as stated in paragraph 7 above.

20. I waive the reading of the indictment/information in open court, and I request the Court to enter my plea of "GUILTY" as set forth in Paragraph 17 of this application.

21. I understand that the Court will address me personally in open court to determine the voluntariness of my guilty plea and to establish a factual basis for it. I understand that the Court may place me under oath, and that the government may use any false statements that I make under oath against me in a prosecution for perjury or false statement (which is a felony).

22. ___ I am proficient enough in English to read the above and have read and fully understand it.

___ I am not proficient enough in English. I speak and understand ____________, which is my native language. The above was read to me in________ and I fully understand it.

Signed by me in open court in the presence of my attorney this____ day of _______, 20__.

____

Defendant

CERTIFICATE OF COUNSEL

I have fully explained to my client the charges in the indictment/information in the case, the defenses he/she may have to the charges, all of the information set forth in this application, and all the rights that a criminal defendant has. In my opinion, my client understands the charges, the defenses, the information in this application, and the rights he or she is giving up by pleading guilty, and, based on the information now known to me, his/her decision to plead guilty is knowing and voluntary.

Signed by me in open court in the presence of the above-named defendant after a full discussion of the contents of this certificate with the defendant this ______ day of____________, 20___ .

____

Attorney for the Defendant

INTERPRETER CERTIFICATION

I, ____________________, hereby certify that I am a certified __________ [language] interpreter and that I accurately translated this plea agreement to the defendant, he/she told me that he/she understood it, and I am satisfied that his/her answer is true and correct.

Date: ______________

____
Interpreter's Signature

ORDER

I find that:

1. The defendant enters this plea of guilty freely and voluntarily and not out of ignorance, inadvertence, fear or coercion.

2. The defendant understands and knowingly, freely and voluntarily waives his/her constitutional rights.

3. The defendant freely and voluntarily executed the attached Application and fully understands its contents.

4. The defendant has admitted the essential elements of the crime charged.

IT IS THEREFORE ORDERED that the defendant's plea of "GUILTY" entered in open court be accepted and entered as requested in this Application and as recommended in the certificate signed by the defendant's lawyer.

Done in open court this___ day of____________, 20__.

____
WILLIAM ALSUP
United States District Judge

Hon. Sandra B. Armstrong

District Judge

Chambers Information

U.S. District Court, Northern District of California
Courtroom 1, 4th Floor
1301 Clay Street
Oakland, CA 94612

Scheduling Information

Courtroom Deputy: (510) 637-3541

Criminal Law and Motion	Tuesdays at 10:00 a.m.
Civil Law and Motion	Tuesdays at 1:00 p.m.
Case Management Conferences	Wednesdays & Thursdays – Telephone Only. Court will schedule time.
Trial Days	Mondays, Wednesdays, Thursdays, and Fridays from 8:30 a.m.-2:00 p.m.

Judge's Biography

Born 1947 in Oakland, CA

Federal Judicial Service:

-Judge, U. S. District Court, Northern District of California
-Nominated by George H.W. Bush on April 25, 1991, to a seat vacated by William A. Ingram; Confirmed by the Senate on June 14, 1991, and received commission on June 18, 1991.

Education:

-Merritt College, A.A., 1967
-California State University, Fresno, B.A., 1969
-University of San Francisco School of Law, J.D., 1977

Professional Career:

-Policewoman, Oakland Police Department, Oakland, California, 1970-1977
-Judicial Extern, California Court of Appeals, 1977
-Deputy District Attorney, Alameda County, California, 1978-1979, 1980-1982
-Senior Consultant, California Assembly Committee on Criminal Justice, 1979-1980
-Trial Attorney, Public Integrity Section, U.S. Department of Justice, 1982-1983
-Commissioner, Consumer Product Safety Commission, 1983-1986
-Commissioner, U.S. Parole Commission, 1986-1989
-Judge, Alameda Superior Court, California, 1989-1991

I. Judge Armstrong's Procedures and Practices

A. *Criminal Standing Order*

JUDGE ARMSTRONG'S CRIMINAL STANDING ORDER

(Effective April 2, 2010)

Criminal Law & Motion will be held on Tuesdays:

9:00 a.m. Calendar is for Status, Trial Setting, Motion Setting and Status or Setting of Supervised Release and/or Probation Revocations

10:00 a.m. Calendar is for Judgment & Sentencings

11:00 a.m. Calendar is for Motion Hearings, Pretrial Conferences and Changes of Plea. Prior to a plea being entered in a criminal case, a copy of the plea agreement **must** be submitted to chambers no later then the Friday before the plea is to be taken. All persons pleading guilty **must** complete an application for permission to enter plea of guilty, which is available on the Court's website at www.cand.uscourts.gov.

Stipulation and proposed order for continuance and exclusion of time in criminal actions. In criminal actions, any stipulation and request for a continuance and exclusion of time under the Speedy Trial Act, 18 U.S.C. § 3161 et seq., shall be submitted in accordance with the following requirements:

a. Prior to submitting any stipulation and request for a continuance and exclusion of time, at least one of the parties shall contact Judge Armstrong's deputy courtroom clerk to ascertain whether the date to which the parties desire to continue the matter is available on Judge Armstrong's calendar.

b. The submission shall bear the title "STIPULATION AND [PROPOSED] ORDER FOR CONTINUANCE AND EXCLUSION OF TIME UNDER THE SPEEDY TRIAL ACT, 18 U.S.C. § 3161 ET SEQ."

c. The format of the submission shall be substantially that of a stipulation and proposed order set out in Civil L.R. 7-11, with the following modifications and additional provisions:

(1) Above the signatures of the individuals signing the stipulation, the following shall appear: (a) specification of the statutory provisions providing the legal basis or bases for the continuance and exclusion of time; (b) in substantial detail, the reasons for the continuance and exclusion of time; and (c) a statement that the parties agree that the matter should be continued and time should be excluded for the statutory reason(s) invoked in the stipulation and proposed order (e.g., a stipulation and proposed order for a continuance and exclusion of time under 18 U.S.C. § 3161(h)(8)(A) and (B)(iv) for continuity of defense counsel may contain this statement: "For the foregoing reasons, the parties stipulate and agree that the ends of justice served by the continuance requested herein outweigh the best interests of the public and the defendant in a speedy trial because the failure to grant such a continuance would unreasonably deny the defendant continuity of counsel.").

(2) Below the signatures of the individuals signing the stipulation, there shall appear the statement "Based on the reasons provided in the stipulation of the parties above, the Court hereby FINDS" followed by all findings required to be made by the Court to warrant an exclusion of time under the provision(s) of the Speedy Trial Act invoked by the parties. These findings must track the language of the relevant statutory provision(s) invoked.

(3) Below the findings, there shall appear the statement "Based on these findings, IT IS HEREBY ORDERED THAT" followed by the requested action(s) (i.e., that the relevant date is continued to the desired date and that time is excluded under the Speedy Trial Act pursuant to specified statutory provisions). On the line below this matter shall appear: "IT IS SO ORDERED."

(4) Below the aforementioned text, there shall appear a signature line and date line for Judge Armstrong.

(5) The phrase "PURSUANT TO STIPULATION, IT IS SO ORDERED" or a similar phrase shall not appear in the stipulation and proposed order.

d. Any stipulation and request for continuance and exclusion of time shall be lodged with the Court no later than the beginning of the period of time sought to be excluded. THE COURT WILL NOT EXCLUDE TIME RETROSPECTIVELY.

e. Any stipulation and request for continuance and exclusion of time shall be lodged with the Court no later than noon on the day before the hearing or other matter sought to be continued.

Any failure to comply with any of these requirements may result in summary denial of the request for the continuance and/or the exclusion of time. Full compliance with these requirements, however, does not guarantee that the Court will grant the requested action(s), as the Court will independently evaluate the matter provided in the parties' stipulation.

B. Patent Standing Order

JUDGE ARMSTRONG'S PATENT STANDING ORDER

(Effective November 8, 2010)

The following instructions shall apply to all patent cases assigned to Judge Saundra Brown Armstrong.

Joint Claim Construction Statement

1. The joint claim construction statement required by Pat. L.R. 4-3 shall be truly joint. Disputed terms, phrases, and clauses shall be clearly designated as disputed. All other terms shall be presumed undisputed. For any term in dispute, the parties must agree on what the term actually is. With regard to disputed terms, phrases, or clauses, the joint statement shall list each disputed term, phrase, or clause (listed by claim); each party's proposed construction; and support for each party's proposed construction side by side. A model construction statement is attached to this order.

2. Parties shall attach to the joint claim construction statement copies of all patents in dispute. Parties shall also make a complete prosecution history for each patent available to the court upon request.

Claim Construction

3. As an initial matter, the court will construe no more than ten terms total. If more than ten terms are at issue, the parties shall meet and confer before the preparation of the joint claim construction statement on narrowing the selection of terms to be construed by the court and shall jointly propose the ten terms requiring construction.

4. If a party genuinely believes that it will require that more than ten terms be construed, that party may, after meeting and conferring with opposing counsel, file a motion for administrative relief, pursuant to Civ. L.R. 7-11, for leave to designate additional terms for construction. The requesting party must demonstrate good cause and explain why other methods of limiting the claims at issue (such as the selection of representative claims or any grouping of claims by issues presented) would be ineffective. The request must be filed no later than two weeks before the deadline for filing the joint claim construction statement. If good cause is shown, the court will either agree to construe all terms or schedule a second claim construction proceeding on the terms that exceed ten. If more than ten terms are submitted for construction without leave of court, the court will construe the first ten terms listed in the joint claim construction statement and sanctions may be imposed.

5. Claim construction briefs shall address each disputed term, but only those that are truly disputed, following the order of the joint statement. The court anticipates that a meaningful meet and confer preceding the preparation of the joint claim construction statement will obviate the need for a party to propose in its briefs a claim construction that differs from that proposed in the statement.

While the court encourages the parties to negotiate mutually agreeable constructions, the court discourages the parties from proposing new constructions for the first time in reply briefs or other filings which do not afford the opposing party an opportunity to respond. However, if it becomes necessary for a party to propose a different construction in its brief than that found in the joint claim construction statement, that party must clearly set forth the new construction and explain the basis for the change. Additionally, that party shall revise the joint claim construction statement, so that the court will have one document reflecting all current proposed constructions.

Tutorial and Claim Construction Hearing

6. If required, the court will schedule a tutorial to occur prior to the claim construction hearing. Each side will be permitted 30-45 minutes to present a short summary and explanation of the technology at issue. The patent holder makes the first presentation. Visual aids are encouraged. The court prefers that someone other than counsel make the presentation. No argument will be permitted. The proceeding is not recorded and parties may not rely on statements made at the tutorial in other aspects of the litigation.

7. Prehearing conferences are not generally held. However, either party may request a telephone conference two weeks prior to the hearing, or the parties may address any prehearing issues at the tutorial, if any.

8. The patent holder will act as the moving party for the purposes of claim construction. Opening briefs in support of claim construction must be filed at least six weeks before the date of the claim construction hearing, and the briefing schedule set forth at Patent L.R. 4-5 will apply. Interactive, hyperlinked briefs on CD-ROM are encouraged when practicable, but not required.

9. The court will not ordinarily hear extrinsic evidence at the claim construction hearing. Should it become apparent that testimony will be necessary, counsel may request a telephone conference with the court within two weeks of the hearing to seek the court's approval.

10. Demonstrative exhibits and visual aids are permissible at the hearing as long as they are based on information contained in the papers already filed. Counsel shall exchange copies of exhibits no later than forty eight hours prior to the hearing.

11. The claim construction hearing will generally be scheduled for no longer than three (3) hours. Counsel shall contact Courtroom Deputy Lisa Clark at 510-637-3541 to schedule the hearing.

Subsequent Case Management Report

12. With thirty (30) days of the filing date of the claim construction ruling, the parties shall file a further joint case management status report. In that report, the parties must address the following topics:

    a) whether either party wishes to certify the claim construction ruling for immediate appeal to the Federal Circuit;

    b) the filing of dispositive motions, and if multiple dispositive motions will be filed, any proposed grouping and timing of those motions and their hearings;

c) if willful infringement has been asserted, whether the allegedly-infringing party wishes to rely on the advice of counsel defense. If so, the parties should be prepared to address proposals for resolving any attorney-client privilege issues that arise, and whether the parties believe bifurcation of the trial into liability and damages phases would be appropriate;

d) anticipated post-claim construction discovery;

e) any other pretrial matters; and

f) the progress of settlement discussions, if any.

The court will review the reports and, if necessary, schedule a further case management conference and enter any appropriate orders.

Miscellaneous

13. All stipulated protective orders and filings shall comply with Civ. L.R. 79-5. Parties shall also submit an unredacted chambers copy of any brief lodged under seal with all confidential material highlighted. The parties shall refer to General Order 62 regarding the electronic filing of documents under seal.

IT IS SO ORDERED.

Dated: 11-8-10

SAUNDRA BROWN ARMSTRONG
United States District Judge

Sample Claim Chart

Claim Language (Disputed Terms in **Bold**) 'xxx Patent	Plaintiff's Proposed Construction and Evidence in Support	Defendant's Proposed Construction and Evidence in Support
1. A method for counting **ducks**, comprising the steps of: [or] **ducks** Found in claim numbers: 'xxx Patent: y, z 'yyy Patent: a, b	**duck** PROPOSED CONSTRUCTION: a bird that quacks. DICTIONARY/TREATISE DEFINITIONS: Webster's Dictionary ("duck: bird that quacks"); Field Guide ("bird call: quack"); INTRINSIC EVIDENCE: 'xxx Patent col. _:_ ("distinctive honking"); Prosecution History at __ ("This patent is distinguished from the prior art in that the quacking of the bird is featured"). EXTRINSIC EVIDENCE: McDonald Depo. at xx:xx ("I'd say the quacking makes it a duck"); '123 Patent at col _:__; Donald Decl. at ¶ __ .	**duck** PROPOSED CONSTRUCTION: a bird that swims DICTIONARY/TREATISE DEFINITIONS: Random House Dictionary ("an aquatic bird"); Field Guide (same) INTRINSIC EVIDENCE: 'xxx Patent col _:__ ("ducks may be found on or near bodies of water"); Prosecution History at __ ("water fowl are particularly amenable to being counted by this method"). EXTRINSIC EVIDENCE: G. Marx Depo at xx:xx ("like a duck to water"); '456 Patent at col _:__; Daffy Decl. at ¶ __.

(Or any other substantively similar format that permits the court to compare terms side by side)

NOT:

Claim Language (Disputed Terms in **Bold**) 'xxx Patent	Plaintiff's Proposed Construction and Evidence in Support	Defendant's Proposed Construction and Evidence in Support
1. A method for counting **ducks** . . .	**duck**	**counting duck**

C. *Standing Order*

JUDGE ARMSTRONG'S STANDING ORDER

(Effective July 1, 2011)

1. **Compliance with Local Rules:** Counsel are expected to consult and comply with all provisions of the Local Rules of Court relating to continuances, motions and all other matters.

2. **Scheduling:**

   a. Criminal: The criminal law and motion calendar is held on Tuesdays beginning at 10:00 a.m.

   b. Civil: The civil law and motion calendar is held on Tuesdays beginning at 1:00 p.m. Civil matters shall not be noticed for hearing on a Tuesday following an official court holiday that falls on a Monday. The Court may resolve motions without a hearing. See Fed. R. Civ. P. 78(b); Civ. L.R. 7-1(b).

   c. Case Management Conferences: Case Management Conferences are conducted telephonically, and are held on Wednesdays and Thursdays, beginning at 2:30 p.m.

   d. Trial: The Court's trial days are Mondays, Wednesdays, Thursdays and Fridays. Trial hours are from 8:30 a.m. to 2:30 p.m., which includes one fifteen (15) minute break in the morning and a thirty (30) minute lunch break.

3. **Setting Motions for Hearing:** The Court does not reserve hearing dates. To schedule a matter on the Court's civil law and motion calendar, the parties are directed to review the Court's calendar at www.cand.uscourts.gov to determine the next available hearing date. Matters are calendared on a first come first serve basis.

4. **Checking the Calendar Before You Appear:** Before appearing for a matter before this Court all parties shall check the court's calendar at www.cand.uscourts.gov to confirm that their matters are still on calendar.

5. **Meet and Confer Requirement:** All parties shall meet and confer before filing any motion before the Court. The motion and any other non-stipulated request shall include a certification, which may be included in the body of the document, that the parties have complied with the meet and confer requirement. The Court may disregard any papers submitted that do not comply with this rule.

6. **Guilty Pleas:** Prior to a plea being entered in a criminal case, a copy of the plea agreement must be submitted to chambers no later than the Friday before the plea is to be taken. All persons pleading guilty must complete an application for permission to enter plea of guilty, which is available on the Court's website at www.cand.uscourts.gov.

7. **Courtesy Copies in e-Filing Cases:** When filing papers in connection with any motion or case management conference, the parties shall, in addition to filing papers electronically, lodge with the Clerk's Office a printed copy of the papers by the close of business the following day the papers are filed electronically. These printed copies shall be marked "Chambers Copy" and shall be submitted to the Clerk's Office, in an envelope clearly marked with the judge's name, case number and "E-Filing Chambers

Copy." Parties shall not file a paper copy of any other document with the Clerk's Office that has already been filed electronically. You MUST submit a hard copy of all motion papers filed in E-FILED cases in order to be placed on calendar.

OTHER REQUIREMENTS

In addition to the requirements set forth in the Civil L.R. 16-10, counsel are expected to comply with the following:

A. Filing Case Management Conference Statements

Counsel are expected to comply with this Standing Order concerning the joint filing of the Case Management Statement. In preparing the Case Management Statement, the parties shall use the Standing Order for all Judges of the Northern District of California provided herewith. Note that no party may submit a separate Case Management Statement. Disagreements among parties with respect to any of the matters contained in the Case Management Statement shall be set forth in the appropriate sections.

Counsel are further expected to file a Case Management Statement at least ten (10) days before each and every scheduled Case Management Conference. If there is no change in the status of the case from the time the last statement was filed, counsel shall indicate as such in a pleading and attach a copy of the most recently filed Case Management Statement to the pleading. Failure to timely file a Case Management Statement may result in sanctions.

B. Appearance at the Case Management Conference

Each party shall be represented at the Case Management Conference by Counsel prepared to address all of the matters referred to in this and the Civil L.R. 16-10(b), and with authority to enter into stipulations and make admissions pursuant to this and Fed. R. Civ. P. 16(a) and (c). Representatives of the parties may, but are not required to, attend. Unless otherwise specified, all Case Management Conferences shall take place via telephone. Plaintiff or his/her counsel is responsible for setting up the conference call. Plaintiff or his/her counsel will be notified of the date and time of the telephone conference call by Clerk's Notice shortly after the case is filed.

Any request to reschedule the above dates shall be made in compliance with Civil L.R. 16-2(e) and must be made at least ten days prior to the date sought to be modified. A request to continue a Case Management Conference shall be made in a separately-filed request, separate from the Case Management Conference Statement. Counsel shall not contact the chambers of Judge Armstrong regarding requests to modify provisions of this Standing Order; all requests must be submitted in writing and served on all parties to the action.

The parties should be prepared to address and resolve at the Case Management Conference the following: Setting the date and the estimated length of the trial; setting the deadline for joining parties and amending the pleadings; setting the date for discovery and motion cutoff; setting the date to designate experts and other witnesses; setting the date for the pretrial conference.

Other matters which the Court will take up at the Case Management Conference, in addition to those specified in the Joint Case Management Statement and Proposed Order Form, will include the following:

1. **Jurisdiction:** Does this Court have subject matter jurisdiction over all of the plaintiff's claim(s) and defendant's counter-claim(s)? What is the basis of such

jurisdiction? Are all the parties subject to the Court's jurisdiction? Do any parties remain to be served?

2. **Substance of the Action:** What are the factual and legal bases for plaintiff's claims, defendant's defenses, defendant's counter-claims and plaintiff's defenses to the counterclaims?

3. **Identification of Issues:** What are the factual and legal issues genuinely in dispute?

4. **Narrowing of Issues:** What are the issues that can be narrowed by agreement or by motions? Are there dispositive or partially dispositive issues appropriate for a decision by motion?

5. **Motions:** What are the motion(s) anticipated by the parties?

6. **Relief:** What relief does the plaintiff seek? What is the amount of damages sought by plaintiff's claim(s)? What is the amount of damages sought by defendant's counter-claim(s)? How are the damages computed?

7. **Discovery:** What discovery does each party intend to pursue? Can discovery be limited in any manner? Are there any alternative methods available to obtain the necessary information? Should a discovery order and conference be entered pursuant to Fed. R. Civ. P. 26(f)?

8. **Alternative Means of Disposition:** Is the case suitable for reference to binding arbitration, to a master, or to a magistrate for trial? Is the case suitable for reference to the Judicial Panel on Multidistrict Litigation?

9. **Pretrial Conference and Trial Setting:** Will this case be tried by a jury? What is the anticipated length of trial? Is it possible to reduce the length of the trial by stipulation, use of summaries or statements, or other expedited means of presenting evidence? Is it feasible and desirable to bifurcate issues for trial?

10. **Related Cases:** Are there any related cases pending before the judges of this Court? See Civil L.R. 3-12.

11. **Cut-Off Dates:** When are the earliest reasonable dates for amendment to the pleadings, discovery cutoff, motion cutoff, expert disclosures, pretrial conference and trial?

12. **Settlement:** What are the prospects for settlement? Does any party wish to have a settlement conference with a magistrate? How can settlement efforts be assisted? See ADR L.R. 7-3.

13. **Other Matters:** Such other matters as any party considers conducive to the just, speedy and inexpensive determination of this action. See Fed.R.Civ.P. 16(a) and (c).

C. **Law and Motion**

1. **Scheduling:** Law and Motion matters will be heard on Tuesdays at 1:00 p.m., in Courtroom 1 of the United States Courthouse, 1301 Clay Street, 4th Floor, Oakland, California. The parties need not reserve hearing dates. The parties are advised to check the court's calendar at

www.cand.uscourts.gov [Judges | Saundra Brown Armstrong | Judge's Calendar | View Scheduling Notes] for the next available hearing date. Matters are calendared on a first come first serve basis. <u>You must submit a hard copy of all motion papers filed in EFILED cases in order to be placed on calendar.</u>

2. **Page Limits:** All noticed motions (other than motions for summary judgment) and any opposition thereto, shall not exceed **fifteen (15) pages** in length, exclusive of the table of contents, table of authorities, exhibits and declarations, if required. Reply briefs may not exceed **ten (10) pages** in length. Motions for summary judgment are subject to the page limits set forth in Civil Local Rule 7.

3. **Meet and Confer Requirement:** All parties are required to meet and confer before filing any motion or any non-stipulated request with this court, and to certify that they have complied with this requirement.

4. **Proposed Orders:** Each party filing or opposing a motion shall also serve and file a proposed order which sets forth the relief of action which includes that the party requests the Court to adopt, a short statement of the rationale of decision including citation to authority.

5. **Summary Judgment Motions:** Parties are limited to filing one motion for summary judgment. Any party wishing to exceed this limit must request leave of Court. The parties are not required to file statements of undisputed facts in connection with a motion for summary judgment. However, if the parties desire to file a statement of undisputed facts, only one joint statement of undisputed facts signed by all parties shall be filed. All separate statements will be stricken. If the parties are unable to agree that a fact is undisputed, they should assume that fact is in dispute.

6. **Failure to File Opposition:** <u>The failure of the opposing party to file a memorandum of points and authorities in opposition to any motion shall constitute a consent to the granting of the motion.</u>

7. **Appearances:** The Court may, in its discretion, adjudicate motions without oral argument. Fed. R. Civ. P. 78(b); Civ. L.R. 7-1(b). The parties are advised to check the Court's website www.cand.uscourts.gov [Judges | Saundra Brown Armstrong | Judge's Calendar] to determine whether an appearance on the motion is required. NOTE: If a Case Management Conference is scheduled to follow the hearing on the motion, and the motion has been removed from the calendar, the Case Management Conference is deemed to have been taken off calendar as well, and will be rescheduled, if appropriate.

8. **Non-Compliant Papers:** Any pleading or brief sought to be filed with the Court after the required time, or in an improper manner or form, shall not be received or considered by the Court. Any attorney in violation of such requirements will be subject to other sanctions. Civil L.R. 1-4.

9. **Sanctions:** Failure to comply with this Order or the Local Rules of this Court may result in sanctions. See Fed.R.Civ.P. 16(f); Civil L.R. 1-4.

D. Discovery Motions

All discovery disputes will be referred to a Magistrate Judge of this Court.

____

SAUNDRA BROWN ARMSTRONG
United States District Judge

II. Judge Armstrong's Case Management Orders

A. *Order for Pretrial Preparation in Civil Cases*

IN THE UNITED STATES DISTRICT COURT
FOR THE NORTHERN DISTRICT OF CALIFORNIA

No. C_________ SBA

Plaintiff,

v.

ORDER FOR PRETRIAL PREPARATION

Defendant.

______________________________________/

Pursuant to Rule 16(e) of the Federal Rules of Civil Procedure ("FRCP"), IT IS HEREBY ORDERED AS FOLLOWS:

A. DISCOVERY CUT-OFF

All discovery, except for expert discovery, shall be completed and all depositions taken on or before _____________. The parties are responsible for scheduling discovery so that motions to resolve discovery disputes can be heard before the above discovery cut-off.

B. EXPERT DESIGNATION AND DISCOVERY

Plaintiff shall designate any experts by ___________; defendant by ____________; rebuttal disclosure by ___________. Any expert not so named may be disallowed as a witness. No expert will be permitted to testify to any opinion, or basis or support for an opinion, that has not been disclosed in response to an appropriate question or interrogatory from the opposing party. Expert discovery shall be completed by ________________.

C. MOTION CUT-OFF

All dispositive motions shall be ***heard*** on or before ____________, at 1:00 p.m. The parties must meet and confer *prior* to filing any motion. The movant shall certify to the Court in its moving papers that it has complied with this requirement. Should the parties fail to meet and confer, the Court may decline to entertain the motion.

THIS COURT DOES NOT RESERVE MOTION HEARING DATES. The parties are advised to contact Judge Armstrong's Deputy Clerk, Lisa Clark, to determine the next available hearing date, particularly in the case of a dispositive motion. The parties are advised *not* to wait until 35 days prior to the law and motion cut-off date to file and serve their motion. As the Court's law and motion calendar tends to fill quickly, there is ***no*** guarantee that a hearing date within the law and motion cut-off date will be available. You MUST submit a hard copy of all motion papers filed in E-FILED cases in order to be placed on calendar.

Pursuant to Civil Local Rule 7-1, 7-2 and 7-3, all civil motions shall be noticed for a hearing not less than thirty-five (35) calendar days after service. The opposition and supporting papers shall be filed not less than twenty-one (21) days before the noticed hearing date. The reply shall be filed not less than fourteen (14) days before the hearing date. Documents not filed in compliance with these time specifications will not be considered by the Court.

The failure of the opposing party to file a memorandum of points and authorities in opposition to any motion shall constitute a consent to the granting of the motion.

The parties are not required to file a statement of undisputed facts in connection with a motion for summary judgment. However, if the parties desire to file a statement of undisputed facts, only one joint statement of undisputed facts signed by all parties, shall be filed. All separate statements will be stricken. If the parties are unable to agree that a fact is undisputed, they should assume that fact is in dispute.

Note that pursuant to Civil L.R. 7-1(b), the Court may, in its discretion, adjudicate motions *without* oral argument.

D. MANDATORY SETTLEMENT CONFERENCES

All parties are ordered to participate in a mandatory settlement conference during the following time period: ________________________________.

E. PRETRIAL CONFERENCE

All Counsel who will try the case shall appear for a pretrial conference in Courtroom 3 on__________________at 1:00 p.m.. All Counsel shall be fully prepared to discuss all aspects of the trial. Failure to file the requisite pretrial documents in advance of the pretrial conference may result in vacation of the pretrial conference and/or the imposition of sanctions. ***ALL PARTIES ARE REQUIRED TO ATTEND THE PRETRIAL CONFERENCE.***

F. PRETRIAL PREPARATION DUE

1. Not less that *thirty (30) calendar days* prior to the pretrial conference, Counsel shall meet and confer in good faith in advance of complying with the following pretrial requirements in order to clarify and narrow the issues for trial, arrive at stipulations of facts, simplify and shorten the presentation of proof at trial, and explore possible settlement. In addition, Counsel shall meet and confer regarding anticipated motions *in limine*, objections to evidence, jury instructions, and any other matter which may require resolution by the Court.

2. The following matters shall be accomplished no later than *twenty-one (21) calendar days* prior to the pretrial conference:

a. Joint Pretrial Statement

Counsel are required to file a pretrial conference statement containing the following information:

(1) **The Action**

(A) Substance of the Action. A brief description of the substance of claims and defenses which remain to be decided.

(B) Relief Prayed. A detailed statement of all the relief claimed, particularly itemizing all elements of damages claimed as well as witnesses, documents or other evidentiary material to be presented concerning the amount of those damages.

(2) **The Factual Basis of the Action**

(A) Undisputed Facts. A plain and concise statement of all relevant facts not reasonably disputable, as well as which facts parties will stipulate for incorporation into the trial record without the necessity of supporting testimony or exhibits.

(B) Disputed Factual Issues. A plain and concise statement of all disputed factual issues which remain to be decided.

(C) Agreed Statement. A statement assessing whether all or part of the action may be presented upon an agreed statement of facts.

(D) Stipulations. A statement of stipulations requested or proposed for pretrial or trial purposes.

(3) **DISPUTED LEGAL ISSUES**

(A) Points of Law. Without extended legal argument, a concise statement of each disputed point of law concerning liability or relief, citing supporting statutes and decisions. Unless otherwise ordered, parties should cite to briefs served and lodged setting forth briefly the nature of each party's contentions concerning each disputed point of law, including procedural and evidentiary issues.

(B) Proposed Conclusions of law. If the case is to be tried without jury, unless otherwise ordered, parties should briefly indicate objections to proposed conclusions of law lodged with this Court.

b. Trial Briefs

Each party shall serve and file a trial brief which shall briefly state their contentions, the relevant facts to be proven at trial, and the law on the issues material to the decision.

c. Findings of Fact

In non-jury cases, each party shall serve and lodge with the Court proposed findings of fact and conclusions of law on all material issues. Findings shall be brief, clear, written in plain English and free of pejorative language, and argument.

d. Witnesses

Each party shall serve and file with the Court a list of all persons who may be called as witnesses. The list shall include a summary of the substance of each witness' proposed testimony. (Civil L.R. 16-15(4)(A))

e. **Designation of Discovery Excerpts**

Each party expecting to use discovery excerpts as part of its case in chief shall serve and lodge with the Court a statement identifying (1) by witness and page and line, all deposition testimony and (2) by lodged excerpt, all interrogatory answers and request for admissions to be used as part of its direct case. Each interrogatory answer intended to be offered as an exhibit shall be copied separately and marked as an exhibit. The original of any deposition to be used at trial must be produced at the time of trial, as well as a copy for the Court. Counsel shall indicate any objections to the use of these materials and advise the Court that counsel has conferred respecting such objections.

f. **Jury Instructions**

The parties shall file a joint set of proposed jury instructions as to those instructions on which the parties have reached agreement. As to any disputed instructions, each party shall separately submit its "proposed" instruction(s) supported by a memorandum setting forth the authority for its use. Responses or objections to any "proposed" jury instruction shall be filed no later than the date of the pretrial conference. All instructions shall be written in plain English which is comprehensible to jurors, concise and free of argument, and shall be organized in a logical fashion so as to aid jury comprehension, and are also to be provided on a CD in a word format. The Court's practice is to utilize, whenever possible, instructions found in the Ninth Circuit Manual of Model Jury Instructions.

g. **Jury Voir Dire and Verdict Forms**

Each party shall submit proposed questions for jury voir dire and a proposed form of verdict.

h. **Exhibits**

Each party shall provide every other party one set of all exhibits, charts, schedules, summaries and diagrams and other similar documentary materials to be used at the trial together with a complete list of all such exhibits. The Court requires one original version of exhibits (as described above) for the Clerk and two copies (one for the Bench and one for the witness stand). All such versions of the exhibits, including the originals, should be indexed into a binder for easy and quick reference by all parties. The first page of each binder should have a copy of the exhibit list (see attached) appropriately completed with each exhibit description and its designated number. Plaintiffs shall refer to their exhibits numerically and Defendants shall label theirs alphabetically. Exhibit labels are also attached for your convenience. Exhibits should be brought to Court on the first day of trial.

3. The following matters shall be accomplished no later than *fourteen (14) calendar days* prior to the pretrial conference: **Motions *in Limine* and Objections to Evidence due:** __________. Each party anticipating making motion(s) *in limine* and/or objection(s) to any testimony or exhibits expected to be offered shall file and serve a statement briefly identifying each item objected to and the grounds for the objection.

4. Responses to motions *in limine* or objections to evidence shall be filed and served no less than *seven (7) calendar days* prior to the pretrial conference due:____________.

H. TRIAL DATE

Trial before the Court or Jury? will begin on ______________, at 8:30 a.m., for an estimated ________ trial days, or as soon thereafter as the Court may designate. The parties are advised that they must be prepared to go to trial on a trailing basis. The trial will take place in Courtroom 3 of the United States Courthouse, 1301 Clay Street, 3rd Floor, Oakland, California, 94612. The Court's trial hours are from 8:30 a.m. to 2:00 p.m., with two fifteen-minute breaks, on Monday, Wednesday, Thursday and Friday.

I. TRANSCRIPTS

If transcripts will be requested during or immediately after the trial, arrangements must be made with the Court Reporter Coordinator (Telephone No. 510-637-3534) at least one week prior to the commencement of trial commences.

J. STATUS AND DISCOVERY CONFERENCES

Any party desiring to confer with the Court may, upon notice to all other parties, arrange a conference through the courtroom deputy (Telephone No. 510-637-3541). Conferences may be conducted telephonically, upon request (preferably in writing).

K. SANCTIONS

Failure to comply with this order may result in the imposition of sanctions pursuant to FRCP 16(f).

IT IS SO ORDERED.

Dated: ____________________

____
SAUNDRA BROWN ARMSTRONG
United States District Judge

B. Order for Pretrial Preparation in Criminal Cases

IN THE UNITED STATES DISTRICT COURT
FOR THE NORTHERN DISTRICT OF CALIFORNIA

No. CR__________ SBA

Plaintiff,

ORDER FOR PRETRIAL PREPARATION IN CRIMINAL CASES

v.

Defendant.
____________________________________/

Good cause appearing, it is hereby ORDERED that:

A. Trial Date. Trial before the COURT or JURY trial? shall begin on Trial Date, at 8:30 a.m., in Courtroom No. 3 of the United States Courthouse, 1301 Clay Street, 3rd Floor, Oakland, California, 94612. The Court's trial hours are from 8:30 a.m. to 2:00 p.m., with two fifteen-minute breaks, on Monday, Wednesday, Thursday and Friday.

B. Trial Length. The estimated length of trial is Length of Trial - Days/Weeks.

C. Discovery. By the close of business, Date of Discovery Cutoff, the parties will exchange the information, documents, and tangible objects authorized by Fed. R. Crim. P. 16. Additional discovery shall be by motion accompanied by affidavits setting for the unusual circumstances justifying discovery beyond the limits of Fed. R. Crim. P. 16. COUNSEL SHALL MEET AND CONFER REGARDING ANY DISCOVERY MATTERS PRIOR TO FILING OF ANY DISCOVERY MOTIONS.

D. Motions. All motions will be heard on Tuesday, Date for Hearing Motions, at 9:00 a.m. in Courtroom No. 3, and shall comply with Local Rule 320-3. Motions, affidavits and memoranda shall be served, filed and an extra copy lodged with the Court by the moving party by 4:00 p.m. On Date for Filing Moving Papers. Any opposition shall be filed and an extra copy lodged with the Court by 12:00 noon on Date for Filing Opposition Papers.

E. Pretrial Preparation. The motions will comply with the following schedule for pretrial preparation.

All Counsel who will try the case shall appear for a pretrial conference in Courtroom 3 on Tuesday, Date of Pretrial Conference, at 9:00 a.m. Counsel for defendant(s) and for the government are directed to confer on all applicable pretrial agenda matters enumerated in Criminal Local Rule 17.1-7 prior to the pretrial conference and be prepared to discuss them at that conference. The following pretrial preparation shall be accomplished by the counsel for the government no later than Deadline for Pretrial Preparations.

(1) Serve and file a trial memorandum briefly stating the legal basis for the charges and the anticipated evidence, and addressing any evidentiary or other anticipated legal

issues;

(2) Serve and file a list of all witnesses which may be called together with a brief summary of the testimony of each;

(3) Serve and lodge requested jury instructions in the following form:

(a) the parties shall file a **joint** set of jury instructions as to those instructions on which the parties have reached agreement. As to any disputed instructions, each party shall separately submit its "proposed" instruction(s) supported by a memorandum setting forth the authority for its use. Responses or objections to any "proposed" jury instruction shall be filed no later than the date of the pretrial conference. All instructions shall be written in plain English which is comprehensible to jurors, concise and free of argument, and shall be organized in a logical fashion so as to aid jury comprehension, and are also to be provided on a 3.5" computer disk (formatted for Word Perfect 6.1). The Court's practice is to utilize, whenever possible, instructions found in the Ninth Circuit Manual of Model Jury Instructions;

(4) Serve and lodge proposed voir dire of the jury panel;

(5) Serve and lodge a proposed form of verdict:

(6) Serve copies of all exhibits to be offered at trial together with a completed list of exhibits (in the form attached). Each item shall be premarked using the form of marker attached; generally, the government will use numbers, defendant letters. The Court requires one original version of exhibits for the Clerk and two copies (one for the Bench and one for the witness stand). All such versions of the exhibits, including the originals, should be indexed into a binder for easy and quick reference by all parties. The first page of each binder should have a copy of the exhibit list appropriately completed with each exhibit description and its designated number or letter. Exhibits should be brought to Court on the first day of trial.

No later than Deadline for Defense Counsel to Comply, the defense counsel shall comply with paragraphs (3) and (4), above, and, to the extent consistent with the defendant's right to an effective defense, with paragraphs (1), (2) and (6).

In particular, counsel will be expected to confer in advance and be prepared to discuss with the court any anticipated evidentiary objections and means for shortening and simplifying the trial (*e.g.*, by stipulations to such matters as chain of custody, the nature of substances, the use of the mail, *etc.*). See Crim. L.R. 17.1-1.

F. **COPIES.** Each document filed or lodged with the court must be accompanied by a copy for use in the judge's chambers. In addition, one copy of the witness and exhibit lists should be provided to the court reporter.

G. **TRANSCRIPTS.** If transcripts will be requested during or immediately after the trial, arrangements must be made with the court reporter at least one week before trial commences.

H. **CHANGE OF PLEA.** Defense Counsel shall give prompt notice to the United States attorney and the Court of any intention to change a previously entered not guilty plea. Government Counsel shall provide the Court with a copy of the plea agreement on the Friday before the defendant is set to change his/her plea.

***MOTIONS IN LIMINE AND/OR OBJECTIONS TO EVIDENCE DUE Deadline for IN LIMINE Motions.

***RESPONSES TO OBJECTIONS TO EVIDENCE AND/OR MOTIONS *IN LIMINE* DUE Deadline for IN LIMINE Responses.

Dated: ______________________

____
SAUNDRA BROWN ARMSTRONG
United States District Judge

C. Order for Pretrial Preparation in Patent Cases

IN THE UNITED STATES DISTRICT COURT
FOR THE NORTHERN DISTRICT OF CALIFORNIA

No. C__________ SBA

Plaintiff,

ORDER FOR PRETRIAL PREPARATION IN PATENT CASES

v.

Defendant.

_______________________________________/

Pursuant to Rule 16(e) of the Federal Rules of Civil Procedure ("FRCP"), IT IS HEREBY ORDERED AS FOLLOWS:

A. DISCOVERY CUT-OFF

All discovery, except for expert discovery, shall be completed and all depositions taken on or before _____________. The parties are responsible for scheduling discovery so that motions to resolve discovery disputes can be heard before the above discovery cut-off.

B. EXPERT DESIGNATION AND DISCOVERY

Plaintiff shall designate any experts by ___________; defendant by ____________; rebuttal disclosure by ___________. Any expert not so named may be disallowed as a witness. No expert will be permitted to testify to any opinion, or basis or support for an opinion, that has not been disclosed in response to an appropriate question or interrogatory from the opposing party. Expert discovery shall be completed by _______________.

C. MOTION CUT-OFF

All dispositive motions shall be ***heard*** on or before ____________, at 1:00 p.m. The parties must meet and confer *prior* to filing any motion. The movant shall certify to the Court in its moving papers that it has complied with this requirement. Should the parties fail to meet and confer, the Court may decline to entertain the motion.

THIS MOTION DATE IS NOT RESERVED. The parties are advised to contact Judge Armstrong's Deputy Clerk, Lisa Clark, to determine the next available hearing date, particularly in the case of dispositive motion. The parties are advised *not* to wait until 35 days prior to the law and motion cut-off date to file and serve their motion. As the Court's law and motion calendar tends to fill quickly, there is ***no*** guarantee that a hearing date within the law and motion cut-off date will be available.

Pursuant to Civil Local Rule 7-1, 7-2 and 7-3, all civil motions shall be noticed for a hearing not less than thirty-five (35) calendar days after service. The opposition and supporting papers shall be filed not less than twenty-one (21) days before the noticed hearing date. The reply shall be filed not less than fourteen (14) days before the hearing date. Documents not filed in compliance with these time specifications will not be considered by the Court.

The failure of the opposing party to file a memorandum of points and authorities in opposition to any motion shall constitute a consent to the granting of the motion.

The parties are not required to file a statement of undisputed facts in connection with a motion for summary judgment. However, if the parties desire to file a statement of undisputed facts, only one joint statement of undisputed facts signed by all parties shall be filed. All separate statements will be stricken. If the parties are unable to agree that a fact is undisputed, they should assume that fact is in dispute.

Note that pursuant to Civil L.R. 7-1(b), the Court may, in its discretion, adjudicate motions *without* oral argument.

D. MANDATORY SETTLEMENT CONFERENCES

All parties are ordered to participate in a mandatory settlement conference during the following time period: _________________________________.

E. PRETRIAL CONFERENCE

All Counsel who will try the case shall appear for a pretrial conference in Courtroom 3 on____________________at 1:00 p.m.. All Counsel shall be fully prepared to discuss all aspects of the trial. Failure to file the requisite pretrial documents in advance of the pretrial conference may result in vacation of the pretrial conference and/or the imposition of sanctions. ***ALL PARTIES ARE REQUIRED TO ATTEND THE PRETRIAL CONFERENCE.***

F. PRETRIAL PREPARATION DUE

1. Not less that *thirty (30) calendar days* prior to the pretrial conference, Counsel shall meet and confer in good faith in advance of complying with the following pretrial requirements in order to clarify and narrow the issues for trial, arrive at stipulations of facts, simplify and shorten the presentation of proof at trial, and explore possible settlement. In addition, Counsel shall meet and confer regarding anticipated motions *in limine*, objections to evidence, jury instructions, and any other matter which may require resolution by the Court.

2. The following matters shall be accomplished no later than *twenty-one (21) calendar days* prior to the pretrial conference:

a. Joint Pretrial Statement

Counsel are required to file a pretrial conference statement containing the following information:

(1) The Action

(A) Substance of the Action. A brief description of the substance of claims and defenses which remain to be decided.

(B) Relief Prayed. A detailed statement of all the relief claimed, particularly itemizing all elements of damages claimed as well as witnesses, documents or other evidentiary

material to be presented concerning the amount of those damages.

(2) **The Factual Basis of the Action**

(A) Undisputed Facts. A plain and concise statement of all relevant facts not reasonably disputable, as well as which facts parties will stipulate for incorporation into the trial record without the necessity of supporting testimony or exhibits.

(B) Disputed Factual Issues. A plain and concise statement of all disputed factual issues which remain to be decided.

(C) Agreed Statement. A statement assessing whether all or part of the action may be presented upon an agreed statement of facts.

(D) Stipulations. A statement of stipulations requested or proposed for pretrial or trial purposes.

(3) **DISPUTED LEGAL ISSUES**

(A) Points of Law. Without extended legal argument, a concise statement of each disputed point of law concerning liability or relief, citing supporting statutes and decisions. Unless otherwise ordered, parties should cite to briefs served and lodged setting forth briefly the nature of each party's contentions concerning each disputed point of law, including procedural and evidentiary issues.

(B) Proposed Conclusions of law. If the case is to be tried without jury, unless otherwise ordered, parties should briefly indicate objections to proposed conclusions of law lodged with this Court.

b. Trial Briefs

Each party shall serve and file a trial brief which shall briefly state their contentions, the relevant facts to be proven at trial, and the law on the issues material to the decision.

c. Findings of Fact

In non-jury cases, each party shall serve and lodge with the Court proposed findings of fact and conclusions of law on all material issues. Findings shall be brief, clear, written in plain English and free of pejorative language, and argument.

d. Witnesses

Each party shall serve and file with the Court a list of all persons who may be called as witnesses. The list shall include a summary of the substance of each witness' proposed testimony. (Civil L.R. 16-15(4)(A))

e. **Designation of Discovery Excerpts**

Each party expecting to use discovery excerpts as part of its case in chief shall serve and lodge with the Court a statement identifying (1) by witness and page and line, all deposition testimony and (2) by lodged excerpt, all interrogatory answers and request for admissions to be used as part of its direct case. Each interrogatory answer intended to be offered as an exhibit shall be copied separately and marked as an exhibit. The original of any deposition to be used at trial must be produced at the time of trial, as well as a copy for the Court. Counsel shall indicate any objections to the use of these materials and advise the Court that counsel has conferred respecting such objections.

f. **Jury Instructions**

The parties shall file a joint set of proposed jury instructions as to those instructions on which the parties have reached agreement. As to any disputed instructions, each party shall separately submit its "proposed" instruction(s) supported by a memorandum setting forth the authority for its use. Responses or objections to any "proposed" jury instruction shall be filed no later than the date of the pretrial conference. All instructions shall be written in plain English which is comprehensible to jurors, concise and free of argument, and shall be organized in a logical fashion so as to aid jury comprehension, and are also to be provided on a CD in a word format. The Court's practice is to utilize, whenever possible, instructions found in the Ninth Circuit Manual of Model Jury Instructions.

g. **Jury Voir Dire and Verdict Forms**

Each party shall submit proposed questions for jury voir dire and a proposed form of verdict.

h. **Exhibits**

Each party shall provide every other party one set of all exhibits, charts, schedules, summaries and diagrams and other similar documentary materials to be used at the trial together with a complete list of all such exhibits. The Court requires one original version of exhibits (as described above) for the Clerk and two copies (one for the Bench and one for the witness stand). All such versions of the exhibits, including the originals, should be indexed into a binder for easy and quick reference by all parties. The first page of each binder should have a copy of the exhibit list (see attached) appropriately completed with each exhibit description and its designated number. Plaintiffs shall refer to their exhibits numerically and Defendants shall label theirs alphabetically. Exhibit labels are also attached for your convenience. Exhibits should be brought to Court on the first day of trial.

3. The following matters shall be accomplished no later than *twenty-eight (28) calendar days* prior to the pretrial conference: **Motions *in Limine* and Objections to Evidence due: __________**. Each party anticipating making motion(s) *in limine* and/or objection(s) to any testimony or exhibits expected to be offered shall file and serve a statement briefly identifying each item objected to and the grounds for the objection.

4. Responses to motions *in limine* or objections to evidence shall be filed and served no less than *twenty-one (21) calendar days* prior to the pretrial conference due:____________.

H. <u>TRIAL DATE</u>

Trial before the Court or Jury? will begin on ______________, at 8:30 a.m., for an estimated ________ trial days, or as soon thereafter as the Court may designate. The parties are advised that they must be prepared to go to trial on a trailing basis. The trial will take place in Courtroom 3 of the United States Courthouse, 1301 Clay Street, 3rd Floor, Oakland, California, 94612. The Court's trial hours are from 8:30 a.m. to 2:00 p.m., with two fifteen-minute breaks, on Monday, Wednesday, Thursday and Friday.

I. <u>TRANSCRIPTS</u>

If transcripts will be requested during or immediately after the trial, arrangements must be made with the Court Reporter Coordinator (Telephone No. 510-637-3534) at least one week prior to the commencement of trial commences.

J. <u>STATUS AND DISCOVERY CONFERENCES</u>

Any party desiring to confer with the Court may, upon notice to all other parties, arrange a conference through the courtroom deputy (Telephone No. 510-637-3541). Conferences may be conducted telephonically, upon request (preferably in writing).

K. <u>SANCTIONS</u>

Failure to comply with this order may result in the imposition of sanctions pursuant to FRCP 16(f).

L. <u>OTHER DEADLINES</u>

IT IS SO ORDERED.

Dated: ____________________

____

SAUNDRA BROWN ARMSTRONG
United States District Judge

III. Judge Armstrong's Forms

A. *Application for Permission to Enter Plea of Guilty and Order Accepting Plea*

IN THE UNITED STATES DISTRICT COURT
FOR THE NORTHERN DISTRICT OF CALIFORNIA

UNITED STATES OF AMERICA,

Plaintiff,

v.

Defendant.

______________________________/

No. CR_________ SBA

APPLICATION FOR PERMISSION TO ENTER PLEA OF GUILTY AND ORDER ACCEPTING PLEA

(Fed. R. Crim. P., Rules 10 and 11)

The defendant represents to the Court:

1. My full true name is _______________. I am _____ years of age. I have gone to school up to and including ______________________________. My most recent occupation has been______________________________. I request that all proceedings against me be in my true name.

2. I am represented by a lawyer. His/her name is____________________.

3. I received and read a copy of the indictment/information. *If applicable:* An interpretator who speaks_________________ read it to me in ______________, and I have discussed it with my lawyer.

I fully understand every charge made against me. I understand these charges to be as follows:_________________________.

4. I have told my lawyer all the facts and circumstances known to me about the charges made against me in the indictment/information. I believe that my lawyer is fully informed on all such matters.

5. I know that the Court must be satisfied that there is a factual basis for a plea of "GUILTY" before my plea can be accepted. I represent to the Court that I took the following actions in connection with the charges made against me in Count[s] __________ and that these facts are true and correct:________________________.

6. My lawyer has counseled and advised me on the nature of each charge, all lesser included charges, all penalties and consequences of each charge, all possible defenses that I may have in this case and constitutional rights I am waiving.

7. I understand that my constitutional rights are as follows:

(a) the right to plead not guilty or, having already so pleaded, to persist in that plea;

(b) the right to a jury trial;

(c) the right to represented by counsel – and if necessary have the Court appoint counsel – at trial and at every other stage of the proceeding; and

(d) the right at trial to confront and cross-examine adverse witnesses, to testify and present evidence, to compel the attendance of witnesses, to be protected from compelled self-incrimination, and to remain silent, such that if I do not take the witness stand, no inference of guilt may be drawn from such failure and the jury must be so advised.

8. I know that I may plead "NOT GUILTY" to any offense charged against me and exercise all of my rights as listed above.

9. I know that if I plead "GUILTY," I am giving up all of the trial rights enumerated in paragraph 7 and that there will be no trial either before a court or jury.

10. I know that if I plead "GUILTY," the result of my plea is more than just an admission or confession of guilt. I understand that it will result in my conviction, and the Court may impose the same punishment as if I had pleaded "NOT GUILTY," stood trial and been convicted by a jury.

11. My lawyer has informed me that the maximum and minimum, if any, punishments which the law provides for the offense charged in Count(s) __________ are as follows:

(For multiple counts, include the following information for each count)
(a) Maximum prison sentence: ______ years
(b) Mandatory minimum prison sentence (if applicable): ______ years
(c) Maximum supervised release term: ______ years
(d) Minimum supervised release term (if applicable): ______ years
(e) Mandatory special assessment: $__________
(f) Restitution: $__________ (or determined by the Court))

(g) Maximum fine equal to the greater of the following:

(1) $_____________ (generally $250,000 for a felony, $100,000 for a Class A misdemeanor, or $5,000 for a Class B misdemeanor or lower; see 18 U.S.C. § 3571)); or

(2) $__________ (twice the gross pecuniary gain I derived from the offense); or

(3) $_____________ (twice the gross pecuniary loss caused by the offense to another person or persons).

If applicable: I understand that, because I am pleading guilty to more than one count, the Court may order the sentences on those counts to run consecutively.

I understand that if I violate any condition of supervised release, the release may be revoked, and I may be sentenced to all or part of the term of supervised release imposed in addition to any other term of imprisonment which I have received. I understand that if I violate any term of probation, the probation may be revoked, and I may be sentenced up to the maximum statutory term of imprisonment for the offense.

I understand that I may be assessed the costs of confinement and/or supervision. I understand I may be ordered to pay restitution in an amount determined by the Court.

12. I know that the sentence I will receive will be decided solely by the Judge. I understand that the Judge will make no decision regarding my sentence until the Judge has read and considered the pre-sentence investigation report prepared and submitted to the Court by the Probation Department. I also understand that the Court and counsel cannot promise me now what sentence will be imposed. I understand that in deciding what sentence it will impose, the Court will calculate my sentencing range under the Sentencing Guidelines. I understand that while the Court is not bound to apply the Guidelines, it must take them into consideration when sentencing me, together with the factors set forth in 18 U.S.C. § 3553(a).

13. I understand that under provisions of certain criminal statutes, certain property of mine may be forfeited to the United States. I have been advised by my lawyer whether, and to what extent, my property may be subject to forfeiture.

14. If I am on probation, supervised release or parole in this or any other Court, I know that by pleading guilty here, my probation, release or parole may be revoked, and I may be required to serve time in that case, which may be consecutive (that is, in addition to) any sentence imposed upon me in this case.

15. I declare that no officer or agent of any branch of government (federal, state or local) has promised or suggested that I will receive a lighter sentence, or probation, or any other form of leniency, nor have any other promises been made if I plead "GUILTY" except as follows:_________.

(In the space above, insert any promises or concessions made to the defendant or to his/her attorney).

If anyone else made such a promise or suggestion, except as noted in the previous sentence, I know that it was entirely without authority or effect.

16. I believe that my lawyer has done all that a lawyer could do to counsel and assist me, and I am satisfied with the advice and help he/she has given me.

17. I know that the Court will not permit anyone to plead "GUILTY" who maintains he/she is innocent and, with that in mind and because I am "GUILTY," I respectfully request the Court to accept my plea of "GUILTY" and to have the clerk enter my plea of "GUILTY" as follows:_______.

18. My mind is clear. I am not under the influence of alcohol or drugs, and I am not under a doctor's care. The only drugs, medicines, or pills that I have taken within the past seven days are:____________________________________. (*If none, so state.*)

19. I confirm that my decision to plead guilty is made voluntarily, and no one coerced or

threatened me to enter into this Agreement. I offer my plea of "GUILTY" freely and voluntarily and of my own accord, and with full understanding of all the matters set forth in the indictment/information, in this application, and in the certificate of my lawyer which is attached to this application. In offering my plea of "GUILTY," I freely and voluntarily waive (that is, give up) the constitutional rights guaranteed to me as stated in paragraph 7 above.

20. I waive the reading of the indictment/information in open court, and I request the Court to enter my plea of "GUILTY" as set forth in Paragraph 17 of this application.

21. I understand that the Court will address me personally in open court to determine the voluntariness of my guilty plea and to establish a factual basis for it. I understand that the Court may place me under oath, and that the government may use any false statements that I make under oath against me in a prosecution for perjury or false statement (which is a felony).

22.__________I am proficient enough in English to read the above and have read and fully understand it.

__________I am not proficient enough in English. I speak and understand __________, which is my native language. The above was read to me in________ and I fully understand it.

Signed by me in open court in the presence of my attorney this____ day of __________, 20__.

____

Defendant

CERTIFICATE OF COUNSEL

I have fully explained to my client the charges in the indictment/information in the case, the defenses he/she may have to the charges, all of the information set forth in this application, and all the rights that a criminal defendant has. In my opinion, my client understands the charges, the defenses, the information in this application, and the rights he or she is giving up by pleading guilty, and, based on the information now known to me, his/her decision to plead guilty is knowing and voluntary.

Signed by me in open court in the presence of the above-named defendant after a full discussion of the contents of this certificate with the defendant this ______ day of________ , 20___ .

____

Attorney for the Defendant

INTERPRETER CERTIFICATION

I, ____________________, hereby certify that I am a certified __________ [language] interpreter and that I accurately translated this plea agreement to the defendant, he/she told me that he/she understood it, and I am satisfied that his/her answer is true and correct.

Date: _______________

____
Interpreter's Signature

ORDER

I find that:

1. The defendant enters this plea of guilty freely and voluntarily and not out of ignorance, inadvertence, fear or coercion.

2. The defendant understands and knowingly, freely and voluntarily waives his/her constitutional rights.

3. The defendant freely and voluntarily executed the attached Application and fully understands its contents.

4. The defendant has admitted the essential elements of the crime charged.

IT IS THEREFORE ORDERED that the defendant's plea of "GUILTY" entered in open court be accepted and entered as requested in this Application and as recommended in the certificate signed by the defendant's lawyer.

Done in open court this___ day of____________, 20__.

____
SANDRA B. ARMSTRONG
United States District Judge

B. Exhibit List

UNITED STATES DISTRICT COURT
for the Northern District of California

Case No. ______________________ Date ______________________

______________________ vs. ______________________

EXHIBIT LIST

☐ Plaintiff ☐ Defendant

EXHIBIT NUMBER	DESCRIPTION	SPONSORING WITNESS	DATE	
			Marked for Identification	Admitted in Evidence

C. Forms for Plaintiff's and Defendant's Exhibit Markers

Plaintiff's Exhibit Markers

PLAINTIFF

United States District Court
Northern District of California

Case No. ______________________

Case Title ______________________

Exhibit No. ______________________

Date Entered ______________________

Richard W. Wieking, Clerk

By: ______________________, Deputy Clerk

Defendant's Exhibit Markers

DEFENDANT

United States District Court
Northern District of California

Case No. ______________________

Case Title ______________________

Exhibit No. ______________________

Date Entered ______________________

Richard W. Wieking, Clerk

By: ______________________, Deputy Clerk

Hon. Charles R. Breyer

District Judge

Chambers Information

U.S. District Court, Northern District of California
Courtroom 6, 17th Floor
450 Golden Gate Avenue
San Francisco, CA 94102

Scheduling Information

Courtroom Deputy: (415) 522-2062

Case Management Conferences	Fridays at 8:30 a.m.
Civil Law and Motion	Fridays at 10:00 a.m.
Criminal Law and Motion	Wednesdays at 2:00 p.m.

Judge's Biography

Born 1941 in San Francisco, CA

Federal Judicial Service:

-Judge, U. S. District Court, Northern District of California
-Nominated by William J. Clinton on July 24, 1997, to a seat vacated by D. Lowell Jensen; Confirmed by the Senate on November 8, 1997, and received commission on November 12, 1997.

Education:

-Harvard College, A.B., 1963
-University of California, Berkeley, Boalt Hall School of Law, J.D., 1966

Professional Career:

-Law Clerk, Hon. Oliver Carter, U.S. District Court, N.D. of California, 1966-1967
-Counsel, Legal Aid Society of San Francisco, California, 1967
-Assistant District Attorney, District Attorney's Office, San Francisco, CA, 1967-1973
-Assistant Special Prosecutor, Watergate Special Prosecution Force, 1973-1974
-Private Practice, San Francisco, California, 1974-1979
-Chief Assistant District Attorney, District Attorney's Office, San Francisco, CA, 1979
-Private Practice, San Francisco, California, 1980-1997

I. Judge Breyer's Procedures and Practices

A. *Guidelines for Trial and Final Pretrial Conference in Civil Bench Cases*

GUIDELINES FOR TRIAL AND FINAL PRETRIAL CONFERENCE IN CIVIL BENCH CASES BEFORE THE HONORABLE CHARLES R. BREYER

FINAL PRETRIAL CONFERENCE

1. Please do not prepare a joint pretrial conference statement. Nor should counsel invest time on deposition designations or extracts from interrogatories or requests for admissions at the pretrial conference stage. Instead, please file SEVEN calendar days in advance of the final pretrial conference the following:

(a) In lieu of preparing a joint pretrial conference statement, the parties shall meet and confer and prepare a joint proposed final pretrial order that contains: (i) a brief description of the substance of claims and defenses which remain to be decided, (ii) a statement of all relief sought, (iii) all stipulated facts, (iv) a list of all factual issues which remain to be tried, (v) a joint exhibit list in numerical order, including a brief description of the exhibit, a column for when it is offered in evidence, a column for when it is received in evidence, and a column for any limitations on its use, and (vi) each party's separate witness list for its case-in-chief witnesses (including those appearing by deposition) providing, for all such witnesses other than an individual plaintiff and an individual defendant, a short statement of the substance of his/her testimony and, separately, what, if any, noncumulative testimony the witness will give. If non-cumulative testimony is not spelled out, then the Court will presume the witness is cumulative. For each witness, state an hour/minute time estimate for the direct examination (only). Items (v) and (vi) should be appendices to the proposed order. The objective is to convert the proposed order to a final order with the benefit of any discussion at the final pretrial conference.

(b) Each side's proposed findings of fact and conclusions of law.

(c) Each side's trial brief.

(d) Any motion *in limine*, with the opposition, filed as follows: At least TWENTY calendar days before the conference, serve, but do not file, the moving papers. At least TEN calendar days before the conference, serve the oppositions. When the oppositions are received, the moving party should collate the motion and the opposition together, back to back, and then file the paired sets at least SEVEN calendar days before the conference. Each motion should be presented in a separate memo and numbered, as in, for example, "Plaintiff's Motion in Limine No. 1 to Exclude . . . ." **Please** be sure to three hole punch the chambers copies so they can go into a trial notebook. For bench trials, motions *in limine* are rarely needed or useful.

2. The joint proposed final pretrial order and the proposed findings of fact and conclusions of law shall be submitted on a 3-3/4-inch disk in WordPerfect 8.0 format, as well as in hard copies. All hard-copy submissions should be three-hole punched on the left, so the chambers' copy can be put in binders.

3. At the final pretrial conference, the above submissions shall be considered and argued. The parties must take notes on rulings and submit a joint summary of all rulings in proposed order format.

PRETRIAL ARRANGEMENTS

4. Should a daily transcript and/or real-time reporting be desired, the parties shall make arrangements with Debra Campbell, Supervisor of the Court Reporting Services, at (415) 522-2079, at least ten calendar days prior to the trial date.

5. During trial, counsel may wish to use overhead projectors, laser-disk/computer graphics, poster blow-ups, models or specimens of devices. The Courtroom is set up with equipment which allows evidence presentation. If equipment is necessary the United States Marshal requires a court order to allow equipment into the courthouse. If both overhead projector and video equipment are to be used, then a single projection screen is best, thus requiring a projection-type video rather than a large monitor. If video equipment is used, equipment capable of instantly accessing the relevant portions of transcripts and graphics should be used (rather than, for example, raw video tapes made at depositions which take time to forward or to rewind). For electronic equipment, either know how to fix it or have a technician handy at all times. For overhead projectors, have a spare bulb. Tape extension cords to the carpet for safety. Please take down and store the equipment (in the courtroom) at the end of each court day. Please work with Barbara Espinoza (415-522-2062) on courtroom-layout issues.

SCHEDULING

6. The normal trial schedule will be 9:00 a.m. to 12:00 p.m.. (or slightly longer to finish a witness) with two fifteen-minute breaks and ending before lunch. For bench trials, counsel must arrive by 8:15 a.m., or earlier as needed for any matters to be heard before the evidence begins. If an afternoon trial schedule is scheduled, it will run from 1:30 p.m. to 4:00 p.m. (or slightly longer) with two fifteen-minute breaks. The trial week is Monday through Thursday except for any Wednesday afternoon and all federal court holidays.

OPENING STATEMENTS

7. If openings are permitted, each side will have a predetermined time limit for its opening statement. Counsel must cooperate and meet and confer to exchange any visuals, graphics or exhibits to be used in the opening statements, allowing for time to work out objections and any reasonable revisions.

WITNESSES

8. Throughout the trial, all counsel are entitled to know a firm order of witnesses for the next two full court days and the exhibits that will be used on direct examination (other than for impeachment of an adverse witness). Within 24 hours of such notice, all other counsel shall provide any objections to such exhibits and shall provide a list of all exhibits to be used with the same witness on cross-examination (other than for impeachment). This requires that the first such notice be provided before trial actually begins. All such notice should be provided in writing.

9. Always have your next witness ready and in the courthouse. Failure to have the next witness ready or to be prepared to proceed with the evidence will usually constitute resting. If counsel plans to read in a transcript of a deposition anyway, it is advisable to have a deposition prepared and vetted early on to read just in case.

10. A witness or exhibit not listed in the joint pretrial statement may not be used without good cause. This rule does not apply to rebuttal witnesses (other than experts).

11. When there are multiple parties, counsel are responsible for coordination of the cross-examination to avoid duplication.

12. Stand at or near the podium to ask questions, straying only to point out material on charts or overheads. Please request permission to approach the witness or the bench.

13. On the first day of trial, be sure to bring the original and clean copies of any deposition(s) for which you are responsible. Any corrections must be readily available. If you are likely to need to use the deposition during a witness examination, then give the Court and the witness a copy with any corrections at the outset of the examination.

14. In lieu of direct testimony, the Court will consider receiving "prepared direct" testimony in the form of declarations. When the witness is presented, the proponent must verbally summarize the direct. Live cross-examination and redirect shall then occur.

DEPOSITION DESIGNATION

15. The following procedure applies only to witnesses who appear by deposition. It does not apply to live witnesses whose depositions are read in while they are on the stand. To save time and avoid unnecessary work, it is not necessary to make all deposition designations before trial. Instead, the following steps should be followed.

(a) To designate deposition testimony, photocopy the cover page, the page where the witness is sworn, and then each page from which any testimony is proffered. Line through or x-out any portions of such pages not proffered. Also, line through objections or colloquy unless they are needed to understand the question. Please make sure any corrections are interlineated and that references to exhibit numbers are conformed to the trial numbers. Such interlineations should be done by hand. The finished packet should then be the actual script and should smoothly present the identification and swearing of the witness and testimony desired. The packet should be provided to all other parties at least five calendar days before it will be used in court. For the rare case of voluminous designations, more lead time will be required. Please be reasonable.

(b) All other parties must then promptly review the packet and highlight in yellow any passages objected to and write in the margin the legal basis for the objections. If any completeness objection is made, the objecting party must insert into the packet the additional passages as needed to cure the completeness objection. A completeness objection should normally be made only if a few extra lines will cure the problem. Such additions shall be highlighted in blue and an explanation for the inclusion shall be legibly handwritten in the margin. Please line out or x-out any irrelevant portions of the additional pages.

(c) The packets, as adjusted, must then be returned to the proffering party, who must then decide the extent to which to accept the adjustments. The parties must meet and confer as reasonable. Counsel forth proffering party must collate and assemble a final packet that covers the proffer and all remaining issues. At least two calendar days before the proffer will be used, the proponent must provide the Court with the final packet, with any objected-to portions highlighted and annotated as described above. If exhibits are needed to resolve the objections, include copies and highlight and tag the relevant passages. Alert the Court on the record that the packet is being provided and whether any rulings are needed. If so, the Court will then read the packet and indicate its rulings in the margin in a distinctive manner. Ordinarily, argument will not be needed.

(d) Counter designations must be made by providing a packet with the counter-designated passages to the proponent at the same time any objections to the original proffer are returned to the first proffering party, who must then supply its objections in the same manner.

(e) When the packet is read in court, the examiner reads the questions (and any relevant colloquy) from the lectern and a colleague sits in the witness stand and reads the answers. When a video-taped deposition is to be played instead, the packets must still be prepared, as above, in order to facilitate rulings on objections. The video should omit any dead time, long pauses, and objections/colloquy not necessary to understand the answers. The Court may decide, instead, to take the designations under submission and simply read them.

REQUESTS FOR ADMISSIONS AND INTERROGATORIES

16. Please designate responses to requests for admissions and interrogatory answers in the same manner and under the same timetable as depositions.

EXHIBITS

17. Prior to the final pretrial conference, counsel must meet and confer in person over all exhibit numbers and objections and to weed out duplicate exhibits. Please be reasonable.

18. Use numbers only, not letters, for exhibits, preferably the same numbers as were used in depositions. Blocks of numbers should be assigned to fit the need of the case (*e.g.*, Plaintiff has 1 to 100, Defendant A has 101 to 200, Defendant B has 201 to 300, etc.). A single exhibit should be marked only once. If the plaintiff has marked an exhibit, then the defendant should not re-mark it. Different versions of the same document, *e.g.*, a copy with additional handwriting, must be treated as different exhibits. To avoid any party claiming "ownership" of an exhibit, all exhibits shall be marked and referred to as "Trial Exhibit No. _____," not as "Plaintiff's Exhibit" or "Defendant's Exhibit." If an exhibit number differs from that used in a deposition transcript, however, then the latter must be conformed to the new trial number if and when the deposition testimony is used (so as to avoid confusion over exhibit numbers).

19. The exhibit tag shall be in the following form:

> United States District Court
> Northern District of California
>
> **TRIAL EXHIBIT 100**
>
> Case No. ______________________
> Date Entered________________
> By ___________________________
> Deputy Clerk

Counsel preferably will make the tag up in a color that will stand out (yet still allow for photocopying) but that is not essential. Place the tag on or near the lower right-hand corner or, if a photograph, on the back. Counsel should fill in the tag but leave the last two spaces blank. Deposit your exhibits with the deputy clerk (Barbara Espinoza) on the first day of trial. The tags can be adhesive or stapled on.

20. Counsel must consult with each other and with the deputy clerk at the end of each trial day and compare notes as to which exhibits are in evidence and any limitations thereon. If there are any differences, counsel should bring them promptly to the Court's attention.

21. In addition to the record copies of exhibits, one or more bench binders containing a copy of each side's exhibits must be provided to the Court on the first day of trial. Each exhibit must be separated with a label divider (an exhibit tag is unnecessary for the bench set). Please use 1-1/2-inch binders with locking rings. (Heavier binders are too hard to handle.)

22. At the close of evidence, counsel shall jointly provide a revised list of all exhibits actually in evidence (and no others) stating the exhibit number and a brief, non-argumentative description (*e.g.*, letter from A. B. Case to D. E. Frank, dated August 17,1999).

OBJECTIONS

23. Counsel shall stand when making objections. State the legal basis only. Speak up promptly.

24. There can only be one lawyer per witness per party for all purposes, including objections.

TIME LIMITS

25. Ordinarily, the Court shall set fixed time limits at the final pretrial conference. All of your examination time (whether direct, cross, re-direct or re-cross) for all witnesses must fit within your time limit and you may allocate it as you wish. Opening and closing time limits shall be separately considered. Counsel must keep track of everyone's usage. At the end of each day, counsel must confer over the time used and the time remaining for all parties and advise the Court daily. The Court will also try to keep track.

SETTLEMENTS AND CONTINUANCES

26. Shortly before trial or a final pretrial conference, counsel occasionally wish jointly to advise the clerk that a settlement has been reached and seek to take the setting off calendar but it turns out later that there was only a settlement "in principle" and disputes remain. Cases, however, cannot be taken off calendar in this manner. Unless and until a stipulated dismissal or judgment is filed or placed on the record, all parties must be prepared to proceed with the final pretrial conference as scheduled and to proceed to trial on the trial date, on pain of dismissal of the case for lack of prosecution or default judgment. Only an advance continuance expressly approved by the Court will release counsel and the parties from their obligation to proceed. If counsel expect that a settlement will be final by the time of trial or the final pretrial conference, they should notify the Court immediately in writing or, if it occurs over the weekend before the trial or conference, by voice mail to the deputy courtroom clerk. The Court will attempt to confer with counsel as promptly as circumstances permit to determine if a continuance will be in order. Pending such a conference, however, counsel must prepare and make all filings and be prepared to proceed with the trial.

CHANGE OF TRIAL DATE

27. Because of scheduling conflicts with other cases on the docket, the Court retains the discretion to change the trial date, either by way of ADVANCEMENT or continuance. In the event the trial date is changed, the parties may seek adjustment of the time limits for compliance with the requirements of this order, which shall be effective only upon Court approval.

IT IS SO ORDERED.

CHARLES R. BREYER
United States District Judge

B. Guidelines for Trial and Final Pretrial Conference in Civil Jury Cases

GUIDELINES FOR TRIAL AND FINAL PRETRIAL CONFERENCE IN CIVIL JURY CASES BEFORE THE HONORABLE CHARLES R. BREYER

FINAL PRETRIAL CONFERENCE

1. Please do not prepare a joint pretrial conference statement. Nor should counsel invest time on deposition designations or extracts from interrogatories or requests for admissions at the pretrial conference stage. Instead, please file SEVEN calendar days in advance of the final pretrial conference the following:

(a) In lieu of preparing a joint pretrial conference statement, the parties shall meet, confer and prepare a joint proposed final pretrial order, signed and vetted by all counsel, that contains: (i) a brief description of the substance of claims and defenses which remain to be decided, (ii) a statement of all relief sought, (iii) all stipulated facts, (iv) a list of all factual issues which remain to be tried, stating the issues with the same generality/specificity as any contested elements in the relevant jury instructions, all organized by counts, (v) a joint exhibit list in numerical order, including a brief description of the exhibit and Bates number, a column for when it is offered in evidence, a column for when it is received in evidence, and a column for any limitations on its use, and (vi) each party's separate witness list for its case-in-chief witnesses (including those appearing by deposition) providing, for all such witnesses other than an individual plaintiff and an individual defendant, a short statement of the substance of his/her testimony and, separately, what, if any, non-cumulative testimony the witness will give. If non-cumulative testimony is not spelled out, then the Court will presume the witness is cumulative. Time limits will be set based on the noncumulative descriptions. Items (v) and (vi) should be appendices to the proposed order. The proposed order should also state which issues, if any, are for the Court to decide, rather than the jury. The objective is to convert the proposed order to a final order with the benefit of any discussion at the final pretrial conference.

(b) A joint set of proposed instructions on substantive issues of law arranged in a logical sequence. If undisputed, an instruction shall be identified as "Stipulated Instruction No. ____ Re __________," with the blanks filled in as appropriate. Even if stipulated, the instruction shall be supported by citation. If disputed, each version of the instruction shall be inserted together, back to back, in their logical place in the overall sequence. Each such disputed instruction shall be identified as, for example, "Disputed Instruction No. ___ Re _________ Offered by ___________," with the blanks filled in as appropriate. All disputed versions of the same basic topic shall bear the same number. Citations with pin cites are required. Any modifications to a form instruction must be plainly identified. If a party does not have a counter version and simply contends no such instruction in any version should be given, then that party should so state (and explain why) on a separate page inserted in lieu of an alternate version. With respect to form preliminary instructions, general instructions, or concluding instructions, please simply cite to the numbers of the requested instructions in the current edition of the *Ninth Circuit Manual of Model Jury Instructions (Civil)*, except the instruction on a simplified statement of the case (No. 1.2 in the 2001 edition). Other than citing the numbers, do not include preliminary, general or concluding instructions in the packet.

(c) A separate memorandum of law in support of each party's disputed instructions, organized by instruction number. Please quote exact, controlling passages from the authorities and give pin cites. No ellipses, please.

(d) A joint special verdict form with the questions arranged in a logical sequence.

(e) A joint set of proposed voir dire questions supplemented as necessary by separate requests. Keep these to a minimum, please. The Court, in its discretion, may use a juror questionnaire.

(f) Any motion *in limine*, with the opposition, filed as follows: At least TWENTY calendar days before the conference, serve, but do not file, the moving papers. At least TEN calendar days before the conference, serve the oppositions. When the oppositions are received, the moving party should collate the motion and the opposition together, back to back, and then file the paired sets at least SEVEN calendar days before the conference. Each motion should be presented in a separate memo and numbered as in, for example, "Plaintiff's Motion *in Limine* No. 1 to Exclude . . . ." Please limit motions *in limine* to circumstances that really need a ruling in advance. Usually five or fewer motions per side is sufficient. Each motion should address a single topic, be separate, and contain no more than seven pages of briefing per side. Advance permission will be needed for more or longer motions. **Please** be sure to three-hole punch the chambers copies so they can go into a trial notebook.

(g) Trial briefs are optional but most helpful to the Court on any controlling issues of law.

2. The joint proposed final pretrial order and instructions shall be submitted (A) on a CD in WordPerfect 10.0 format, (B) in Judge Breyer's proposed order email address, as well as (C) in hard copies. All hard-copy submissions should be three-hole punched on the left, so the chambers' copy can be put in binders.

3. At the final pretrial conference, the above submissions shall be considered and argued. The parties must take notes on rulings and submit a joint summary of all rulings in proposed order format.

PRETRIAL ARRANGEMENTS

4. Should a daily transcript and/or real-time reporting be desired, the parties shall make arrangements with Debra Campbell, Supervisor of the Court Reporting Services, at (415) 522-2079, at least ten calendar days prior to the trial date.

5. During trial, counsel may wish to use overhead projectors, laser-disk/computer graphics, poster blow-ups, models or specimens of devices. The Courtroom is set up with equipment which allows evidence presentation. If equipment is necessary the United States Marshal requires a court order to allow equipment into the courthouse. If both overhead projector and video equipment are to be used, then a single projection screen is best, thus requiring a projection-type video rather than a large monitor. If video equipment is used, equipment capable of instantly accessing the relevant portions of transcripts and graphics should be used (rather than, for example, raw video tapes made at depositions which take time

to forward or to rewind). For electronic equipment, either know how to fix it or have a technician handy at all times. For overhead projectors, have a spare bulb. Tape extension cords to the carpet for safety. Please take down and store the equipment (in the courtroom) at the end of each court day. Please work with Barbara Espinoza (415-522-2062) on courtroom layout issues.

SCHEDULING

6. The normal trial schedule will be 9:00 a.m. to 12:00 p.m. (or slightly longer to finish a witness) with two fifteen-minute breaks and ending before lunch. Counsel must arrive by 8:15 a.m., or earlier as needed for any matters to be heard out of the presence of the jury. Please be prepared to start with the jury at 9:00 a.m. The trial week is Monday through Thursday except for any Wednesday afternoon and all federal court holidays.

THE JURY

7. No later than on the first day of trial, counsel shall jointly submit a simplified statement of the case to be read to the jury during voir dire as part of the proposed jury instructions. Unless the case is extremely complex, this statement should not exceed one page. The Court will usually conduct the voir dire.

8. In civil cases, there are no alternate jurors and the jury is selected as follows: All potential jurors are called and seated in the jury box and courtroom benches in the order their names are drawn from the drum. This placement will now determine their order in the selection process. The Court will then conduct its voir-dire of the entire panel. Once this questioning is accomplished, the Court will advise counsel at side-bar which potential jurors it would excuse for cause. This determination is preliminary only. Counsel are then permitted to conduct limited voir-dire of the entire panel. Once all voir-dire is completed, the Court will then address all challenges for cause and excuse those potential jurors who have been successfully challenged. The Court will then advise counsel as to the number of jurors which will be seated. After a short recess, each side may exercise its allotment of peremptory challenges. Challenges must be made in writing by each side at the same time (without knowing how the other side is exercising its challenges). Write down the names and numbers of the candidates to be stricken. The eight (or such other size as will constitute the jury) surviving the challenge process with the lowest numbers become the final jury. For example, if the plaintiff strikes 1, 5 and 7 and the defendant strikes 2, 4 and 9, then 3, 6, 8, 10, 11, 12, 13 and 14 become the final jury. If both sides strike one or more of the same jurors, then the eight unstruck jurors with the lowest numbers will be seated. If more than eight jurors (or less) are to be seated, then the starting number will be adjusted. So too if more than a total of six peremptories is allowed. Once the jury selection is completed, the jurors' names will be read again and they will be seated in the jury box and sworn. The Court may alter the procedure in its discretion.

9. Jurors may take notes. Steno notebooks will be distributed at the beginning of each trial. The pads will remain in the jury room at the end of each day. Jurors will be instructed on the use of notes both in the preliminary and final jury instructions.

OPENING STATEMENTS

10. Each side will have a predetermined time limit for its opening statement. Counsel must cooperate and meet and confer to exchange any visuals, graphics or exhibits to be used in the opening statements, allowing for time to work out objections and any reasonable revisions. Be prepared for opening statements as soon as the jury is sworn.

WITNESSES

11. Throughout the trial, all counsel are entitled to know a firm order of witnesses for the next two full court days and the exhibits that will be used on direct examination (other than for impeachment of an adverse witness). Within 24 hours of such notice, all other counsel shall provide any objections to such exhibits and shall provide a list of all exhibits to be used with the same witness on cross-examination (other than for impeachment). This requires that the first such notice be provided before trial actually begins. All such notice should be provided in writing.

12. Always have your next witness ready and in the courthouse. Failure to have the next witness ready or to be prepared to proceed with the evidence will usually constitute resting. If counsel plans to read in a transcript of a deposition anyway, it is advisable to have a deposition prepared and vetted early on to read just in case.

13. A witness or exhibit not listed in the joint pretrial statement may not be used without good cause. This rule does not apply to true rebuttal witnesses (other than experts). Defense witnesses are normally case-in-chief witnesses, not "rebuttal" witnesses.

14. When there are multiple parties, counsel are responsible for coordination of the cross-examination to avoid duplication.

15. Stand at or near the podium to ask questions, straying only to point out material on charts or overheads.

EXPERTS

16. A recurring problem in trials is the problem of expert witnesses trying to go beyond the scope of their expert reports on direct examination. FRCP 26(a)(2) and FRCP 37(c) limit experts to the opinions and bases contained in their timely reports (absent substantial justification or harmlessness). The Court regularly enforces these rules. FRCP 26(a) even requires that any "exhibits to be used as summary of or support for the opinions" be included in the report. Accordingly, at trial, the direct testimony of experts will be limited to the matters disclosed in their reports. Omitted material may not ordinarily be added on direct examination. This means the reports must be complete and sufficiently detailed Illustrative animations, diagrams, charts and models may be used on direct examination only if they were part to the expert's report, with the exception of simple drawings and tabulations that plainly illustrate what is already in the report, which can be drawn by the witness at trial or otherwise shown to the jury. If cross-examination fairly opens the door, however, an expert may go beyond the written report on cross-examination and/or re-direct examination. By written stipulation, of course, all sides may relax these requirements.

17. As to damages studies, the cut-off date for *past damages* will be as of the expert report (or such earlier date as the expert may select). In addition, the experts may try to project *future damages* (*i.e.*, after the cut-off date) if the substantive standards for future damages can be met. With timely leave of Court or by written stipulation, the experts may update their reports (with supplemental reports) to a date closer to the time of trial.

18. The case management order will already have set out the timetable for expert reports.

USE OF DEPOSITIONS TO IMPEACH AND SHORT READ-INS

19. Depositions can be used at trial to impeach a witness testifying at trial or, in the case of a party deponent, "for any purpose." Please follow the following procedure:

(a) On the first day of trial, be sure to bring the original and clean copies of any deposition(s) for which you are responsible. Any corrections must be readily available. If you are likely to need to use the deposition during a witness examination, then give the Court a copy with any corrections at the outset of your examination. This will minimize delay between the original question and the read-ins of the impeaching material. Opposing counsel should have their copy immediately available.

(b) When you wish to read in a passage, simply say, for example: "I wish to read in page 210, lines 1 to 10 from the witness' deposition." A brief pause will be allowed for any objection.

(c) The first time a deposition is read, state the deponent's name, the date of the deposition, the name of the lawyer asking the question, and if it was FRCP 30(b)(6) deposition, please say so. The first time a deposition is read, the Court will give an appropriate explanation to the jury about depositions.

(d) When reading in the passage, state "question" and then read the question exactly. Then state "answer" and then read the answer exactly. Stating "question" and "answer" is necessary so the jury and the court reporter can follow who was talking at the deposition.

(e) Please do **NOT** ask, "Didn't you say XYZ in your deposition?" The problem with such a question is that the "XYZ" rarely turns out to be exactly what the deponent said. Instead, ask for permission to read in a passage, as above, and read it in exactly, so that the jury can hear what was actually testified to.

(f) Subject to Rule 403, party depositions may be read in whether or not they contradict (and regardless of who the witness is on the stand). For example, a short party deposition excerpt may be used as foundation for questions for a different witness on the stand.

(g) Rather than reading the passage, counsel are free to play an audiovisual digitized version of the passage, but counsel must have a system for immediate display of the precise passage.

DEPOSITION DESIGNATION

20. The following procedure applies only to witnesses who appear by deposition. It does not apply to live witnesses whose depositions are read in while they are on the stand. To save

time and avoid unnecessary work, it is not necessary to make all deposition designations before trial. Instead, the following steps should be followed.

(a) To designate deposition testimony, photocopy the cover page, the page where the witness is sworn, and then each page from which any testimony is proffered. Line through or x-out any portions of such pages not proffered. Also, line through objections or colloquy unless they are needed to understand the question. Please make sure any corrections are interlineated and that references to exhibit numbers are conformed to the trial numbers. Such interlineations should be done by hand. The finished packet should then be the actual script and should smoothly present the identification and swearing of the witness and testimony desired. The packet should be provided to all other parties at least five calendar days before it will be used in court. For the rare case of voluminous designations, more lead time will be required. Please be reasonable.

(b) All other parties must then promptly review the packet and highlight in yellow any passages objected to and write in the margin the legal basis for the objections. If any completeness objection is made, the objecting party must insert into the packet the additional passages as needed to cure the completeness objection. A completeness objection should normally be made only if a few extra lines will cure the problem. Such additions shall be highlighted in blue and an explanation for the inclusion shall be legibly handwritten in the margin. Please line out or x-out any irrelevant portions of the additional pages.

(c) The packets, as adjusted, must then be returned to the proffering party, who must then decide the extent to which to accept the adjustments. The parties must meet and confer as reasonable. Counsel for the proffering party must collate and assemble a final packet that covers the proffer and all remaining issues. At least two calendar days before the proffer will be used, the proponent must provide the Court with the final packet, with any objected-to portions highlighted and annotated as described above. If exhibits are needed to resolve the objections, include copies and highlight and tag the relevant passages. Alert the Court on the record that the packet is being provided and whether any rulings are needed. Tag all passages that require a ruling. The Court will then read the packet and indicate its rulings in the margin in a distinctive manner. Ordinarily, argument will not be needed.

(d) Counter designations must be made by providing a packet with the counter-designated passages to the proponent at the same time any objections to the original proffer are returned to the first proffering party, who must then supply its objections in the same manner.

(e) When the packet is read to the jury, the examiner reads the questions (and any relevant colloquy) from the lectern and a colleague sits in the witness stand and reads the answers. When a video-taped deposition is to be played instead, the packets must still be prepared, as above, in order to facilitate rulings on objections. The video should omit any dead time, long pauses, and objections/colloquy not necessary to understand the answers.

REQUESTS FOR ADMISSIONS AND INTERROGATORIES

21. Please designate responses to requests for admissions and interrogatory answers in the same manner and under the same timetable as depositions.

EXHIBITS

22. Prior to the final pretrial conference, counsel must meet and confer in person over all exhibit numbers and objections and to weed out duplicate exhibits. Please be reasonable.

23. Use numbers only, not letters, for exhibits, preferably the same numbers as were used in depositions. Blocks of numbers should be assigned to fit the need of the case (*e.g.*, Plaintiff has 1 to 100, Defendant A has 101 to 200, Defendant B has 201 to 300, etc.). A single exhibit should be marked only once. If the plaintiff has marked an exhibit, then the defendant should not re-mark it. Different versions of the same document, *e.g.*, a copy with additional handwriting, must be treated as different exhibits. To avoid any party claiming "ownership" of an exhibit, all exhibits shall be marked and referred to as "Trial Exhibit No. ___," not as "Plaintiff's Exhibit" or "Defendant's Exhibit." If an exhibit number differs from that used in a deposition transcript, however, then the latter must be conformed to the new trial number if and when the deposition testimony is read to the jury (so as to avoid confusion over exhibit numbers). The jury should always hear any given exhibit referred to by its unique number. You cannot have competing versions of the same exhibit numbers.

24. The exhibit tag shall be in the following form:

United States District Court
Northern District of California

TRIAL EXHIBIT 100

Case No. ____________________
Date Entered________________
By ________________________
Deputy Clerk

Counsel preferably will make the tag up in a color that will stand out (yet still allow for photocopying) but that is not essential. Place the tag on or near the lower right-hand corner or, if a photograph, on the back. Counsel should fill in the tag but leave the last two spaces blank. Deposit your exhibits with the deputy clerk (Barbara Espinoza) on the first day of trial. The tags can be adhesive or stapled on.

25. Counsel must consult with each other and with the deputy clerk at the end of each trial day and compare notes as to which exhibits are in evidence and any limitations thereon. If there are any differences, counsel should bring them promptly to the Court's attention.

26. In addition to the record copies of exhibits, one or more bench binders containing a copy of each side's exhibits must be provided to the Court on the first day of trial. Each exhibit must be separated with a label divider (an exhibit tag is unnecessary for the bench set). Please use 1-1/2-inch binders with locking rings. (Heavier binders are too hard to handle.)

27. Before the case goes to the jury, counsel must confer with the clerk to make sure the exhibits to go into the jury room are all in evidence and in good order. Counsel may, but are

not required to, jointly provide a revised list of all exhibits actually in evidence (and no others) stating the exhibit number and a brief, non-argumentative description (*e.g.*, letter from A. B. Case to D. E. Frank, dated August 17, 1999). This list may go into the jury room to help the jury sort through exhibits.

28. Publication must be by poster blow-up, overhead projection, or such other method as is allowed in the circumstances. Poster blow-ups should be about 3' x 4' to be seen by all jurors. Any overhead projector should have a powerful light to help in jury viewing. Counsel must have a practical means for all important documents to be published to the jury. It is permissible to highlight, circle or underscore in the enlargements so long as it is clear that it was not on the original. Exhibit notebooks for the jury will not be permitted without prior permission by the Court.

OBJECTIONS

29. Counsel shall stand when making objections and shall not make speeches. State the legal basis only. Speak up promptly.

30. There can only be one lawyer per witness per party for all purposes, including objections.

31. Side bar conferences are discouraged. The procedure described above should eliminate the need for most side bars.

32. To maximize jury time, counsel must alert the Court in advance of any problems that will require discussion outside the presence of the jury, so that the conference can be held before court begins or after the jury leaves for the day.

TIME LIMITS

33. Ordinarily, the Court shall set fixed time limits at the final pretrial conference. All of your examination time (whether direct, cross, re-direct or re-cross) for all witnesses must fit within your time limit and you may allocate it as you wish. Opening and closing time limits shall be separately considered. Counsel must keep track of everyone's usage. At the end of each day, counsel must confer over the time used and the time remaining for all parties and advise the Court daily. The Court will also try to keep track. The time taken at a side bar or on objections will still be charged to the examining party unless otherwise ordered.

SETTLEMENTS AND CONTINUANCES

34. Shortly before trial or a final pretrial conference, counsel occasionally wish jointly to advise the clerk that a settlement has been reached and seek to take the setting off calendar but it turns out later that there was only a settlement "in principle" and disputes remain. Cases, however, cannot be taken off calendar in this manner. Unless and until a stipulated dismissal or judgment is filed or placed on the record, all parties must be prepared to proceed with the final pretrial conference as scheduled and to proceed to trial on the trial date, on pain of dismissal of the case for lack of prosecution or entry of default judgment. Only an advance continuance expressly approved by the Court will release counsel and the parties from their

obligation to proceed. If counsel expect that a settlement will be final by the time of trial or the final pretrial conference, they should notify the Court immediately in writing or, if it occurs over the weekend before the trial or conference, by voice mail to the deputy courtroom clerk. The Court will attempt to confer with counsel as promptly as circumstances permit to determine if a continuance will be in order. Pending such a conference, however, counsel must prepare and make all filings and be prepared to proceed with the trial.

35. Local rule 40-1 provides that jury costs may be assessed as sanctions for failure to provide the Court with timely written notice of a settlement. Please be aware that any settlement reached on the day of trial, during trial, or at any time after the jury or potential jurors have been summoned without sufficient time to cancel, will normally require the parties to pay juror costs.

CHANGE OF TRIAL DATE

36. Because of scheduling conflicts with other cases on the docket, the Court retains the discretion to change the trial date, either by way of advancement or continuance. In the event the trial date is changed, the parties may seek an adjustment of the time limits for compliance with the requirements of this order, which shall be effective only upon Court approval.

IT IS SO ORDERED.

CHARLES R. BREYER
United States District Judge

C. Standing Orders

STANDING ORDERS

1. Counsel shall consult and comply with all provisions of the Local Rules relating to continuance, motions, briefs, and all other matters, unless superseded by these Standing Orders.
2. Scheduling Days:
   a. Criminal Law and Motion Calendar is conducted on Wednesdays at **2:15 p.m.** **ORDER OF CALL IS DETERMINED BY THE COURT.**
   b. Civil Law and Motion Calendar is conducted on Fridays at **10:00 a.m. ORDER OF CALL IS DETERMINED BY THE COURT.**
   c. Case Management Conferences are conducted on Fridays at 8**:30 a.m. ORDER OF CALL IS DETERMINED BY THE COURT.**
   d. Pretrial conferences are generally conducted at **2:30 p.m.** on days determined by the Court.
   e. Counsel need not reserve a hearing date for motions, however, counsel are advised to check the legal papers for unavailable dates. Noticed dates may be reset as the Court's calendar requires.
3. Motions to compel discovery are referred to a Magistrate Judge for assignment and shall be noticed for hearing before the assigned Magistrate Judge.
4. No changes in the Court's schedule shall be made ***except by signed order of the Court and only upon a showing of good cause***. Parties seeking to continue hearings, request special status conferences, modify briefing schedules, or make other procedural changes shall submit a signed stipulation and proposed order, or, if stipulation is not possible, an *ex parte* application in writing.
5. Briefs or Memoranda of Points and Authorities in support of, or in opposition to, any motions filed in this action must be typed on 28-line, double-spaced pleading paper and, except for summary judgment motions, may not exceed **FIFTEEN** (15) pages in length, exclusive of title pages, indexes of cases, table of contents, exhibits, affidavits, and summaries of argument, if required. Briefs exceeding ten (10) pages in length must contain an **additional** summary of argument, including reference to any important cases cited. Summary judgment memoranda may not exceed 25 pages. Counsel shall submit a proposed form of order with all motion and opposition papers.
6. ll chambers copies should be three-hole punched along the left side of the page, and should bear the ECF filing "stamp" (case number, docket number, date, and ECF page number) along the top of the page.
7. Counsel in civil matters shall comply with the Court's Guidelines for trial and pre-trial conference.

PLAINTIFF IS DIRECTED TO SERVE COPIES OF THIS ORDER AT ONCE UPON ALL PARTIES TO THIS ACTION AND UPON THOSE SUBSEQUENTLY JOINED IN ACCORDANCE WITH THE PROVISIONS OF RULES 4 AND 5, FEDERAL RULES OF CIVIL PROCEDURE, AND TO FILE WITH THE CLERK OF THE COURT A CERTIFICATE REFLECTING SUCH SERVICE.

IT IS SO ORDERED.

Dated: May 9, 2011

CHARLES R. BREYER,
United States District Judge

SPECIAL NOTICE REGARDING MOTIONS

Except for summary judgment motions, all briefs or memoranda of points and authorities shall not exceed FIFTEEN (15) pages in length, exclusive of title pages, indexes of cases, table of contents, exhibits, affidavits and summaries of argument. Counsel shall submit a proposed form of order with all motion and opposition papers.

IT IS SO ORDERED.

Dated: February 11, 2003

CHARLES R. BREYER,
United States District Judge

D. Standing Order Regarding Rule 11(c)(1)(B) Plea Agreements

STANDING ORDER REGARDING
RULE 11(c)(1)(B) PLEA AGREEMENTS

Plea agreements pursuant to Federal Rule of Criminal Procedure 11(c)(1)(B) must include the following:

1. If the agreement includes a Sentencing Guidelines calculation, then it must also state that the parties agree that the adjusted offense level results in a Guidelines range of___to___months depending on the defendant's Criminal History Category.

2. If the agreement includes a waiver of appellate rights as to sentence, it must also reserve the defendant's right to appeal a sentence of more than a certain number of months imprisonment.

IT IS SO ORDERED.

Dated: June 7, 2004

CHARLES R. BREYER
United States District Judge

II. Judge Breyer's Case Management Orders

A. *Order Setting Case Management Conference*

IN THE UNITED STATES DISTRICT COURT
FOR THE NORTHERN DISTRICT OF CALIFORNIA

No. _________ CRB

Plaintiff,

ORDER SETTING CASE MANAGEMENT CONFERENCE

v.

Defendant.
_______________________________________/

The above matter having been assigned to Judge Charles R. Breyer,

IT IS HEREBY ORDERED, pursuant to Rule 16, Federal Rules of Civil Procedure, and Civil Local rule 16, that a case management conference will be held before Judge Charles R. Breyer on Friday, ____________________at 8:30 a.m., in Courtroom 6, 17th floor, 450 Golden Gate Avenue, San Francisco, California.

Lead trial counsel shall meet and confer not less than thirty (30) days in advance of the conference and shall file a joint case management statement in the form contained in the Civil Local rules as supplemented by this order not less than seven (7) days in advance of the conference.

If the conference is inconveniently scheduled, it may be rescheduled by stipulation and order to another date or time convenient to the Court's calendar.

At the conclusion of the conference, an order will be entered setting dates either for a further case management conference, or for close of discovery, pre-trial conference, and trial. Other orders regulating and controlling future proceedings may be entered.

Plaintiff(s) shall serve copies of this order at once on all parties to this action, and on any parties subsequently joined, in accordance with Federal Rules of Civil Procedure 4 and 5. Following service, plaintiff(s) shall file a certificate of service with the Clerk of this Court.

SUPPLEMENTAL TO INITIAL CASE MANAGEMENT STATEMENT

1. At the initial case management conference, the parties or at least one attorney of record for each party must appear in person. See FRCP 26(f); Civil LR 16-10(a).

2. The case management statement may not exceed ten pages. It should briefly describe the parties' controversy. Any party seeking damages must set forth in the statement the amount sought and the basis for its calculation.

3. If the case was removed from a state court, and the applicable state law has not required the parties to make an express demand for a jury trial at the time of removal, any party claiming right to a jury trial must make the request therefor within ten days after service of the notice of removal. FRCP 81(c).

4. NOTICE TO PRO SE LITIGANTS IN NON-PRISONER ACTIONS:

If you are proceeding in this lawsuit without an attorney, then the following directives apply to you in the prosecution of your case.

The court hereby ORDERS you to comply with the service requirements of Rule 4 of the Federal Rules of Civil Procedure as set forth below. Failure to follow the procedures set forth in this order may result, under Rule 4(m), in dismissal of your case.

It is your responsibility to obtain a valid summons from the clerk and to effect service of the summons and complaint on all defendants in accordance with Rule 4 of the Federal Rules of Civil Procedure. If you have named the United States government, a federal agency, a federal official or a federal employee as a defendant, you must comply with the special requirements of Rule 4(i).

Service may be effected by any person who is not a party and who is at least 18 years of age, which means that you, as a party, may not effect service. If service of the summons and complaint is not made upon a defendant within 120 days after the filing of the complaint, your action will, under Rule 4(m), be dismissed as to that defendant.

Within 125 days after the filing of the complaint, you must file proof of service indicating which defendants were served within the 120 days allowed under Rule 4(m) and showing, in accordance with Rule 4(l), how each of those defendants was served (for example, by attaching appropriate certificates of service). You must also show cause why a defendant not served within the 120 days allowed under Rule 4(m) should not be dismissed without prejudice. Failure to do these things within the designated time will result in the dismissal of your case under Rule 4(m) and Rule 41(b).

5. NOTICE FOR AMERICANS WITH DISABILITIES ACT LITIGATION:

If this action seeks accommodation or other relief, including attorney fees, pursuant to Title III of the American with Disabilities Act, 42 U.S.C. § 12191-89, the court ORDERS, pursuant to FRCP 16, the following:

a. Each plaintiff shall, pursuant to FRCP 4(m), forthwith complete service on any unserved defendant;

b. Discovery, except for initial disclosures required by FRCP 26(a), and all other proceedings are until further order STAYED;

c. If not previously done, each plaintiff shall forthwith serve upon each defendant a demand for accommodation and statement of attorney fees incurred to date (42 U.S.C. § 12205; Hensly v. Eckerhart, 461 U.S. 424, 429-30, 433-37 (1983));

d. Each defendant shall, no later than the date for the conference of the parties specified above, serve a response to the demand for accommodation;

e. The joint case management statement shall contain, in addition to the information called for by FRCP 26(f), the information set forth in paragraphs c and d.

Sanctions. **FAILURE TO COMPLY WITH THIS ORDER** may be deemed sufficient grounds for dismissal of this cause, default or other appropriate sanctions. See Federal Rules of Civil Procedure 16(f), 41(b); Civ LR 1-4.

IT IS SO ORDERED.

Date: May 9, 2011

CHARLES R. BREYER
United States District Judge

III. Judge Breyer's Forms

A. *Application for Permission to Enter Plea of Guilty and Order Accepting Plea*

IN THE UNITED STATES DISTRICT COURT
FOR THE NORTHERN DISTRICT OF CALIFORNIA

Plaintiff,	No. CR________ CRB
v.	**APPLICATION FOR PERMISSION TO ENTER PLEA OF GUILTY AND ORDER ACCEPTING PLEA**
Defendant.	(Fed. R. Crim. P., Rules 10 and 11)
______________________________/	

The defendant represents to the Court:

1. My full true name is ____________. I am years of age _____. I have gone to school up to and including _________________________. My most recent occupation has been . I request that all proceedings against me be in my true name.

2. I am represented by a lawyer; his/her name is ___________________.

3. I received a copy of the indictment/information (as used in the Application the term indictment includes information) before being called upon to plead. I have read the indictment or a translator who speaks _____________ read it to me, and I have discussed the indictment with my lawyer.

I fully understand every charge made against me. I understand these charges to be: _______________________.

4. I have told my lawyer all the facts and circumstances known to me about the charges made against me in the indictment. I believe that my lawyer is fully informed on all such matters.

5. I know that the Court must be satisfied that there is a factual basis for a plea of "GUILTY" before my plea can be accepted. I represent to the Court that I did the following acts in connection with the charges made against me in Counts__ ____.

(In the above space defendant must set out in detail in his/her own handwriting what he/she did. If more space is needed, add a separate page.)

6. My lawyer has counseled and advised me on the nature of each charge, all lesser included charges, all penalties and consequences of each charge, all possible defenses that I may have in this case and the constitutional rights I am waiving.

7. I understand that my constitutional rights are as follows:

(a) the right to a speedy and public trial by jury;

(b) the right to see all of the evidence against me and to hear all witnesses called to testify against me and to have my attorney cross-examine them;

(c) the right to use the power and process of the court to compel the production of any evidence, including the attendance of any witnesses in my favor;

(d) the right to the assistance of a lawyer at all stages of the proceedings including trial and appeal and if I cannot afford one, to have the court appoint one to represent me without cost to me or based upon my ability to pay;

(e) the right to remain silent or to take the witness stand at my sole option and if I do not take the witness stand, no inference of guilt may be drawn from such failure and the jury must be so advised;

(f) the right against self-incrimination;

(g) the right to appeal from an adverse judgment;

(h) the right to appeal my sentence without any limitation contained in my plea agreement.

8. I know that I may plead "NOT GUILTY" to any offense charged against me and exercise all of my rights as listed above.

9. I know that if I plead "GUILTY" I am giving up all of the rights enumerated in paragraph 7 and that there will be no trial either before a court or jury.

10. I know that if I plead "GUILTY" the result of my plea is more than just an admission or confession of guilt and that it will result in my conviction, and that further, the court may impose the same punishment as if I had pleaded "NOT GUILTY," stood trial and been convicted by a jury.

11. My lawyer has discussed with me the maximum and minimum, if any, punishments which the law provides and the various provisions of the Sentencing Guidelines that may apply to me. I understand that the maximum punishment for the offense(s) charged in Count(s) ______________ of the indictment is ____________ years of imprisonment, a fine of $______________, and a period of ________years supervised release. I understand that there is a mandatory minimum punishment of _____________years imprisonment for the offense(s) charged in Count(s) ______________. I also understand that the minimum period of supervised release which the court may impose is _____________ (if applicable) and that if I violate any condition of supervised release the release may be revoked and I may be sentenced to all or a part of the term of supervised release imposed in addition to any other term of imprisonment which I have received.

I understand that I may be assessed the costs of confinement and/or supervision. I understand that I must pay a penalty assessment of $100.00 per count to which I plead (or $25.00 in the case of misdemeanor counts). I understand that I may be ordered to pay restitution in an amount determined by the court.

I know that the sentence I will receive is solely a matter within the control of the Judge. I understand that the Judge will make no decision regarding my sentence until the Judge has read and considered the pre-sentence investigation report prepared and submitted to the court by the Probation Department.

I also understand that the court and counsel cannot promise what sentence or sentencing range will be set and that these calculations will depend upon the Sentencing Guidelines as they apply to me. I have been advised that the court may sentence within the guideline range determined by the Probation Department or may depart upward or downward from the range. However, no promises have been made to me as to the range or departure.

12. If I am on probation, supervised release or parole in this or any other court, I know that by pleading guilty here my probation, release or parole may be revoked and I may be required to serve time in that case, which may be consecutive, that is, in addition to any sentence imposed upon me in this case.

13. I declare that no officer or agent of any branch of government (federal, state or local) has promised or suggested that I will receive a lighter sentence, or probation, or any other form of leniency, nor have any other promises been made if I plead "GUILTY," except as stated in the Plea Agreement I have signed, stated on the record in my entry of plea or as follows: ________________.

(In the space above insert any promises or concessions made to the defendant or to his/her attorney.)

If anyone else made such a promise or suggestion, except as noted in the previous sentence, I know that person had no authority to do it. No one has forced or coerced me into entering this plea. My willingness to plead guilty (does) (does not) result from prior discussions between my attorney and
the government's attorney. (If it does, state any factors that influenced you that are not reflected in the plea agreement.) ____.

14. I believe that my lawyer has done all that a lawyer could do to counsel and assist me, and I am satisfied with the advice and help he/she has given me.

15. I know that the court will not permit anyone to plead "GUILTY" who maintains he/she is innocent and, with that in mind and because I am "GUILTY," I respectfully request the court to accept my plea of "GUILTY" and to have the clerk enter my plea of "GUILTY" as follows: ____.

16. My mind is clear. I am not under the influence of alcohol or drugs and I am not under a doctor's care. The only drugs, medicines or pills that I took within the past seven days are:________________. (If none, so state.)

17. **I OFFER MY PLEA OF "GUILTY" FREELY AND VOLUNTARILY AND OF MY OWN ACCORD AND WITH FULL UNDERSTANDING OF ALL THE MATTERS SET FORTH IN THE INDICTMENT AND IN THIS APPLICATION AND IN THE CERTIFICATE OF MY LAWYER WHICH IS ATTACHED TO THIS APPLICATION. IN OFFERING MY PLEA OF "GUILTY" I FREELY AND VOLUNTARILY WAIVE (give up) THE CONSTITUTIONAL RIGHTS**

GUARANTEED TO ME AS STATED IN PARAGRAPH 7 ABOVE.

18. I waive the reading of the indictment in open court, and I request the court to enter my plea of "GUILTY" as set forth in Paragraph 15 of this application.

19. I understand that all of the above statements will be made in open court under oath and that any false statements may be used against me in a prosecution for perjury or false statement which is a felony.

20. ______I am proficient enough in English to read the above and have read and fully understand it.

______I am not proficient enough in English. I speak and understand______________ which is my native language. The above was read to me in____________________ and I fully understand it.

Signed by me in open court in the presence of my attorney this day of __________, 20___.

____
Defendant

INTERPRETER CERTIFICATION

I, ____________________, hereby certify that I am a duly ______________ interpreter in the English and ________________ languages and that I read all of the above to the defendant, that he/she stated he/she fully understood it, and I am satisfied that his/her answer is true and correct.

____
Date

____
Interpreter's signature

CERTIFICATE OF COUNSEL

The undersigned, as lawyer and counselor for the defendant ____________, hereby certifies:

1. I have read and fully explained to the defendant and believe he/she fully understands the allegations contained in the indictment of this case, the defenses he/she may have to each and every one of the allegations and the consequences of a plea of "GUILTY," including the pertinent Sentencing Guidelines provisions and maximum and minimum penalties.

2. I believe the defendant fully understands the constitutional rights he/she is waiving and that by entering a plea of "GUILTY" he/she is waiving each and every one of those rights.

3. Nothing has come to my attention which causes me to believe that the defendant lacks the ability to understand anything contained in the attached application or that at the time of entering his/her plea he/she is under the influence of any drug or alcohol.

4. The plea of "GUILTY" offered by the defendant in Paragraph 15 accords with my

understanding of the facts he/she related to me and is consistent with my advice to the defendant.

5. In my opinion the defendant's waiver of reading of the indictment in open court as provided by Rule 10 is voluntarily and understandingly made, and I recommend to the court that the waiver be accepted by the court.

6. Defendant has read the Plea Agreement she/he signed in the matter and I believe she/he fully understands it. I certify that no promises have been made to the defendant by the government or myself other than those contained in the Plea Agreement and if there are such other promises I must state them on the record before my client and the court.

7. In my opinion the plea of "GUILTY" offered by the defendant in Paragraph 15 of the application is voluntarily and understandingly made. I recommend that the court accept the plea of "GUILTY."

Signed by me in open court in the presence of the defendant above-named and after full discussion of the contents of this certificate with the defendant this day of __________, 20 ___.

____
Attorney for the Defendant

ORDER

I find that:

1. The defendant enters this plea of guilty freely and voluntarily and not out of ignorance, inadvertence, fear or coercion.

2. The defendant understands and knowingly, freely and voluntarily waives his constitutional rights.

3. The defendant freely and voluntarily executed the within Application and understands its contents.

4. The defendant has admitted the essential elements of the crime charged.

IT IS THEREFORE ORDERED that the defendant's plea of "GUILTY" be accepted and entered as prayed for in the Application and as recommended in the certificate of his lawyer.

Done in open court this ____ day of __________, 20___.

Dated: ____________________

____
CHARLES R. BREYER
United States District Judge

Hon. Edward M. Chen

District Judge

Chambers Information

U.S. District Court, Northern District of California
Courtroom 5, 17th Floor
450 Golden Gate Avenue
San Francisco, CA 94102

Scheduling Information

Courtroom Deputy: (415) 415-522-2034

Criminal Law and Motion	Wednesdays at 2:30 p.m.
Civil Law and Motion	Fridays at 1:30 p.m.
Initial Case Management Conferences	Fridays at 9:00 a.m.
Further Case Management Conferences/ Status Conferences	Fridays at 10:30 a.m.
Pretrial Conferences	Tuesdays at 2:30 p.m.
Trials	8:30 a.m. to 2:00 p.m.

Judge's Biography

Born 1953 in Oakland, CA

Federal Judicial Service:

-Judge, U. S. District Court, Northern District of California
-Nominated by Barack Obama on January 5, 2011, to a seat vacated by Martin J. Jenkins; Confirmed by the Senate on May 10, 2011, and received commission on May 12, 2011.
-U.S. Magistrate Judge, U.S. District Court, Northern District of California, 2001-2011

Education:

-University of California, Berkeley, A.B., 1975
-University of California, Berkeley, Boalt Hall School of Law, J.D., 1979

Professional Career:

-Law clerk, Hon. Charles B. Renfrew, U.S. District Court, Northern District of California, 1979-1980
-Attorney, Asian Law Caucus, San Francisco, California, 1980-1981
-Law clerk, Hon. James R. Browning, U.S. Court of Appeals for the Ninth Circuit, 1981-1982
-Private practice, San Francisco, California, 1982-1985
-Staff attorney, American Civil Liberties Union Foundation of Northern California, 1985-2001

I. Judge Chen's Procedures and Practices

A. *Civil Pretrial Instructions*

CIVIL PRETRIAL INSTRUCTIONS

A. MEET AND CONFER

At least thirty (30) days prior to the final pretrial conference, lead counsel who will try the case shall meet and confer regarding the following:

- Preparation and content of the joint pretrial conference statement, *see* Part B, *infra*;
- Preparation and exchange of pretrial materials, *see* Part C, *infra*; and
- Settlement of the action.

B. JOINT PRETRIAL CONFERENCE STATEMENT

At least fourteen (14) days prior to the final pretrial conference, the parties shall file a joint pretrial conference statement. The statement shall contain the following information:

1. **The Action.**

   a. Substance of the Action. A brief description of the substance of claims and defenses which need to be decided.

   b. Relief Prayed. A statement of all relief sought, particularly itemizing all elements of damages claimed.

2. **Factual Basis of the Action.**

   a. Undisputed Facts. A list of all stipulated facts, *i.e.*, all facts parties to which the parties will stipulate to for incorporation into the trial record without the necessity of supporting testimony or exhibits.

   b. Disputed Factual Issues. A list of all factual issues that remain to be tried, stating the issues with the same generality/specificity as any contested elements in the relevant jury instructions and organized by counts.

3. **Disputed Legal Issues.** *Without extended legal argument*, a concise statement of each disputed point of law concerning liability or relief, citing supporting statutes and decisions.

4. **Estimate of Trial Time.** An estimate of the number of hours needed for the presentation of each party's case.

5. **Trial Alternatives and Options.**

   a. Settlement Discussion. A statement summarizing the status of settlement negotiations and indicating whether further negotiations are likely to be productive.

   b. Consent to Trial Before a Magistrate Judge. A statement whether reference of all or part of the action to a master or magistrate judge is feasible, including whether the parties consent to a court or jury trial before a magistrate judge, with appeal directly to the Ninth Circuit.

c. Amendments or Dismissals. A statement of requested or proposed amendments to pleadings or dismissals of parties, claims, or defenses.

d. Bifurcation or Separate Trial of Issues. A statement of whether bifurcation or a separate trial of specific issues is feasible and desired.

6. **Witnesses.** *The following information should be provided as an appendix to the joint pretrial conference statement.* For each party, a list of all witnesses likely to be called at trial, including those appearing by deposition. For each witness, there should be a short statement of the substance of his or her testimony and an estimate regarding the length of testimony (including direct and cross-examination). If the witness is an expert witness, the short statement should clearly state the expert's theories and conclusions and the bases therefor; in addition, the expert's curriculum vitae and report (if any) should be attached. If there are objections to a live witness's testimony, whether in whole or in part, that objection should be raised through a motion in limine. For objections to deposition testimony, *see* Part B.8, *infra.*

7. Exhibits. *The following information should be provided as an appendix to the joint pretrial conference statement.* A joint exhibit list in tabular form, with (a) a column that briefly describes the exhibit; (b) a column that describes for what purpose the party will offer the exhibit and identifies its sponsoring witness; (c) a column that states any objections to the exhibit; (d) a column that briefly responds to the objections; and (e) a blank column for the Court's use. Before this list is filed with the Court, the parties shall meet and confer, in person, to consider exhibit numbers, to eliminate duplicate exhibits and confusion over exhibits, and to make a good faith effort to stipulate to admissibility. If stipulation is not possible, the parties shall make every effort to stipulate to authenticity and foundation absent a legitimate (not tactical) objection.

8. Use of Discovery Responses. *The following information should be provided as an appendix to the joint pretrial conference statement.* Excerpts of interrogatory responses, responses to requests for admission, and deposition testimony (with specific line references identified) that each party intends to present at trial. If there are objections to the use of written responses, the parties should include a joint memorandum that briefly states the objecting party's objection and the opposing party's response. If there is an objection to the general subject matter of a deponent's testimony, the objection should be made through a motion in limine. If specific objections were made during the deposition that are still in need of a Court ruling, the parties should include a joint memorandum that identifies the deposition testimony at issue and that briefly states the objecting party's objection (including any counter-designation) and the opposing party's response (including any counter-designation). The Court expects the parties to meet and confer in good faith in the attempt to resolve those specific objections regarding deposition testimony before any memorandum regarding objections are filed.

C. PRETRIAL MATERIALS

At least fourteen (14) days prior to the final pretrial conference, the parties shall file the following pretrial materials.

1. **Motions in Limine.** The following procedure should be used with respect to motions in limine. At least twenty-five (25) days before the pretrial conference, serve – but do not file – the moving papers. At least eighteen (18) days before the conference, serve – but do not file – the oppositions. When the oppositions are received, the moving party should collate the motion and opposition together, back to back, and then file the paired sets (each under separate cover) at least fourteen (14) days prior to the conference.

   Each motion in limine should address a single topic and contain no more than seven pages of briefing per side. Reply briefs are not permitted. Usually, each party or side should not need to file more than five motions in limine. Each party shall number its motions in limine in order of importance, the first being the most important.

2. **Preliminary Statement to the Jury.** In a jury trial, the parties shall provide a simplified statement of the case to be read to the jury during voir dire and as a part of the proposed jury instructions. Unless the case is extremely complex, this statement should not exceed one paragraph.

3. **Jury Instructions.** In a jury trial, a *joint* set of proposed jury instructions on substantive issues of law, arranged in a logical sequence.

   If undisputed, an instruction shall be identified as "Stipulated Instruction No. ____ re ______________________," with the blanks filled in as appropriate. Even if stipulated, the instruction shall be supported by citation.

   If disputed, each version of the instruction shall be inserted together, back to back, in their logical place in the overall sequence. A disputed instruction shall be identified as "Disputed Instruction No. ____ re ________________ offered by ___________," with the blanks filled in as appropriate. All disputed versions of the same basic instruction shall bear the same number. If a party does not have a counter-version and simply contends that no such instruction in any version should be given, then that party should so state on a separate page inserted in lieu of an alternate version. Each party should support its version of a disputed instruction, and/or oppose the version offered by the opposing party, with a brief argument and citation to any relevant authority. The argument and citation should be provided immediately following the disputed instructions. The parties are encouraged to keep disputed instructions to a minimum.

   Finally, absent objection, the Court shall give the following jury instructions from the Ninth Circuit Manual of Model Civil Jury Instructions (2007 ed.): 1.1-1.2, 1.6-1.14, 1.18-1.19, 3.1-3.3.

4. **Voir Dire.** In a jury trial, the Court will conduct a voir dire based on the attached (or a similar) questions/subjects. Counsel may also submit for the Court's consideration an *agreed upon* set of additional voir dire questions to be posed by the Court. Any voir dire questions on which counsel cannot agree may be submitted separately. Counsel will be allowed a brief (15 minutes) follow-up voir dire after the Court's questioning.

5. **Verdict Form.** In a jury trial, the parties shall submit a *joint* proposed verdict

form. If the parties are unable to stipulate to a verdict form, then each party or side shall submit a proposed verdict form.

6. **Proposed Findings of Fact and Conclusions of Law.** In a bench trial, each party or side shall submit proposed findings of fact and conclusions of law.

7. **Exhibits.** The parties shall submit *two* sets of all exhibits. Exhibits are not to be filed but rather shall be submitted to chambers. *Exhibits must be premarked. In addition, one set of exhibits must be tagged.* Exhibits shall be three-hole punched and shall be submitted in binders. Sample tags may be obtained from the Courtroom Deputy and are attached as Exhibit A hereto.

8. **Trial Brief.** Each party shall submit a trial brief not to exceed 15 pages absent court order. A trial brief is most helpful to the Court when it: (1) summarizes the party's theory of the case, (2) identifies key evidence, and (3) provides summary briefing on any controlling issues of law.

JUROR QUESTIONNAIRE

1. Name.
2. City of residence.
3. Occupational status.
4. Organizations.
5. Hobbies.
6. Marital status.
7. Spouse's occupation.
8. Children (including ages).
9. If a juror on another case.
10. If ever a grand juror.
11. If ever in the military.

EXHIBIT A

UNITED STATES DISTRICT COURT NORTHERN DISTRICT OF CALIFORNIA	UNITED STATES DISTRICT COURT NORTHERN DISTRICT OF CALIFORNIA
Case Number:	Case Number:
PLTF / DEFT EXHIBIT NO.____________	PLTF / DEFT EXHIBIT NO.____________
Date Admitted:____________________	Date Admitted:____________________
By:________________________ Betty Lee, Deputy Clerk	By:________________________ Betty Lee, Deputy Clerk

B. Civil Standing Order – General

CIVIL STANDING ORDER – GENERAL
U.S. DISTRICT JUDGE EDWARD M. CHEN

1. **Conformity to Rules.** Parties shall follow the Federal Rules of Civil Procedure, the Civil Local Rules, and the General Orders of the Northern District of California, except as superseded by these Standing Orders. Any failure to comply with any of the rules and orders may be deemed sufficient grounds for monetary sanctions, dismissal, entry of default judgment, or other appropriate sanctions.

2. **Communication with the Court.** Parties shall not attempt to make *ex parte* contact with the Judge or his chambers staff by telephone, facsimile, or any other means but may contact the Courtroom Deputy Clerk, Betty Lee, at (415) 522-2034 with appropriate inquiries (*e.g.*, scheduling inquiries).

All counsel listed on the parties' briefing must be fully apprised of the status of the pending matter and must be authorized to respond to calendar settings by the Court.

With the exception of discovery disputes (see the Civil Standing Orders on Discovery), or unless expressly permitted by the Court, parties shall not submit letters to the Court, and any communication with the Court must be in pleading form, including but not limited to status reports, requests for continuances, and requests for telephonic appearances.

3. **Scheduling Days.**

   a. Civil law-and-motion calendar is conducted on Fridays at 1:30 p.m. Order of call is to be determined by the Court. Parties may *jointly* ask for a motion to be considered on the papers, but such requests are not automatically granted. The Court may, in its discretion, vacate a hearing on a motion and rule on the papers.

   b. Initial case management conferences are conducted on Fridays at 9:00 a.m.

   c. Further status conferences are conducted on Fridays at 10:30 a.m.

   d. Pretrial conferences are conducted on Tuesdays at 2:30 p.m.

4. **Changes to the Court Calendar.** No changes to the Court's schedule shall be made except by order of the Court. Parties seeking to continue hearings, request special status conferences, modify briefing schedules, or make any other procedural changes shall submit a signed stipulation and proposed order or, if stipulation is not possible, a motion for administrative relief. *See* Civ. L.R. 7-11. Parties seeking to enlarge a filing deadline by way of a motion for administrative relief are admonished to file such a motion in advance of the filing deadline rather than on the day a brief or other matter is due. Continuances will be granted only upon a showing of good cause, with a particular focus on diligence by the party seeking the continuance and prejudice that may result if the continuance is denied.

5. **Chambers Copy.** A copy of all documents filed, whether electronically or manually, shall be submitted to the Clerk's Office in an envelope clearly marked with the case number and "EMC Chambers Copy" no later than noon on the next business day after the

document is filed. The chambers copy must be three-hole punched on the left-hand side. Exhibits to declarations must be tabbed.

6. **Case Management Conference Statement.** The *joint* case management statement must be filed one week in advance of the case management conference date. The statement must include all elements requested in the "Standing Order for All Judges of the Northern District of California – Contents of Joint Case Management Statement." *See* Civ. L.R. 16-9. In cases involving pro se litigants, parties shall attempt to file a joint statement; if after due diligence, an agreement cannot be reached, the parties may file separate case management statements, with each statement not to exceed seven (7) pages. Unless proceeding pro se, each party shall be represented at the case management conference by counsel with full and complete authority to address all of the matters referred to in (a) Federal Rules of Civil Procedure 16(c) and 26(f) and (b) the "Standing Order for All Judges of the Northern District of California – Contents of Joint Case Management Statement." Counsel must also have full and complete authority to enter stipulations and made admissions.

7. **Motions. All declarations shall be filed as separate documents.** Tabs *must* be used for exhibits attached to declarations, including chambers copies.

8. **Discovery and Discovery Motions.** *See* the "Civil Standing Orders on Discovery."

9. **Motions for Summary Judgment.** Each party or side is limited to filing one summary judgment motion. Any party wishing to exceed this limit must request leave of the Court. Briefing shall comply with Civil Local Rules 7-2 through 7-5. Separate statements of undisputed facts will not be considered by the Court. Joint statements of undisputed facts are not required, but are helpful if agreed upon.

10. **Proposed Orders Required.** Each party filing or opposing a motion shall also serve a proposed order that sets forth the relief or action sought and a short statement of the rationale of decision. The proposed order should be filed at the same time as the motion or Opposition.

11. **Grounds for Recusal.** Parties are directed to inform the Court of any and all reasonable bases for recusal at the earliest possible date.

12. **Service of Standing Orders.** Plaintiff (or in the case of removed cases, any removing defendant) is directed to serve copies of: (1) this standing order, (2) this Court's "Civil Standing Order on Discovery," and (3) the "Standing Order for All Judges of the Northern District of California – Contents of Joint Case Management Statement" at once upon all parties to the action, and upon those subsequently joined, in accordance with the provisions of Federal Rules of Civil Procedure 4 and 5. The plaintiff (or in the case of removed cases, any removing defendant) shall also file with the Clerk of the Court a certificate reflecting such service, in accordance with Civil Local Rule 5-6(a).

IT IS SO ORDERED.

EDWARD M. CHEN
United States District Judge

C. Civil Standing Order on Discovery

CIVIL STANDING ORDER ON DISCOVERY
U.S. DISTRICT JUDGE EDWARD M. CHEN

These Standing Orders on Discovery are a supplement to this Court's "Civil Standing Orders – General."

These Standing Orders apply only to cases in which discovery is supervised by this Court rather than the magistrate judge. The Court, at its discretion, may elect to transfer discovery matters to a magistrate judge or a special master.

1. **Conformity to Rules.** Parties shall follow the Federal Rules of Civil Procedure, the Civil Local Rules, and the General Orders of the Northern District of California, except as superseded by these Standing Orders. Any failure to comply with any of the rules and orders may be deemed sufficient grounds for monetary sanctions, dismissal, entry of default judgment, or other appropriate sanctions.

2. **Production of Documents.**
   a. **Responses.** In responding to requests for production of documents, *see* Fed. R. Civ. P. 34, a party shall affirmatively state in a written response the full extent to which the party will produce materials. In addition, the party shall, promptly after the production, confirm in writing that the party has produced all such materials so described that have been located after a diligent search of all locations where such materials might plausibly be found.

3. **Depositions.**
   a. **Scheduling.** The parties shall comply with Civ. L.R. 30-1. Generally, the party seeking the deposition may notice it at least ten (10) days in advance.

   b. **Documents.** Witnesses subpoenaed or requested to produce documents should ordinarily be served at least 30 days before the scheduled deposition unless otherwise stipulated, and arrangements should be made to permit inspection of the documents before the deposition commences. Extra copies of documents used during the deposition should ordinarily be provided to opposing counsel and the deponent.

   c. **Conduct.** During the deposition, parties are expected to cooperate with and be courteous to each other and deponents. Each party should designate one attorney to conduct the examination of the deponent. Parties should cooperate in the allocation of time to comply with any time limit set by the Court.

   d. **Marking of Exhibits.** Counsel shall comply with Civil Local Rule 30-2.

   e. **Objections.** Parties shall comply with Federal Rule of Civil Procedure 30(c)(2). Deposition objections shall be preserved except as to privilege or as to form. Speaking objections or those calculated to coach the deponent are prohibited.

      A person may *not* instruct a deponent not to answer a question except when necessary to preserve a privilege, to enforce a limitation directed by the Court, or to present a motion under Federal Rule of Civil Procedure 30(d)(3). When a privilege is claimed, the witness should nevertheless answer questions relevant to the existence, extent, or waiver of the privilege, such as the date of the communication, who made the statement, to whom and in whose presence the statement was made, other persons to whom the contents of the statement have been disclosed, and the general subject matter of the statement, unless such information itself is privileged.

A party may be subject to sanctions if the party consistently impedes, or otherwise unreasonably delays, the fair examination of the deponent.

f. **Private Consultation.** Private conferences between deponents and their attorneys in the course of deposition are improper and prohibited except for the sole purpose of determining whether a privilege should be asserted.

g. **Requests for Intervention by the Court.** If a dispute arises during a deposition and involves a persistent obstruction of the deposition or a refusal to answer a question in violation of this Standing Order, parties may arrange a telephonic conference with the Court through the Courtroom Deputy, Betty Lee, at (415) 522-2034.

4. **Discovery Motions.**

Except as specifically set forth below, no motions regarding discovery disputes may be filed without prior leave of the Court.

If there is an emergency discovery dispute, parties may request a telephonic conference with the Court through the Courtroom Deputy. If possible, the parties shall provide a short (one paragraph) description of the dispute prior to any conference call. An emergency discovery dispute is a discovery dispute that is in need of *immediate* attention by the Court. *This process should not be abused.*

All other requests for discovery relief (including requests for discovery-related sanctions) must be made by the parties in a *joint* letter brief no longer than four pages. Discovery letter briefs must be e-filed under the Civil Events category of Motions and Related Filings > Motions – General > "Discovery Letter Brief." The joint letter brief:

a. Must attest that, prior to filing the request for relief, counsel with full and complete authority on discovery matters met and conferred *in person*. A telephone meet and confer is permitted only where there is good cause (*e.g.*, plaintiff's counsel is located on the West coast while defense counsel is located on the East coast). The letters must certify that *lead trial counsel* have concluded no agreement can be reached.

b. Must concisely summarize those remaining issues that the parties were unable to resolve and state each party's last offer of compromise.

c. May cite to limited and specific legal authority.

d. May not be accompanied by declarations, unless a party declaration is needed to support a specific claim of undue burden.

e. May include as an attachment the specific excerpt of disputed discovery material.

f. No other attachments are permitted absent authorization by the Court.

The Court will advise the parties if additional briefing or a telephonic conference will be necessary. The Court may order the parties to further meet and confer at the federal courthouse with lead trial counsel in attendance.

5. **Service of Standing Orders.** Plaintiff (or in the case of removed cases, any removing defendant) is directed (a) to serve copies of this standing order at once upon all parties to the action, and upon those subsequently joined, in accordance with the provisions of Federal Rules of Civil Procedure 4 and 5 and (b) to file with the Clerk of the Court a certificate reflecting such service, in accordance with Civil Local Rule 5-6(a).

IT IS SO ORDERED.

____
EDWARD M. CHEN
United States District Judge

D. *Guidelines for Trial in Civil Cases (Jury and Bench)*

GUIDELINES FOR TRIAL IN CIVIL CASES (JURY AND BENCH)

PRETRIAL ARRANGEMENTS

1. Should a daily transcript and/or real-time reporting be desired, the parties shall make arrangements with the Supervisor of the Court Reporting Services at (415) 522-2079, at least ten calendar days prior to the trial date.

2. During trial, parties may wish to use, *e.g.*, overhead projectors, laserdisk/ computer graphics, poster blow-ups, models, or specimens of devices. The United States Marshal requires a court order to allow equipment into the Courthouse. Parties should be prepared to fix any equipment, if necessary.

SCHEDULING

1. Trial will normally be conducted from 8:30 a.m. to 2:00 p.m. (or slightly longer to finish a witness), with one 15-minute break and one 40-minute lunch break. Parties must arrive by 8:00 a.m. or, in a jury trial, earlier as needed for any matters to be heard out of the presence of the jury. The jury will be called at 8:30 a.m. The trial week is Monday through Thursday, excluding holidays. Fridays are dark.

JURY SELECTION

1. In civil jury cases, there are no alternate jurors, and the jury is typically selected as follows. At the outset, 18 potential jurors are called and seated in the jury box and front courtroom bench in the order their names are drawn from the drum. This placement will determine their order in the selection process. The Court will first conduct its voir dire of the entire panel (not just the seated 18) to determine hardships. Jurors excused from the seated 18 will be replaced from those drawn from the panel. The Court will then voir dire the seated 18 for cause. Afterwards, the parties will be allowed a brief follow-up voir dire (15 minutes). Once all voir dire is completed, the Court will address all challenges for cause and excuse those potential jurors who have been successfully challenged. After a short recess, each side may exercise its allotment of peremptory challenges. The plaintiff has the first challenge, the defendant the next two, the plaintiff the next two, and so forth. The default number of peremptory challenges per party or side is three. Any party that passes will be deemed to have used a challenge. The eight (or such other size as will constitute the jury) surviving the challenge process with the lowest numbers become the final jury. Once the jury selection is completed, the jurors' names will be read again, and they will be seated in the jury box and sworn in. The Court may alter the above procedure in its discretion.

2. Jurors may take notes. Note pads will be distributed at the beginning of each trial. The pads will remain in the jury room at the end of each day. Jurors will be instructed on the use of notes both in the preliminary and final jury instructions.

TIME LIMITS

1. Ordinarily, the Court shall set fixed time limits for the presentation of evidence by each side at the final pretrial conference. The time limit includes all examination

time (whether direct, cross, re-direct, or re-cross) for each witness regardless of which party called the witness. Opening and closing time limits shall be separately considered.

OPENING STATEMENTS

1. Each side may be subject to a predetermined time limit for its opening statement.

2. Parties must cooperate and meet and confer to exchange any visuals, graphics, or exhibits to be used in the opening statements, allowing for time to work out objections and any reasonable revisions one court day in advance of trial.

3. In a jury case, parties should be prepared to give opening statements as soon as the jury is sworn.

WITNESSES

1. At the close of each trial day (at 2:00 p.m.), parties shall exchange a list of witnesses for the next full court day and the exhibits that will be used on direct and cross-examination (other than for impeachment of an adverse witness). By 4:00 p.m. that same day, opposing parties shall provide any objections to such exhibits and further shall provide a list of all exhibits to be used with the same witnesses on cross-examination (other than for impeachment). The Court will address objections before 8:30 a.m. on the following day. The first notice of objection shall be provided one court day prior to the first day of trial. All notices should be provided in writing and filed with the Court, and a courtesy copy should be given to chambers immediately.

2. Parties should always have their next witness ready and in the Courthouse. Failure to have the next witness ready may constitute resting.

3. Parties are expected to cooperate with each other in the scheduling and production of witnesses. Witnesses may be taken out of order if necessary. Every effort shall be made to avoid calling a witness twice (as an adverse witness and later as a party's witness).

4. If a witness is testifying at the time of a recess or adjournment and has not been excused, the witness shall be seated back on the stand when court reconvenes. If a new witness is to be called immediately following recess or adjournment, the witness should be seated in the front row, ready to be sworn.

5. Immediately before each new witness takes the stand, counsel calling the witness shall place on the witness stand a clearly marked copy of each exhibit that counsel expects to have the witness refer to during his or her direct examination. Immediately before beginning cross-examination, counsel conducting cross-examination shall do the same with any additional exhibits to be referenced on cross.

6. If counsel intends to have the witness draw diagrams or put markings on visual exhibits or diagrams prepared by the party calling the witness, the witness shall do so before taking the stand. Once on the stand, the witness shall adopt the diagrams and/or markings and explain what they represent. If the diagram or visual exhibit is prepared by the opposing party, the witness shall not make any markings on the diagram or visual exhibit without leave of the Court.

7. A witness or exhibit not listed in the joint pretrial conference statement may not be called or used without good cause. This rule does not apply to true rebuttal witnesses (other than experts). Defense witnesses are normally considered case-in-chief witnesses, not "rebuttal" witnesses.

USE OF DEPOSITIONS TO IMPEACH OR SHORT READ-INS

1. Depositions used at trial for impeachment shall comply with the following procedure:

- **a.** On the first day of trial, bring the original and clean copies of any deposition(s) intended to be used. A sealed original copy shall be provided to the Judge.
- **b.** The first time a deposition is read, counsel should state the deponent's name, the date of the deposition, and the name of the lawyer asking the question. If the deposition was a Rule 30(b)(6) deposition, counsel should so state.
- **c.** When counsel reads a passage into the record, counsel should simply say, for example, "I wish to read in page ____, lines ____ to ____ from the witness's deposition." A brief pause will be allowed for any objection.
- **d.** Counsel should then proceed by stating "question" and reading the question exactly, then stating "answer" and reading the answer exactly. Stating "question" and "answer" is necessary so that the court reporter, the Court, and the jury (in a jury trial) can follow who was talking at the deposition.
- **e.** Rather than reading a passage, counsel is free to play a videotaped version of the passage, but counsel must have a system for immediate display of the precise passage.

DEPOSITION DESIGNATIONS

1. The following procedure applies only to witnesses who appear by deposition. It does not apply to live witnesses whose depositions are read in while they are on the stand. To prepare designated deposition testimony, counsel shall photocopy the cover page, the page where the witness is sworn, and each page from which any testimony is proffered, including pages containing a counter-designation made by opposing counsel. Counsel should redact objections or colloquy unless needed to understand the question. In addition, counsel should redact any testimony that has not been designated or any testimony to which an objection has been made and sustained by the Court. Any corrections must be interlineated and references to exhibit numbers must conform to the trial numbers. The finished packet should then be the actual script and should smoothly present the identification and swearing of the witness and testimony desired.

2. Counsel is free to play a videotaped version of any deposition testimony, but counsel must have a system for immediate display of the precise testimony omitting any properly redacted passages.

EXHIBITS

1. Use numbers only, not letters, for exhibits, preferably the same numbers as were used in depositions. Blocks of numbers should be assigned to fit the need of the case (*e.g.*, Plaintiff has 1 to 100, Defendant A has 101 to 200, Defendant B has 201 to 300, etc.). A single exhibit should be marked only once. If the plaintiff has marked an exhibit, then the defendant should not re-mark it. Different versions of the same document, *e.g.*, a copy with additional handwriting, must be treated as different exhibits. To avoid any party claiming "ownership" of an exhibit, all exhibits shall be marked and referred to as "Trial Exhibit No. ____," not as "Plaintiff's Exhibit" or "Defendant's Exhibit." If an exhibit number differs from that used in a deposition transcript, however, then the latter must be conformed to the new trial number if and when the deposition testimony is read (so as to avoid confusion over exhibit numbers).

2. Exhibits are not to be filed but rather shall be submitted to chambers (two sets). *Exhibits must be premarked. In addition, one set of exhibits must be tagged.* Exhibits shall be three-hole punched and shall be submitted in binders. Sample tags may be obtained from the Courtroom Deputy and are attached as Exhibit A hereto.

3. Parties must consult with each other and with the Courtroom Deputy at the end of each trial date and compare notes as to which exhibits are in evidence and any limitations thereon. If there are any differences, parties should bring them promptly to the Court's attention.

4. In a jury trial, before the case goes to the jury, parties must confer with the Courtroom Deputy to make sure the exhibits going to the jury room are all in evidence and in good order. Parties may, but are not required to, jointly provide a revised list of all exhibits actually in evidence (and no others) stating the exhibit number and a brief, non-argumentative description (*e.g.*, letter from A to B, dated August 17, 1999). This list may go into the jury room to help the jury sort through exhibits. In a bench trial, parties may follow a similar procedure to help the Court sort through exhibits.

OBJECTIONS

1. Counsel shall stand when making objections and briefly state the basis of the objection.

2. Counsel shall not make speaking objections.

3. There can be only one lawyer per witness per party for all purposes, including objections.

4. In a jury trial, sidebar conferences are discouraged. The procedures outlined in these guidelines should eliminate the need for most sidebars.

5. In a jury trial, to maximize jury time, parties must alert the Court in advance of any problems that will require discussion outside the presence of the jury so that the conference can be held before court begins or after the jury leaves for the day.

SETTLEMENTS AND CONTINUANCES

1. Shortly before trial or a final pretrial conference, parties occasionally wish

jointly to advise the Courtroom Deputy that a settlement has been reached and seek to take the matter off calendar, but it turns out later that there was only a settlement "in principle" and disputes remain. Cases, however, cannot be taken off calendar in this manner. Unless and until a legally binding settlement is reached, all parties must be prepared to proceed with the final pretrial conference as scheduled and to proceed to trial on the trial date, or face dismissal of the case for lack of prosecution or entry of default judgment. To facilitate settlement, the Court is available to place the material terms of a settlement on the record. Only an advance continuance expressly approved by the Court will release parties from their obligation to proceed to trial. If parties expect that a settlement will be final by the time of trial or the final pretrial conference, they should notify the Court immediately in writing or, if it occurs over the weekend before the trial or conference, by voicemail to the Courtroom Deputy. The Court will attempt to confer with the parties as promptly as circumstances permit to determine if a continuance will be in order or if it can assist the parties in putting the settlement on the record. Pending such a conference, however, parties must prepare and make all filings and be prepared to proceed with trial.

2. Civil Local Rule 40-1 provides that jury costs may be assessed as sanctions for failure to provide the Court with timely written notice of a settlement. Please be aware that any settlement reached on the day of trial, during trial, or at any time after the jury or potential jurors have been summoned will normally require the parties to pay juror costs.

EXHIBIT A

UNITED STATES DISTRICT COURT
NORTHERN DISTRICT OF CALIFORNIA

Case Number:

PLTF / DEFT EXHIBIT
NO.____________

Date
Admitted:________________________

By:______________________________
Betty Lee, Deputy Clerk

UNITED STATES DISTRICT COURT
NORTHERN DISTRICT OF CALIFORNIA

Case Number:

PLTF / DEFT EXHIBIT
NO.____________

Date
Admitted:________________________

By:______________________________
Betty Lee, Deputy Clerk

Hon. Maxine M. Chesney

District Judge

Chambers Information

U.S. District Court, Northern District of California
Courtroom 7, 19th Floor
450 Golden Gate Avenue
San Francisco, CA 94102

Scheduling Information

Courtroom Deputy: (415) 522-2041

Criminal Law and Motion	Wednesdays at 2:15 p.m.
Civil Law and Motion	Fridays at 9:00 a.m.

Judge's Biography

Born 1942 in San Francisco, CA

Federal Judicial Service:

-Judge, U.S. District Court, Northern District of California
-Nominated by William J. Clinton on January 24, 1995, to a seat vacated by John P. Vukasin, Jr.; Confirmed by the Senate on May 8, 1995, and received commission on May 10, 1995.
-Assumed senior status on June 30, 2009.

Education:

-University of California, Berkeley, B.A., 1964
-University of California, Berkeley, Boalt Hall School of Law, J.D., 1967

Professional Career:

-Attorney, Office of the San Francisco District Attorney, California, 1968-1979
-Trial Attorney, 1968-1969
-Senior Trial Attorney, 1969-1971
-Principal Trial Attorney, 1971-1976
-Head Trial Attorney, 1976
-Assistant Chief Deputy, 1976-1979
-Judge, San Francisco Municipal Court, California, 1979-1983
-Judge, Superior Court of California, City and County of San Francisco, appointed and subsequently elected, 1983-1995
-Nominated to U.S. District Court for the Northern District of California, 1994; Senate took no action.

I. Judge Chesney's Procedures and Practices

A. *Standing Order for Civil Cases*

STANDING ORDER FOR CIVIL CASES ASSIGNED TO THE HONORABLE MAXINE M. CHESNEY

1. Counsel shall consult and comply with all provisions of the Local Rules relating to continuance, motions, briefs, and all other matters, unless superseded by these Standing Orders.

2. **Electronic Case Filing - Lodging Hard Copies for Chambers**
In all cases that have been assigned to the Electronic Case Filing Program, the parties are required to provide for use in chambers one paper copy of each document that is filed electronically. The paper copy of each such document shall be delivered no later than noon on the day after the document is filed electronically. The paper copy shall be marked **"Chambers Copy"** and shall be delivered to the Clerk's Office in an envelope clearly marked with the judge's name, case number, and "E-Filing Chambers Copy."

3. **Scheduling Days:**
a. Criminal Law and Motion Calendar is conducted on Wednesdays at 2:30 p.m.
b. Civil Law and Motion Calendar is conducted on Fridays at **9:00 a.m.**
c. Case Management Conferences are conducted on Fridays at **10:30 a.m.**, with order of call determined by the Court.
d. Pretrial conferences are generally conducted on Tuesday afternoons at **3:00 p.m.**
e. Counsel need not reserve a hearing date for motions, but noticed dates may be reset as the Court's calendar requires.

4. **Proposed Orders Required:** Each party filing or opposing a motion shall also serve and file a proposed order which sets forth the relief or action sought and a short statement of the rationale of decision, including citation of authority, that the party requests the Court to adopt.

5. **Discovery:** Discovery motions will be referred to a Magistrate Judge.

6. **Summary Judgment:** Unless specific leave has been requested and granted, the Court will address only one motion for summary judgment/adjudication per party or side. Examples of issues the Court may deem appropriate for determination by separate motion, particularly if raised early in the case, include such affirmative defenses as the statute of limitations and failure to exhaust administrative remedies.

7. **Procedural Matters:** Parties seeking to continue hearings, request special status conferences, modify briefing schedules, or make other procedural changes shall submit a signed stipulation and proposed order, or, if stipulation is not possible, an administrative request in accordance with Civil Local Rule 7-11. In either case, no changes in the Court's schedule or procedures shall be made except by signed order of the Court and only upon a

showing of good cause.

8. **Service of Standing Orders:** Plaintiff is directed to serve copies of these standing orders at once upon all parties to this action and upon those subsequently joined, in accordance with the provisions of Rules 4 and 5, Federal Rules of Civil Procedure, and to file with the Clerk of the Court a certificate reflecting such service.

IT IS SO ORDERED.

Dated: March 16, 2009

MAXINE M. CHESNEY
United States District Judge

II. Judge Chesney's Case Management Orders

A. *Order for Criminal Pretrial Preparation*

IN THE UNITED STATES DISTRICT COURT
FOR THE NORTHERN DISTRICT OF CALIFORNIA

UNITED STATES OF AMERICA,

Plaintiff,

v.

Defendant.
______________________________/

No. CR _________ MMC

ORDER FOR CRIMINAL PRETRIAL PREPARATION

Good cause appearing, IT IS HEREBY ORDERED that:

TRIAL:

Trial will begin on **MONDAY**, _____________, **201__, at 9:00 a.m.** Estimated length of trial is____________ days.

DISCOVERY:

By the close of business, **THURSDAY**, _________, 200__, the parties will exchange the information, documents and tangible objects authorized by Rule 16 of the Federal Rules of Criminal Procedure. Additional discovery shall be by motion accompanied by affidavits setting forth the unusual circumstances justifying discovery beyond the limits of Rule 16.

PRIOR TO FILING ANY DISCOVERY-RELATED MOTIONS, COUNSEL SHALL:

1. Meet and confer with opposing counsel, and

2. File a declaration, under penalty of perjury, that counsel has conferred with opposing counsel with respect to each and every issue on an informal basis. Said declaration may be filed contemporaneously with the motion. If no such declaration is filed, the Court will return the motion papers to counsel.

MOTIONS:

All motions will be heard on **WEDNESDAY**, ______________, 200__, **at 2:30 p.m.** Motions, affidavits and memoranda shall be served, filed and an extra copy lodged with the Court by the moving party by 4:00 p.m. On __________, 201__. Any opposition shall be filed and an extra copy lodged with the Court by 12 o'clock noon on _____________, 201__.

PRETRIAL CONFERENCE:

A Pretrial Conference will be held on **TUESDAY**, _________, 200___, **at 3:00 p.m.** At the Pretrial Conference the parties shall be prepared to discuss the matters set forth in Criminal Local Rule 17.1-1(b).

PRETRIAL PREPARATION:

Not less than **five court days** before the Pretrial Conference, counsel for the government shall:

(1) Serve and file a trial memorandum briefly stating the legal bases for the charges and the anticipated evidence, and addressing any evidentiary, procedural or other anticipated legal issues;

(2) Serve and file a list of all witnesses who may be called, together with a brief summary of the testimony of each;

(3) Serve and lodge a proposed form of verdict on pleading paper containing no reference to the party submitting it;

(4) Serve and lodge proposed questions for jury voir dire; and

(5) Serve and lodge copies of all exhibits to be offered at trial, together with a complete list (**see attached form**) of those exhibits. Each exhibit shall be premarked with an exhibit sticker (**see attached form**), the government's with numbers and the defendant's with letters.

Not less than **five court days** before the Pretrial Conference, defense counsel shall comply with subparagraphs (3) and (4) above, and, to the extent consistent with the defendant's right to an effective defense, with subparagraphs (1), (2) and (5) above.

JURY INSTRUCTIONS:

All proposed jury instructions and any objections thereto are to be filed and served no later than **five court days** before the pretrial conference.

In advance of the pretrial filings the parties shall do the following:

(1) Meet and confer and resolve all jury instructions to the extent possible. Parties are expected to resolve technical or semantic differences.

(2) Prepare **one joint** set of instructions upon which the parties agree.

(3) The parties shall submit separately only those instructions upon which there is substantive disagreement. Each separate instruction shall note on its face the identity of the party submitting such instruction. The party or parties objecting to an instruction shall file a written objection. The form of the objection shall be as follows:

(a) Set forth in full the instruction to which the objection is made;

(b) Provide concise argument and citation to authority explaining why the instruction is improper.

(c) Set forth in full an alternative instruction, if any;

(4) All instructions should be concise, understandable and neutral statements of law. Argumentative instructions will not be given and should not be submitted.

(5) Any modifications of instructions from the Ninth Circuit Model Jury Instructions or other form instructions must identify the modifications made to the original form instruction and the authority supporting the modification.

TRANSCRIPTS:

If transcripts will be requested during or immediately after trial, arrangements must be made with the court reporter at least **one week** before trial commences.

CHANGE OF PLEA:

Defendant's counsel shall give prompt notice to the United States Attorney and to the Court of any intention to change a previously entered not guilty plea.

EXHIBITS:

Each party is responsible for their exhibits. Upon the conclusion of the trial, each party shall retain their exhibits. Should an appeal be taken, it is the party's responsibility to make arrangements with the clerk of the Court to file the record on appeal.

IT IS SO ORDERED.

DATED: ___________________

____
MAXINE M. CHESNEY
United States District Judge

B. Pretrial Preparation Order

IN THE UNITED STATES DISTRICT COURT
FOR THE NORTHERN DISTRICT OF CALIFORNIA

No. C _________ MMC

Plaintiff(s),

v.

PRETRIAL PREPARATION ORDER

Defendant(s).

____/

It is hereby **ORDERED** pursuant to Federal Rules of Civil Procedure and the Local Rules of this Court:

JURY/COURT TRIAL DATE: Monday, _____________ at 9:00 a.m., Courtroom 7, 19th floor.

TRIAL LENGTH is estimated to be ____________ days.

DISCOVERY PLAN: Per Federal Rules of Civil Procedure and Local Rules, subject to any provisions below.

NON-EXPERT DISCOVERY CUTOFF is ________________.

DESIGNATION OF EXPERTS:

Plaintiff/Defendant: No later than __________________.

Plaintiff/Defendant: Rebuttal no later than ___________________.

Parties shall conform to Federal Rule of Civil Procedure 26(a)(2).

EXPERT DISCOVERY CUTOFF : ______________________.

DISCOVERY MATTERS are referred to a Magistrate Judge and are to be noticed for hearing before the assigned Magistrate Judge.

DISPOSITIVE MOTIONS shall be filed no later than ___________, and shall be noticed for hearing 35 days thereafter.

SETTLEMENT CONFERENCE shall be held before Magistrate Judge _____________and scheduled to take place no later than 30 days prior to the Pretrial Conference.

PRETRIAL CONFERENCE DATE: _________________at **3:00 p.m.**

> **COUNSEL WHO INTEND TO TRY THE CASE MUST ATTEND THE PRETRIAL CONFERENCE.** Counsel shall be prepared to discuss all aspects of the case, including settlement. Pretrial shall conform to the attached instructions.

MEET AND CONFER (Civil L.R. 16-10(b)(5): Lead trial counsel shall meet and confer no later than ____________________.

FURTHER STATUS CONFERENCE: Friday, ______________at 10:30 a.m.

FURTHER STATUS CONFERENCE STATEMENT DUE: Friday, __________.

ADDITIONAL ORDERS: ____________________.

PLAINTIFF IS ORDERED TO SERVE A COPY OF THIS ORDER ON ANY PARTY SUBSEQUENTLY JOINED IN THIS ACTION.

DATED: ____________________

____
MAXINE M. CHESNEY
United States District Judge

PRETRIAL INSTRUCTIONS

Counsel SHALL meet and confer in good faith in advance of complying with the following pretrial requirements for the purpose of preparing for the Pretrial Conference and to discuss settlement.

A. PRETRIAL STATEMENT: The parties shall file a joint pretrial statement which shall set forth:

1. The substance of the action;
2. The relief claimed, including the particular elements of the damages claimed;
3. The factual issues remaining, as well as any stipulations of fact;
4. The legal issues, including a concise statement of each disputed point of law concerning liability or relief and citing supporting statutory and case law;
5. A current estimate as to the length of the trial;
6. The status of the case with respect to alternative dispute resolution.
7. A list of witnesses likely to be called at trial. Expert witnesses shall be listed separately. Witnesses not included on the list may be excluded from testifying.

B. JURY INSTRUCTIONS:

1. Joint Set of Agreed Upon Instructions: The parties shall jointly prepare a set of agreed upon jury instructions, which shall be filed **ten Court days** prior to the Pretrial Conference.
2. Separate Instructions: Separate instructions may be submitted only as to those instructions upon which the parties cannot agree. Each separate instruction shall note on its face the identity of the party submitting such instruction. Separate instructions shall be filed **ten Court days** prior to the Pretrial Conference.

No later than **ten Court days** prior to the Pretrial Conference, the party or parties objecting to an instruction shall file a written objection to such instruction. The form of the objection shall be as follows:

(a) Set forth in full the instruction to which the objection is made;

(b) Provide concise argument and citations to authority explaining why the opposing party's instruction is improper; and

(c) Set forth in full an alternative instruction, if any.

3. Substance and Format of Instructions: The instructions shall cover all substantive issues. Proposed instructions shall be consecutively numbered. Each proposed instruction shall be typed in full on a separate page and cover only one subject, to be indicated in the title. Citations to the authorities upon which the instruction is based shall be included. Instructions shall be brief, clear, written in plain English and free of argument. Pattern or form instructions shall be revised to address the particular facts and issues of this

C. VOIR DIRE AND VERDICT FORMS: No later than ten Court days prior to the Pretrial Conference each party shall serve and file proposed questions for jury voir dire and a proposed form of verdict.

D. FINDINGS OF FACT and CONCLUSIONS OF LAW: In non-jury cases, no later than **ten Court days** prior to the Pretrial Conference, each party shall serve and lodge with the Court proposed findings of fact and conclusions of law on all material issues. Proposed findings shall be brief, written in plain English and free of pejorative language and argument. Whenever possible, parties shall deliver to the Courtroom Deputy copies of proposed findings of fact and conclusions of law on a CD in WordPerfect format. The disk label shall include the name of the parties, the case number and a description of the documents.

E. EXHIBITS:

1. Provide Copies of Exhibits to Other Parties: No later than ten Court days prior to the Pretrial Conference, each party shall provide every other party with one set of all proposed exhibits, charts, schedules, summaries, diagrams and other similar documentary materials to be used in its case in chief at trial, together with a complete list (**see attached form**) of all such proposed exhibits. Voluminous exhibits shall be reduced by elimination of irrelevant portions or through the use of summaries. Each item shall be pre-marked with an exhibit sticker (**see attached form**), plaintiff's exhibits with numbers, defendant's exhibits with letters or with numbers sequenced to begin after plaintiff's exhibit numbers. If there are numerous exhibits, they should be provided in three-ring binders with marked tab separators. All exhibits which have not been provided as required are subject to exclusion.

2. Stipulations re Admissibility: Prior to the Pretrial Conference, the parties shall make a good faith effort to stipulate exhibits into evidence and be prepared to place their admission on the record at the Pretrial Conference. If stipulation to admission in evidence is not possible, the parties shall make every effort to stipulate to authenticity and foundation absent a legitimate (not tactical) objection.

3. Provide Copies of Exhibits to Court: Two sets of exhibits shall be provided to the Court on the **first day of trial**. Each set shall be in binders, tabbed and indexed.

4. Disposition of Exhibits After Trial: Upon the conclusion of the trial, each party shall retain its exhibits through the appellate process. It is each party's responsibility to make arrangements with the Clerk of the Court to file the record on appeal.

F. **WITNESSES:**

1. Jury Trials: The Pretrial Conference Statement shall include a list of witnesses likely to be called at trial, other than solely for impeachment or rebuttal. Expert witnesses shall be listed separately. Witnesses not included on the list may be excluded from testifying.

2. Non-Jury Trials: In non-jury cases, each party shall serve and lodge with the Court a written narrative statement of the proposed direct testimony of each witness under that party's control. Each statement shall be marked as an exhibit and shall be in a form suitable to be received into evidence.

G. **MOTIONS IN LIMINE:** Motions in limine are limited to motions to exclude specific items of evidence (i.e., specific testimony or exhibits) on a ground and upon such authority as would be sufficient to sustain an objection to such evidence at trial.

1. Motions in limine shall be filed and served no later than **ten Court days** prior to the date set for the Pretrial Conference. Any party opposing such a motion in limine shall file and serve its opposition papers no later than **five Court days** prior to the Pretrial Conference. No reply papers will be considered.

2. Format of motions in limine: Each motion in limine and each opposition thereto, shall be separately filed and numbered.

H. **LIST OF EXHIBITS WITH STIPULATIONS AND OBJECTIONS:** No later than **one Court day** prior to the Pretrial Conference the parties shall file with the Court a list of all exhibits admitted by stipulation; and a list of all exhibits as to which objections have been made, with a brief notation indicating which party objects and for what reason.

I. **OTHER PRETRIAL MATTERS**

1. Settlement Conferences - Any party utilizing another form of Alternative Dispute Resolution who wishes to arrange a settlement conference

before a judge or magistrate judge thereafter may do so by contacting the Courtroom Deputy.

2. Daily Transcripts - If transcripts will be requested during or immediately after trial, arrangements must be made with the court reporter at least **one week** before trial commences.

Attachments

[1. Exhibit List]

IN THE UNITED STATES DISTRICT COURT
FOR THE NORTHERN DISTRICT OF CALIFORNIA

CASE NO. **C-__________ MMC** DATE: ________________

______________________ vs. ______________________

EXHIBIT LIST

( ) Plaintiff ( ) Defendant

EXHIBIT NUMBER	Marked	Admitted	Sponsoring Witness	DESCRIPTION

[2. Forms of Exhibit Tags for Plaintiffs and Defendants]

Case No. ________________ **PLNTF** Exhibit No. __________ Date Entered ______________ Signature ________________	Case No. ________________ **DEFT** Exhibit No. __________ Date Entered ______________ Signature ________________
Case No. ________________ **PLNTF** Exhibit No. __________ Date Entered ______________ Signature ________________	Case No. ________________ **DEFT** Exhibit No. __________ Date Entered ______________ Signature ________________

III. Judge Chesney's Forms

A. *Application for Permission to Enter Plea of Guilty and Order Accepting Plea*

IN THE UNITED STATES DISTRICT COURT
FOR THE NORTHERN DISTRICT OF CALIFORNIA

No. CR_________ MMC

Plaintiff,

v.

Defendant.

______________________________________/

APPLICATION FOR PERMISSION TO ENTER PLEA OF GUILTY AND ORDER ACCEPTING PLEA

(Fed. R. Crim. P., Rules 10 and 11)

The defendant represents to the Court:

1. My full true name is ______________. I am years of age ____. I have gone to school up to and including ______________. My most recent occupation has been ______________. I request that all proceedings against me be in my true name.

2. I am represented by a lawyer; his/her name is __________________.

3. I received a copy of the indictment/information (as used in the Application the term indictment includes information) before being called upon to plead. I have read the indictment or a translator who speaks _____________ read it to me, and I have discussed the indictment with my lawyer.

I fully understand every charge made against me. I understand these charges to be: ______________________________________.

4. I have told my lawyer all the facts and circumstances known to me about the charges made against me in the indictment. I believe that my lawyer is fully informed on all such matters.

5. I know that the Court must be satisfied that there is a factual basis for a plea of "GUILTY" before my plea can be accepted. I represent to the Court that I did the following acts in connection with the charges made against me in Counts____.

(In the above space defendant must set out in detail in his/her own handwriting what he/she did. If more space is needed, add a separate page.)

6. My lawyer has counseled and advised me on the nature of each charge, all lesser included charges, all penalties and consequences of each charge, all possible defenses that I may have in this case and the constitutional rights I am waiving.

7. I understand that my constitutional rights are as follows:

(a) the right to a speedy and public trial by jury;

(b) the right to see all of the evidence against me and to hear all witnesses called to testify against me and to have my attorney cross-examine them;

(c) the right to use the power and process of the court to compel the production of any evidence, including the attendance of any witnesses in my favor;

(d) the right to the assistance of a lawyer at all stages of the proceedings including trial and appeal and if I cannot afford one, to have the court appoint one to represent me without cost to me or based upon my ability to pay;

(e) the right to remain silent or to take the witness stand at my sole option and if I do not take the witness stand, no inference of guilt may be drawn from such failure and the jury must be so advised;

(f) the right against self-incrimination;

(g) the right to appeal from an adverse judgment;

(h) the right to appeal my sentence without any limitation contained in my plea agreement.

8. I know that I may plead "NOT GUILTY" to any offense charged against me and exercise all of my rights as listed above.

9. I know that if I plead "GUILTY" I am giving up all of the rights enumerated in paragraph 7 and that there will be no trial either before a court or jury.

10. I know that if I plead "GUILTY" the result of my plea is more than just an admission or confession of guilt and that it will result in my conviction, and that further, the court may impose the same punishment as if I had pleaded "NOT GUILTY," stood trial and been convicted by a jury.

11. My lawyer has discussed with me the maximum and minimum, if any, punishments which the law provides and the various provisions of the Sentencing Guidelines that may apply to me. I understand that the maximum punishment for the offense(s) charged in Count(s) ______________ of the indictment is ____________ years of imprisonment, a fine of $______________, and a period of ________years supervised release. I understand that there is a mandatory minimum punishment of _____________years imprisonment for the offense(s) charged in Count(s) ______________. I also understand that the minimum period of supervised release which the court may impose is ______________ (if applicable) and that if I violate any condition of supervised release the release may be revoked and I may be sentenced to all or a part of the term of supervised release imposed in addition to any other term of imprisonment which I have received.

I understand that I may be assessed the costs of confinement and/or supervision. I understand that I must pay a penalty assessment of $100.00 per count to which I plead (or $25.00 in the case of misdemeanor counts). I understand that I may be ordered to pay restitution in an amount determined by the court.

I know that the sentence I will receive is solely a matter within the control of the Judge. I understand that the Judge will make no decision regarding my sentence until the Judge has read and considered the pre-sentence investigation report prepared and submitted to the court by the Probation Department.

I also understand that the court and counsel cannot promise what sentence or sentencing range will be set and that these calculations will depend upon the Sentencing Guidelines as they apply to me. I have been advised that the court may sentence within the guideline range determined by the Probation Department or may depart upward or downward from the range. However, no promises have been made to me as to the range or departure.

12. If I am on probation, supervised release or parole in this or any other court, I know that by pleading guilty here my probation, release or parole may be revoked and I may be required to serve time in that case, which may be consecutive, that is, in addition to any sentence imposed upon me in this case.

13. I declare that no officer or agent of any branch of government (federal, state or local) has promised or suggested that I will receive a lighter sentence, or probation, or any other form of leniency, nor have any other promises been made if I plead "GUILTY," except as stated in the Plea Agreement I have signed, stated on the record in my entry of plea or as follows: ________________.

(In the space above insert any promises or concessions made to the defendant or to his/her attorney.)

If anyone else made such a promise or suggestion, except as noted in the previous sentence, I know that person had no authority to do it. No one has forced or coerced me into entering this plea. My willingness to plead guilty (does) (does not) result from prior discussions between my attorney and the government's attorney. (If it does, state any factors that influenced you that are not reflected in the plea agreement.) ____________________.

14. I believe that my lawyer has done all that a lawyer could do to counsel and assist me, and I am satisfied with the advice and help he/she has given me.

15. I know that the court will not permit anyone to plead "GUILTY" who maintains he/she is innocent and, with that in mind and because I am "GUILTY," I respectfully request the court to accept my plea of "GUILTY" and to have the clerk enter my plea of "GUILTY" as follows: ____.

16. My mind is clear. I am not under the influence of alcohol or drugs and I am not under a doctor's care. The only drugs, medicines or pills that I took within the past seven days are:_________________. (If none, so state.)

17. **I OFFER MY PLEA OF "GUILTY" FREELY AND VOLUNTARILY AND OF MY OWN ACCORD AND WITH FULL UNDERSTANDING OF ALL THE MATTERS SET FORTH IN THE INDICTMENT AND IN THIS APPLICATION AND IN THE CERTIFICATE OF MY LAWYER WHICH IS ATTACHED TO THIS APPLICATION. IN OFFERING MY PLEA OF "GUILTY" I FREELY AND**

VOLUNTARILY WAIVE (give up) THE CONSTITUTIONAL RIGHTS GUARANTEED TO ME AS STATED IN PARAGRAPH 7 ABOVE.

18. I waive the reading of the indictment in open court, and I request the court to enter my plea of "GUILTY" as set forth in Paragraph 15 of this application.

19. I understand that all of the above statements will be made in open court under oath and that any false statements may be used against me in a prosecution for perjury or false statement which is a felony.

20. ______I am proficient enough in English to read the above and have read and fully understand it.

______I am not proficient enough in English. I speak and understand______________ which is my native language. The above was read to me in______________________ and I fully understand it.

Signed by me in open court in the presence of my attorney this day of ______, 20__.

____
Defendant

INTERPRETER CERTIFICATION

I, ____________________, hereby certify that I am a duly ______________ interpreter in the English and _________________ languages and that I read all of the above to the defendant, that he/she stated he/she fully understood it, and I am satisfied that his/her answer is true and correct.

____
Date

____
Interpreter's signature

CERTIFICATE OF COUNSEL

The undersigned, as lawyer and counselor for the defendant ____________, hereby certifies:

1. I have read and fully explained to the defendant and believe he/she fully understands the allegations contained in the indictment of this case, the defenses he/she may have to each and every one of the allegations and the consequences of a plea of "GUILTY," including the pertinent Sentencing Guidelines provisions and maximum and minimum penalties.

2. I believe the defendant fully understands the constitutional rights he/she is waiving and that by entering a plea of "GUILTY" he/she is waiving each and every one of those rights.

3. Nothing has come to my attention which causes me to believe that the defendant lacks the ability to understand anything contained in the attached application or that at the

time of entering his/her plea he/she is under the influence of any drug or alcohol.

4. The plea of "GUILTY" offered by the defendant in Paragraph 15 accords with my understanding of the facts he/she related to me and is consistent with my advice to the defendant.

5. In my opinion the defendant's waiver of reading of the indictment in open court as provided by Rule 10 is voluntarily and understandingly made, and I recommend to the court that the waiver be accepted by the court.

6. Defendant has read the Plea Agreement she/he signed in the matter and I believe she/he fully understands it. I certify that no promises have been made to the defendant by the government or myself other than those contained in the Plea Agreement and if there are such other promises I must state them on the record before my client and the court.

7. In my opinion the plea of "GUILTY" offered by the defendant in Paragraph 15 of the application is voluntarily and understandingly made. I recommend that the court accept the plea of "GUILTY."

Signed by me in open court in the presence of the defendant above-named and after full discussion of the contents of this certificate with the defendant this day of __________, 20 ___.

____
Attorney for the Defendant

ORDER

I find that:

1. The defendant enters this plea of guilty freely and voluntarily and not out of ignorance, inadvertence, fear or coercion.

2. The defendant understands and knowingly, freely and voluntarily waives his constitutional rights.

3. The defendant freely and voluntarily executed the within Application and understands its contents.

4. The defendant has admitted the essential elements of the crime charged.

IT IS THEREFORE ORDERED that the defendant's plea of "GUILTY" be accepted and entered as prayed for in the Application and as recommended in the certificate of his lawyer.

Done in open court this ____ day of __________, 20___.

Dated: ____________________

____
MAXINE M. CHESNEY
United States District Judge

Hon. Samuel Conti

District Judge

Chambers Information

U.S. District Court, Northern District of California
Courtroom 1, 17th Floor
450 Golden Gate Avenue
San Francisco, CA 94102

Scheduling Information

Courtroom Deputy: (415) 522-2077

Law and Motion	Fridays at 10:00 a.m. **NOTE: Dates must be reserved with the Courtroom Deputy Clerk.**

Judge's Biography

Born 1922 in Los Angeles, CA

Federal Judicial Service:

-Judge, U. S. District Court, Northern District of California
-Nominated by Richard M. Nixon on October 7, 1970, to a new seat created by 84 Stat. 294; Confirmed by the Senate on October 13, 1970, and received commission on October 16, 1970. Assumed senior status on November 1, 1987.

Education:

-University of Santa Clara, B.S., 1945
-Stanford Law School, LL.B., 1948

Professional Career:

-United States Army
-Private Practice, San Francisco, California, 1948-1967
-Chairman, Civil Service Board of Appeals, Pittsburg, California, 1956-1958
-City Attorney, Concord, California, 1960-1969
-Superior Court Judge, Contra Costa County, California, 1968-1970

I. Judge Conti's Procedures and Practices

A. *Standing Order*

JUDGE CONTI'S STANDING ORDER

Judge Conti does not permit appearances by telephone. All appearances shall be in person.

Electronic Case Filing

In all cases that have been assigned to the Electronic Case Filing System, the parties are required to provide one paper copy of each document that is filed electronically for use in chambers. The paper copy of each document shall be delivered no later than noon on the day after the document is filed electronically. Delivery shall be made directly to Judge Conti's chambers.

Hon. Edward J. Davila

District Judge

Chambers Information

U.S. District Court, Northern District of California
Courtroom 4, 5th Floor
280 South First Street
San Jose, CA 95113

Scheduling Information

Courtroom Deputy: (408) 535-5356

Criminal Law and Motion	Mondays at 1:30 p.m.
Civil Law and Motion	Fridays at 9:00 a.m. (by reservation only)
Case Management Conferences	Fridays at 10:00 a.m.
Pretrial Conferences	Fridays at 11:00 a.m.
Trial Jury Selection	Mondays at 9:00 a.m.

Judge's Biography

Born 1952 in Palo Alto, CA

Federal Judicial Service:

-Judge, U. S. District Court, Northern District of California
-Nominated by Barack Obama on January 5, 2011, to a seat vacated by Marilyn Hall Patel. Confirmed by the Senate on February 14, 2011, and received commission on March 3, 2011.

Education:

-California State University, San Diego, B.A., 1976
-University of California, Hastings College of the Law, J.D., 1979

Professional Career:

-Deputy Public Defender, Santa Clara County Office of the Public Defender, California, 1981-1988
-Private Practice, San Jose, California, 1988-2001
-Judge, Superior Court of California, County of Santa Clara, 2001-2011

I. Judge Davila's Procedures and Practices

A. Standing Order Regarding Preliminary and Final Pretrial Conferences and Trial Preparation in Civil Cases

STANDING ORDER RE: PRELIMINARY AND FINAL PRETRIAL CONFERENCES AND TRIAL PREPARATION IN CIVIL CASES

I. PRELIMINARY PRETRIAL CONFERENCES

A. Civil actions will be scheduled for a Preliminary Pretrial Conference approximately 30 days before the close of fact discovery. The purpose of the Preliminary Pretrial Conference is to determine the parties' readiness for trial and schedule final pretrial and trial dates.

B. No later than 10 days before the Preliminary Pretrial Conference, the parties shall file a Joint Preliminary Pretrial Conference Statement, not to exceed 10 pages in length, containing the following information:

- Jurisdiction: A short statement explaining the basis for the court's subject matter jurisdiction over plaintiff's claims and defendant's counterclaims.
- Substance of the Action: A brief description of the parties, a recitation of the facts and a statement of the principal factual issues in dispute, as well as a description of the relief sought.
- Legal Issues: A brief statement, without extended legal argument, of the disputed points of law, including reference to specific statutes and decisions.
- Motions: All prior and pending motions, their current status, and any anticipated motions.
- Discovery: The status of discovery. If discovery has not been completed, the scope of any anticipated further discovery, and proposed modifications to the discovery plan, and a realistic estimate of when discovery will be complete.
- Settlement and ADR: A description of all ADR efforts to date and whether further ADR efforts should be pursued prior to trial.
- Bifurcation and Separate Trial of Issues: A statement addressing whether bifurcation or a separate trial of specific issues is appropriate or desired.
- Trial: A brief statement describing each party's readiness for trial, whether the case will be tried before a jury or to the court, and a realistic estimate of the length of the trial.
- Scheduling: Any proposed modifications to the Case Management Schedule, as well as proposed dates for the Final Pretrial Conference and Trial.
- Other Matters: Such other matters that may facilitate the just, speedy and inexpensive disposition of the matter.

II. FINAL PRETRIAL CONFERENCES

A. The Final Pretrial Conference requirements described in this section apply to ***civil cases only***. Please refer to Criminal Local Rule 17.1-1 for pretrial requirements in criminal cases.

B. No later than 21 days before the Final Pretrial Conference, lead counsel who will try the case shall meet and confer with respect to:

- Settlement of the case;
- The preparation of the Joint Final Pretrial Conference Statement;
- Preparation and exchange of pretrial materials to be served and lodged;
- Clarifying and narrowing of the contested issued and disputes for trial.

C. No later than 14 days before the Final Pretrial Conference, unless otherwise ordered, the parties shall file and serve a Joint Final Pretrial Conference Statement containing the following information:

- Substance of the Action: A brief description of the parties and the claims and defenses that remain to be decided with reference to the operative pleadings that raises the claims and defenses.
- Relief Sought: A detailed description of all relief claimed, particularly itemizing all elements of damages claimed as well as witnesses, documents, or other evidentiary material to be presented concerning the amount of damages.
- Undisputed Facts: A concise statement of all relevant facts to which the parties will stipulate for incorporation into the trial record without the necessity of supporting testimony or exhibits, as well as which facts can be presented at trial upon an agreed statement.
- Disputed Factual Issues: A concise list of the issues of facts that are contested and remain to be determined at trial.
- Disputed Legal Issues: A brief statement, without extended legal argument, of the disputed points of law, including reference to specific statutes and decisions.
- Trial Stipulations: A statement of the proposed stipulations or agreements that will expedite the presentation of evidence.
- Witnesses: A list of witnesses likely to be called at trial, other then solely for impeachment or rebuttal, together with a brief statement following each name describing the substance of the testimony to be given. No party shall be permitted to call any witness in its case-in-chief, without leave of court for good cause shown, if that witness is not disclosed on the Joint Final Pretrial Conference Statement.
- Exhibits: A list of all documents and other items to be offered as exhibits at trial, other than solely for impeachment or rebuttal, along with a brief statement for each describing its substance or purpose and the identity of the sponsoring witness.
- Further Discovery or Motions: A statement describing any remaining discovery or any motion or other matters that must be resolved prior to trial, including motions in limine.
- Disputed Evidentiary Issues: A concise statement of each disputed evidentiary issue, even if a motion in limine will not be filed on that issue,

including reference to specific statutes and decisions.

- Trial Estimate: An updated statement of the total amount of days/hours needed for the trial.
- Other Matters: Such other matters that may facilitate the just, speedy and inexpensive disposition of the matter.

D. Trial Exhibits

No later than 14 days before the Final Pretrial Conference, the parties shall exchange copies of all exhibits, summaries, charts, and diagrams to be used at trial other than solely for impeachment or rebuttal.

Each exhibit shall be pre-marked for identification. Counsel shall meet and confer and reach an agreement on the method for marking exhibits as to each side (i.e., Plaintiff's exhibits will be numbered, Defendant's exhibits will be alphabetized).

No later than 7 days before the commencement of trial, unless otherwise ordered, the parties shall deliver three sets of all pre-marked exhibits in three-ring binders to Elizabeth C. Garcia, Courtroom Deputy Clerk.

No party shall be permitted to offer any exhibit, without leave of court for good cause shown, if such exhibit is not disclosed on the Joint Final Pretrial Conference Statement unless the exhibit is offered solely for impeachment or rebuttal.

E. Motions in Limine

No later than 14 days before the Final Pretrial Conference, unless otherwise ordered, the parties shall file and serve any motions in limine. Oppositions to motions in limine shall be filed and served no later than 10 days before the Final Pretrial Conference. Each motion in limine should be separate, address a single topic, and contain no more than 7 pages of briefing.

F. Deposition and Discovery Designations

No later than 14 days before the commencement of trial, unless otherwise ordered, the parties shall file and serve any excerpts of deposition testimony or other discovery to be offered at trial, other than solely for impeachment or rebuttal.

Any objections to the use of designated experts and any counter-designations or deposition testimony shall be filed and served no later than 10 days prior to the commencement of trial.

G. Jury Materials

No later than 10 days before the Final Pretrial Conference, unless otherwise ordered, the parties shall file and serve:

- Jury Voir Dire Questions;
- Proposed Jury Instructions;
- Proposed Jury Verdict Forms.

The court will ordinarily give the standard preliminary and closing jury instructions contained in the Model Jury Instructions of the Ninth Circuit prior to opening statements and closing arguments.

For substantive case-specific instructions, the parties shall meet and confer regarding an agreed set of jury instructions using the Model Jury Instructions of the Ninth Circuit where appropriate. In the event the parties are unable to agree to the language of a particular instruction, the objecting party shall submit a written objection or an alternative proposed instruction placed in sequence following the disputed instruction.

Sets of jury instructions shall be submitted both on paper and in electronic word-processing format to Elizabeth C. Garcia, Courtroom Deputy Clerk.

H. Proposed Findings of Fact and Conclusions of Law

In any case to be tried without a jury, each party shall file and serve proposed findings of fact and conclusions of law no later than 7 days before the Final Pretrial Conference.

The findings of fact shall set forth in simple separately-numbered declarative sentences all factual contentions relied upon by the party in support of its claims or defenses and shall be free from pejorative language and argument. Conclusions of law shall be supported by appropriate citation to legal authority.

Proposed findings of fact and conclusions of law shall be submitted both on paper and in electronic word-processing format to Elizabeth C. Garcia, Courtroom Deputy Clerk.

I. Trial Briefs

Trial briefs are optional. Any party wishing to submit a trial brief must do so no later than 7 days prior to the commencement of trial.

Trial briefs shall be submitted to Elizabeth C. Garcia, Courtroom Deputy Clerk.

J. Time Limits

The court will ordinarily set fixed time limits at the Final Pretrial Conference. Examination time for witnesses, including direct, cross, re-direct, and re-cross, must be completed within the designated time. Opening and closing time limits are excluded from witness examination time.

K. Scheduling

The regular trial schedule is:

- Tuesday and Wednesday from 9:00 a.m. to 4:30 p.m., with a break from 12:00 p.m to 1:30 p.m.
- Thursday from 9:00 a.m. to 12:00 p.m.

Jury selection is held Monday from 9:00 a.m. to 12:00 p.m. Additional times may be scheduled on a case-by-case basis.

L. Settlement and Continuances

If counsel expect that a settlement of the action will be finalized or a continuance will be requested prior to the Final Pretrial Conference or trial date, they shall immediately notify the court in writing. If settlement occurs on a weekend or court holiday, counsel shall leave a voicemail message for Elizabeth C. Garcia, Courtroom Deputy Clerk.

The court will determine whether appearance by counsel is necessary upon receiving a notice of settlement or continuance. Pending such determination, however, counsel must continue preparations and be prepared to proceed with the Final Pretrial Conference and trial.

M. Opportunities for Junior Lawyers

The court strongly encourages parties to permit less experienced lawyers to examine witnesses at trial and to have an important role at trial. Counsel should be prepared to discuss such opportunities at the Final Pretrial Conference.

IT IS SO ORDERED.

DATED: September 15, 2011

EDWARD J. DAVILA
United States District Judge

Hon. Jeremy D. Fogel

District Judge

Chambers Information

U.S. District Court, Northern District of California
Courtroom 3, 5th Floor
280 South First Street
San Jose, CA 95113

Scheduling Information

Administrative Law Clerk: (408) 535-5426

Civil Law and Motion	Specially Set
Case Management Conferences	Specially Set
Criminal Law and Motion	Specially Set
Pretrial Conferences	Specially Set
Jury Selection	Specially Set
All Other Hearings	Specially Set

Judge's Biography

Born 1949 in San Francisco, CA

Federal Judicial Service:

-Judge, U. S. District Court, Northern District of California
-Nominated by William J. Clinton on September 8, 1997, to a seat vacated by Robert P. Aguilar; Confirmed by the Senate on March 16, 1998, and received commission on March 17, 1998.

Education:

-Stanford University, B.A., 1971
-Harvard Law School, J.D., 1974

Professional Career:

-Private Practice, San Jose, CA, 1974-1978
-Lecturer, Human Development, California State University, 1977-1978
-Law Foundation, Inc., Santa Clara County, CA Bar Association, 1978-1981
-Directing Attorney, Mental Health Advocacy Project, 1978-81; Executive Director, 1980-81
-Judge, Santa Clara County, CA Municipal Court, 1981-1986
-Judge, Santa Clara, CA Superior Court, 1986-1998

I. Judge Fogel's Procedures and Practices

A. *Standing Order Regarding Pretrial Preparation*

STANDING ORDER RE PRETRIAL PREPARATION

I. REQUIREMENTS PRIOR TO THE PRETRIAL CONFERENCE

Prior to the pretrial conference, counsel (or parties appearing *pro se*) shall comply in all respects with the following requirements:

(A) Required Meet and Confer Prior to Pretrial Conference.

At least twenty (20) days before the Pretrial Conference, lead counsel who will try the case shall meet and confer with respect to:

(1) preparation and content of the joint pretrial conference statement;

(2) preparation, exchange and lodging of pretrial materials discussed in this order; and

(3) settlement of the action.

(B) Pretrial Conference Statement.

Unless otherwise ordered, not less than fourteen (14) days prior to the Pretrial Conference, the parties shall file a joint pretrial conference statement containing the following information:

(1) The Action.

(a) Substance of the Action. A brief description of the substance of the issues that remain to be decided.

(b) Relief Sought. For civil actions, a detailed statement of all the relief sought, particularly itemizing all elements of damages claimed as well as witnesses, documents or other evidentiary material to be presented concerning the amount of such damages.

(2) The Factual Basis of the Action.

(a) Undisputed Facts. A plain and concise statement of all relevant facts not reasonably disputable, as well as facts to which parties will stipulate for incorporation into the trial record without the necessity of supporting testimony or exhibits.

(b) Disputed Factual Issues. A plain and concise statement of all disputed factual issues that remain to be decided.

(c) Agreed Statement. A statement assessing whether all or part of the action may be presented upon an agreed statement of facts.

(d) Stipulations. A statement of stipulations requested or proposed for pretrial or trial purposes.

(3) Disputed Legal Issues.

(a) Points of Law. Without extended legal argument, a concise statement of each disputed point of law concerning liability or relief, citing supporting statutes and decisions. Unless otherwise ordered, parties should cite to briefs served and lodged with the Court setting forth briefly the nature of each party's contentions concerning each disputed point of law, including procedural and evidentiary issues.

(b) Proposed Conclusions of Law. If the case is to be tried without a jury, unless otherwise ordered, parties should provide proposed conclusions of law.

(C) Trial Preparation.

(1) Witnesses to be Called. A list of all witnesses likely to be called at trial, other than solely for impeachment or rebuttal, together with a brief statement following each name describing the substance of the testimony to be given.

(2) Exhibits, Schedules and Summaries. A list of all documents and other items to be offered as exhibits at trial, other than solely for impeachment or rebuttal, with a brief statement following each, describing its substance or purpose and the identity of the sponsoring witness. Unless otherwise ordered, parties should indicate any objections to the receipt in evidence of exhibits and materials lodged with the Court and that counsel have conferred with respect to such objections. Three sets of premarked, joint exhibits, numbered consecutively starting with number one (1), shall be delivered to the Courtroom Deputy Clerk on or before the date of the Pretrial Conference. (In cases involving a large number of exhibits, exhibits should be placed in binders).

(3) Unless otherwise ordered, if the trial is to be a jury trial, proposed jury instructions, and proposed content of a jury questionnaire and proposed voir dire questions should be submitted to the Court not later than ten (10) days prior to trial. If the parties cannot agree as to these materials, counsel shall state that they have met and conferred for the purpose of resolving their differences.

(4) Estimate of Trial Time. An estimate of the number of court hours in fractions thereof for the direct examination and cross-examination of each witness identified in the witness list submitted.

(5) Use of Discovery Responses. A statement as to any intended use, other than solely for impeachment or rebuttal, of excerpts from depositions, interrogatory answers, or responses to requests for admission. Counsel shall indicate any objections to use of such materials and that they have conferred with respect to such objections.

(6) Further Discovery and Motions In Limine. A statement of all remaining discovery or any motions *in limine* shall be filed not later than seven (7) days prior to the Pretrial Conference.

(D) Trial Alternatives and Options.

(1) Settlement. Without revealing the substance of the parties' settlement positions, a statement summarizing the status of settlement negotiations and indicating whether further negotiations are likely to be productive.

(2) Consent to Trial Before a Magistrate Judge. A statement as to whether reference of all or part of the action to a master or magistrate judge is feasible, including whether the parties consent to a court or jury trial before a magistrate judge, with appeal directly to the Ninth Circuit.

(3) Amendments and Dismissals. A statement of requested or proposed amendments to pleadings or dismissals of parties, claims or defenses.

II. AGENDA FOR THE PRETRIAL CONFERENCE

At the pretrial conference, the Court will:

(1) Set a schedule for the receipt of opposition to and determination of any contested motions *in limine* or other pretrial motions;

(2) Allocate a fixed number of hours to each side for the direct examination and cross-examination of witnesses;

(3) Set specific dates and times when the trial will be in session;[1]

(4) For jury trials, determine the number of prospective jurors to be summoned, the number of jurors to be seated and whether a jury questionnaire will be used to assist in jury selection;

(5) Consider any other trial management matter which is likely to promote fair and efficient resolution of the case.

DATED: 1/19/2010

JEREMY FOGEL
United States District Judge

1 Jury selection normally commences at 1:30 p.m. on the Friday on which the trial is set. The Court normally conducts trials between 9:00 a.m. and 4:30 p.m. on Monday, Tuesday and Thursday, and between 10:00 a.m. and 4:30 p.m. on Wednesday.

Hon. Phyllis J. Hamilton

District Judge

Chambers Information

U.S. District Court, Northern District of California
Courtroom 3, 3rd Floor
1301 Clay Street
Oakland, CA 94612

Scheduling Information

Courtroom Deputy: (510) 637-1296

Civil Law and Motion	Wednesdays at 9:00 a.m.
Criminal Law and Motion	Wednesdays at 1:30 p.m.

Judge's Biography

Born 1952 in Jacksonville, IL

Federal Judicial Service:

-Judge, U. S. District Court, Northern District of California
-Nominated by William J. Clinton on February 9, 2000, to a new seat created by 104 Stat. 5089, 5105. Confirmed by the Senate on May 24, 2000, and received commission on May 25, 2000.
-U.S. Magistrate Judge, U.S. District Court for the Northern District of California, 1991-2000

Education:

-Stanford University, B.A., 1974
-Santa Clara University School of Law, J.D., 1976

Professional Career:

-Deputy Public Defender, Office of the Public Defender, CA, 1976-1980
-Manager, EEO Programs, Farinon Electric Corporation, 1980
-Administrative Judge, U.S. Merit Systems Protection Board, San Francisco Regional Office, CA, 1980-1985
-Court Commissioner, Municipal Court, Oakland-Piedmont-Emeryville Judicial District, 1985-1991

I. Judge Hamilton's Procedures and Practices

A. Pretrial Instructions

PRETRIAL INSTRUCTIONS
JUDGE HAMILTON

A. PRETRIAL MOTIONS

1. All dispositive motions are heard **no later than 120 days before trial**, unless leave of court is obtained for another deadline.

2. Only **one** summary judgment motion may be filed by each side, absent leave of court. Leave of court may be sought if multiple parties comprise one or both sides. Leave of court may be obtained by filing a motion for administrative relief pursuant to Civ. L. R. 7-11, or by requesting a case management conference or informal telephone conference.

3. **Separate** statements of undisputed facts in support of or in opposition to motions for summary judgment shall NOT be filed. See Civil L. R. 56-2. The parties may file a truly joint statement of undisputed facts only if all parties agree that the facts are undisputed.

4. **Objections** to evidence may no longer be filed separately but must be contained within the opposition or reply brief or memorandum. Civil L. R. 7-3.

5. Each party filing or opposing a motion shall also serve and file a **proposed order** which sets forth the relief or action sought and a short statement of the rationale of decision, including citation of authority that the party requests the court to adopt.

6. **Chambers copies** of each electronically-filed document must include on each page the running header created by the ECF system and must be delivered to the Clerk's Office by noon the day following its filing. All documents must be stapled or bound by a two-pronged fastener, and all exhibits to declarations or requests for judicial notice must be tabbed.

7. **Footnotes** in briefs appearing in smaller than the 12-point font required for the text, will be stricken, see Civil L. R. 3-4(c)(2), as will footnotes that are so numerous as to be clearly designed to defeat the page limits found at Civil L. R. 7-2 - 7-4.

8. Motions pursuant to **Daubert v. Merrill Dow Pharmaceuticals, Inc.**, 509 U.S. 579 (1993), challenging the reliability of expert testimony, may be noticed for hearing on the date dispositive motions will be heard or on any available hearing date up to and including the date of the final pretrial conference. Irrespective of the hearing date, the briefs shall be filed in accordance with Civil L. R. 7-2 - 7-5, on a 35-day briefing schedule.

9. **Motions *in limine*** are limited to motions to exclude specific items of evidence on a ground and upon such authority as would be sufficient to sustain an objection to such evidence at trial. The court will not generally consider a motion presenting a purely legal issue in the guise of a motion *in limine.*

10. **Discovery motions** will be referred to a Magistrate Judge for resolution. The words "Discovery Matter" shall appear in the caption of all documents relating to discovery to insure proper routing.

11. **Confidential and/or sealed documents** shall be handled in accordance

with this court's standing order and Civil L.R. 79-5, both of which the parties shall consult before moving for a protective order or requesting a sealing order. Requests to seal documents used in conjunction with dispositive motions are rarely granted and then only upon a showing of the most compelling of reasons.

B. FINAL PRETRIAL CONFERENCE

1. Each party shall attend personally or by counsel who will try the case.

2. Not less 35 days prior to the pretrial conference, all counsel and/or parties shall meet and confer regarding preparation of the joint pretrial statement.

3. Not less than 28 days prior to the pretrial conference, counsel and/or parties shall:

a. Serve and file a joint pretrial statement. (Separately filed statements will not be accepted by the court and monetary sanctions will be imposed upon the party failing to cooperate in the preparation of a joint statement). The pretrial statement shall include the following:

i) A brief description of the substance of the claims and defenses which remain to be decided.

ii) A detailed statement of all relief sought, itemizing all elements of damages claimed.

iii) A statement of all relevant undisputed facts to which the parties will stipulate for incorporation into the trial record without the necessity of supporting testimony or exhibits.

iv) A statement of all relevant disputed facts which remain to be decided.

v) A statement of stipulations requested or proposed.

vi) A brief statement of disputed points of law concerning liability and relief. Legal argument on these points shall be reserved for the trial briefs.

vii) A statement of whether bifurcation or a separate trial of specific issues is feasible and desired.

viii) A statement summarizing the status of settlement negotiations and indicating whether further negotiations are likely to be productive.

b. Serve and file trial briefs (not to exceed 25 pages), which shall specify each cause of action and defense remaining to be tried along with a statement of the applicable legal standard (no opposition shall be filed);

c. Serve and file no more than ten motions *in limine*, which shall be filed in one document not to exceed 25 pages;

d. Serve and file a list of deposition excerpts for witnesses who will not testify in person, (specifying the witness, page and line references) and other discovery responses that will be offered at trial;

e. Serve and file a list of all witnesses to be called at trial, in person or by deposition, other than solely for impeachment or rebuttal, with a brief statement describing the substance of the testimony to be given;

f. Serve and file a numerical list of exhibits that will be offered as evidence in a party's case in chief in support of a claim or defense, with a brief statement describing the substance and purpose of each exhibit and the name of the sponsoring witness;

g. Exchange exhibits which shall be premarked with an exhibit sticker tabbed and in binders. Plaintiff shall use numbers (1, 2, 3, etc.) and defendant shall use numbers preceded by a letter (A-1, A-2, A-3, etc.). Additional parties shall also use a letter preceding numbers (B-1, B-2, B-3, or C-1, C-2, C-3, etc.).

h. Submit two sets for jury trials and three sets for court trials of all premarked exhibits to the Clerk's Office (exhibits are not filed);

i. Serve and file any request regarding the treatment of confidential or sealed documents.

j. Serve and file proposed joint voir dire questions and joint jury instructions for cases to be tried by jury;

k. Serve and file proposed findings of fact and conclusions of law for cases or claims to be tried by the court.

l. Serve and file a proposed verdict form which contains no reference to submitting party.

4. No party shall be permitted to call any witness or offer any exhibit in its case in chief that is not disclosed in these pretrial filings without leave of court and for good cause.

5. **Not less than 14 days** prior to the pretrial conference, counsel and/or parties shall serve and file any opposition to a motion *in limine* and any counter deposition designations. No replies shall be filed. All motions shall be heard at the pretrial conference unless otherwise ordered. The parties shall not file separate objections, apart from those contained in the motions *in limine*, to the opposing party's witness list, exhibit list or discovery designations.

C. JURY TRIAL

Jury Selection shall proceed as follows: The Jury Commissioner will summon 20 to 25 prospective jurors. The Courtroom Deputy will select their names at random and seat them in the courtroom in the order in which their names are called. Voir dire will be conducted of sufficient venire members so that six to eight will remain after all peremptory challenges and an anticipated number of hardship dismissals and cause challenges have been made.

The court will then take cause challenges and discuss hardship claims at side bar. The court will inform counsel which hardship claims and cause challenges will be granted, but will not announce those dismissals until the selection process is completed. Peremptory challenges will be made in writing. The court will strike at one time those with meritorious hardship claims, those excused for cause, and those challenged peremptorily, and then seat the first six to eight people remaining in numerical order.

The attached voir dire questionnaire shall be given to the venire members and copies of the responses will be made available to counsel at the beginning of voir dire. Counsel shall submit a joint set of additional voir dire questions to be posed by the court. Any voir dire questions on which counsel cannot agree may be submitted separately. Counsel will be permitted brief follow-up voir dire after the court's questioning.

The following jury instructions from the Ninth Circuit Manual of Model Jury Instructions Civil (2007 Edition) shall be given absent objection: 1.0 - 1.4, 1.6 - 1.14, 1.18 - 1.19, 3.1 – 3.4. Counsel shall submit a **joint set** of these instructions along with a joint set of case specific instructions using the Ninth Circuit Manual where appropriate. Any instructions on which counsel cannot agree may be submitted separately. Each instruction shall be typed in full on a separate page with citations to the authority upon which it is based **and** a reference to the party submitting it. A second blind copy of each instruction shall also be submitted omitting the citation to authority and the reference to the submitting party, but retaining the title of the instruction.

D. TRIAL SCHEDULE

The court's trial schedule is 8:30 a.m. to 1:30 p.m. with two fifteen-minute breaks, on Monday, Tuesday, Thursday and Friday.

B. Standing Order for Cases Involving Sealed or Confidential Documents

STANDING ORDER FOR CASES INVOLVING SEALED OR CONFIDENTIAL DOCUMENTS

Proposed Protective Orders

1. The court will not approve a broad protective order that essentially gives each party carte blanche to decide which portions of the record will be sealed and, therefore, not made part of the public record. See Civ. L. R. 79-5; Citizens First Nat'l Bank v. Cincinnati Ins. Co., 178 F.3d 943 (7th Cir. 1999). Fed. R. Civ. Pro. 26(c) as well as the local rules require the court to determine whether good cause exists to seal any portion of the record. Therefore, all proposed protective orders submitted for court approval which contain provisions for filing documents under seal, must also provide a procedure for obtaining the sealing order that complies with Civ. L. R. 79-5.

Requests to File Documents Under Seal

2. Parties are reminded that court proceedings are presumptively public, and no document shall be filed under seal without request for a court order that is narrowly tailored to cover only the document, the particular portion of the document, or category of documents for which good cause exists for filing under seal. To that end, if a party wishes to file a document under seal, that party shall first file a written request for a sealing order setting forth the good cause and accompanied by a proposed order that is narrowly tailored as specified above.

3. However, if the sole ground for the sealing order is that the opposing party (or non-party) has designated the document as confidential, the opposing party (or nonparty) shall file a declaration establishing good cause for the sealing along with a proposed order, or shall withdraw the designation. The declaration shall be filed within seven days of service on the opposing party (or non-party) of the request for a sealing order. If the declaration is not filed as required, the court may order that the document be filed in the public record.

Use of Sealed Documents in Motion Papers

4. The court cautions parties that documents designated as confidential that are attached as exhibits to case-dispositive motions, or redacted portions of casedispositive briefs that contain confidential information, must meet the high "compelling reasons" threshold. See Kamakana v. City of Honolulu, 447 F.3d 1172 (9th Cir. 2006). A good cause showing, without more, will not satisfy a compelling reasons test, but will only suffice to maintain the confidentiality of documents attached to non-dispositive motions. Documents designated as confidential in conjunction with case-dispositive motions and/or briefs that do not satisfy the compelling reasons test may accordingly be re-designated as public information upon proper request. See Foltz v. State Farm Mut. Automobile Ins. Co., 331 F.3d 1122 (9th Cir. 2003).

Use of Sealed or Confidential Documents at Trial

5. Notwithstanding any provision of a protective order to the contrary, any document, whether previously designated confidential or previously sealed, will be unsealed

and/or will lose its confidential status if offered as an exhibit at trial, absent a showing of the "most compelling" reasons. See Manual for Complex Litigation § 21.432; Foltz, 331 F.3d at 1135-36. Any party believing that a document, portions thereof, or witness testimony should remain confidential or sealed during trial must request in advance of trial that the court take extraordinary measures, such as closing the courtroom to the public or sealing the trial transcript, to protect the confidentiality of that information. The request must be made in writing and filed no later than the date on which pretrial papers are due.

If previously sealed documents are ordered unsealed for use at trial, counsel for the party offering the document as evidence shall within two business days of the conclusion of the trial identify which entries on the docket represent the exhibits actually received. Counsel are required to cooperate with the deputy clerk in order to complete the unsealing process in cases involving voluminous sealed documents.

C. Standing Order – Criminal Cases

STANDING ORDER
CRIMINAL CASES

1. CALENDAR

Criminal matters are heard on Wednesdays -- in custody matters at 1:30 p.m. and out of custody matters at 2:30 p.m.

If either party wishes to have a matter placed on the Court's calendar and if the defendant is in custody, counsel must contact the courtroom deputy **by 1:30 p.m., the day before the defendant is to be transported to court by the U.S. Marshal**.

2. MOTIONS

Except for hearing and briefing dates set by the court, the parties may stipulate to any briefing schedule they wish as long as all briefing is complete at least **7** days in advance of the hearing. In the absence of a stipulation, motions (except those pertaining to sentencing) shall be filed at least **21** days in advance of the hearing date. Opposition briefs shall be filed at least **14** days in advance of the hearing date. Reply briefs shall be filed at least 7 days in advance of the hearing date.

Motions pertaining to sentencing and sentencing memoranda shall be filed at least **7** days before the date on which Judgment and Sentencing is scheduled. Responses or objections shall be filed at least **5** days before the date on which Judgment and Sentencing is scheduled.

A courtesy copy of all briefs shall be delivered to the Clerk's Office, in an envelope clearly marked with Judge Hamilton's name.

3. CHANGE OF PLEA

Judge Hamilton does not use an Application for Entry of Plea. However, counsel for the government shall deliver a copy of the Plea Agreement to chambers **by 5:00 p.m., the day before the plea is to be entered**. Should the plea not involve a Plea Agreement, counsel for the defendant shall notify the courtroom deputy of the entry of an open plea **by 5:00 p.m., the day before the plea is to be entered**.

4. CONFORMITY WITH LOCAL RULES RE: EVIDENTIARY SUBMISSIONS

All motions and oppositions to motions shall comply with Crim. L.R. 47-2(b), which requires that motions "presenting issues of fact . . . be supported by affidavits or declarations which comply with the requirements of Civil L.R. 7-5." Civil L.R. 7-5, in turn, requires that "[f]actual contentions made in support of or in opposition to any motion must be supported by an affidavit or declaration and by appropriate references to the record." Moreover, other evidence in support of or in opposition to any motion "must be appropriately authenticated by an affidavit or declaration." That rule further requires that affidavits and declarations contain factual contentions only, avoiding conclusions and legal argument, and "conform as much as possible to the requirements of FRCivP 56(e)."

5. CHAMBERS COPIES OF E-FILED DOCUMENTS

In all "E-Filing" cases, in addition to filing papers electronically, the parties are required to lodge a courtesy paper copy of each document no later than noon on the day following the day that the papers are filed electronically. These copies shall be marked "Chambers" or "Courtesy" copy and **shall be submitted to the Clerk's Office**, in an envelope clearly marked with Judge Hamilton's name.

D. Standing Order for Patent Cases

STANDING ORDER FOR PATENT CASES

The following instructions shall apply to all patent cases assigned to Judge Phyllis Hamilton.

Joint Claim Construction Statement

1. The joint claim construction statement required by Pat. L. R. 4-3 must be truly joint. Disputed terms, phrases, and clauses must be clearly designated as disputed. All other terms will be presumed undisputed. For any term in dispute, the parties must agree on what the term actually is. With regard to disputed terms, phrases, or clauses, the joint statement must list each disputed term, phrase, or clause (listed by claim); each party's proposed construction; and support for each party's proposed construction side by side. A model joint claim construction statement is attached to this order.

2. Parties must attach to the joint claim construction statement copies of all patents in dispute. Parties must also make a complete prosecution history for each patent available to the court upon request.

Claim Construction

3. As an initial matter, the court will construe no more than ten terms. If more than ten terms are in dispute, the parties must meet and confer before the preparation of the joint claim construction statement on narrowing the selection of terms to be construed by the court and must jointly propose the ten terms requiring construction.

4. If a party genuinely believes that it will require that more than approximately ten terms be construed, that party may move pursuant to Civ. L. R. 7-11 for leave to designate additional terms for construction. The requesting party must demonstrate good cause and explain why other methods of limiting the claims at issue (such as selecting representative claims or grouping claims by issues presented) would be ineffective. The request must be filed no later than two weeks before the deadline for filing the joint claim construction statement. If good cause is shown, the court will either agree to construe all terms or, if necessary, schedule a second claim construction proceeding on the terms that exceed ten. If more than approximately ten terms are submitted for construction without leave of court, the court will construe the first ten terms listed in the joint claim construction statement and sanctions may be imposed.

5. Claim construction briefs must address each disputed term, but only those that are truly disputed, following the order of the joint statement. The court anticipates that a meaningful meet and confer preceding the preparation of the joint claim construction statement will obviate the need for a party to propose in its briefs a claim construction that differs from that proposed in the statement. While the court encourages the parties to negotiate mutually agreeable constructions, the court discourages the parties from proposing new constructions for the first time in reply briefs or other filings which do not afford the opposing party an opportunity to respond. However, if it becomes necessary for a party to propose a different construction in its brief than that found in the joint claim construction statement, that party must clearly set forth the new construction and explain the basis for the

change. Additionally, that party shall revise the joint claim construction statement, so that the court will have one document reflecting all current proposed constructions.

<u>Tutorial and Claim Construction Hearing</u>

6. The court will schedule a tutorial to occur two to four weeks prior to the claim construction hearing. Each side will be permitted 30-45 minutes to present a summary of the background of the technology involved, an explanation of the nature of the problem the inventor sought to solve, and reference to the prior art in existence at the time of conception. The patent holder will make the first presentation. Visual aids are encouraged. The court prefers that someone other than counsel make the presentation. No argument or examination will be permitted. The proceeding is not recorded and statements made during the tutorial may not be cited as judicial admissions against a party.

7. Prehearing conferences are not generally held. However, either party may request a telephone conference within two weeks prior to the hearing, or the parties may address any prehearing issues at the tutorial.

8. The patent holder will act as the moving party for the purposes of claim construction. Opening briefs in support of claim construction must be filed at least six weeks before the date of the claim construction hearing, and the briefing schedule set forth at Patent L. R. 4-5 will apply.

9. The court will not ordinarily hear extrinsic evidence at the claim construction hearing. Should it become apparent that testimony will be necessary, counsel may request a telephone conference with the court within two weeks of the hearing to seek the court's approval.

10. Demonstrative exhibits and visual aids are permissible at the hearing as long as they are based on information contained in the papers already filed. Counsel shall exchange copies of exhibits no later than forty eight hours prior to the hearing.

11. The claim construction hearing will generally be scheduled for no longer than 3 hours on Wednesday's law and motion calendar. However, the court will specially set the hearing on a different day and for a longer period of time if warranted. Counsel should request a telephone conference with the court as soon as it is apparent that a special setting is necessary.

<u>Subsequent Case Management Conference</u>

12. Upon issuance of the claim construction ruling, the court will also set a date for a further case management conference. In the case management statement to be filed 7 calendar days prior to the conference, the parties must address the following topics:

a) anticipated post-claim construction discovery;

b) the filing of dispositive motions

c) if willful infringement has been asserted, whether the allegedly infringing party wishes to rely on the advice of counsel defense. If so, the parties should be prepared to address proposals for resolving any attorney-client privilege issues that arise, and whether the parties believe bifurcation of the trial into liability and damages phases would be appropriate;

d) the progress of settlement discussions, if any;

e) any other pretrial matters.

Sample Claim Construction Chart

Claim Language (Disputed Terms in **Bold**) 'xxx Patent	Plaintiff's Proposed Construction and Evidence in Support	Defendant's Proposed Construction and Evidence in Support
1. A method for counting **ducks**, comprising the steps of: [or] **ducks** Found in claim numbers: 'xxx Patent: y, z 'yyy Patent: a, b	**duck** PROPOSED CONSTRUCTION: a bird that quacks. DICTIONARY/TREATISE DEFINITIONS: Webster's Dictionary ("duck: bird that quacks"); Field Guide ("bird call: quack"); INTRINSIC EVIDENCE: 'xxx Patent col. _:_ ("distinctive honking"); Prosecution History at __ ("This patent is distinguished from the prior art in that the quacking of the bird is featured"). EXTRINSIC EVIDENCE: McDonald Depo. at xx:xx ("I'd say the quacking makes it a duck"); '123 Patent at col _:__; Donald Decl. at ¶ __ .	**duck** PROPOSED CONSTRUCTION: a bird that swims DICTIONARY/TREATISE DEFINITIONS: Random House Dictionary ("an aquatic bird"); Field Guide (same) INTRINSIC EVIDENCE: 'xxx Patent col _:__ ("ducks may be found on or near bodies of water"); Prosecution History at __ ("water fowl are particularly amenable to being counted by this method"). EXTRINSIC EVIDENCE: G. Marx Depo at xx:xx ("like a duck to water"); '456 Patent at col _:__; Daffy Decl. at ¶ __.

(Or any other substantively similar format that permits the court to compare terms side by side)

NOT:

Claim Language (Disputed Terms in **Bold**) 'xxx Patent	Plaintiff's Proposed Construction and Evidence in Support	Defendant's Proposed Construction and Evidence in Support
1. A method for counting **ducks** . . .	**duck**	**counting duck**

E. Standing Order for Securities Class Action Settlements

STANDING ORDER FOR SECURITIES CLASS ACTION SETTLEMENTS

This order is intended to facilitate disposition of class action securities cases in the event that a settlement is reached. Voluntary settlement between the parties is the preferred method of resolution in all cases. However, once settlement is achieved, the adversarial process which usually acts to inform the court's rulings may cease to function. Because a settlement affects the rights of absent class members, the court must ensure that the settlement is fair and reasonable with respect to their interests. This court will approve notices, plans of allocation, settlements and fee requests only if the court is first presented with information sufficient to allow a meaningful evaluation of the questions put before it.

Certain issues arise with some frequency in these cases, and the court addresses them here. This discussion is in no way exhaustive regarding the duties of counsel in securing approval of a class action settlement. Counsels' goal should always be to facilitate a meaningful evaluation by the court.

A. Preliminary and Final Approval of Settlements.

Traditionally, the most thorough review of the terms of the proposed settlement, the plan of allocation, and any application for attorneys' fees and/or costs has occurred at the final approval stage. However, this court believes it is preferable to conduct a thorough evaluation of these issues at the preliminary approval stage, before notice is given to the class. Conducting such an inquiry at this stage will help ensure that the class notice is as complete as possible, thus enabling each member to engage in their own meaningful evaluation of the proposed settlement. See Manual For Complex Litigation, § 30.42 (3d ed. 1995). In addition, if such a review is not conducted until after notice has been mailed, there is a risk that the notice process will need to be repeated, thus further depleting the settlement fund, should the court disapprove any of the components of the settlement. Guidelines for briefing of these issues are discussed below.

1. Preliminary Approval of Settlement.

At the preliminary approval stage, the parties must provide sufficient information to permit a meaningful preliminary fairness evaluation of the settlement. Such information must include, at a minimum, the relevant claims and defenses, an honest assessment of the strengths and weaknesses of each side's position (bolstered by the results of discovery if any has occurred), each side's views regarding the risks of proceeding to trial, an indication of the total amount of damages sought by plaintiffs and, if different, plaintiffs' anticipated recovery at trial, and whether any part of the settlement fund is to be paid through insurance proceeds. Because both sides have an interest in obtaining approval of the settlement, and because information from both sides is critical to the court's evaluation, both sides shall participate in this process. The parties shall file a brief in support of the application for preliminary approval of the settlement that specifically addresses the factors mentioned above. The parties may file separate briefs or they may file a single joint brief. In either case counsel from each side who participated in the settlement process shall file a sworn declaration attesting to the facts in the brief(s) and further declaring that the settlement is fair, reasonable, and was achieved through arms-length negotiations. Plaintiffs' counsel shall in addition submit a declaration by the lead plaintiff(s) attesting to and describing that person's involvement in the settlement process and stating whether the lead plaintiff objects to or concurs with the settlement.

2. Final Approval of Settlement.

At the final approval stage, the court's primary concern is the response of the class to the proposed settlement. Accordingly, in the motion for final approval the court must be provided with a status report on the notice and opt-out process that reports any matters that may have arisen in the interim period. This report should include, at a minimum: the number of notices sent out in the original mailing; the number of requests for notice received by the administrator; the dates and number of notices sent in subsequent mailings; the date the summary notice was published; a copy of the published summary notice; the number of requests for exclusion received; the number of proof of claim forms received to date; a detailed description or copy of all objections received; and any final revisions or modifications to applications for fee and cost awards. The parties need not reiterate the same arguments made in briefs filed at the preliminary approval stage.

B. Approval of Plans of Allocation.

The court will review the plan of allocation at the preliminary approval stage. To enable that review, plaintiffs must specifically describe the plan and explain why the ultimate plan was selected. If an expert was used in formulating the plan of allocation, that expert shall submit a declaration describing his or her work in formulating the plan and explaining why the court should approve it.

C. Approval of Proposed Notice.

The court will review the proposed notice at the preliminary approval stage. The court will not approve any notice which conditions participation at the final approval hearing upon the filing of written objections. Any class member who wishes to be heard at the hearing, regardless of whether he/she has filed an objection, will be given that opportunity. Notices may, however, encourage that written objections be submitted first. See Manual For Complex Litigation, §30.41. Additionally, when drafting proof of claim and request for exclusion forms, counsel should be careful not to make either process more onerous than is absolutely necessary. If a member requesting exclusion is required to submit more information than a member seeking to file a claim, counsel must provide an explanation.

D. Application for Attorneys' Fees and/or Costs.

The court will initially review any application for fees and/or costs at the preliminary approval stage. When presented with an application for fees and/or costs, the court has "the responsibility of reviewing the fees . . . to ensure that they are fair to the class and otherwise meet the Reform Act's standards." In re Cavanaugh, 306 F.3d 726, 733, n.13 (9th Cir. 2002). In performing this review, the court "must assume the role of fiduciary for the class of plaintiffs" because "the relationship between plaintiffs and their attorneys turns adversarial at the fee setting stage." In re Washington Public Power Supply Sys. Lit., 19 F.3d 1291, 1302 (9th Cir.1994). To aid the court in fulfilling this role, counsel shall comply the with the following minimum guidelines.

Preliminarily, counsel should review the following opinions prior to preparing any application for fees or costs: In re Quantum Health Resources, 962 F. Supp. 1254 (C.D. Cal. 1997); and In re Brooktree Securities Litigation, 915 F. Supp. 193 (S.D.Cal. 1996). These cases accurately describe the difficulties often faced by the court in reviewing a fee and/or cost application.

Fee applications are "subject to close judicial scrutiny based on counsel's actual work done and results achieved." In re Cavanaugh, 306 F.3d at 733. Plaintiffs' submissions must permit such scrutiny. This court will not grant a fee request supported only by boilerplate that does not focus on the particular case under review.

String cites or lengthy exhibits listing other litigation in which particular fees were approved are not helpful. See In re Brooktree Securities Litigation, 915 F. Supp. at 197. Rather, counsel must take pains to describe why the requested fee is appropriate in the case currently before the court. Counsel must describe with particularity the risks posed by the instant litigation and explain how they justify the requested fee. See In re Quantum Health Resources, 962 F. Supp. at 1258-59 ("The Ninth Circuit's 25% benchmark assumes a genuine degree of risk. . . . it is appropriate for a court to depart significantly from the 25% benchmark . . . unless genuine risk exists in a particular securities class action case."); see also In re Cavanaugh, 306 F.3d at 733, n.13 ("the court has wide latitude to go below the agreed amount in actually awarding fees.").

Regarding cost applications, the court will not award costs for any item unless counsel provides the following: (1) documentation in support of each substantial item;[1] (2) a description of each item and an explanation as to why it was necessary; and (3) legal authority establishing that such an item is a compensable cost. See In re Fleet/Norstar Securities Litigation, 974 F. Supp. 155, 158 (D.R.I. 1997) ("Noncompensable expenses include those which are not adequately supported by detailed records showing the amount of each expense, the reason for the expenditure, and the relationship between the expense and some reasonable benefit to the class."). By way of illustration, if counsel requests expert fees as an item of reimbursable costs, counsel shall provide proof regarding the hours worked, rate charged, tasks performed, an explanation why such tasks were necessary, and citation to legal authority supporting the request.[2] Moreover, all documentation provided to the court must be properly authenticated and presented in a usable format (*i.e.*, indexed and tabbed). See Orr v. Bank of America, NT & SA, 285 F.3d 764, 775 (9th Cir. 2002) ("The efficient management of judicial business mandates that parties submit evidence responsibly.").

---

[1] In providing documentation, counsel must exercise good judgment and assist the court. The court is not interested in pouring through every receipt for copies of late night take-out. However, where the expenses are more substantial, such expenses normally are and should be substantiated with copies of invoices, billing statements, etc.

[2] Counsel are reminded that any cost award will diminish the recovery of the individual class members and are cautioned to keep the interests of the class in mind when paying for items such as airfare, hotels and meals. See generally In re Horizon/CMS Healthcare Corp. Securities Litigation, 3 F. Supp. 2d 1208, 1212 (D.N.M. 1998) (finding that "the style in which the attorneys travel and dine is a lifestyle choice not necessarily shared by the class members," and "limit[ing] the attorneys to travel, meal, and hotel expenses at the United States Government per diem rate."); see also In re Media Vision Technology Securities Litigation, 913 F. Supp. 1362 , 1370 (N.D.Cal. 1996).

E. Timing of certain events.

When preparing the schedule for class notice and final hearing, counsel shall be careful to allow sufficient time for class members to receive and respond to the notices before the deadline for requests for exclusion. Typically, the initial mailing to institutions and potential nominees results in a subsequent mailing to individuals and other entities, the names for which are provided by the initial recipients well after the date class notice is ordered. Because the subsequent notice cannot be sent until the identities of the recipients are received by the administrator, counsel should be mindful of scheduling the deadlines in such a manner as to permit the vast majority of class members an opportunity to opt-out before the deadline for doing so.

Additionally, the court requires at least two weeks between the filing of the final approval papers and the final hearing.

F. Hearings.

Counsel who actively litigated and have first hand knowledge of the settlement are required to appear at all hearings related to the matters discussed above.

Hon. Thelton E. Henderson

District Judge

Chambers Information

U.S. District Court, Northern District of California
Courtroom 12, 19th Floor
450 Golden Gate Avenue
San Francisco, CA 94102

Scheduling Information

Courtroom Deputy: (415) 522-2047

Civil Law and Motion	Mondays at 10:00 a.m.
Case Management Conferences	Mondays at 1:30 p.m.
Pretrial Conferences	Mondays at 3:00 p.m.

Judge's Biography

Born 1933 in Shreveport, LA

Federal Judicial Service:

-Judge, U. S. District Court, Northern District of California
-Nominated by Jimmy Carter on May 9, 1980, to a seat vacated by Cecil F. Poole; Confirmed by the Senate on June 26, 1980, and received commission on June 30, 1980. Served as chief judge, 1990-1997. Assumed senior status on Nov. 28, 1998.

Education:

-University of California, Berkeley, B.A., 1956
-University of California, Berkeley, Boalt Hall School of Law, J.D., 1962

Professional Career:

-U.S. Army Corporal, 1956-1958
-Attorney, Civil Rights Division, U.S. Department of Justice, 1962-1963
-Private Practice, Oakland, California, 1964-1966
-Directing Attorney, East Bayshore Neighborhood Legal Center, East Palo Alto, California, 1966-1969
-Assistant Dean, Stanford Law School, 1968-1977
-Private Practice, San Francisco, California, 1977-1980
-Associate Professor, Golden Gate University School of Law, 1978-1980

I. Judge Henderson's Procedures and Practices

A. *Standing Order*

STANDING ORDER FOR THE HONORABLE THELTON E. HENDERSON

1. Counsel shall consult and comply with all provisions of the Local Rules for the Northern District of California. The parties are reminded that most procedural questions are answered in the Local Rules. The Court will not accept any pleadings that are untimely or presented in an improper manner or form. The Local Rules are available on the Court's website and may also be obtained from the Clerk's Office. Any attorney who violates the Local Rules may be subject to sanctions pursuant to Civil Local Rule 1-4.

2. Counsel shall notice their motions for a Monday morning at 10:00 AM and need not reserve a specific motion hearing date. Case management conferences are held on Mondays at 1:30 PM, and pretrial conferences are held on Mondays at 3:00 PM.

3. Parties wanting to continue hearings, request special status conferences, or make other procedural changes shall do so either by a signed stipulation and proposed order or, if a stipulation is not possible, by a written *ex parte* application and order. Briefing schedules may not be changed by stipulation. Any change in the hearing date does not alter the original briefing schedule unless otherwise ordered by the Court.

4. Any request to reschedule a case management conference shall be made in writing, and by stipulation if possible, at least ten calendar days prior to the scheduled case management conference date.

5. For Electronic Case Filing ("ECF") cases, the parties shall comply with General Order 45, including the requirement regarding courtesy copies: "In all cases subject to ECF, in addition to filing papers electronically, the parties are required to lodge for chambers **no later than noon on the business day following the day that the papers are filed electronically**, one paper copy of each document that is filed electronically. These printed copies shall be marked 'Chambers Copy' and shall be clearly marked with [Judge Henderson's] name, case number, and 'Chambers Copy-Do Not File.' **The printed copies shall be delivered to the Clerk's Office.** Parties shall not file a paper copy of any document with the Clerk's Office that has already been filed electronically." General Order 45, Section VI.G (emphasis added).

6. All discovery matters are hereby referred to a magistrate judge. If a discovery dispute arises, the parties shall call this Court's courtroom deputy, at (415) 522-2047, for referral to a magistrate.

7. Plaintiff is directed to serve copies of this order at once upon all parties to this action, and upon those subsequently joined, in accordance with Federal Rules of Civil Procedure 4 and 5. Plaintiff shall file with the Court a certificate reflecting such service.

Failure to comply with this order may be deemed sufficient grounds for dismissal of this case, entry of default, or other appropriate sanctions.

IT IS SO ORDERED.

Dated: March 9, 2007

THELTON E. HENDERSON
United States District Judge

Hon. Susan Y. Illston

District Judge

Chambers Information
U.S. District Court, Northern District of California
Courtroom 10, 19th Floor
450 Golden Gate Avenue
San Francisco, CA 94102

Scheduling Information
Courtroom Deputy: (415) 522-2028

Civil Law and Motion	Fridays at 9:00 a.m.
Criminal Law and Motion	Fridays at 11:00 a.m.
Case Management Conferences (Initial)	Fridays at 2:30 p.m.
Case Management Conferences (Further)	Fridays at 3:00 p.m.

Judge's Biography
Born 1948 in Tokyo, Japan

Federal Judicial Service:
-Judge, U. S. District Court, Northern District of California
-Nominated by William J. Clinton on January 23, 1995, to a seat vacated by Barbara A. Caulfield; Confirmed by the Senate on May 25, 1995, and received commission on May 26, 1995

Education:
-Duke University, B.A., 1970
-Stanford Law School, J.D., 1973

Professional Career:
-Private Practice, Burlingame, California, 1973-1995

I. Judge Illston's Procedures and Practices

A. *Pretrial Instructions*

PRETRIAL INSTRUCTIONS
The Honorable Susan Illston

COUNSEL SHALL MEET AND CONFER IN GOOD FAITH IN ADVANCE OF COMPLYING WITH THE FOLLOWING PRETRIAL REQUIREMENTS.

1. **PRETRIAL CONFERENCE and STATEMENT** – The parties shall comply in all respects with F.R.Civ.P 16. The statement is due **fourteen days** prior to the Pretrial Conference. The Pretrial Statement must contain the following:

(a) **Pretrial Conference Statement:** The parties shall file a joint pretrial conference statement containing the following information:

(1) **The Action**

(A) **Substance of the Action.** A brief description of the substance of claims and defenses which remain to be decided.

(B) **Relief Prayed.** A detailed statement of all the relief claimed, particularly itemizing all elements of damages claimed as well as witnesses, documents or other evidentiary material to be presented concerning the amount of those damages.

(2) **The Factual Basis of the Action**

(A) **Undisputed Facts.** A plain and concise statement of all relevant facts not reasonably disputable, as well as which facts parties will stipulate for incorporation into the trial record without the necessity of supporting testimony or exhibits.

(B) **Disputed Factual Issues.** A plain and concise statement of all disputed factual issues which remain to be decided.

(C) **Agreed Statement.** A statement assessing whether all or part of the action may be presented upon an agreed statement of facts.

(D) **Stipulations.** A statement of stipulations requested or proposed for pretrial or trial purposes.

(3) **Disputed Legal Issues**

(A) **Points of Law.** Without extended legal argument, a concise statement of each disputed point of law concerning liability or relief, citing supporting statutes and decisions setting forth briefly the nature of each party's contentions concerning each disputed point of law, including procedural and evidentiary issues.

(B) **Proposed Conclusions of Law.** If the case is to be tried without a jury, unless otherwise ordered, parties should briefly indicate objections to proposed conclusions of law.

(4) Trial Preparation

(A) **Witnesses to be Called.** A list of all witnesses likely to be called at trial, other than solely for impeachment or rebuttal, together with a brief statement following each name describing the substance of the testimony to be given.

(B) **Exhibits, Schedules and Summaries.** A list of all documents and other items to be offered as exhibits at the trial, other than solely for impeachment or rebuttal, with a brief statement following each, describing its substance or purpose and the identity of the sponsoring witness. Unless otherwise ordered, parties will indicate their objections to the receipt in evidence of exhibits and materials lodged and that counsel have conferred respecting such objections.

(C) **Estimate of Trial Time.** An estimate of the number of court days needed for the presentation of each party's case, indicating possible reductions in time through proposed stipulations, agreed statements of facts, or expedited means of presenting testimony and exhibits.

(D) **Use of Discovery Responses.** Counsel shall cite possible presentation at trial of evidence, other than solely for impeachment or rebuttal, through use of excerpts from depositions, from interrogatory answers, or from responses to requests for admission. Counsel shall indicate any objections to use of these materials and that counsel has conferred respecting such objections.

(E) **Further Discovery or Motions.** A statement of all remaining discovery or motions, including motions in limine.

(5) Trial Alternatives and Options

(A) **Settlement Discussion.** A statement summarizing the status of settlement negotiations and indicating whether further negotiations are likely to be productive.

(B) **Consent to Trial Before a Magistrate Judge.** A statement whether reference of all or part of the action to a master or magistrate judge is feasible, including whether the parties consent to a court or jury trial before a magistrate judge, with appeal directly to the Ninth Circuit.

(C) **Amendments, Dismissals.** A statement of requested or proposed amendments to pleadings or dismissals of parties, claims or defenses.

(D) **Bifurcation, Separate Trial of Issues.** A statement of whether bifurcation or a separate trial of specific issues is feasible and desired.

2. WITNESSES

a. **Jury Trials.** The Pretrial Conference Statement shall include the witness list required in part by 1(a)(4)(A) above. In addition, in the case of expert witnesses, the summary shall clearly state the expert's theories and conclusions and the basis therefore and shall be accompanied by a curriculum vitae; if the expert has prepared a report in preparation for the testimony, a copy thereof shall be furnished to opposing counsel. Witnesses not included on the list may be excluded from testifying.

b. **Non-Jury Trials.** In non-jury cases, any party may serve and lodge with the Court a written narrative statement of the proposed direct testimony of each witness under that party's control in lieu of a summary. Each statement shall be marked as an exhibit and shall be in a form suitable to be received into evidence.

3. JURY INSTRUCTIONS

a. **Joint Set of Instructions.** The parties shall jointly prepare a set of jury instructions, and shall file an original and two copies of same **fourteen days** prior to the Pretrial Conference. The submission shall contain both agreed upon instructions (which shall be so noted), and contested instructions, all in the order in which they should be read to the jury. Where contested instructions are included, they should be annotated both with the proponent's authority for seeking the instruction and the opponent's reason for opposition. Counsel shall deliver to Chambers a copy of the joint submission, on a CD/DVD in WordPerfect format. The label shall include the case number and a description of the documents.

b. **Substance and Format of Instructions.** The instructions shall cover all substantive issues and other points not covered by the Ninth Circuit Manual of Model Jury Instructions. Each requested instruction shall be typed in full on a separate page and citations to the authorities upon which the instruction is based shall be included. Instructions shall be brief, clear, written in plain English and free of argument. Pattern or form instructions shall be revised to address the particular facts and issues of this case.

c. **Preliminary Statement and Instructions.** If the parties wish to have a preliminary statement read to the jury, and/or preliminary instructions given to the jury, they shall jointly prepare and submit to the Court, **fourteen days** prior to the pretrial conference, the text of the statement and instructions, clearly marked.

d. **Voir Dire and Verdict Forms.** Each party shall serve and file proposed questions for jury voir dire and a proposed Form of Verdict not later than **fourteen days** prior to the Pretrial Conference.

4. FINDINGS OF FACT and CONCLUSIONS OF LAW

In **non-jury cases**, each party shall serve and lodge with the Court fourteen days prior to the Pretrial Conference, proposed Findings of Fact and Conclusions of Law on all material issues. Proposed Findings shall be brief, written in plain English and free of pejorative language, conclusions and argument. Parties shall deliver to Chambers copies of proposed Findings of Fact and Conclusions of Law on a CD/DVD in WordPerfect format. The label shall include the name of the parties, the case number and a description of the documents.

5. EXHIBITS

a. **Provide Copies of Exhibits to Other Parties.** Each party shall provide every other party with one set of all proposed exhibits, charts, schedules, summaries, diagrams and other similar documentary materials to be used in its case in chief at trial, together with a complete list of all such proposed exhibits. Voluminous exhibits shall be reduced by elimination of irrelevant portions or through the use of summaries. Each item shall be pre-marked with a trial exhibit sticker (not deposition exhibit label), defendant's exhibit numbers shall be sequenced to begin after plaintiff's exhibit numbers. If there are numerous exhibits, they should be provided in three-ring binders with marked tab separators. All exhibits which have not been provided as required are subject to exclusion.

b. **Stipulations re Admissibility. Fourteen days** prior to the Pretrial Conference, the parties shall make a good faith effort to stipulate to exhibits' admissibility. If stipulation is not possible, the parties shall make every effort to stipulate to authenticity and foundation absent a legitimate (not tactical) objection.

c. **Objections to Exhibits.** In addition to the exhibit list, counsel shall confer with respect to any other objections to exhibits in advance of the Pretrial Conference. Each party shall file and serve a statement briefly identifying each item objected to, the grounds for the objection and the position of the offering party **fourteen days** prior to the date set for the Pretrial Conference.

d. **Provide Copies of Exhibits to Court.** Three sets of exhibits shall be provided to the Court on the **Friday prior to the trial date**. Each set shall be in binders, marked, tabbed and indexed and shall be **delivered/mailed directly to Chambers**. Parties are to comply with Local Rule 16-10(b)(7).

e. **Disposition of Exhibits after Trial.** Upon the conclusion of the trial, each party shall retain its exhibits through the appellate process. It is each party's responsibility to make arrangements with the Clerk of Court to file the record on appeal.

6. MOTIONS IN-LIMINE

Any party wishing to have motions in limine heard prior to the commencement of trial must file and serve same no later than **fourteen days** prior to the date set for the Pretrial Conference. Any party opposing such a motion in limine shall file and serve its opposition papers no later than **seven days** prior to the Pretrial Conference. Reply papers are not required. The motions will be heard at the Pretrial Conference or at such other time as the Court may direct. Nothing in this provision prevents a party from noticing its motions in limine regularly for hearing on or prior to the final date for hearing dispositive motions. **NO LEAVE TO FILE UNDERSEAL WILL BE GRANTED WITH RESPECT TO MOTIONS IN-LIMINE.**

7. OTHER PRETRIAL MATTERS

a. **Status/Discovery Conferences.** Any party desiring to confer with the Court may, upon notice to all other parties, arrange a conference through the Courtroom Deputy, Ms. Tracy Forakis (415-522-2028).

b. **Settlement Conferences.** Any party wishing to arrange a settlement conference before another judge or Magistrate Judge may do so by contacting the courtroom deputy.

c. **Daily Transcripts.** If transcripts will be requested during or immediately after trial, arrangements must be made with the court reporter at least **seven days** before trial commences.

8. MISCELLANEOUS

a. The Court takes a photograph of each witness prior to the witness' testimony.

b. Please **DO NOT** call Chambers. If you need to contact the courtroom deputy, please call the number above and leave a message if the deputy is not available.

B. *Standing Order*

JUDGE ILLSTON'S STANDING ORDER

1. Scheduling Days:
Civil Law and Motion Calendar is conducted on Fridays at 9:00 a.m.

Criminal Law and Motion Calendar is conducted on Fridays at 11:00 a.m.

Civil Case Management Conferences are generally conducted on Fridays at 2:30 p.m. with the order of call determined by the Court.

Pretrial Conferences are generally conducted on Tuesday afternoons at 3:30 p.m.

Counsel need not reserve motion hearing dates, but may call the clerk to obtain the next available law and motion calendar. Motions may be reset as the Court's calendar requires.

All parties are directed to comply with the Civil Local Rules except as identified in this Order.

2. Discovery Disputes:
The parties shall meet and confer in person, or, if counsel are located outside the Bay Area, by telephone, to attempt to resolve their dispute informally. A mere exchange of letters, e-mails, telephone calls, or facsimile transmissions does not satisfy the requirement to meet and confer.

If, after a good faith effort, the parties have not resolved their dispute, they shall prepare a concise joint statement of 5 pages or less, stating the nature and status of their dispute. Absent an order of this Court, parties shall not file affidavits or exhibits, other than copies of the written requests for discovery and the answers or objections thereto.

If a joint statement is not possible, each side may submit a brief individual statement of 2 pages or less. The joint statement or individual statements shall be filed or e-filed, if in an e-filing case, and courtesy copies submitted as provided by the Civil Local Rules.

The Court will advise the parties regarding the need, if any, for more formal briefing or a hearing, pursuant to Civil Local Rule 7-1(b).

3. Sealed Documents (Civil L.R. 79-5; G.O. 62):
This Court does not require the filing of Administrative Motions to seal (Civil L.R. 7-11). The Court will accept stipulations (Civ. L.R. 7-12) or an ex-parte application (Civ. L.R. 7-10) with proposed orders in lieu of the administrative motion. In the event an agreement and stipulation for leave to file under seal is not possible, an ex-parte application shall be filed instead. Oppositions to ex-parte applications and proposed order must be submitted to the Court immediately.

4. Courtesy Copies:
All courtesy copies must be three-hole punched at the left margin. All courtesy copies

must bear the ECF stamp (case number, document number, date and page number) on the top of each page.

5. Summary Judgment Motions:
Parties are limited to filing one motion for summary judgment. Any party wishing to exceed this limit must request leave of Court.

IT IS SO ORDERED

Dated: July 28, 2011

____
SUSAN ILLSTON
United States District Judge

II. Judge Illston's Case Management Orders

A. *Case Management Conference Order*

IN THE UNITED STATES DISTRICT COURT
FOR THE NORTHERN DISTRICT OF CALIFORNIA

Plaintiff,	No. C _________ SI
v.	**CASE MANAGEMENT CONFERENCE ORDER**
Defendant. __________________________________/	

IT IS HEREBY ORDERED that, pursuant to Rule 16(b), Federal Rules of Civil Procedure, and Civil L.R. 16-10, a Case Management Conference will be held in this case before the Honorable Susan Illston on _________ at 2:30 p.m. in Courtroom No. 10, 19th floor Federal Building.

Plaintiff(s) shall serve copies of this Order at once on all parties to this action, and on any parties subsequently joined, in accordance with the provisions of Fed.R.Civ.P. 4 and 5. Following service, plaintiff(s) shall file certificate of service with the Clerk of this Court.

Counsel are directed to confer in advance of the Case Management Conference. Not less than seven days before the conference, counsel shall file a joint case management statement in compliance with the Civil Local Rules and the Standing Order for All Judges of the Northern District of California. Failure to file a joint statement shall be accompanied by a signed declaration setting forth the grounds for such failure. Failure to show good cause for such failure may subject the parties to sanctions.

Each party shall be represented at the Case Management Conference by counsel prepared to address all of the matters referred to in this Order, and with authority to enter stipulations and make admissions pursuant to this Order. The parties are encouraged to attend.

Any request to reschedule the above dates should be made in writing, and by stipulation, if possible, not less than ten days before the conference date. Good cause must be shown.

At the case management conference the parties should be prepared to address and resolve the following: setting the date and the estimated length of the trial; setting the date for discovery cutoff; setting the date to designate experts and other witnesses; and setting the date for the pretrial conference.

Standing Orders: All parties shall comply with the Standing Order for All Judges of the Northern District of California concerning the contents of the joint case management conference statement and Judge Illston's Standing Order. Failure to comply with this Order or the Local Rules of this Court may result in sanctions. See Fed.R.Civ.P. 16(f), Civil L.R. 1-4.

NOTICE TO PRO SE LITIGANTS IN NON-PRISONER ACTIONS: If you are proceeding in this lawsuit without an attorney, and have not been granted leave to proceed *in forma pauperis*, then the following directives apply to you in the prosecution of your case.

The court hereby ORDERS you to comply with the service requirements of Rule 4 of the Federal Rules of Civil Procedure as set forth below. Failure to follow the procedures set forth in this order may result, under Rule 4 (m), in dismissal of your case.

It is your responsibility to obtain a valid summons from the clerk and to effect service of the summons and complaint on all defendants in accordance with Rule 4 of the Federal Rules of Civil Procedure. If you have named the United States government, a federal agency, a federal official or a federal employee as a defendant, you must comply with the special requirements of Rule 4 (i).

Service may be effected by any person who is not a party and who is at least 18 years of age, which means that you, as a party, may not effect service. If service of the summons and complaint is not made upon a defendant within 120 days after the filing of the complaint, your action will, under Rule 4 (m), be dismissed as to that defendant.

Within 125 days after the filing of the complaint, you must file proof of service indicating which defendants were served within the 120 days allowed under Rule 4 (m) and showing, in accordance with Rule 4 (i), how each of those defendants was served (for example, by attaching appropriate certificates of service). You must also show cause why a defendant not served within the 120 days allowed under Rule 4 (m) should not be dismissed without prejudice.

Failure to do these things within the designated time will result in the dismissal of your case under Rule 4 (m) and Rule 41 (b).

For additional information on procedures for litigating in Federal Court, pro se litigants are encouraged to call the Court's Federal Pro Bono Project at 415-782-9000 x 8657 or visit the Legal Help Center in the Federal Courthouse, 450 Golden Gate Avenue, 15th Floor, Room 2796, San Francisco, CA 94102.

IT IS SO ORDERED.

Dated: 8/1/11

____

SUSAN ILLSTON
United States District Judge

B. ***Order for Pretrial Preparation in Criminal Cases***

IN THE UNITED STATES DISTRICT COURT
FOR THE NORTHERN DISTRICT OF CALIFORNIA

UNITED STATES OF AMERICA, Plaintiff, v. Defendant. _______________________________/	No. CR _________ SI **ORDER FOR PRETRIAL PREPARATION**

Good cause appearing, IT IS HEREBY ORDERED that:

TRIAL DATE: On ___________ at ________ Courtroom 10, 19th floor, and will be before the JURY.

TRIAL LENGTH is estimated to be ____________ days.

MOTIONS IN LIMINE:

Any party wishing to have motions in limine heard prior to the commencement of trial must file and serve same no later than **five court days** prior to the date set for the Pretrial Conference. Any party opposing such a motion in limine shall file and serve its opposition papers no later than **two court days** prior to the Pretrial Conference(with personal service directly on chambers). No reply papers will be considered, and the motions will be heard at the Pretrial Conference or at such other time as the Court may direct.

PRETRIAL CONFERENCE: A Pretrial Conference SHALL be held at on in Courtroom 10. Not less than three days before the Pretrial Conference, counsel for the government **SHALL**:

(1) Serve and file a trial memorandum briefly stating the legal bases for the charges and the anticipated evidence, and addressing any evidentiary, procedural or other anticipated legal issues;

(2) Serve and file a list of all witnesses who may be called, together with a brief summary of the testimony of each;

(3) Serve and file proposed jury instructions on all substantive issues and on any procedural issue not adequately covered by the Court's standard instructions (which are published in the Ninth Circuit Manual of Model Jury Instructions). Counsel shall deliver to the Courtroom Deputy a copy of their proposed jury instructions on a CD/DVD in WordPerfect format;

(4) Serve and lodge a proposed form of verdict and proposed questions for jury voir dire; and,

(5) Serve and file exhibit lists; and serve copies of all marked exhibits on all parties. Each item **SHALL** be premarked; generally, the government **SHALL** use numbers, the defendant, letters. The exhibits **SHOULD NOT** be filed with the Court, only the exhibit lists must be filed with the Court. However, counsel shall lodge with the Court two copies of the exhibits in binders the Friday before trial, for the Court's use and witnesses use during trial. The original exhibits admitted by the Court shall be collected by the Court during trial.

Not less than **three days** before the Pretrial Conference, defense counsel **SHALL** comply with subparagraphs (3) and (4) above, and, to the extent consistent with the defendant's right to an effective defense, with subparagraphs (1), (2) and (5) above.

Counsel **SHALL** confer in advance and be prepared to discuss with the Court any anticipated evidentiary objections and any means for shortening and simplifying the trial (e.g., by stipulating to such matters as chain of custody, nature of substances, use of the mails, etc.).

Counsel should submit an agreed upon set of additional requested voir dire questions to be posed by the Court. Any voir dire questions on which counsel cannot agree shall be submitted separately. Voir dire by counsel will not be permitted absent leave of Court.

MOTIONS: All motions **SHALL** be heard on ____________ at _______ in Courtroom 10, and **SHALL** comply with Crim. L.R. 47-2. Before filing any motion, counsel for defendant and for the government SHALL confer concerning any matter covered by Crim. L.R. 17.1-1, relevant to the case, in particular, subparagraphs (a), (b) and (c).

The party filing any motion or other paper in this case shall show on the first page beneath the file number which, if any, of the exclusions under 18 U.S.C. § 3161 may be applicable to the action sought or opposed by the motion or other paper, and his or her calculation of the amount of excludable time to the hearing date.

The party filing an opposition or other paper shall also show on the first page beneath the file number which, if any, of the exclusions under 18 U.S.C. § 3161 may be applicable to the action sought or opposed by the motion or other paper, and his or her calculation of the amount of excludable time to the hearing date. Crim. L.R. 47-2(c).

COPIES: Each document filed or lodged with the Court must be accompanied by a **three-hole punched** copy for use in the Judge's chambers. In addition, one copy of the witness and exhibit lists should be furnished to the court reporter.

TRANSCRIPTS: If transcripts will be requested during or immediately after trial, arrangements must be made with the court reporter at least one week before trial commences.

CHANGE OF PLEA: Counsel **SHALL** give prompt notice to the United States Attorney and to the Court of any intention to change a previously entered not guilty plea.

EXHIBITS: Upon the conclusion of the trial, the admitted exhibits are filed by the Court. The exhibits not admitted are returned to counsel.

Dated: 8/1/11

SUSAN ILLSTON
United States District Judge

Hon. D. Lowell Jensen

District Judge

Chambers Information

U.S. District Court, Northern District of California

Oakland courthouse	San Jose Courthouse
(See weekly calendar for courtroom)	Courtroom 7, 4th Floor
1301 Clay Street	280 South First Street
Oakland, CA 94612	San Jose, CA 95113

Scheduling Information

Courtroom Deputy: (408) 535-5375

San Jose Criminal Law and Motion	Thursdays at 9:00 a.m.

Judge's Biography

Born 1928 in Brigham City, UT

Federal Judicial Service:

-Judge, U. S. District Court, Northern District of California

-Nominated by Ronald Reagan on June 2, 1986, to a seat vacated by William H. Orrick, Jr.; Confirmed by the Senate on June 24, 1986, and received commission on June 25, 1986. Assumed senior status on June 27, 1997.

Education:

-University of California, Berkeley, A.B., 1949

-University of California, Berkeley, Boalt Hall School of Law, LL.B., 1952

Professional Career:

-United States Army Corporal, 1952-1954

-Private Practice, Oakland, California, 1954-1955

-Deputy District Attorney, Alameda County, California, 1955-1966

-Assistant District Attorney, Alameda County, California, 1966-1969

-District Attorney, Alameda County, California, 1969-1981

-Assistant U.S. Attorney General, Criminal Division, U.S. Dept. of Justice, 1981-1983

-Associate U.S. Attorney General, U.S. Department of Justice, 1983-1985

-Deputy U.S. Attorney General, U.S. Department of Justice, 1985-1986

I. Judge Jensen's Procedures and Practices

A. Standing Order

Judge Jensen's Standing Order

1. Counsel shall comply with all provisions of the Local Rules.

2. No party shall submit a statement of "undisputed" facts unless such statement has been jointly prepared by all parties pursuant to Civil L.R. 56-2. Any other statement of "undisputed" facts will be disregarded by the Court.

Hon. Lucy H. Koh

District Judge

Chambers Information

U.S. District Court, Northern District of California
Courtroom 8, 4th Floor
280 South First Street
San Jose, California 95113

Scheduling Information

Courtroom Deputy: (408) 535-5346

Civil Law & Motion	Thursdays at 1:30 p.m.
Criminal Law and Motion	Wednesdays at 9:00 a.m.
Civil Case Management and Pretrial Conferences	Wednesdays at 2:00 p.m.
Trials	Mondays, Tuesdays, and Fridays: 9:00 a.m. – 4:30 p.m.

Judge's Biography

Born 1968 in Washington, DC

Federal Judicial Service:

-Judge, U. S. District Court, Northern District of California
-Nominated by Barack Obama on January 20, 2010, to a seat vacated by Ronald M. Whyte. Confirmed by the Senate on June 7, 2010, and received commission on June 9, 2010.

Education:

-Harvard University, B.A., 1990
-Harvard Law School, J.D., 1993

Professional Career:

-Fellow, Committee on the Judiciary, U.S. Senate, 1993-1994
-Special Counsel, Office of Legislative Affairs, U.S. Department of Justice, 1994-1996
-Special Assistant to the Deputy Attorney General, U.S. Department of Justice, 1996-1997
-Assistant U. S. Attorney, Central District of California, 1997-2000
-Private practice, Palo Alto, California, 2000-2008
-Judge, Superior Court of California, County of Santa Clara, 2008-2010

I. Judge Koh's Procedures and Practices

A. *Civil Standing Order Regarding Motions to File Under Seal*

CIVIL STANDING ORDER REGARDING MOTIONS TO FILE UNDER SEAL

1. **Conformity to Rules.** Parties shall follow the Federal Rules of Civil Procedure, the Civil Local Rules, and the General Orders of the Northern District of California, except as superseded by this Order.

2. **E-filing Administrative Motions to File Under Seal.** Beginning December 1, 2011, for all civil cases, a party seeking to file documents under seal shall also publicly e-file, as an exhibit to the administrative motion to file under seal, a proposed public redacted version of the documents that the party is seeking to file under seal. In all other respects, parties shall follow G.O. 62 and Local Rule 79-5.

IT IS SO ORDERED.

Dated: December 1, 2011

LUCY H. KOH
United States District Judge

B. *Guidelines for Final Pretrial Conference in Bench Trials*

GUIDELINES FOR FINAL PRETRIAL CONFERENCE IN BENCH TRIALS BEFORE DISTRICT JUDGE LUCY H. KOH

A. Meeting and Disclosure Prior to Pretrial Conference: At least 21 days[1] before the final Pretrial Conference, lead counsel who will try the case shall meet and confer with respect to:

1. Settlement of the Case;
2. Preparation of the Joint Pretrial Statement;
3. Preparation and exchange of pretrial materials to be served and lodged pursuant to Federal Rule of Civil Procedure 26(a)(3); and
4. Clarifying and narrowing the contested issues for trial in order to achieve a just, speedy, and efficient determination of the case.

B. Joint Pretrial Statement and Order: At least 14 days before the Pretrial Conference, unless otherwise ordered, the parties shall lodge and serve a Joint Pretrial Statement and Proposed Order containing the following information:

1. Substance of the Action. A brief description of the parties, the substance of claims and defenses that remain to be decided, and the operative pleadings that raise the issues;
2. Relief Sought. A detailed statement of all relief claimed, particularly itemizing all elements of damages claimed as well as witnesses, documents, or other evidentiary material to be presented concerning the amount of damages;
3. Undisputed Facts. A plain and concise statement of all relevant facts to which the parties will stipulate for incorporation into the trial record without the necessity of supporting testimony or exhibits;
4. Disputed Factual Issues. A plain and concise list of the issues of fact that are contested and remain to be litigated at trial;
5. Agreed Statement. A statement assessing whether all or part of the action may be presented upon an agreed statement of facts;
6. Stipulations. A statement of proposed stipulations or agreements that will expedite the presentation of evidence;
7. Witnesses to be Called. A list of witnesses likely to be called at trial, other than solely for impeachment or rebuttal, together with a brief statement following each name describing the substance of the testimony to be given. No party shall be permitted to call any witness in its case in chief who is not disclosed in its Joint Pretrial Statement without leave of the Court for good cause;
8. Exhibits, Schedules, Summaries. A list of all documents and other items to be offered as exhibits at the trial, other than solely for impeachment or rebuttal, with a

[1] Time shall be computed according to Federal Rule of Civil Procedure 6(a).

brief statement following each, describing its substance or purpose and the identity of the sponsoring witness;

9. Disputed Legal Issues. Without extended legal argument, a concise statement of each disputed point of law concerning liability or relief, citing supporting statutes and decisions;

10. Further Discovery or Motions. A statement of all remaining discovery, if any, or any motions or matters that must be resolved prior to trial, including motions in limine;

11. Disputed Evidentiary Issues. A concise statement of each disputed evidentiary issue (even if a motion in limine will not be filed on that issue), citing supporting statutes and decisions or referring to the appropriate motion in limine;

12. Bifurcation, Separate Trial of Issues. A statement of whether bifurcation or a separate trial of specific issues is feasible and desired;

13. Estimate of Trial Time. An estimate of the total number of hours or days needed for the trial; and

14. Miscellaneous. Any other matters that will facilitate the just, speedy and efficient determination of the action.

C. Binding Effect of the Joint Pretrial Statement and Order: The Joint Pretrial Statement and Order described above shall recite, directly above the signature lines of each party, the following:

> *The foregoing admissions having been made by the parties, and the parties having specified the foregoing issues of fact and law remaining to be litigated, this order shall supplement the pleadings and govern the course of trial of this action, unless modified to prevent manifest injustice.*

D. Preparation for Trial

1. Exhibits:

a) At least 14 days before the final Pretrial Conference, the parties shall exchange copies of all exhibits, summaries, charts, and diagrams to be used at trial other than solely impeachment or rebuttal.

b) Each exhibit shall be pre-marked for identification. Counsel shall meet and confer and reach agreement upon a method for marking exhibits (for example, Plaintiff shall use numbers and Defendant shall use letters, or Plaintiff shall use numbers 100-199 and Defendant shall use numbers 200-299, etc.).

c) Unless otherwise ordered, at least 7 days prior to the commencement of trial, the parties shall deliver three sets of all pre-marked exhibits contained in three ring binders to Martha Parker Brown, Courtroom Deputy to Judge Koh.

d) No party shall be permitted to offer any exhibit at trial that is not disclosed in its Joint Pretrial Statement without leave of the Court for good cause, unless it is offered solely for impeachment or rebuttal.

2. Motions in Limine. Unless otherwise ordered, the parties shall file and serve any motions in limine at least 14 days before the final Pretrial Conference, and any opposition thereto at least 10 days before the final Pretrial Conference. Ordinarily, these motions will be deemed submitted without oral argument. Each motion should be presented in a separate memo and numbered as, for example, "Plaintiff's Motion in Limine No. 1 to Exclude . . . ." Please limit motions in limine to circumstances that actually require a ruling in advance of trial. Usually five or fewer motions per side are sufficient at the Pretrial Conference stage (without prejudice to raising matters as the trial progresses). Each motion should address a single topic, be separate, and contain no more than seven pages of briefing per side.

3. Deposition and Discovery Designations: Unless otherwise ordered, at least 14 days before the commencement of trial, the parties shall file and serve any excerpts of deposition testimony or other discovery to be offered at trial, other than solely for impeachment or rebuttal. (A hard copy of the designated deposition testimony with page and line references, or the interrogatory response or admission shall be provided.) Any objections to the use of designated excerpts and any counter-designations of deposition testimony shall be filed and served at least 10 days prior to the commencement of trial.

4. Proposed Findings of Fact and Conclusions of Law. At least 7 days prior to the Pretrial Conference, each party shall file and serve proposed findings of fact and conclusions of law. The findings of fact shall set forth in simple declarative sentences, separately numbered, all factual contentions relied upon by the party in support of its claims or defenses and shall be free of pejorative language and argument. Conclusions of law shall be supported by appropriate citation to legal authority. The proposed findings of fact and conclusions of law shall be submitted in hard copy as well as in word processing format via e-mail to LHKpo@cand.uscourts.gov.

5. Trial Briefs: Trial briefs are optional, but any party wishing to file a trial brief must do so not less than 7 days prior to the commencement of trial.

6. Time Limits: Ordinarily, the Court shall set fixed time limits at the final Pretrial Conference. All of your examination time (whether direct, cross, re-direct, or recross) for all witnesses must fit within your time limit and you may allocate the time as you wish. Opening and closing time limits are *in addition* to your examination time.

E. Scheduling

The normal trial schedule will be 9:00 a.m. to 4:30 p.m., with a lunch break from 12:00 p.m. to 1:30 p.m., on Monday, Tuesday, and Friday, and from 9:00 a.m. to 12:00 p.m. on Thursday.

F. Settlement and Continuances

Shortly before trial or a final Pretrial Conference, counsel occasionally wish to jointly advise the Court that a settlement has been reached and seek to take the matter off calendar based on a settlement "in principle" with disputes remaining. Cases, however, cannot be taken off calendar in this manner. Unless and until a stipulated dismissal is filed or placed on the record, all parties must be prepared to proceed as scheduled. Only an advance continuance *expressly approved by the Court* will release counsel and the parties from their obligation to proceed. If counsel expect that a settlement will be final by the time of Pretrial Conference or trial, they should notify the Court immediately in writing, or, if settlement occurs over the weekend, by voice mail to Martha Parker Brown, Courtroom Deputy to Judge Koh. The Court will attempt to confer with counsel promptly to determine whether a continuance is in order. Pending such a conference, however, counsel must prepare and make all filings and be prepared to proceed with the trial.

G. Opportunities for Junior Lawyers

The Court strongly encourages parties to permit less experienced lawyers to examine witnesses at trial and to have an important role at trial. Counsel should be prepared to discuss such opportunities at the Pretrial Conference.

IT IS SO ORDERED.

Dated: January 3, 2011

LUCY H. KOH
United States District Judge

C. *Guidelines for Final Pretrial Conference in Jury Trials*

GUIDELINES FOR FINAL PRETRIAL CONFERENCE IN JURY TRIALS BEFORE DISTRICT JUDGE LUCY H. KOH

A. Meeting and Disclosure Prior to Pretrial Conference: At least 21 days[1] before the final Pretrial Conference, lead counsel who will try the case shall meet and confer with respect to:

1. Settlement of the Case;
2. Preparation of the Joint Pretrial Statement;
3. Preparation and exchange of pretrial materials to be served and lodged pursuant to Federal Rule of Civil Procedure 26(a)(3); and
4. Clarifying and narrowing the contested issues for trial in order to achieve a just, speedy, and efficient determination of the case.

B. Joint Pretrial Statement and Order: At least 14 days before the Pretrial Conference, unless otherwise ordered, the parties shall lodge and serve a Joint Pretrial Statement and Proposed Order containing the following information:

1. Substance of the Action. A brief description of the parties, the substance of claims and defenses that remain to be decided, and the operative pleadings that raise the issues;
2. Relief Sought. A detailed statement of all relief claimed, particularly itemizing all elements of damages claimed as well as witnesses, documents, or other evidentiary material to be presented concerning the amount of damages;
3. Undisputed Facts. A plain and concise statement of all relevant facts to which the parties will stipulate for incorporation into the trial record without the necessity of supporting testimony or exhibits;
4. Disputed Factual Issues. A plain and concise list of the issues of fact that are contested and remain to be litigated at trial;
5. Agreed Statement. A statement assessing whether all or part of the action may be presented upon an agreed statement of facts;
6. Stipulations. A statement of proposed stipulations or agreements that will expedite the presentation of evidence;
7. Witnesses to be Called. A list of witnesses likely to be called at trial, other than solely for impeachment or rebuttal, together with a brief statement following each name describing the substance of the testimony to be given. No party shall be permitted to call any witness in its case in chief who is not disclosed in its Joint Pretrial Statement without leave of the Court for good cause;
8. Exhibits, Schedules, Summaries. A list of all documents and other items to be offered as exhibits at the trial, other than solely for impeachment or rebuttal, with a

[1] Time shall be computed according to Federal Rule of Civil Procedure 6(a).

brief statement following each, describing its substance or purpose and the identity of the sponsoring witness;

9. Disputed Legal Issues. Without extended legal argument, a concise statement of each disputed point of law concerning liability or relief, citing supporting statutes and decisions;

10. Further Discovery or Motions. A statement of all remaining discovery, if any, or any motions or matters that must be resolved prior to trial, including motions in limine;

11. Disputed Evidentiary Issues. A concise statement of each disputed evidentiary issue (even if a motion in limine will not be filed on that issue), citing supporting statutes and decisions or referring to the appropriate motion in limine;

12. Bifurcation, Separate Trial of Issues. A statement of whether bifurcation or a separate trial of specific issues is feasible and desired;

13. Estimate of Trial Time. An estimate of the total number of hours or days needed for the trial; and

14. Miscellaneous. Any other matters that will facilitate the just, speedy and efficient determination of the action.

C. Binding Effect of the Joint Pretrial Statement and Order: The Joint Pretrial Statement and Order described above shall recite, directly above the signature lines of each party, the following:

> *The foregoing admissions having been made by the parties, and the parties having specified the foregoing issues of fact and law remaining to be litigated, this order shall supplement the pleadings and govern the course of trial of this action, unless modified to prevent manifest injustice.*

D. Preparation for Trial

1. Exhibits:

   a) At least 14 days before the final Pretrial Conference, the parties shall exchange copies of all exhibits, summaries, charts, and diagrams to be used at trial other than solely for impeachment or rebuttal.

   b) Each exhibit shall be pre-marked for identification. Counsel shall meet and confer and reach agreement upon a method for marking exhibits (for example, Plaintiff shall use numbers and Defendant shall use letters, or Plaintiff shall use numbers 100-199 and Defendant shall use numbers 200-299, etc.).

   c) Unless otherwise ordered, at least 7 days prior to the commencement of trial, the parties shall deliver three sets of all pre-marked exhibits contained in three ring binders to Martha Parker Brown, Courtroom Deputy to Judge Koh.

   d) No party shall be permitted to offer any exhibit at trial that is not disclosed in its Joint Pretrial Statement without leave of the Court for good cause, unless it is offered solely for impeachment or rebuttal.

2. Motions in Limine. Unless otherwise ordered, the parties shall file and serve any motions in limine at least 14 days before the final Pretrial Conference, and any opposition thereto at least 10 days before the final Pretrial Conference. Ordinarily, these motions will be deemed submitted without oral argument. Each motion should be presented in a separate memo and numbered as, for example, "Plaintiff's Motion in Limine No. 1 to Exclude . . . ." Please limit motions in limine to circumstances that actually require a ruling in advance of trial. Usually five or fewer motions per side are sufficient at the Pretrial Conference stage (without prejudice to raising matters as the trial progresses). Each motion should address a single topic, be separate, and contain no more than seven pages of briefing per side.

3. Deposition and Discovery Designations: Unless otherwise ordered, at least 14 days before the commencement of trial, the parties shall file and serve any excerpts of deposition testimony or other discovery to be offered at trial, other than solely for impeachment or rebuttal. (A hard copy of the designated deposition testimony with page and line references, or the interrogatory response or admission shall be provided.) Any objections to the use of designated excerpts and any counter-designations of deposition testimony shall be filed and served at least 10 days prior to the commencement of trial.

4. Jury Materials:

a) Unless otherwise ordered, at least 7 days prior to the final Pretrial Conference, the parties shall file and serve:

1) Jury Voir Dire Questions
2) Proposed Jury Instructions
3) Proposed Jury Verdict Forms

b) Ordinarily, the Court will give the standard preliminary jury instructions contained in the Model Jury Instructions of the Ninth Circuit prior to opening statements and will give the standard closing instructions in the Model Jury Instructions of the Ninth Circuit before closing arguments.

c) As to substantive case-specific instructions, the parties shall meet and confer and submit jointly an agreed set of instructions, using the Model Jury Instructions of the Ninth Circuit where appropriate. In the event the parties are unable to agree to the language of a particular instruction, the objecting party shall submit a written objection or an alternative proposed instruction placed in sequence immediately following the disputed instruction. The joint set of jury instructions shall be submitted in hard copy as well as word processing format via e-mail to LHKpo@cand.uscourts.gov.

5. Trial Briefs: Trial briefs are optional, but any party wishing to file a trial brief must do so not less than 7 days prior to the commencement of trial.

6. Time Limits: Ordinarily, the Court shall set fixed time limits at the final Pretrial Conference. All of your examination time (whether direct, cross, re-direct, or recross) for all witnesses must fit within your time limit and you may allocate the time as you wish. Opening and closing time limits are *in addition* to your examination time.

E. Scheduling

The normal trial schedule will be 9:00 a.m. to 4:30 p.m., with a lunch break from 12:00 p.m. to 1:30 p.m., on Monday, Tuesday, and Friday, and from 9:00 a.m. to 12:00 p.m. on Thursday.

F. Settlement and Continuances

Shortly before trial or a final Pretrial Conference, counsel occasionally wish to jointly advise the Court that a settlement has been reached and seek to take the matter off calendar based on a settlement "in principle" with disputes remaining. Cases, however, cannot be taken off calendar in this manner. Unless and until a stipulated dismissal is filed or placed on the record, all parties must be prepared to proceed as scheduled. Only an advance continuance *expressly approved by the Court* will release counsel and the parties from their obligation to proceed. If counsel expect that a settlement will be final by the time of the Pretrial Conference or trial, they should notify the Court immediately in writing, or, if settlement occurs over the weekend, by voice mail to Martha Parker Brown, Courtroom Deputy to Judge Koh. The Court will attempt to confer with counsel promptly to determine whether a continuance is in order. Pending such a conference, however, counsel must prepare and make all filings and be prepared to proceed with the trial.

G. Opportunities for Junior Lawyers

The Court strongly encourages parties to permit less experienced lawyers to examine witnesses at trial and to have an important role at trial. Counsel should be prepared to discuss such opportunities at the Pretrial Conference.

IT IS SO ORDERED.

Dated: January 3, 2011

____

LUCY H. KOH
United States District Judge

Hon. Marilyn Hall Patel

District Judge

Chambers Information

U.S. District Court, Northern District of California
Courtroom 15, 18th Floor
450 Golden Gate Avenue
San Francisco, CA 94102

Scheduling Information

Courtroom Deputy: (415) 522-3140

Civil Law and Motion	Mondays at 2:00 p.m.
Criminal Law and Motion	Mondays at 10:00 a.m.
Case Management Conferences	Mondays at 3:00 p.m.

Judge's Biography

Born 1938 in Amsterdam, NY

Federal Judicial Service:

-Judge, U. S. District Court, Northern District of California
-Nominated by Jimmy Carter on May 9, 1980, to a seat vacated by Lloyd Hudson Burke; Confirmed by the Senate on June 26, 1980, and received commission on June 30, 1980.
-Served as chief judge, 1997-2004. Assumed senior status on October 30, 2009.

Education:

-Wheaton College, B.A., 1959
-Fordham University School of Law, J.D., 1963

Professional Career:

-Private Practice, New York City, 1963-1967
-Attorney, Immigration and Naturalization Service, U.S. Department of Justice, San Francisco, 1967-1971
-Private Practice, San Francisco, California, 1971-1976
-Adjunct Professor of Law, University of California, San Francisco, Hastings College of Law, 1974-1976
-Judge, Municipal Court, Oakland-Piedmont Judicial District, State of California, 1976-1980

I. Judge Patel's Procedures and Practices

A. *Standing Orders – Notices*

STANDING ORDERS
NOTICES

1. Civil Law and Motion Calendar is held on Monday at 2:00 p.m. for Motions; 3:00 p.m. for Status Conferences; 4:00 p.m. for Case Management Conferences. The Criminal Calendar will be called every Monday at 9:00 a.m.

2. Counsel should listen to the recorded message at 415-522-3140 for the first available dates for motions.

3. Counsel are expected to consult and conform with all provisions of the Local Rules relating to continuances and motions, including motions for reconsideration, and all other matters.

4. Motions to dismiss shall not be filed before the initial Case Management Conference except by leave of court.

5. All evidentiary submissions on motions and for trial shall be filed in accordance with the court's instructions. Copies of the instructions are available from the docket clerk.

6. Discovery disputes are governed by Civ. LR 37-1(a) and (b). Parties must comply with the meet and confer requirements of 37-1(a) before contacting the court. If it is necessary to involve the court, the parties shall arrange a phone conference through the Courtroom Deputy. Written letter briefs shall not be filed unless requested by the court.

7. Summary Judgment motions: Only one joint statement of undisputed facts, signed by all parties, shall be filed at time of filing of oppositions. If the parties are unable to agree that a fact is undisputed, then that fact shall be in dispute.

8. Counsel must submit courtesy copies of pleadings, motions, or other papers to chambers in cases designated as "E-File" only.

II. Judge Patel's Forms

A. *Application for Permission to Enter Plea of Guilty and Order Accepting Plea*

IN THE UNITED STATES DISTRICT COURT
FOR THE NORTHERN DISTRICT OF CALIFORNIA

No. CR________ MHP

Plaintiff,

v.

Defendant.
_________________________________/

APPLICATION FOR PERMISSION TO ENTER PLEA OF GUILTY;

ORDER ACCEPTING PLEA
(FRCrP, Rules 10 and 11)

The defendant represents to the Court:

1. My full true name is ____________. I am years of age _____. I have gone to school up to and including __________________________. My most recent occupation has been . I request that all proceedings against me be in my true name.

2. I am represented by a lawyer; his/her name is ___________________.

3. _____ I am proficient enough in English to read the above and have read and fully understand it.

_____ I am not proficient enough in English. I speak and understand ____________, which is my native language. The above was read to me in ______________, and I fully understand it.

4. I received a copy of the indictment/information (as used in the Application the term indictment includes information) before being called upon to plead. I have read the indictment or a translator who speaks _____________ read it to me, and I have discussed the indictment with my lawyer. I fully understand every charge made against me. I understand these charges to be:_________.

5. I have told my lawyer all the facts and circumstances known to me about the charges made against me in the indictment. I believe that my lawyer is fully informed on all such matters.

6. I know that the Court must be satisfied that there is a factual basis for a plea of "GUILTY" before my plea can be accepted. I represent to the Court that I did the following acts in connection with the charges made against me in Counts____.

(In the above space, defendant must set out in detail in his/her own handwriting what he/she did. If more space is needed, add a separate page.)

7. My lawyer has counseled and advised me on the nature of each charge, all lesser included charges, all penalties and consequences of each charge, all possible defenses that I may have in this case and the constitutional rights I am waiving.

8. I understand that my constitutional rights are as follows:

A. The right to a speedy and public trial by jury;

B. The right to see and hear all witnesses called to testify against me;

C. The right to use the power and process of the Court to compel the production of any evidence, including the attendance of any witnesses in my favor;

D. The right to the assistance of a lawyer at all stages of the proceedings, and if I cannot afford one, to have the court appoint one to represent me without cost to me or based upon my ability to pay;

E. The right to take the witness stand at my sole option, and if I do not take the witness stand, no inference of guilt may be drawn from such failure;

F. The right against self-incrimination;

G. The right to appeal from an adverse judgment;

H. The right to raise available defenses, including defenses which may be raised by motion.

I. The right to appeal my sentence as limited by my plea agreement;

J. If plea entered pursuant to a plea agreement, the right to discovery of materials in the possession of or available to the government, including materials that may be exculpatory, and which I may receive in the future, but have not yet received because of entering into a plea agreement.

9. I know that I may plead "NOT GUILTY" to any offense charged against me.

10. I know that if I plead "GUILTY," I am giving up all of the rights enumerated in paragraph 8 and that there will be no trial either before a court or jury.

11. I know that if I plead "GUILTY" the result of my plea is more than just an admission or confession of guilt and that it will result in my conviction. Further, the Court may impose the same punishment as if I had pleaded "NOT GUILTY," stood trial, and been convicted by a jury.

12. My lawyer has discussed with me the maximum and minimum, if any, punishments which the law provides, and the various provisions of the Sentencing Guidelines that may apply to me. I understand that the maximum punishment for the offense(s) charged in Count(s) ______________ of the indictment is ____________ months of imprisonment, a fine in the amount of $______________, and a period of _____ years supervised release. I understand that there is a mandatory minimum punishment of _________ months imprisonment for the offense(s) charged in Count(s) ___________. I also understand that the minimum period of supervised release which the court may impose is ___________ (if applicable) and that if I violate any condition of supervised release, the release may be revoked and I may be sentenced to a part or all of the term of supervised release imposed in addition to any other term of imprisonment which I have received.

I understand that I may be assessed the costs of confinement and/or supervision. I understand that I must pay a penalty assessment of $__________ per count to which I plead (or $_________ per count in the case of misdemeanor counts). I also understand that I may be ordered to pay restitution in an amount determined by the court.

I also understand that the court and counsel cannot promise what sentence or sentencing range will be set and that these calculations will depend upon the Sentencing Guidelines as they apply to me. I have been advised that the Court may sentence within the guideline range determined by the U.S. Probation Office, or may depart upward or downward from the range. However, no promises have been made to me as to the range or departure.

13. If I am on probation, supervised release or parole in this or any other court, I know that by pleading guilty here my probation, release or parole may be revoked and I may be required to serve time in that case, which may be consecutive (that is, in addition) to any sentence imposed upon me in this case.

14. I declare that no officer or agent of any branch of government (Federal, State or Local) has promised or suggested that I will receive a lighter sentence, or probation, or any other form of leniency if I plead "GUILTY," except as stated in the Plea Agreement I have signed, stated on the record in my entry of plea or as follows: ________________.
(In the space above, insert any promises or concessions made to the defendant or to his/her attorney.)

If anyone else made such a promise or suggestion, except as noted in the previous sentence, I know that that person had no authority to do it. No one has forced or coerced me into entering this plea. I enter this plea of my own free will. My willingness to plead guilty:

_____ does not result from prior discussions between my attorney and the government's attorney.

_____ does result from prior discussion between my attorney and the government's attorney. (If it does, state any factors that influenced you that are not reflected in the plea agreement.)______________________________.

If a plea agreement has been entered into, please answer the following:

15. I have read in full the plea agreement I have entered into with the government or an interpreter has translated the entire agreement into the __________ language, and I fully understand it. No one has made any promises to me that are not included in the agreement except: ____________________. **(Set forth all promises or state "None" if no other promises made.)**

16. I believe that my lawyer has done all that a lawyer could do to counsel and assist me, and I am satisfied with the advice and help he/she has given me.

17. I know that the court will not permit anyone to plead "GUILTY" who maintains he/she is innocent and, with that in mind and because I am "GUILTY," I respectfully request the court to accept my plea of "GUILTY" and to have the clerk enter my plea of "GUILTY" as follows: ____.

18. I understand that I may not withdraw my plea unless the plea agreement I have entered into provides otherwise or the court permits me to withdraw my plea.

19. My mind is clear. I am not under the influence of alcohol or drugs and I am not under a doctor's care. The only drugs, medicines or pills that I took within the past seven days are:________________. **(If none, so state.)**

20. **I OFFER MY PLEA OF "GUILTY" FREELY AND VOLUNTARILY, AND**

OF MY OWN ACCORD AND WITH FULL UNDERSTANDING OF ALL THE MATTERS SET FORTH IN THE INDICTMENT AND IN THIS APPLICATION AND IN THE CERTIFICATE OF MY LAWYER WHICH IS ATTACHED TO THIS APPLICATION. IN OFFERING MY PLEA OF "GUILTY," I FREELY AND VOLUNTARILY WAIVE (give up) THE CONSTITUTIONAL RIGHTS GUARANTEED TO ME AS STATED IN PARAGRAPH 8 ABOVE.

21. I waive the reading of the indictment in open court, and I request the court to enter my plea of "GUILTY" as set forth in Paragraph 15 of this application.

22. I understand that all of the above statements will be made in open court under oath and that any false statements may be used against me in a prosecution for perjury or false statement, which is a felony.

Signed by me in open court in the presence of my attorney this day of ___________, 20___.

____
Defendant's Signature

INTERPRETER CERTIFICATION

I, _____________________, hereby certify that I am a duly _____________ interpreter in the English and ________________ languages and that I read all of the above to the defendant, that he/she stated he/she fully understood it, and I am satisfied that his/her answer is true and correct.

____
Date

____
Interpreter's Signature

CERTIFICATE OF COUNSEL

The undersigned, as lawyer and counselor for the defendant ____________, hereby certifies:

1. I have read and fully explained to the defendant and believe he/she fully understands the allegations contained in the indictment of this case, the defenses he/she may have to each and every one of the allegations and the consequences of a plea of "GUILTY," including the pertinent Sentencing Guidelines provisions and maximum and minimum penalties.

2. I believe the defendant fully understands the constitutional rights he/she is waiving and that by entering a plea of "GUILTY" he/she is waiving each and every one of those rights.

3. Nothing has come to my attention which causes me to believe that the defendant lacks the ability to understand anything contained in the attached application or that at the time of entering his/her plea he/she is under the influence of any drug or alcohol.

4. The plea of "GUILTY" offered by the defendant in Paragraph 15 accords with my understanding of the facts he/she related to me and is consistent with my advice to the defendant.

5. In my opinion, the defendant's waiver of reading of the indictment in open court as provided by FRCrP 10 is voluntarily and understandingly made, and I recommend to the court that the waiver be accepted by the court.

6. Defendant has read the Plea Agreement she/he signed in the matter and I believe she/he fully understands it. I certify that no promises have been made to the defendant by the government or myself other than those contained in the Plea Agreement and if there are such other promises I must state them on the record before my client and the court.

7. In my opinion the plea of "GUILTY" offered by the defendant in Paragraph 15 of the application is voluntarily and understandingly made. I recommend that the court accept the plea of "GUILTY."

Signed by me in open court in the presence of the defendant above-named and after full discussion of the contents of this certificate with the defendant this day of __________, 20 ___.

____
Attorney's (for the Defendant) Signature

ORDER

I find that:

1. The defendant enters this plea of guilty freely and voluntarily and not out of ignorance, inadvertence, fear or coercion.
2. The defendant understands and knowingly, freely and voluntarily waives his constitutional rights.
3. The defendant freely and voluntarily executed the within Application and understands its contents.
4. The defendant has admitted the essential elements of the crime charged.

IT IS THEREFORE ORDERED that the defendant's plea of "GUILTY" be accepted and entered as prayed for in the Application and as recommended in the certificate of his lawyer.

IT IS FURTHER ORDERED that the plea agreement entered into in this matter is:

______ Accepted at this time.
______ Taken under submission until the time of sentencing.

Done in open court this ____ day of __________, 20___.

____
MARILYN HALL PATEL
United States District Judge

Hon. Yvonne Gonzalez Rogers

District Judge

Chambers Information

U.S. District Court, Northern District of California
Oakland Courthouse
1301 Clay Street
Oakland, CA 94612

Scheduling Information

Courtroom Deputy: (510) 637-3540

Civil Law and Motion	Tuesdays at 2:00 p.m.
Criminal Law and Motion	Thursdays at 2:00 p.m.
Case Management Conferences	Mondays at 2:00 p.m.
Trials	Mondays through Thursdays from 8:30 a.m. to 1:30 p.m.

Judge's Biography

Born 1965 in Houston, TX

Federal Judicial Service:

-Judge, U. S. District Court, Northern District of California
-Nominated by Barack Obama on May 4, 2011, to a seat vacated by Vaughn R. Walker; Confirmed by the Senate on November 15, 2011, and received commission on November 21, 2011.

Education:

-Princeton University, A.B., 1987
-University of Texas School of Law, J.D., 1991

Professional Career:

-Private practice, San Francisco, California, 1991-2003
-Judge pro tem, California Superior Court, Alameda County, 2007-2008
-Judge, California Superior Court, Alameda County, 2008-2011

I. Judge Rogers' Procedures and Practices

A. *Pretrial Instructions in Civil Cases*

PRETRIAL INSTRUCTIONS IN CIVIL CASES
Judge Yvonne Gonzalez Rogers

1. **PRETRIAL CONFERENCE:** Trials are scheduled to begin Monday mornings at 8:30 a.m. through 1:30 p.m. with two 15-minute breaks. Generally, Fridays are dark. Pretrial Conferences are scheduled on the third Friday preceding the trial at 9:00 a.m. Parties shall comply in all respects with Fed. R. Civ. P 16.

2. **PRETRIAL CONFERENCE STATEMENT:** The parties shall file a joint Pretrial Conference Statement containing the information listed below. To comply with this requirement, trial counsel shall meet and confer at least twentyone (21) days in advance of the Pretrial Conference. The Statement is due **fourteen (14) days** prior to the Pretrial Conference.

   a. **The Action.**
      i. **Substance of the Action.** A brief description of the substance of claims and defenses which remain to be decided, including a list of the causes of action to be tried.

      ii. **Relief Prayed.** A detailed statement of all the relief claimed, particularly itemizing all elements of damages claimed as well as witnesses, documents or other evidentiary material to be presented concerning the amount of those damages.

   b. **The Factual Basis of the Action.**
      i. **Undisputed Facts.** A plain and concise statement of all relevant facts not reasonably disputable, as well as which facts the parties will stipulate for incorporation into the trial record without the necessity of supporting testimony or exhibits.

      ii. **Disputed Factual Issues.** A plain and concise statement of all disputed factual issues which remain to be decided.

      iii. **Agreed Statement.** A statement assessing whether all or part of the action may be presented upon an agreed statement of facts.

      iv. **Stipulations.** A statement of stipulations requested or proposed for pretrial or trial purposes.

   c. **Disputed Legal Issues.**
      i. **Points of Law.** Without extended legal argument, a concise statement of each disputed point of law concerning liability or relief, citing supporting statutes and decisions setting forth the nature of each party's contentions concerning each disputed point of law, including procedural and evidentiary issues. Supporting statutes and decisions and the parties' contentions regarding the same shall be brief and provided in an outline or bullet point format.

      ii. **Proposed Conclusions of Law.** If the case is to be tried without a jury, unless otherwise ordered, parties should briefly indicate objections to Proposed Conclusions of Law. *See* Rule 7 below.

d. **Further Discovery or Motions.** A statement of all remaining discovery and/or pending motions.

e. **Estimate of Trial Time.** An estimate of the number of court days needed for the presentation of each party's case, indicating possible reductions in time through proposed stipulations, agreed statements of facts, or expedited means of presenting testimony and exhibits.

f. **List of Motions *in Limine*.** *See* Rule 4 below. The list shall include only contested non-duplicative motions.

g. **Juror Questionnaire.** Whether the parties intend to file proposed additional questions for jury voir dire. *See* Rule 3.h.i below.

h. **Trial Alternatives and Options.**

   i. **Settlement Discussion.** A statement summarizing the status of settlement negotiations and indicating whether further negotiations are likely to be productive.

   ii. **Consent to Trial Before a Magistrate Judge.** A statement of whether reference of all or part of the action to a master or magistrate judge is feasible, including whether the parties consent to a court or jury trial before a magistrate judge, with appeal directly to the Ninth Circuit. The Court will entertain requests for reference to a specific magistrate.

   iii. **Amendments, Dismissals.** A statement of requested or proposed amendments to pleadings or dismissals of parties, claims or defenses and any objections thereto.

   iv. **Bifurcation, Separate Trial of Issues.** A statement of whether bifurcation or a separate trial of specific issues is feasible and desired.

3. **TRIAL READINESS FILINGS AND BINDER and PROPOSED ORDER THEREON:** The parties shall file each of the documents listed below and deliver to chambers a JOINT TRIAL READINESS BINDER. To provide the Court with sufficient time to prepare, the documents and binder with said documents are due no less than **seven (7) days** prior to the Pretrial Conference.

   a. **Proposed Order Re Trial Stipulations.** During the meet and confer process, the Court expects that the parties will agree to a variety of stipulations regarding the conduct of the trial. A Proposed Order outlining all such stipulations shall be presented to the Court.

   b. **Witness List.** A list of all witnesses likely to be called at trial (other than solely for impeachment or rebuttal), with a brief statement following each name describing the substance of the testimony to be given and a time estimate of the direct and cross examinations. This information shall be presented in chart format and organized by party.

   c. **Expert Witness List.** A list of all expert witnesses with a summary which shall clearly state the expert's theories and conclusions and the basis therefore and shall be accompanied by a curriculum vitae; if the expert has prepared a report in preparation for the testimony, a copy thereof shall be furnished to opposing counsel. Witnesses not included on the list may be excluded from testifying.

d. **Exhibit Lists Annotated with Stipulations/Objections.** A list of all documents and other items to be offered as exhibits at the trial (other than solely for impeachment or rebuttal) shall be provided with a brief description of each exhibit's contents, and the identity of each sponsoring witness. As applicable, the Exhibit List shall specify whether the parties stipulate to admit the exhibit or the grounds for any objections to the exhibit. The Exhibit List shall also include an additional column so that the Court can track the date on which each exhibit is admitted. Prior to submitting the list, the parties shall meet and confer and attempt to stipulate as to the admissibility of each exhibit. This information shall be presented in chart format and organized numerically. The parties should consult the Appendix for a suggested format of the Exhibit List.

   Parties shall meet and confer and agree on numeric designations for exhibits, such as plaintiffs shall have numbers 1-99, defendant one: numbers 100-199, defendant two: numbers 200-299, etc. The agreed upon designations shall be noted for the Court.

e. **List of Discovery Excerpts.** The parties shall list those excerpts from depositions, from interrogatory answers, or from responses to requests for admission (other than those solely for impeachment or rebuttal) likely to be used at trial.

   Prior to submitting the list, the parties shall meet and confer and attempt to resolve any disagreements regarding designations or counter-designations. The parties shall (i) identify any remaining legal objections to the excerpts on the list itself and (ii) attach in a separate appendix copies of the disputed excerpts so that the Court can review the disputed materials. The parties should consult the Appendix for a suggested format of the List of Discovery Excerpts.

   The parties shall provide a single proposed order with each disputed designation which will allow the Court to rule whether permission to use each is granted, granted with modification, or denied. The parties should consult the Appendix for a suggested format of a chart to be contained within the Proposed Order Re Discovery Excerpts.

f. **Jury Instructions.**

   i. **Joint and Disputed Sets of Instructions.**

      (A) The parties shall meet and confer and prepare a Joint Set of Jury Instructions which shall be so designated. Authority shall be provided even for these stipulated instructions.

      (B) For disputed instructions, the parties shall jointly submit a separate document entitled "Joint Set of Requested and Disputed Jury Instructions." These jury instructions should be annotated both with the proponent's authority for seeking the instruction and the opponent's reason for opposition. It shall be clearly identified which party is proposing each disputed instruction.

ii. **Substance and Format of Instructions.** The instructions shall cover all substantive issues and other points not covered by the Ninth Circuit Manual of Model Jury Instructions. All instructions submitted to the Court, whether stipulated or disputed, shall contain a table of contents. Each requested instruction shall be typed in full on a separate page with annotations or citations to the authorities upon which the instruction is based included below the instruction. Instructions shall be brief, clear, written in plain English and free of argument. Model Instructions shall be revised to address the particular facts and issues of this case. The parties shall give a brief explanation of its authorities and any revisions to Model Instructions.

iii. Routine Instructions. Absent objection, the Court will give Model Instructions 1.1B, 1.2, 1.3 and/or 1.4, 1.6–1.12, 1.14–1.15, 1.19, and 3.1–3.3 from the Manual of Model Civil Jury Instructions for the Ninth Circuit (2007 Edition). If any party seeks to alter the above-referenced Model Instructions, that party (or parties, if stipulated) shall provide the Court with a redline in Word reflecting the proposed changes to the Model Instructions. The parties should not file this document, but should send an electronic copy to ygrchambers@cand.uscourts.gov.

The Court will read Model Instructions 1.1B, 1.2, 1.3 and/or 1.4, 1.6–1.12, 1.14–1.15, 1.19 before opening statements. Model Instructions 3.1–3.3 shall be read immediately before the jury begins its deliberations.

g. **Preliminary Statement of the Case and Instructions.** The parties shall propose a joint statement of the case to be read to the jury. The parties may also propose additional preliminary instructions where appropriate.

h. **Voir Dire.**

i. The Court will conduct most of the voir dire and will provide additional time for attorney follow-up. Parties may file proposed additional questions for jury voir dire. If any party has advised the Court that it requests a juror questionnaire, the party shall submit a proposed form herewith. To determine whether prospective jurors know any of the parties, attorneys or potential trial witnesses, the parties shall provide the Court with one alphabetical list of all names for distribution to the prospective jurors.

ii. Generally, in civil cases, the jury commissioner will summon 20 to 25 prospective jurors. The Court will seat 8 jurors and no alternates.

i. **Proposed Verdict Forms.** The parties shall meet and confer and prepare a joint proposed Verdict Form with as few questions as possible. If an agreement cannot be reached, each may file their own proposed verdict form.

4. **MOTIONS *IN LIMINE*.**

a. Any party wishing to have motions *in limine* heard prior to the commencement of trial must exchange (but not file or serve) the same no later than twenty-eight (28) days prior to the date set for the Pretrial Conference. Each motion may not exceed more than four (4) pages. No more than fifteen (15) motions may be filed, and each motion shall be numbered. The parties shall then meet and confer and attempt to resolve the issues raised in the motions prior to the filing of the

Pretrial Statement.

b. Any motions not resolved shall be filed and served in conjunction with the Pretrial Conference Statement. Any party opposing such a motion *in limine* shall file and serve its opposition papers no later than nine (9) days prior to the Pretrial Conference. Each opposition shall reference the moving party's motion *in limine* number. Reply papers are not permitted.

c. The Chambers Copies shall be included in a separate binder entitled MOTIONS *IN LIMINE* and collated with the opposition papers following the motion papers. Said binder shall be delivered no later than **seven (7) days** prior to the Pretrial Conference.

d. One Proposed Order on Motions *in Limine* per side shall be provided briefly identifying the requested relief and the legal basis therefor. Said Order shall be formatted to allow the Court to rule whether the motion is granted, granted with modification, or denied.

5. **ELECTRONIC COPIES OF TRIAL DOCUMENTS.** Parties shall send an electronic copy in **Word** format to ygrchambers@cand.uscourts.gov of the following documents listed above: (i) Proposed Order Re Trial Stipulations, (ii) Proposed Order Re Discovery Excerpts, (iii) Joint Set of Jury Instructions, (iv) Joint Set of Requested and Disputed Jury Instructions, (v) redline of proposed changes to Model Instructions (if any), (vi) Proposed Juror Questionnaire (if any), (vii) Proposed Verdict Forms, and (viii) Proposed Order(s) on Motions *in Limine.*

6. **EXHIBITS.**

a. **Copies of Exhibits to Other Parties.** At least twenty-eight (28) days before the Pretrial Conference, the parties shall exchange with every other party one set of all proposed exhibits, charts, schedules, summaries, diagrams, and other similar documentary materials to be used in its case in chief at trial, together with a complete list of all such proposed exhibits. To the extent the parties agree, the parties may exchange the above-referenced documents by providing only a complete list of proposed exhibits through reference to bates labels or other identification. Any party may request that the exchange occur by hard copy documents. Voluminous or lengthy exhibits shall be reduced by the elimination of irrelevant portions and/or through the use of summaries. For particularly lengthy exhibits, the Court may inquire as to why a summary could not have been used as an exhibit. All exhibits which have not been exchanged as required are subject to exclusion.

b. **Stipulations re Admissibility.** The parties shall make a good faith effort to stipulate to exhibits' admissibility. If stipulation is not possible, the parties shall make every effort to stipulate to authenticity and foundation absent a legitimate (not tactical) objection. NO EXHIBIT may be shown to the jury until it is admitted, included during Opening Statements.

c. **Copies of Exhibits to Court.**

i. Three sets of exhibits shall be provided to the Court on the **Friday prior to the trial date**. Each set shall be in binders, marked, tabbed and indexed, and shall be **delivered/mailed directly to Chambers**. Parties are to comply with Local Rule 16-10(b)(7).

ii. Each exhibit shall be pre-marked with an exhibit tag placed in the top right corner of the first page of a document. Parties are to use a color other than white for the exhibit tags. A page of blank trial exhibit tags can be found on the Court's website.

iii. If an exhibit is a physical object (rather than a document), a picture should be taken and placed in the binder.

iv. Updated Exhibit Lists shall be included in the binders.

d. **Disposition of Exhibits after Trial.** Upon the conclusion of the trial, each party shall retain its exhibits through the appellate process. It is each party's responsibility to make arrangements with the Clerk of Court to file the record on appeal.

7. NON-JURY TRIALS. In non-jury cases, each party shall serve and lodge with the Court **fourteen (14) days** prior to the Pretrial Conference, proposed Findings of Fact and Conclusions of Law on all material issues. Proposed Findings shall be brief, written in plain English and free of pejorative language, conclusions and argument. In addition to the copy in the binder, parties shall send an electronic copy in Word format to ygrchambers@cand.uscourts.gov.

8. MISCELLANEOUS.

a. The Court takes a photograph of each witness prior to the witness' testimony to assist the trier of fact with recalling the testimony. Please advise your witnesses.

b. If a party wishes to use internet, electronic equipment, or other large items (such as bookshelves), the party must file a request and proposed order with the Court by the second Friday preceding the trial. Equipment not provided by the Court must be tested in the courtroom prior to the day when it will be used. Arrangements may be made with the Courtroom Deputy, Frances Stone, at (510) 637-3540 as to an appropriate time for doing so.

c. Please DO NOT call Chambers. If you need to contact the Courtroom Deputy, please call (510) 637-3540 and leave a message if the Deputy is not available.

IT IS SO ORDERED.

Dated: January 13, 2012

____

YVONNE GONZALEZ ROGERS
United States District Court Judge

APPENDIX

(SAMPLE EXHIBIT LIST)

Ex. No.	Description	Sponsoring Witness	Stipulation to Admit	Objection	Date Admitted

(SAMPLE LIST OF DISCOVERY EXCERPTS)

No.	Form of Excerpt	Designation in Dispute	Legal Objection

(SAMPLE PROPOSED ORDER RE DISCOVERY EXCERPTS)

No.	Form of Excerpt	Designation in Dispute	Court's Ruling

B. Standing Order in Civil Cases

STANDING ORDER IN CIVIL CASES
Judge Yvonne Gonzalez Rogers

1. **Conformity to Rules.** Parties are expected to consult and comply with all provisions of the Local Rules and the Federal Rules of Civil Procedure relating to motions, briefs, continuances, and all other matters, unless specifically superceded by this Standing Order. Any failure to comply with any of the rules and the Court's Standing Order may be deemed sufficient grounds for monetary sanctions, dismissal, entry of default judgment, or other appropriate sanctions.

2. **Scheduling days.** Prior to noticing a motion, parties shall check the scheduling information on this Court's website to confirm open and available dates. However, noticed days may be reset as the Court's calendar requires, with order of call to be determined by the Court. Generally, the Court will schedule as follows:

    a. Case Management Conferences are conducted on Mondays at 2:00 p.m.

    b. Civil Law and Motion calendar is conducted on Tuesdays at 2:00 p.m.

    c. Pretrial conferences are conducted on Fridays at 9:00 a.m. Trials are set to commence on Mondays at 8:30 a.m.

    d. Before appearing for a matter before this Court, all parties shall check the Court's calendar at www.cand.uscourts.gov or the posting in the Clerk's Office to confirm that their matter is still on calendar. Frequently, the Court will issue a written order and vacate the hearing unless oral argument appears to be necessary. Where argument is allowed, the Court will attempt to advise counsel in advance of the issues to be addressed. In addition, if a written request for oral argument is filed, before issuance of a ruling, stating that a lawyer of four or fewer years out of law school will conduct all or most of the oral argument, the Court will entertain oral argument on the principle that young lawyers need more opportunities for appearances than they typically receive.

3. **Changes to Court Calendar.** No changes to the Court's schedule shall be made except by signed order of the Court and only upon a showing of good cause. Parties seeking to continue hearings, request special status conferences, modify briefing schedules, or make any other procedural changes shall submit a signed stipulation and proposed order, or, if stipulation is not possible, a Motion for Administrative Relief, as contemplated by Civil Local Rule 7-11. Continuances will be granted only upon a showing of good cause, particularly focusing on evidence of diligence by the party seeking delay and of prejudice that may result if the continuance is denied. Briefing schedules may not be changed by stipulation. The parties must obtain leave of court. Parties seeking to enlarge a filing deadline by way of a Motion for Administrative Relief are admonished to file such a motion in advance of the filing deadline, rather than on the day a brief or other matter is due. ***Parties are advised that requests which, in effect, decrease the Court's time to consider a motion in advance of the hearing date are denied routinely.***

4. **Notice of Hearing Location/Construction.** Only four courtrooms currently exist

in the Oakland courthouse. An additional courtroom is currently under construction. Parties shall notice hearings for appearance at the Oakland courthouse. The exact courtroom location will be assigned the day of the hearing.

5. **Chambers Copies.** A chambers copy of all documents filed, whether electronically filed or manually filed at the Clerk's Office, shall be submitted to the Clerk's Office in an envelope clearly marked with the case number and "YGR Chambers Copy" for receipt no later than 12 noon the second business day after the document is filed. Submission by overnight delivery such as Federal Express or UPS is sufficient.

   a. **All chambers' copies must be 3-hole punched** in the left margin in a manner suitable for placement in a 3-ring binder.

   b. Chambers copies must include tabs between exhibits and must fasten or attach pages of individual documents together so as to distinguish between separate documents. Please do not use bottom tabs as they do not work well in binders.

   c. In addition to the above, the Chambers Copy of **the initial complaint or pleading must be submitted in a 3" 3-ring binder (black) with the copy of the initial complaint or pleading behind tab 1, and an additional 10 tabs in consecutive order thereafter**. The binder shall include a label on the spine in the following format and placed so that it can be read horizontally:

      Case No.
Short Title
Chambers Copy

      This requirement applies to cases reassigned to Judge Gonzalez Rogers, including cases reassigned as a result of declination to proceed before a magistrate judge.

      This requirement does not apply to habeas corpus petitions and Social Security cases.

   d. Chambers copies submitted without meeting the above requirements may be rejected, and the party may be required to re-submit. Failure to comply may also result in monetary or other appropriate sanctions.

6. **Case Management Conference.** Joint case management statements are required and must be filed fourteen days in advance of the case management conference date. In cases involving pro se litigants, the parties may file separate case management statements. The format shall follow the Standing Order for All Judges of the Northern District of California re: Contents of Joint Case Management Statement ("CAND CMC Order") found on the Court's website at http://cand.uscourts.gov/ygr.

   These conferences are intended to be substantive and productive. Accordingly, each party shall be represented at the Case Management Conference by counsel with authority to enter into stipulations and make admissions pursuant to this and Fed. R. Civ. P. 16(a) and (c), as well as fully prepared to address all of the matters referred to the CAND CMC Order and Civil L.R. 16-10(b). Failure to do so shall be considered grounds for sanctions.

7. **Proposed Orders Required.** Each party filing or opposing any motion shall also

serve a proposed order that sets forth the relief or action sought and a short statement of the rationale of decision, including citation of authority that the party requests the Court to adopt, and citations to the record evidence where applicable. The proposed order should be submitted at the same time as the motion or opposition with a courtesy copy emailed to ygrpo@cand.uscourts.gov.

8. **Discovery and Discovery Motions.**
   a. Except as specifically set forth below, no motions regarding discovery disputes may be filed without prior leave of Court. If a dispute arises during a deposition and involves a persistent obstruction of the deposition or a refusal to answer a material question on the basis of any ground other than privilege or the work product doctrine, counsel may arrange a telephonic conference with the Court through contact with the Courtroom Deputy, Frances Stone, at (510) 637-3540. Any such conference shall be attended by the court reporter recording the deposition.

   b. All other requests for discovery relief must be summarized jointly by the parties in a *joint* letter brief no longer than four pages. The joint letter brief must attest that, prior to filing the request for relief, counsel met and conferred *in person* and must concisely summarize those remaining issues that counsel were unable to resolve. The joint letter brief may cite to limited and specific legal authority only for resolution of dispositive issues. The joint letter brief may not be accompanied by declarations; however any specific excerpt of disputed discovery material may be attached. The Court will then advise the parties if additional briefing, a telephonic conference, or a personal appearance will be necessary.

      Note: Discovery letter briefs must be e-filed under the Civil Events category of Motions and Related Filings >Motions - General > "Discovery Letter Brief."

   c. This provision applies only to cases in which discovery is supervised by this Court rather than the magistrate judge. The Court, at its discretion, may elect to transfer discovery matters to a magistrate judge or a special master.

9. **Motions for Summary Judgment.**
   a. **Pre-filing Conference Required:** Except as specifically set forth below, no motion for summary judgment pursuant to Rule 56 of the Rules of Civil Procedure may be filed without prior leave of Court. The moving party must submit a letter to Chambers, with a copy to opposing counsel, to request a pre-motion conference and propose a date and time for such conference. Pre-hearing conferences are normally set for Wednesday or Friday afternoons at 2:00 p.m. unless circumstances and the Court's calendar require otherwise, and should be requested sufficiently in advance of the deadlines established in the Court's initial case management order. Telephonic appearances will not be allowed.

      The moving party's letter shall be submitted at least seven (7) business days prior to the proposed conference date and must explain the grounds for the motion. The letter shall be no more than three single-spaced pages in length, including any attached exhibits or other supporting papers. Within three (3) business days after receipt of the letter, any adversary wishing to oppose the motion must submit a written response to the moving party and a copy to Chambers. This response shall also be limited to three single-spaced pages including any attached exhibits or supporting papers.

This pre-filing requirement does not apply to *either side* in *pro se* cases. This pre-filing requirement does not apply to habeas corpus petitions and motions in Social Security cases.

b. **One Motion Per Side:** All issues shall be contained within one motion, may not exceed twenty-five pages in length, and shall conform to Civil Local Rule 7-2. Only one summary judgment motion may be filed by each side, absent leave of court. Leave of court may be sought if multiple parties comprise one or both sides. This issue will be addressed at the Pre-filing Conference.

c. **Separate Statements:** Parties moving for summary judgment must include a separate, short and concise statement of the material facts as to which the moving party contends there is no genuine issue to be tried. The statement must present, in a two-column format, each asserted fact in an individually numbered paragraph. In the first column, the party shall state the fact asserted and in the second corresponding column, the party shall cite to the documentary support for that assertion by document (e.g., deposition, affidavit, discovery response, etc.), specifying the page and line numbers therein. Upon filing, the moving party shall provide the separate statement to all other parties in an electronic, word processing format for ease of response thereto.

The papers opposing a motion for summary judgment shall provide a responsive separate statement which: (1) incorporates the facts in the moving separate statement and (2) provides a response to each of the facts in the correspondingly numbered paragraph in the moving separate statement. The response shall indicate as to each fact whether the party contends the fact is "disputed" or "undisputed," and shall cite the evidentiary basis for any disputed fact. The statement may include, if necessary, additional paragraphs containing a separate, short, and concise statement of any additional material facts as to which it is contended that there exists a genuine issue to be tried.

Each numbered paragraph in the moving separate statement of material facts will be deemed to be admitted for purposes of the motion unless specifically controverted by a correspondingly numbered paragraph in the responsive separate statement.

Unless a party has obtained prior permission from this Court, opening separate statements are limited to no more than fifteen (15) pages, and opposing separate statements are limited to no more than five (5) additional pages beyond the number of pages in the opening statement.

The moving and responsive separate statements must be signed by counsel (or a party, if proceeding in pro per) as follows: *"I attest that the evidence cited herein fairly and accurately supports [or disputes] the facts as asserted."*

d. **Cross-Motions:** Any cross-motion for summary judgment shall be contained within the opposition to any motion for summary judgment, shall contain twenty-five (25) pages or less, and shall be filed fourteen (14) days after the filing of the motion. The reply to a motion may contain up to fifteen (15) pages, shall include the opposition to any cross-motion, and shall be filed seven (7) days after the filing of the opposition. (See Civil Local Rule 7-3). The Court may, *sua sponte* or pursuant to a motion under Civil L.R. 6-3, reschedule the hearing so as to give a moving party time to file a reply to any cross-motion.

10. **Communication with Court.** Counsel shall not attempt to make contact by telephone, facsimile, or any other *ex parte* means with the Court or its chambers staff, but may contact the Courtroom Deputy, Frances Stone, at (510) 637-3540 with appropriate inquiries. Counsel should list their facsimile transmission numbers as well as their telephone numbers on their papers to facilitate communication with the Courtroom Deputy. All counsel listed on the parties' briefing must be fully apprised of the status of the pending matter and must be authorized to respond to calendar settings by the Court.

11. **Removed Cases.** The removing defendant shall, within five (5) days of filing of the notice of removal, submit to Chambers a copy of all pleadings filed in the state court, three-hole punched in the manner required above for all other Chambers Copies, and placed in a binder and labeled on the spine as set forth in Paragraph 5(c) above.

12. **Service of Standing Orders.** Plaintiff (or in the case of removed cases, any removing defendant) is directed to serve copies of this Standing Order in Civil Cases and the CAND CMC Order at once upon all parties to their action, and upon those subsequently joined, in accordance with the provisions of Federal Rules of Civil Procedure, Rules 4 and 5, and to file with the Clerk of the Court a certificate reflecting such service, in accordance with Civil Local Rule 5-6(a).

IT IS SO ORDERED.

Dated: March 16, 2012

____

YVONNE GONZALEZ ROGERS
United States District Judge

C. *Standing Order for Certain Employment Cases*

STANDING ORDER FOR CERTAIN EMPLOYMENT CASES
Judge Yvonne Gonzalez Rogers

This Court is participating in a Pilot Program for **INITIAL DISCOVERY PROTOCOLS FOR EMPLOYMENT CASES ALLEGING ADVERSE ACTION**, initiated by the Advisory Committee on Federal Rules of Civil Procedure.

The Initial Discovery Protocols will apply to all employment cases pending in this court that challenge one or more actions alleged to be adverse, except:

i. Class actions; or

ii. Cases in which the allegations involve only the following:

1. Discrimination in hiring;
2. Harassment/hostile work environment;
3. Violations of wage and hour laws under the Fair Labor Standards Act (FLSA);
4. Failure to provide reasonable accommodations under the Americans with Disabilities Act (ADA);
5. Violations of the Family Medical Leave Act (FMLA);
6. Violations of the Employee Retirement Income Security Act (ERISA).

Parties and counsel in the Pilot Program shall comply with the Initial Discovery Protocols set forth below. If any party believes that there is good cause why a particular case should be exempted from the Initial Discovery Protocols, in whole or in part, that party may raise the issue with the Court.

Within 30 days following the defendant's submission of a responsive pleading or motion, the parties shall provide to one another the documents and information described in the Initial Discovery Protocols for the relevant time period. This obligation supersedes the parties' obligations to provide initial disclosures pursuant to Federal Rules of Civil Procedure ("F.R.C.P.") 26(a)(1). The parties shall use the documents and information exchanged in accordance with the Initial Discovery Protocols to prepare the F.R.C.P. 26(f) discovery plan.

The parties' responses to the Initial Discovery Protocols shall comply with the F.R.C.P. obligations to certify and supplement discovery responses, as well as the form of production standards for documents and electronically stored information. As set forth in the Protocols, this Initial Discovery is not subject to objections, except upon the grounds set forth in F.R.C.P. 26(b)(2)(B).

The Initial Discovery Protocols are not intended to preclude or to modify the rights of any party for discovery as provided by the F.R.C.P. and other applicable local rules, but they are intended to supersede the parties' obligations to make initial disclosures pursuant to F.R.C.P. 26(a)(1). The purpose of these protocols is to encourage parties and their counsel to exchange the most relevant information and documents early in the case, to assist in framing the issues to be resolved and to plan for more efficient and targeted discovery.

The Initial Discovery Protocols were prepared by a group of highly experienced attorneys from across the country who regularly represent plaintiffs and/or defendants in employment matters. The information and documents identified are those most likely to be requested automatically by experienced counsel in any similar case. They are unlike initial disclosures pursuant to F.R.C.P. 26(a)(1) because they focus on the type of information most likely to be useful in narrowing the issues for employment discrimination cases.

Definitions. The following definitions apply to cases proceeding under the Initial Discovery Protocols.

- **a.** ***Concerning.*** The term "concerning" means referring to, describing, evidencing, or constituting.
- **b.** ***Document.*** The terms "document" and "documents" are defined to be synonymous in meaning and equal in scope to the terms "documents" and "electronically stored information" as used in F.R.C.P. 34(a).
- **c.** ***Identify (Documents).*** When referring to documents, to "identify" means to give, to the extent known: (i) the type of document; (ii) the general subject matter of the document; (iii) the date of the document; (iv) the author(s), according to the document; and (v) the person(s) to whom, according to the document, the document (or a copy) was to have been sent; or, alternatively, to produce the document.
- **d.** ***Identify (Persons).*** When referring to natural persons, to "identify" means to give the person's: (i) full name; (ii) present or last known address and telephone number; (iii) present or last known place of employment; (iv) present or last known job title; and (v) relationship, if any, to the plaintiff or defendant. Once a person has been identified in accordance with this subparagraph, only the name of that person need be listed in response to subsequent discovery requesting the identification of that person.

Instructions.

- **a.** For this Initial Discovery, the relevant time period begins three years before the date of the adverse action, unless otherwise specified.
- **b.** This Initial Discovery is not subject to objections except upon the grounds set forth in F.R.C.P. 26(b)(2)(B).
- **c.** If a partial or incomplete answer or production is provided, the responding party shall state the reason that the answer or production is partial or incomplete.
- **d.** This Initial Discovery is subject to F.R.C.P. 26(e) regarding supplementation and F.R.C.P. 26(g) regarding certification of responses.
- **e.** This Initial Discovery is subject to F.R.C.P. 34(b)(2)(E) regarding form of production.

PART 2: PRODUCTION BY PLAINTIFF

(1) Timing.

- **a.** The plaintiff's Initial Discovery shall be provided within 30 days after the defendant has submitted a responsive pleading or motion, unless the court rules otherwise.

(2) Documents that Plaintiff must produce to Defendant.

- **a.** All communications concerning the factual allegations or claims at issue in this lawsuit between the plaintiff and the defendant.

b. Claims, lawsuits, administrative charges, and complaints by the plaintiff that rely upon any of the same factual allegations or claims as those at issue in this lawsuit.

c. Documents concerning the formation and termination, if any, of the employment relationship at issue in this lawsuit, irrespective of the relevant time period.

d. Documents concerning the terms and conditions of the employment relationship at issue in this lawsuit.

e. Diary, journal, and calendar entries maintained by the plaintiff concerning the factual allegations or claims at issue in this lawsuit.

f. The plaintiff's current resume(s).

g. Documents in the possession of the plaintiff concerning claims for unemployment benefits, unless production is prohibited by applicable law.

h. Documents concerning: (i) communications with potential employers; (ii) job search efforts; and (iii) offer(s) of employment, job description(s), and income and benefits of subsequent employment. The defendant shall not contact or subpoena a prospective or current employer to discover information about the plaintiff's claims without first providing the plaintiff 30 days' notice and an opportunity to file a motion for a protective order or a motion to quash such subpoena. If such a motion is filed, contact will not be initiated or the subpoena will not be served until the motion is ruled upon.

i. Documents concerning the termination of any subsequent employment.

j. Any other document(s) upon which the plaintiff relies to support the plaintiff's claims.

(3) Information that Plaintiff must produce to Defendant.

a. Identify persons the plaintiff believes to have knowledge of the facts concerning the claims or defenses at issue in this lawsuit, and a brief description of that knowledge.

b. Describe the categories of damages the plaintiff claims.

c. State whether the plaintiff has applied for disability benefits and/or social security disability benefits after the adverse action, whether any application has been granted, and the nature of the award, if any. Identify any document concerning any such application.

PART 3: PRODUCTION BY DEFENDANT

(1) Timing.

a. The defendant's Initial Discovery shall be provided within 30 days after the defendant has submitted a responsive pleading or motion, unless the court rules otherwise.

(2) Documents that Defendant must produce to Plaintiff.

a. All communications concerning the factual allegations or claims at issue in this lawsuit among or between:

   i. The plaintiff and the defendant;
   ii. The plaintiff's manager(s), and/or supervisor(s), and/or the defendant's human resources representative(s).

b. Responses to claims, lawsuits, administrative charges, and complaints by the plaintiff that rely upon any of the same factual allegations or claims as those at issue in this lawsuit.

c. Documents concerning the formation and termination, if any, of the employment relationship at issue in this lawsuit, irrespective of the relevant time period.

d. The plaintiff's personnel file, in any form, maintained by the defendant, including files concerning the plaintiff maintained by the plaintiff's supervisor(s), manager(s), or the defendant's human resources representative(s), irrespective of the relevant time period.

e. The plaintiff's performance evaluations and formal discipline.

f. Documents relied upon to make the employment decision(s) at issue in this lawsuit.

g. Workplace policies or guidelines relevant to the adverse action in effect at the time of the adverse action. Depending upon the case, those may include policies or guidelines that address:
   i. Discipline;
   ii. Termination of employment;
   iii. Promotion;
   iv. Discrimination;
   v. Performance reviews or evaluations;
   vi. Misconduct;
   vii. Retaliation; and
   viii. Nature of the employment relationship.

h. The table of contents and index of any employee handbook, code of conduct, or policies and procedures manual in effect at the time of the adverse action.

i. Job description(s) for the position(s) that the plaintiff held.

j. Documents showing the plaintiff's compensation and benefits. Those normally include retirement plan benefits, fringe benefits, employee benefit summary plan descriptions, and summaries of compensation.

k. Agreements between the plaintiff and the defendant to waive jury trial rights or to arbitrate disputes.

l. Documents concerning investigation(s) of any complaint(s) about the plaintiff or made by the plaintiff, if relevant to the plaintiff's factual allegations or claims at issue in this lawsuit and not otherwise privileged.

m. Documents in the possession of the defendant and/or the defendant's agent(s) concerning claims for unemployment benefits unless production is prohibited by applicable law.

n. Any other document(s) upon which the defendant relies to support the defenses, affirmative defenses, and counterclaims, including any other document(s) describing the reasons for the adverse action.

(3) Information that Defendant must produce to Plaintiff.

a. Identify the plaintiff's supervisor(s) and/or manager(s).

b. Identify person(s) presently known to the defendant who were involved in making the decision to take the adverse action.

c. Identify persons the defendant believes to have knowledge of the facts concerning the claims or defenses at issue in this lawsuit, and a brief description of that knowledge.

d. State whether the plaintiff has applied for disability benefits and/or social security disability benefits after the adverse action. State whether the defendant has provided information to any third party concerning the application(s). Identify any documents concerning any such application or any such information provided to a third party.

APPENDIX

The Initial Discovery Protocols for Employment Cases Alleging Adverse Action are designed to achieve the goal of more efficient and targeted discovery. If a protective order will be entered in a case to which the Initial Discovery Protocols applies, immediate entry of the order will allow the parties to commence discovery without delay. In furtherance of that goal, the Employment Protocols Committee offers the following Model Protective Order. Recognizing that the decision to enter a protective order, as well as the parameters of any such order, rests within the Court's sound discretion and is subject to local practice, the following provisions are options from which the Court might select.

MODEL PROTECTIVE ORDER

It is hereby ordered by the Court that the following restrictions and procedures shall apply to certain information, documents and excerpts from documents supplied by the parties to each other in response to discovery requests:

1. Counsel for any party may designate any document, information contained in a document, information revealed in an interrogatory response or information revealed during a deposition as confidential if counsel determines, in good faith, that such designation is necessary to protect the interests of the client. Information and documents designated by a party as confidential will be stamped "CONFIDENTIAL." "Confidential" information or documents may be referred to collectively as "confidential information."

2. Unless ordered by the Court, or otherwise provided for herein, the Confidential Information disclosed will be held and used by the person receiving such information solely for use in connection with the above-captioned action.

3. In the event a party challenges another party's confidential designation, counsel shall make a good faith effort to resolve the dispute, and in the absence of a resolution, the challenging party may thereafter seek resolution by the Court. Nothing in this Protective Order constitutes an admission by any party that Confidential Information disclosed in this case is relevant or admissible. Each party specifically reserves the right to object to the use or admissibility of all Confidential Information disclosed, in accordance with applicable law and Court rules.

4. Information or documents designated as "confidential" shall not be disclosed to any person, except:
   a. The requesting party and counsel, including in-house counsel;
   b. Employees of such counsel assigned to and necessary to assist in the litigation;
   c. Consultants or experts assisting in the prosecution or defense of the matter, to the extent deemed necessary by counsel;
   d. Any person from whom testimony is taken or is to be taken in these actions, except that such a person may only be shown that Confidential Information during and in preparation for his/her testimony and may not retain the Confidential Information; and
   e. The Court (including any clerk, stenographer, or other person having access to any Confidential Information by virtue of his or her position with the Court) or the jury at trial or as exhibits to motions.
5. Prior to disclosing or displaying the Confidential Information to any person, counsel shall:
   a. inform the person of the confidential nature of the information or documents; and
   b. inform the person that this Court has enjoined the use of the information or documents by him/her for any purpose other than this litigation and has enjoined the disclosure of that information or documents to any other person.
6. The Confidential Information may be displayed to and discussed with the persons identified in Paragraphs 4(c) and (d) only on the condition that prior to any such display or discussion, each such person shall be asked to sign an agreement to be bound by this Order in the form attached hereto as Exhibit A. In the event such person refuses to sign an agreement in the form attached as Exhibit A, the party desiring to disclose the Confidential Information may seek appropriate relief from the Court.
7. The disclosure of a document or information without designating it as "confidential" shall not constitute a waiver of the right to designate such document or information as Confidential Information provided that the material is designated pursuant to the procedures set forth herein no later than that latter of fourteen (14) days after the close of discovery or fourteen (14) days after the document or information's production. If so designated, the document or information shall thenceforth be treated as Confidential Information subject to

all the terms of this Stipulation and Order.

8. All information subject to confidential treatment in accordance with the terms of this Stipulation and Order that is filed with the Court, and any pleadings, motions or other papers filed with the Court disclosing any Confidential Information, shall be filed under seal to the extent permitted by law (including without limitation any applicable rules of court) and kept under seal until further order of the Court. To the extent the Court requires any further act by the parties as a precondition to the filing of documents under seal (beyond the submission of this Stipulation and Order Regarding Confidential Information), it shall be the obligation of the producing party of the documents to be filed with the Court to satisfy any such precondition. Where possible, only confidential portions of filings with the Court shall be filed under seal.

9. At the conclusion of litigation, the Confidential Information and any copies thereof shall be promptly (and in no event later than thirty (30) days after entry of final judgment no longer subject to further appeal) returned to the producing party or certified as destroyed, except that the parties' counsel shall be permitted to retain their working files on the condition that those files will remain confidential.

The foregoing is entirely without prejudice to the right of any party to apply to the Court for any further Protective Order relating to confidential information; or to object to the production of documents or information; or to apply to the Court for an order compelling production of documents or information; or for modification of this Order. This Order may be enforced by either party and any violation may result in the imposition of sanctions by the Court.

Dated: February 27, 2012

____
YVONNE GONZALEZ ROGERS
United States District Court Judge

EXHIBIT A

I have been informed by counsel that certain documents or information to be disclosed to me in connection with the matter entitled have been designated as confidential. I have been informed that any such documents or information labeled "CONFIDENTIAL – PRODUCED PURSUANT TO PROTECTIVE ORDER" are confidential by Order of the Court.

I hereby agree that I will not disclose any information contained in such documents to any other person. I further agree not to use any such information for any purpose other than this litigation.

DATED: ________________ ______________________________

Signed in the Presence of: ____________________
(counsel of record)

D. Standing Order for Patent Cases

STANDING ORDER FOR PATENT CASES
Judge Yvonne Gonzalez Rogers

Joint Claim Construction Statement

1. The initial joint claim construction statement required by Patent Local Rule 4-3 shall be truly joint. Disputed terms, phrases, and clauses shall be designated as disputed. All other terms shall be presumed undisputed. For any term in dispute, the parties must agree on the identity of the term. With regard to disputed terms, phrases, or clauses, the joint statement shall list each disputed term, phrase, or clause (listed by claim); each party's proposed construction; and support for each party's proposed construction side by side. A model construction statement is attached to this Order.

2. Parties shall attach to the joint claim construction statement copies of all patents in dispute. Parties shall also make a complete prosecution history for each patent available to the Court upon request.

Claim Construction

3. As an initial matter, the Court will construe no more than ten terms. If more than ten terms are at issue, the parties shall meet and confer before the preparation of the joint claim construction statement on narrowing the selection of terms to be construed by the Court and shall jointly propose the ten terms requiring construction.

4. If a party genuinely believes that it will require that more than ten terms be construed, that party may request leave to designate additional terms for construction, pursuant to Civil Local Rule 7-11(b). The requesting party must demonstrate good cause and explain why other methods of limiting the claims at issue (such as the selection of representative claims or any grouping of claims by issues presented) would be ineffective. The request must be filed no later than two weeks before the deadline for filing the joint claim construction statement. If good cause is shown, the Court will either agree to construe all terms or schedule a second claim construction proceeding on the excess terms. If more than ten terms are submitted for construction without leave of court, the Court will construe the first ten terms listed in the joint claim construction statement and sanctions may be imposed.

5. Claim construction briefs shall address each disputed term, but only those that are truly disputed, following the order of the joint statement. The opening and opposition briefs shall not exceed 25 pages; the reply brief shall not exceed 15 pages. The Court anticipates that a meaningful meet and confer between the parties preceding the preparation of the joint claim construction statement will obviate the need for a party to propose in its briefs a claim construction that differs from that proposed in the statement. While the Court encourages the parties to negotiate mutually agreeable constructions, the Court discourages the parties from proposing new constructions for the first time in reply briefs or other filings which do not afford the opposing party an opportunity to respond. However, if it becomes necessary for a party to propose a different construction in its brief than that found in the joint claim construction statement, that party must clearly set forth the new construction and

explain the basis for the change. Additionally, that party shall revise the joint claim construction statement, so that the Court will have one document reflecting all current proposed constructions.

6. At the time of filing the reply briefs, the parties shall file an amended, final joint claim construction statement, including only the remaining disputed terms, phrases, and clauses.

Tutorial and Claim Construction Hearing

7. The Court will schedule a tutorial to occur one to three weeks prior to the claim construction hearing. Each side will be permitted 45-60 minutes to present a short summary and explanation of the technology at issue. The patent holder makes the first presentation. Visual aids are encouraged. The Court prefers that someone other than counsel make the presentation. Counsel will be permitted to make opening remarks and then a brief summation following the presentation. No argument will be permitted. The proceeding is not recorded and parties may not rely on statements made at the tutorial in other aspects of the litigation. The Court, however, encourages the parties to make a joint presentation and will entertain requests for additional time in those circumstances.

8. Prehearing conferences generally are not held. However, either party may request a telephone conference within two weeks prior to the hearing, or the parties may address any prehearing issues at the tutorial.

9. The patent holder will act as the moving party for the purposes of claim construction. Opening briefs in support of claim construction must be filed at least six weeks before the date of the claim construction hearing, and the briefing schedule set forth at Patent Local Rule 4-5 will apply.

10. The Court will not ordinarily hear extrinsic evidence at the claim construction hearing. Should it become apparent that testimony will be necessary, counsel may request a telephone conference with the Court within two weeks of the hearing to seek the Court's approval.

11. Demonstrative exhibits and visual aids are permissible at the hearing as long as they are based on information contained in the papers already filed. Counsel shall exchange copies of exhibits no later than forty-eight hours prior to the hearing.

12. The claim construction hearing generally will be scheduled for no longer than three (3) hours on either Wednesday or Friday afternoon.

Subsequent Case Management Conference

13. Upon issuance of the claim construction ruling, the Court will also set a date for a further joint case management conference. In a joint case management statement to be filed fourteen (14) days prior to the conference, the parties must address the following topics:

- **a)** whether either party wishes to certify the claim construction ruling for immediate appeal to the Federal Circuit;
- **b)** the filing of dispositive motions, and timing of those motions;

c) if willful infringement has been asserted, whether the allegedly-infringing party wishes to rely on the advice of counsel defense. If so, the parties should be prepared to address proposals for resolving any attorney-client privilege issues that arise, and whether the parties believe bifurcation of the trial into liability and damages phases would be appropriate;

d) anticipated post-claim construction discovery;

e) any other pretrial matters; and

f) the progress of settlement discussions, if any.

The Court will review the reports and, if necessary, schedule a further case management conference and enter any appropriate orders.

Miscellaneous

14. All stipulated protective orders and filings shall comply with Civil Local Rule 79-5. Parties shall also submit a complete unredacted chambers copy of any brief or supporting papers lodged under seal with all confidential material highlighted.

IT IS SO ORDERED.

Dated: 1/13/2012

____

YVONNE GONZALEZ ROGERS
United States District Judge

Sample Claim Construction Chart

Claim Language (Disputed Terms in **Bold**) 'xxx Patent	Plaintiff's Proposed Construction and Evidence in Support	Defendant's Proposed Construction and Evidence in Support
1. A method for counting **ducks**, comprising the steps of: [or] **ducks** Found in claim numbers: 'xxx Patent: y, z 'yyy Patent: a, b	**duck** PROPOSED CONSTRUCTION: a bird that quacks. DICTIONARY/TREATISE DEFINITIONS: Webster's Dictionary ("duck: bird that quacks"); Field Guide ("bird call: quack"); INTRINSIC EVIDENCE: 'xxx Patent col. _:_ ("distinctive honking"); Prosecution History at __ ("This patent is distinguished from the prior art in that the quacking of the bird is featured"). EXTRINSIC EVIDENCE: McDonald Depo. at xx:xx ("I'd say the quacking makes it a duck"); '123 Patent at col _:__; Donald Decl. at ¶ __ .	**duck** PROPOSED CONSTRUCTION: a bird that swims DICTIONARY/TREATISE DEFINITIONS: Random House Dictionary ("an aquatic bird"); Field Guide (same) INTRINSIC EVIDENCE: 'xxx Patent col _:__ ("ducks may be found on or near bodies of water"); Prosecution History at __ ("water fowl are particularly amenable to being counted by this method"). EXTRINSIC EVIDENCE: G. Marx Depo at xx:xx ("like a duck to water"); '456 Patent at col _:__; Daffy Decl. at ¶ __.

(Or any other substantively similar format that permits the court to compare terms side by side)

NOT:

Claim Language (Disputed Terms in **Bold**) 'xxx Patent	Plaintiff's Proposed Construction and Evidence in Support	Defendant's Proposed Construction and Evidence in Support
1. A method for counting **ducks** . . .	**duck**	**counting duck**

Hon. Richard G. Seeborg

District Judge

Chambers Information

U.S. District Court, Northern District of California
Courtroom 3, 17th Floor
450 Golden Gate Avenue
San Francisco, CA 94102

Scheduling Information

Courtroom Deputy: (415) 522-2123

Civil Law and Motion	Thursdays at 1:30 p.m.
Criminal Law and Motion	Tuesdays at 2:30 p.m.
Pretrial Conferences	Thursdays at 10:00 a.m.
Case Management Conferences	Thursdays at 10:00 a.m.

Judge's Biography

Born 1956 in Landstuhl, Germany

Federal Judicial Service:

-Judge, U. S. District Court, Northern District of California
-Nominated by Barack Obama on August 6, 2009, to a seat vacated by Maxine M. Chesney; Confirmed by the Senate on December 24, 2009, and received commission on January 4, 2010.
-U.S. Magistrate Judge, U.S. District Court for the Northern District of California, 2001-2009

Education:

-Yale College, B.A., 1978
-Columbia University School of Law, J.D., 1981

Professional Career:

-Law Clerk to Hon. John H. Pratt, U.S. District Court for the District of Columbia, 1981-1982
-Private Practice of law, San Francisco, Calif., 1982-1991
-Assistant U.S. Attorney, Northern District of California, 1991-1998
-Private Practice, Palo Alto, Calif., 1998-2001

I. Judge Seeborg's Procedures and Practices

A. Guidelines for Final Pretrial Conference in Bench Trials

GUIDELINES FOR FINAL PRETRIAL CONFERENCE IN BENCH TRIALS BEFORE DISTRICT JUDGE RICHARD SEEBORG

A. Meeting and Disclosure Prior to Pretrial Conference: At least 21 days before the final Pretrial Conference, lead counsel who will try the case shall meet and confer with respect to:

1. Settlement of the case;

2. Preparation and content of the Joint Pretrial Statement and Order; and

3. Preparation and exchange of pretrial materials to be served and lodged pursuant to Rule 26(a)(3) F.R. Civ. P.; and

4. Clarifying and narrowing the contested issues for trial in order to achieve a just, speedy and efficient determination of the case.

B. Joint Pretrial Statement and Order: At least ten (10) days before the Pretrial Conference, unless otherwise ordered, the parties shall lodge and serve a Joint Pretrial Statement and Proposed Order containing the following information:

1. Substance of the Action. A brief description of the parties, the substance of claims and defenses that remain to be decided, and the operative pleadings that raise the issues;

2. Relief Prayed. A detailed statement of all relief claimed, particularly itemizing all elements of damages claimed;

3. Undisputed Facts. A plain and concise statement of all relevant facts to which the parties will stipulate for incorporation into the trial record without the necessity of supporting testimony or exhibits. The parties shall exercise good faith in stipulating to facts that are not reasonably disputable;

4. Disputed Factual Issues. A plain and concise list of the issues of fact that are contested and remain to be litigated at trial;

5. Agreed Statement. A statement assessing whether all or part of the action may be presented upon an agreed statement of facts;

6. Stipulations. A statement of proposed stipulations or agreements that will expedite the presentation of evidence;

7. Witnesses to be Called. A list of all witnesses likely to be called at trial, other than solely for impeachment or rebuttal, together with a brief statement following each name describing the substance of the testimony to be given. No party shall be permitted to call any witness in its case in chief who is not disclosed in its pretrial statement without leave of court for good cause;

8. Exhibits, Schedules and Summaries. A list of all documents and other items to be offered as exhibits at the trial, other than solely for impeachment or rebuttal, with a brief statement following each, describing its substance or purpose and the identity of the sponsoring witness;

9. Disputed Legal Issues. Without extended legal argument, a concise statement of each disputed point of law concerning liability or relief, citing supporting statutes and decisions;

10. Pending Motions or Matters. A statement of any motions or matters that must be resolved prior to trial;

11. Bifurcation, Separate Trial of Issues. A statement of whether bifurcation or a separate trial of specific issues is feasible and desired;

12. Estimate of Trial Time. An estimate of the number of hours or days needed for the trial; and,

13. Miscellaneous. Any other matters that will facilitate the just, speedy and efficient determination of the action.

C. Binding Effect of the Joint Pretrial Statement and Order: The Joint Pretrial Statement and Order described above shall recite, directly above the signature lines of each party, the following:

> *The foregoing admissions having been made by the parties, and the parties having specified the foregoing issues of fact and law remaining to be litigated, this order shall supplement the pleadings and govern the course of trial of this cause, unless modified to prevent manifest injustice.*

D. Preparation For Trial

1. Exhibits

a) At least (10) days before the final Pretrial Conference, the parties shall exchange copies of all exhibits, summaries, charts, and diagrams to be used at trial other than solely for impeachment or rebuttal.

b) Each exhibit shall be premarked for identification. Counsel shall meet and confer and reach agreement upon a method for marking exhibits (for example, Plaintiff shall use numbers and Defendant shall use letters, or Plaintiff shall use numbers 100-199 and Defendant shall use numbers 200-299, etc.).

c) Unless otherwise ordered, at least five (5) days prior to the commencement of trial the parties shall deliver three sets of all premarked exhibits contained in three ring binders to the judge's deputy clerk.

d) No party shall be permitted to offer any exhibit at trial that is not disclosed in its pretrial statement without leave of court for good cause, unless it is offered solely for impeachment or rebuttal.

2. Motions in Limine: Ordinarily, motions in limine are unnecessary in a bench trial. However, any party believing motions in limine to be necessary shall file and serve any such motions at least ten (10) days before the final Pretrial Conference. Any oppositions thereto shall be filed and served at least three (3) days before the final

Pretrial Conference. Unless otherwise ordered, these motions will be deemed submitted without oral argument.

3. Deposition and Discovery Designations: Unless otherwise ordered, at least five (5) days before the commencement of trial, the parties shall file and serve any excerpts of deposition testimony or other discovery to be offered at trial, other than solely for impeachment or rebuttal. (A copy of the designated deposition testimony with page and line references, or the interrogatory response or admission shall be provided). Any objections to the use of designated excerpts and any counter-designations of deposition testimony shall be filed and served prior to the commencement of trial.

4. Proposed Findings of Fact and Conclusions of Law: At least five (5) days prior to the pretrial conference, each party shall file and serve proposed findings of fact and conclusions of law. The findings of fact shall set forth in simple declarative sentences, separately numbered, all factual contentions relied upon by the party in support of its claims for relief or defenses and shall be free of pejorative language and argument. Conclusions of law shall be supported by appropriate citation to legal authority. The proposed findings of fact and conclusions of law shall be submitted in hard copy as well as in word processing format via email to RSpo@cand.uscourts.gov.

5. Trial Briefs: Trial briefs are optional, but any party wishing to file a trial brief must do so not less than five (5) days prior to the commencement of trial.

DATED: June 1, 2010

RICHARD SEEBORG
United States District Judge

B. Guidelines for Final Pretrial Conference in Jury Cases

GUIDELINES FOR FINAL PRETRIAL CONFERENCE IN JURY CASES BEFORE DISTRICT JUDGE RICHARD SEEBORG

A. Meeting and Disclosure Prior to Pretrial Conference: At least 21 days before the final Pretrial Conference, lead counsel who will try the case shall meet and confer with respect to:

1. Settlement of the case; :

2. Preparation of the Joint Pretrial Statement; and

3. Preparation and exchange of pretrial materials to be served and lodged pursuant to Rule 26(a)(3) F.R. Civ. P.; and

4. Clarifying and narrowing the contested issues for trial in order to achieve a just, speedy and efficient determination of the case.

B. Joint Pretrial Statement and Order: At least ten (10) days before the Pretrial Conference, unless otherwise ordered, the parties shall lodge and serve a Joint Pretrial Statement and Proposed Order containing the following information:

1. Substance of the Action. A brief description of the parties, the substance of claims and defenses that remain to be decided, and the operative pleadings that raise the issues;

2. Relief Prayed. A detailed statement of all relief claimed, particularly itemizing all elements of damages claimed;

3. Undisputed Facts. A plain and concise statement of all relevant facts to which the parties will stipulate for incorporation into the trial record without the necessity of supporting testimony or exhibits. The parties shall exercise good faith in stipulating to facts that are not reasonably disputable;

4. Disputed Factual Issues. A plain and concise list of the issues of fact that are contested and remain to be litigated at trial;

5. Agreed Statement. A statement assessing whether all or part of the action may be presented upon an agreed statement of facts;

6. Stipulations. A statement of proposed stipulations or agreements that will expedite the presentation of evidence;

7. Witnesses to be Called. A list of all witnesses likely to be called at trial, other than solely for impeachment or rebuttal, together with a brief statement following each name describing the substance of the testimony to be given. No party shall be permitted to call any witness in its case in chief who is not disclosed in its pretrial statement without leave of court for good cause;

8. Exhibits, Schedules and Summaries. A list of all documents and other items to be offered as exhibits at the trial, other than solely for impeachment or rebuttal, with a brief statement following each, describing its substance or purpose and the identity of the sponsoring witness;

9. Disputed Legal Issues. Without extended legal argument, a concise statement of each disputed point of law concerning liability or relief, citing supporting statutes and decisions;

10. Pending Motions or Matters. A statement of any motions or matters that must be resolved prior to trial;

11. Bifurcation, Separate Trial of Issues. A statement of whether bifurcation or a separate trial of specific issues is feasible and desired;

12. Estimate of Trial Time. An estimate of the number of hours or days needed for the trial; and,

13. Miscellaneous. Any other matters that will facilitate the just, speedy and efficient determination of the action.

C. Binding Effect of the Joint Pretrial Statement and Order: The Joint Pretrial Statement and Order described above shall recite, directly above the signature lines of each party, the following:

> *The foregoing admissions having been made by the parties, and the parties having specified the foregoing issues of fact and law remaining to be litigated, this order shall supplement the pleadings and govern the course of trial of this cause, unless modified to prevent manifest injustice.*

D. Preparation For Trial:

1. Exhibits

   a) At least (10) days before the final Pretrial Conference, the parties shall exchange copies of all exhibits, summaries, charts, and diagrams to be used at trial other than solely for impeachment or rebuttal.

   b) Each exhibit shall be pre-marked for identification. Counsel shall meet and confer and reach agreement upon a method for marking exhibits (for example, Plaintiff shall use numbers and Defendant shall use letters, or Plaintiff shall use numbers 100-199 and Defendant shall use numbers 200-299, etc.).

   c) Unless otherwise ordered, at least five (5) days prior to the commencement of trial the parties shall deliver three sets of all pre-marked exhibits contained in three ring binders to the judge's deputy clerk.

   d) No party shall be permitted to offer any exhibit at trial that is not disclosed in its pretrial statement without leave of court for good cause, unless it is offered solely for impeachment or rebuttal.

2. Motions in Limine: Unless otherwise ordered, the parties shall file and serve any motions in limine at least ten (10) days before the final Pretrial Conference, and any oppositions thereto at least three (3) days before the final Pretrial Conference. Ordinarily, these motions will be deemed submitted without oral argument.

3. Deposition and Discovery Designations: Unless otherwise ordered, at least five (5) days before the commencement of trial, the parties shall file and serve any excerpts of deposition testimony or other discovery to be offered at trial, other than solely for impeachment or rebuttal. (A copy of the designated deposition testimony with page and line references, or the interrogatory response or admission shall be provided). Any objections to the use of designated excerpts and any counter-designations of deposition testimony shall be filed and served prior to the commencement of trial.

4. Jury Materials:

a) Unless otherwise ordered, at least five (5) days prior to the pretrial conference, the parties shall file and serve: :

(1) Jury Voir Dire Questions;
(2) Proposed Jury Instructions; and
(3) Proposed Jury Verdict Forms.

b) Ordinarily, the court will give the standard preliminary jury instructions contained in the Model Jury Instructions of the Ninth Circuit prior to opening statements and will give the standard closing instructions in the Model Jury Instructions of the Ninth Circuit before closing arguments.

c) As to substantive case specific instructions, the parties shall meet and confer and submit jointly an agreed set of instructions, using the Model Jury Instructions of the Ninth Circuit where appropriate. In the event the parties are unable to agree to the language of a particular instruction, the objecting party shall submit a written objection or an alternative proposed instruction placed in sequence immediately following the disputed instruction. The joint set of jury instructions shall be submitted in hard copy as well as in word processing format via email to RSpo@cand.uscourts.gov.

5. Trial Briefs: Trial briefs are optional, but any party wishing to file a trial brief must do so not less than five (5) days prior to the commencement of trial.

DATED: June 1, 2010

____
RICHARD SEEBORG
United States District Judge

C. *Standing Order Regarding Initial Case Management*

STANDING ORDER RE: INITIAL CASE MANAGEMENT

1. The civil law and motion calendar is heard on Thursdays at 1:30 p.m. in Courtroom 3, 17th Floor, United States Courthouse, 450 Golden Gate Avenue, San Francisco, California. Motions may be noticed for hearing pursuant to Civil L.R. 7. Counsel need not reserve a hearing date in advance for civil motions. However, noticed dates may be reset as the Court's calendar requires.

2. Civil Case Management Conferences and Civil Pretrial Conferences will be held on Thursdays at 10 a.m. in Courtroom 3, 17th Floor, United States Courthouse, 450 Golden Gate Avenue, San Francisco, California.

3. All scheduling questions should be addressed to Judge Seeborg's courtroom deputy at 415/522-2123.

4. A Case Management Conference will be held on the date and time specified in the Order Setting Initial Case Management Conference and ADR Deadlines. This conference may be continued only by Court Order pursuant to Civil L.R. 16-2(e). Parties may not stipulate to continue a case management conference without Court approval. Parties or counsel may appear personally or file a request to appear by telephone. If any party files such a request, all parties shall appear telephonically and must contact Court Conference at 866/582-6878 at least one week prior to the Conference.

5. Pursuant to Fed. R. Civ. P. 26(f), and Civil L.R. 16-3, no later than 21 days before the Case Management Conference, each party shall confer to consider and discuss: (1) the nature and basis of their claims and defenses; (2) possibilities for a prompt settlement or resolution of the case; (3) exchanging the initial disclosures required by Fed.R.Civ.P. 26(a)(1); (4) developing a proposed discovery plan with suitable limits; and (5) preparation of a joint case management statement.

6. The parties shall also consider the selection of an ADR (Alternate Dispute Resolution) process. *See* "Dispute Resolution Procedures in the Northern District of California Booklet," available on the Court's website at http://www.cand.uscourts.gov. Pursuant to Civil L.R. 16-8(b) and ADR L.R. 3-5, no later than the date specified in the Order Setting Initial Case Management Conference and ADR Deadlines, each party shall file and serve an ADR Certificate.

7. Pursuant to Civil L.R. 16-9, no later than seven (7) days before the Case Management Conference, the parties shall file a Joint Case Management Statement and Proposed Order. If preparation of a joint statement would cause undue hardship, the parties may serve and file separate statements, which shall include a description of the undue hardship. The Statement should not exceed ten pages in length and should address the following items in the following order:

   a. Date case was filed;

b. List or description of all parties;
c. Summary of all claims, counter-claims, cross-claims, third party claims;
d. Brief description of the event underlying the action;
e. Description of relief sought and damages claimed with an explanation as to how damages are computed;
f. Status of discovery (including any proposed limits or cutoff dates);
g. Procedural history of the case including any previous motions decided and/or submitted, ADR proceedings or settlement conferences scheduled or concluded, appellate proceedings pending or concluded, and any previous referral to a magistrate judge;
h. Other deadlines in place (in the event of reassignment), including those for dispositive motions, pretrial conferences, and trials;
i. If no deadlines are in place, a proposed schedule that includes pretrial and trial dates, a deadline by which dispositive motions shall be heard, and any discovery cutoff dates;
j. Whether the parties will consent to a magistrate judge for trial.

8. Plaintiff or removing Defendant shall serve a copy of this Standing Order on all parties to this action and on all parties subsequently joined, in accordance with Fed.R.Civ.P. 4 and 5. Following service, Plaintiff or removing Defendant shall file a certificate of service, in accordance with Civil L.R. 5-6.

IT IS SO ORDERED.

Dated: February 7, 2011

RICHARD SEEBORG
United States District Judge

Hon. James Ware

Chief District Judge

Chambers Information

U.S. District Court, Northern District of California
Courtroom 9, 19th Floor
450 Golden Gate Avenue
San Francisco, California 94102

Scheduling Information

Courtroom Deputy: (415) 522-2036

Civil Law and Motion	Mondays at 9:00 a.m.
Criminal Law and Motion	Mondays at 1:30 p.m.
Case Management Conferences	Mondays at 10:00 a.m.
Final Pretrial Conferences	Two weeks prior, on Mondays at 11:00 a.m.
Trial/Jury Selection	Tuesdays at 9:00 a.m.

Judge's Biography

Born 1946 in Birmingham, AL

Federal Judicial Service:

-Judge, U. S. District Court, Northern District of California
-Nominated by George H.W. Bush on August 3, 1990, to a seat vacated by Robert F. Peckham; Confirmed by the Senate on September 28, 1990, and received commission on October 1, 1990.

Education:

-California Lutheran University, B.A., 1969
-Stanford Law School, J.D., 1972

Professional Career:

-U.S. Army Reserve Second Lieutenant, 1972
-U.S. Army, Military Police, 1973
-U.S. Army Reserve Captain, Military Police, 1973-1986
-Private Practice, Palo Alto, California, 1972-1988
-Judge, Santa Clara County Superior Court, 1988-1990

I. Judge Ware's Procedures and Practices

A. *Standing Order Regarding Case Management in Civil Cases*

**STANDING ORDER REGARDING
CASE MANAGEMENT IN CIVIL CASES**

This order sets forth requirements for initial case management in all civil matters assigned to United States District Chief Judge James Ware. All papers filed must include the case number of the action followed by the initials of the assigned district judge or magistrate judge and, if applicable, the initials of the magistrate judge to whom the action is referred for discovery or other pretrial activity.

Plaintiff shall serve a copy of this Standing Order on all parties to this action and on all parties subsequently joined, in accordance with Fed.R.Civ.P. 4 and 5. Following service, plaintiff shall file a certificate of service in accordance with Civil L.R. 5-6(a).

Before selecting a hearing date for a motion before any of the judges of the San Francisco Division, counsel must confer with opposing counsel to determine that the proposed hearing date will not cause undue prejudice.

Civil motions under Civil L.R. 7-2 in cases assigned to Judge Ware may be noticed for hearing on any Monday at 9:00 a.m. However, counsel must review Judge Ware's on-line calendar to check for availability since it is Judge Ware's practice to close out dates due to high volume of motions.

Pursuant to Fed.R.Civ.P. 16 and 26 and Civil L.R. 16-10(a), a Case Management Conference will be held on Mondays at 10:00am, at the United States Courthouse, 450 Golden Gate Ave., San Francisco, California. This conference may be continued only by court order pursuant to Civil L.R. 16-2(e). Parties may not stipulate to continue a Case Management Conference without court approval.

Pursuant to Civil L.R. 16-3, in advance of the Case Management Conference, counsel shall confer with their respective clients and opposing counsel for the purposes specified in Fed.R.Civ.P. 26(f), Civil L.R. 16-8 and 16-9, and in patent cases, Patent L.R. 3-1 through 3-6. A meaningful meet and confer process prior to the Case Management Conference and good faith compliance with the requirements of this Order are essential elements of effective case management. Failure to meet and confer, to be prepared for the Case Management Conference or to file a Joint Case Management Conference Statement may result in sanctions.

In all "E-filing" cases when filing papers in connection with any motion for determination by a judge, the parties shall, in addition to filing papers electronically, lodge with chambers a printed copy of the papers by the close of the next court day following the day the papers are filed electronically. These printed copies shall be marked "Chambers Copy" and shall be submitted to the Clerk's Office, in an envelope clearly marked with the Judge's name, case number and "E-filing Chambers Copy." Parties shall not file a paper copy of any document with the Clerk's Office that has already been filed electronically.

IT IS SO ORDERED.

Dated: April 28, 2011

JAMES WARE
United States Chief District Judge

Hon. Jeffrey S. White

District Judge

Chambers Information

U.S. District Court, Northern District of California
Courtroom 11, 19th Floor
450 Golden Gate Avenue
San Francisco, CA 94102

Scheduling Information

Courtroom Deputy: (415) 522-4173

Civil Law and Motion	Fridays at 9:00 a.m.
Criminal Law and Motion	Thursdays at 2:00 p.m.
Case Management Conferences	Fridays at 1:30 p.m.
Pretrial Conferences	Mondays at 2:00 p.m.

Judge's Biography

Born 1945 in New York, NY

Federal Judicial Service:

-Judge, U. S. District Court, Northern District of California
-Nominated by George W. Bush on July 25, 2002, to a seat vacated by Charles E. Legge; Confirmed by the Senate on November 14, 2002, and received commission on November 15, 2002.

Education:

-Queens College of City University of New York, B.A., 1967
-State University of New York, J.D., 1970

Professional Career:

-Attorney, Criminal Division, U.S. Department of Justice, 1970-1971
-Assistant U.S. Attorney, District of Maryland, 1971-1977
-Attorney, Criminal Division, U.S. Department of Justice, 1977-1978
-Private Practice, San Francisco, California, 1978-2002

I. Judge White's Procedures and Practices

A. *Civil Standing Order*

CIVIL STANDING ORDER

1. **Conformity to Rules.** Counsel are expected to consult and comply with all provisions of the Local Rules and the Federal Rules of Civil Procedure relating to motions, briefs, continuances, and all other matters, unless specifically superceded by these Standing Orders. Any failure to comply with any of the rules and orders may be deemed sufficient grounds for monetary sanctions, dismissal, entry of default judgment, or other appropriate sanctions.

2. **Scheduling days.** Prior to noticing a motion, counsel shall check the scheduling information on this Court's website to confirm open and available dates. However, noticed days may be reset as the Court's calendar requires, with order of call to be determined by the Court. Motions shall be noticed in accordance with the following times:

a. Civil Law and Motion calendar is conducted on Fridays at 9:00 a.m.

b. Case Management Conferences are conducted on Fridays at 1:30 p.m.

c. Pretrial conferences are conducted on Mondays at 2:00 p.m. Trials are set to commence on Mondays at 8:30 a.m.

d. By 4:00 p.m. on the first court date preceding any hearing, parties participating in the e-filing program shall check the e-filing system to determine whether there has been a tentative ruling issued in their matter (or a ruling with respect to requests for specific issues to be addressed during oral argument).

e. Before appearing for a matter before this Court, all parties shall check the Court's calendar at www.cand.uscourts.gov or the posting in the Clerk's Office to confirm that their matter is still on calendar.

3. **Changes to Court Calendar.** No changes to the Court's schedule shall be made except by signed order of the Court and only upon a showing of good cause. Parties seeking to continue hearings, request special status conferences, modify briefing schedules, or make any other procedural changes shall submit a signed stipulation and proposed order, or, if stipulation is not possible, a Motion for Administrative Relief, as contemplated by Civil Local Rule 7-11. Continuances will be granted only upon a showing of good cause, particularly focusing on evidence of diligence by the party seeking delay and of prejudice that may result if the continuance is denied.

Briefing schedules may not be changed by stipulation; the parties must obtain leave of court. Parties seeking to enlarge a filing deadline by way of a Motion for Administrative Relief are admonished to such a motion in advance of the filing deadline, rather than on the day a brief or other matter is due.

4. **Chambers Copy.** A copy of all documents filed both electronically and manually with the Clerk's Office shall be submitted to the Clerk's Office in an envelope clearly marked with the case number and "JSW Chambers Copy" no later than noon on the next business day after the document is filed.

5. **Case Management Conference Statements.** Joint case management statements are required and must be filed five court days in advance of the case management conference date. Counsel shall conform to all elements requested in the initial case management scheduling order, and particularly with respect to the Court's requirements regarding a discovery plan. In cases involving *pro se* litigants, the parties may file separate case management statements.

6. **Motions.** All briefs, whether in support of, in opposition to, or in reply to any motion, with the exception of summary judgment motions and claims construction briefs, may not exceed fifteen pages in length, exclusive of title pages, indices of cases, table of contents, exhibits, and summaries of argument, if required. All declarations shall be filed as separate documents. Briefs exceeding ten pages in length must contain an additional one-page summary of argument, including reference to any important cases cited.

7. **Discovery and Discovery Motions.** Except as specifically set forth below, no motions regarding discovery disputes may be filed without prior leave of Court.

If a dispute arises during a deposition and involves a persistent obstruction of the deposition or a refusal to answer a material question on the basis of any ground other than privilege or the work product doctrine, counsel may arrange a telephonic conference with the Court through contact with Chambers at (415) 522-4160. Any such conference shall be attended by the court reporter recording the deposition.

All other requests for discovery relief must be summarized jointly by the parties in a joint letter brief no longer than four pages. The joint letter brief must attest that, prior to filing the request for relief, counsel met and conferred in person and must concisely summarize those remaining issues that counsel were unable to resolve. The joint letter brief may cite to limited and specific legal authority only for resolution of dispositive issues. The joint letter brief may not be accompanied by declarations; however any specific excerpt of disputed discovery material may be attached. The Court will then advise the parties if additional briefing or a telephonic conference will be necessary.

This provision applies only to cases in which discovery is supervised by this Court rather than the magistrate judge. The Court, at its discretion, may elect to transfer discovery matters to a magistrate judge or a special master.

8. **Motions for Summary Judgment.** All issues shall be contained within one motion, may not exceed twenty-five pages in length, and shall conform with Civil Local Rule 7-2. Absent of a showing of good cause, the Court will address only one motion for summary judgment per party or side. Separate statements of undisputed facts will not be considered by the Court. Joint statements of undisputed facts are not required, but are helpful if completely agreed upon.

9. **Proposed Orders Required.** Each party filing or opposing a motion shall also serve a proposed order that sets forth the relief or action sought and a short statement of the rationale of decision, including citation of authority, that the party requests the Court to adopt. The proposed order should be filed at the same time as the motion or opposition.

10. **Communication with Court.** Counsel shall not attempt to make contact by

telephone, facsimile, or any other *ex parte* means with the Court or its chambers staff, but may contact the Courtroom Deputy Clerk, Jennifer Ottolini, at (415) 522-4173 with appropriate inquiries. Counsel should list their facsimile transmission numbers as well as their telephone numbers on their papers to facilitate communication with the Courtroom Deputy. All counsel listed on the parties' briefing must be fully apprised of the status of the pending matter and must be authorized to respond to calendar settings by the Court.

11. Grounds for Recusal. Parties are directed to inform the Court of any and all reasonable bases for recusal at the earliest possible date, and no later than the initial case management conference. *See also* Standing Order on Recusal.

12. Service of Standing Orders. Plaintiff (or in the case of removed cases, any removing defendant) is directed to serve copies of these standing orders at once upon all parties to their action, and upon those subsequently joined, in accordance with the provisions of Federal Rules of Civil Procedure, Rules 4 and 5, and to file with the Clerk of the Court a certificate reflecting such service, in accordance with Civil Local Rule 5-6(a).

IT IS SO ORDERED.

____

JEFFREY S. WHITE
United States District Judge

B. Criminal Standing Order

CRIMINAL STANDING ORDER

1. **Conformity to Rules.** Counsel are expected to consult and comply with all provisions of the Local Rules and the Federal Rules of Criminal Procedure relating to disclosure and discovery, motions, continuances, and all other matters, unless specifically superceded by these Standing Orders.

2. **Scheduling.** The criminal law and motion calendar is conducted on Thursdays at 2:30 p.m. Pretrial Conferences are conducted on Mondays at 2:00 p.m. Trials are set to commence on Mondays at 8:30 a.m.

If either party wishes to have a matter placed on the Court's calendar and if the defendant is in custody, counsel must contact the Courtroom Deputy Clerk, Jennifer Ottolini, at (415) 522-4173, by 10:00 a.m., the day before the defendant is to be transported to the Court by the United States Marshal.

3. **Chambers Copy.** A copy of all documents, document, filed manually or electronically or lodged with the Clerk's Office shall be submitted to the Clerk's Office in an envelope clearly marked with the case name and number, and "JSW Chambers Copy" at the time of filing, or for e-filing cases by no later than noon on the next business day after the document is filed.

4. **Change of Plea.** If the plea is being entered pursuant to a plea agreement, counsel for the government shall deliver a copy of the Plea Agreement to chambers on the 17th Floor by 2:30 p.m., the day before the plea is to be entered. If the plea is not pursuant to a plea agreement or if the specifics of the agreement are not yet finalized, counsel for the defendant shall notify the courtroom deputy of the entry of an open plea by 2:30 p.m., the day before the plea is to be entered. An application for Entry of Plea (available at www.cand.uscourts.gov) is required only for open pleas.

5. **Discovery:** The procedures for disclosure and discovery set forth in the Local Criminal Rules, in particular Criminal Local Rule 16-1, and the Federal Rules of Criminal Procedure will be strictly enforced.

6. **Sentencing Memoranda and Motions for or Relating to Sentencing:**

Motions for or relating to sentencing (*e.g.*, under *Blakely v. Washington*, 542 U.S. 296 (2004), or *United States v. Ameline*, 376 F.3d 967 (9th Cir. 2004)) shall be filed at least seven (7) calendar days before the date on which Judgment and Sentencing is scheduled. Responses or objections to motions relating to sentencing shall be filed at least five (5) calendar days before the date on which Judgment and Sentencing is scheduled.

Although the parties are not required to file a Sentencing Memorandum, except as set forth in Criminal Local Rule 32-5(b), the Court encourages the parties to submit a Sentencing Memorandum. If a party chooses to submit a Sentencing Memorandum to the Court, it must be filed at least seven (7) calendar days before the date on which Judgment and Sentencing is scheduled. Responses to Sentencing Memoranda shall be filed at least five (5) calendar days before the date on which Judgment and Sentencing is scheduled.

IT IS SO ORDERED.

____
JEFFREY S. WHITE
United States District Judge

C. *Guidelines for Trial and Final Pretrial Conference in Civil Bench Cases*

GUIDELINES FOR TRIAL AND FINAL PRETRIAL CONFERENCE IN CIVIL BENCH CASES BEFORE THE HONORABLE JEFFREY S. WHITE

FINAL PRETRIAL CONFERENCE AND REQUIRED FILINGS

1. Counsel shall not prepare a joint pretrial conference statement. Instead, please follow the following procedures:

In lieu of preparing a joint pretrial conference statement, the parties shall meet and confer in person and prepare a jointly signed proposed final pretrial order to be filed fourteen (14) calendar days in advance of the final pretrial conference. This joint pretrial conference order should contain: (i) a brief description of the substance of claims and defenses which remain to be decided; (ii) a statement of all relief sought; (iii) all stipulated facts; (iv) a list of all factual issues that remain to be tried, stating the issues with the same generality/specificity as any contested elements in the relevant jury instructions and organized by counts; (v) a joint exhibit list in numerical order, including a brief description of the exhibit and Bates numbers, a blank column for when it will be offered into evidence, a blank column for when it may be received into evidence, and a blank column for any limitations on its use; and (vi) each party's separate witness list for its case-in-chief witnesses (including those appearing by deposition) providing, for all such witnesses other than an individual plaintiff and an individual defendant, a short statement of the substance of his/her testimony and, separately, what, if any, non-cumulative testimony the witness will offer. If non-cumulative testimony is not spelled out, the Court will presume the witness is cumulative. For each witness, state an hour/minute time estimate for both direct and cross examination. The Court uses this information to estimate the time limits to be allocated for trial. Items (v) and (vi) should be appendices to the proposed order. The objective is to convert the proposed order to a final order with the benefit of any discussion at the final pretrial conference.

2. In addition to the joint pretrial order, fourteen (14) days in advance of the final pretrial conference, the parties also shall file the following materials:

(a) In addition to the joint pretrial conference statement, fourteen (14) calendar days in advance of the final pretrial conference, each side shall file their: (i) proposed findings of fact and conclusions of law. The parties shall be prepared to meet and confer at the end of each day of trial in an effort to prepare stipulated findings of fact and conclusions of law and to update the previously submitted proposed findings of fact and conclusions to reflect the proceedings at trial.

(b) A trial brief not to exceed ten pages on any controlling issues of law.

(c) Excerpts of any deposition designations that are to be used in a parties' case in chief as to which there are objections. The parties should include with these excerpts the basis for the objection and the response thereto. If the parties do not have objections to deposition designations, they should follow the procedures set forth in paragraph 25.

(d) Excerpts of responses to interrogatories and requests for admissions that are to be used in a party's case-in-chief as to which there are objections. The parties should include with these excerpts the basis for the objection and the response thereto. If the parties do not have objections to responses to interrogatories or requests for admissions, they should follow the procedures set forth in paragraph 26.

(e) A list of objections to each exhibit, in tabular form. The first column should describe the exhibit, the second column should set briefly set forth the basis of the objection, and the third column should set forth a brief response thereto. The parties shall meet and confer, in person, in an attempt to resolve objections to the exhibits before this list is filed with the Court, to consider exhibit numbers, and to eliminate duplicate exhibits and confusion over the precise exhibit. Unless there is a genuine issue as to the authenticity of exhibits, a party that has produced documents should not object to the other party offering those documents as exhibits on the basis of authenticity or the best evidence rule. Finally, the Court normally will not entertain routine objections to exhibits on the basis of a lack of foundation.

(f) Any motions *in limine*, as to which the parties should follow the following procedure:

The motions *in limine* and all oppositions thereto must be filed no later than fourteen (14) calendar days prior to the Final Pretrial Conference, and shall be submitted to the Court collated and in a binder, as set forth below. Therefore, the parties must serve their motions *in limine* on the opposing party reasonably in advance of the pretrial to permit the opposing party to prepare and serve its opposition.[1] The Court does not permit reply briefs. Each motion should be presented in a separate memo and properly identified, for example, "Plaintiff's Motion *in Limine* No. 1 to Exclude . . . ."

Please limit motions *in limine* to circumstances that really need a ruling in advance. No more than five motions per side will be allowed. If a party seeks to file more than five motions *in limine*, they must file an administrative motion at least fourteen days before the motions *in limine* are due to be filed with the Court demonstrating extraordinarily good cause for allowing the excess motions. The administrative motion should summarize the subject matter of each proposed additional motion *in limine*.

Each motion *in limine* should address a single, separate topic, and contain no more than seven pages of briefing per side. Leave of Court will be required to exceed the page limitations. A binder containing all motions *in limine* should be submitted to the Clerk's office in an envelope clearly marked with the case number and "JSW chambers copy."

3. The proposed findings of fact and conclusions of law, the joint proposed final pretrial order, and objections to exhibits required by paragraph 2(e) of this Order, shall be submitted in WordPerfect 10.0 format on a CD-ROM, as well as in hard copies. All hard-copy submissions should be submitted in a binder to the Clerk's office in an envelope clearly marked with the case number and "JSW chambers copies."

4. At the final pretrial conference, the above submissions shall be considered and argued.

---

[1] The Court suggests, but does not require, that at least thirty (30) calendar days before the Final Pretrial Conference, the moving party serve, but not file, the opening brief and at least twenty (20) calendar days before the Final Pretrial Conference, the responding party serve the opposition.

PRETRIAL ARRANGEMENTS

5. Should a daily transcript and/or real-time reporting be desired, the parties shall make arrangements with the Supervisor of the Court Reporting Services, at (415) 522-2079, at least ten calendar days prior to the trial date.

6. During trial, counsel may wish to use overhead projectors, laser-disk/computer graphics, poster blow-ups, models or specimens of devices. The United States Marshal requires a court order to allow equipment into the courthouse.

If monitor screens are used, there should be a single large screen (not multiple small screens) viewable by the Court, the witness and most counsel. It should be large and bright enough to be seen when placed on the opposite side of the courtroom. If counsel cannot conveniently see the screen, counsel may have a small monitor at counsel table. If both overhead projector and video equipment are to be used, a single projection screen is best, thus requiring a projection-type video rather than a monitor. If video equipment is used, equipment capable of instantly accessing the relevant portions of transcripts and graphics should be used (rather than, for example, raw video tapes made at depositions which take time to forward or to rewind). Equipment should be shared by all counsel to the maximum extent possible. The Court provides no equipment other than an easel. For electronic equipment, parties should be prepared to maintain the equipment or have a technician handy at all times. For overhead projectors, the parties shall provide a spare bulb. The parties shall tape extension cords to the carpet for safety. The parties shall disassemble and store all equipment in the courtroom at the end of each court day. The parties may work with the deputy clerk, Jennifer Ottolini (415-522-4173), on all courtroom-layout issues.

SCHEDULING

7. Trial normally will be conducted from 8:00 a.m. to 1:30 p.m. (or slightly longer to finish a witness) with two fifteen-minute breaks, Monday through Thursday, excluding holidays. Counsel must arrive by 7:30 a.m., or earlier as needed for any matters to be heard before the evidence begins. This schedule may be modified at the discretion of the Court.

GENERAL DECORUM

8. A trial is a rational and civilized inquiry to seek a just result. Counsel are expected to conduct themselves with dignity and decorum at all times. Disruptive tactics or appeals to prejudice are not acceptable.

9. Colloquy between counsel on the record is not permitted – all remarks are to be addressed to the Court.

10. Vigorous advocacy does not preclude courtesy to opposing counsel and witnesses and respect for the Court. Addressing witnesses or parties by first names or the Court by "Judge" or "Sir" on the record is not appropriate.

11. Counsel shall not engage in activity at counsel table or move about the courtroom while opposing counsel is arguing or questioning witnesses, or in other ways cause distraction. Neither counsel nor client should indicate approval, disapproval or otherwise react to any testimony or argument.

OPENING STATEMENTS

12. If openings are permitted, each side will have a predetermined time limit for its opening statement. Counsel should meet and confer to exchange any visuals, graphics or exhibits to be used in the opening statements, allowing for time to work out objections and any reasonable revisions.

WITNESSES

13. At the close of each trial day, all counsel shall exchange a list of witnesses for the next two full court days and the exhibits that will be used during direct examination (other than for impeachment of an adverse witness). Within 24 hours of such notice, all other counsel shall provide any objections to such exhibits and shall provide a list of all exhibits to be used with the same witness on cross-examination (other than for impeachment). The first notice shall be exchanged prior to the first day of trial. All such notice should be provided in writing.

14. The parties shall have all upcoming witnesses on the same day available in the courthouse and ready to testify. Failure to have the next witness ready or to be prepared to proceed with the evidence will usually be deemed to constitute resting. If counsel plans to read in a transcript of a deposition, counsel must have a deposition prepared and vetted early on to read into the record.

15. A witness or exhibit not listed in the joint pretrial order may not be used without good cause. This rule does not apply to true rebuttal witnesses (other than rebuttal experts who must be listed). Defense witnesses are considered case-in-chief witnesses, not "rebuttal" witnesses.

16. When there are multiple parties, counsel are responsible for coordination of the cross-examination to avoid duplication. If there are multiple parties on a side, counsel for only one party may cover a subject matter; reiteration of the examination, whether direct or cross, will not be permitted.

17. Counsel shall stand at or near the podium to ask questions, straying only to point out material on charts or overheads. Counsel should request permission from the Court to approach the witness or the bench.

18. Counsel shall treat witnesses with courtesy and respect, and not become familiar (*e.g.*, avoiding the use of first or nick-names).

19. Counsel shall pose brief, direct and simply stated questions, covering one point at a time. Leading questions may be used for background or routine matters.

20. Cross-examination similarly should consist of brief, simple questions. Cross-examination should not be a restatement of the direct examination and should not be used for discovery.

21. In lieu of direct testimony, the Court will consider receiving "prepared direct" testimony in the form of declarations. When the witness is presented, the proponent must verbally summarize the direct. Live cross-examination and redirect shall then occur.

EXPERTS

22. At trial, direct testimony of experts will be limited to the matters disclosed in their reports. Omitted material may not ordinarily be added on direct examination. Illustrative animations, diagrams, charts and models may be used on direct examination only if they were part of the expert report, with the exception of simple drawings and tabulations that plainly illustrate the content of the report, which can be drawn by the witness at trial or otherwise shown to the Court. If cross-examination fairly opens the door, however, an expert may go beyond the written report on cross-examination and/or re-direct examination. By written stipulation, all parties may relax these requirements. The Court will not permit Federal Rule of Evidence 703 to be used to admit otherwise inadmissible evidence through the expert (*i.e.*, through the "back door"). At its discretion, the Court may require the parties' expert witnesses to testify immediately following one another

23. As to damages studies, the cut-off date for *past damages* will be as of the expert report (or such earlier date as the expert may select). In addition, the experts may try to project *future damages* (*i.e.*, after the cut-off date) if the substantive standards for future damages can be met. With timely leave of Court or by written stipulation, the experts may update their reports (with supplemental reports) to a date closer to the time of trial.

USE OF DEPOSITION DESIGNATIONS AND USE OF DEPOSITIONS FOR IMPEACHMENT OR SHORT READ-INS

24. Depositions can be used at trial to impeach a witness testifying at trial or, in the case of a party deponent, "for any purpose." For depositions to be used for impeachment purposes, the parties shall abide by the following procedure:

(a) On the first day of trial, counsel shall bring the original and clean copies of any deposition(s) intended to be used during the course of the trial. Any corrections must be readily available. If counsel need to use the deposition during a witness examination, they shall provide the Court with a copy and with any corrections at the outset of the examination. This will minimize delay between the original question and the read-ins of the impeaching material. Opposing counsel should have their copy immediately available.

(b) When counsel reads a passage into the record, counsel should seek permission from the Court. For example, counsel should state: "I wish to read in page 210, lines 1 to 10 from the witness' deposition." A brief pause will be allowed for any objection.

(c) The first time a deposition is read, counsel shall state the deponent's name, the date of the deposition, the name of the lawyer asking the question, and if it was a Federal Rule of Civil Procedure 30(b)(6) deposition. The first time a deposition is read, the Court will give an appropriate explanation to the jury about depositions. Do not embellish the deposition testimony with follow-on questions.

(d) When reading in the passage, counsel shall state "question" and then read the question exactly, followed by,"answer" and then read the answer exactly. Stating "question" and "answer" is necessary so the jury and the court reporter can follow who was talking at the deposition. Once the passage is on the record, move on. Opposing counsel may then immediately ask to read such additional testimony as is necessary to complete the context.

(e) To avoid mischaracterizing the record, counsel should not ask, "Didn't you say XYZ in your deposition?" It is unnecessary to ask a witness if he "recalls" the testimony or otherwise to lay a foundation.

(f) Subject to Federal Rule of Evidence 403, party depositions may be read into the record whether or not they contradict (and regardless of who the witness is on the stand). For example, a short party deposition excerpt may be used as foundation for questions for a different witness on the stand.

25. The following procedure applies to the manner in which deposition designations shall be presented. The parties shall have met in conferred sufficiently in advance of trial to ensure that they will be able to submit their objections to the Court at the pretrial conference, see Paragraph 2(c) of this Order. In addition, the parties must have met and conferred regarding counter-designations, and shall submit any objections to counter-designations in accordance with Paragraph 2(c) of this Order. It does not apply to live witnesses whose depositions are read into the record while they are on the stand.

(a) To prepare designated deposition testimony, counsel shall photocopy the cover page, the page where the witness is sworn, and then each page containing any testimony to be proffered, with lines through portions of such pages not proffered. In addition, counsel shall line through objections or colloquy unless they are needed to understand the question. Any corrections must be interlineated and references to exhibit numbers must conform to the trial numbers. Such interlineations should be done by hand. The finished packet should then be the actual script and should smoothly present the identification and swearing of the witness and testimony desired.

(b) When the packet is read into the record, the examiner shall read the questions (and any relevant colloquy) from the lectern while a colleague sits in the witness stand and reads the answers. While reading the deposition the reader and "witness" shall refrain from undue emoting, emphasis or other dramatization. The same procedure shall be followed when a video-taped deposition is to be played instead, in order to facilitate rulings on objections.

The video should omit any dead time, long pauses, and objections/colloquy not necessary to understand the answers.

REQUESTS FOR ADMISSIONS AND INTERROGATORIES

26. Please prepare responses to requests for admissions and interrogatory answers in the same manner for presentation in the same manner as deposition designations.

EXHIBITS

27. Use numbers only, not letters, for exhibits, preferably the same numbers as were used in depositions. Blocks of numbers should be assigned to fit the need of the case (*e.g.*, Plaintiff has 1 to 100, Defendant A has 101 to 200, Defendant B has 201 to 300, etc.). A single exhibit should be marked only once, just as it should have been marked only once in discovery pursuant to this Court's discovery guidelines). If the plaintiff has marked an exhibit, then the defendant should not re-mark the exact document with another number. Different *versions* of

the same document, *e.g.*, a copy with additional handwriting, must be treated as different exhibits with different numbers. To avoid any party claiming "ownership" of an exhibit, all exhibits shall be marked and referred to as "Trial Exhibit No. _____," not as "Plaintiff's Exhibit" or "Defendant's Exhibit." If an exhibit number differs from that used in a deposition transcript, then the latter transcript must be conformed to the new trial number, if and when the deposition testimony is used (so as to avoid confusion over exhibit numbers). There should be no competing versions of the same exhibit number; any discrepancies must be brought to the Court's attention promptly.

28. The exhibit tag shall be in the following form:

UNITED STATES DISTRICT COURT
NORTHERN DISTRICT OF
CALIFORNIA

TRIAL EXHIBIT 100

CASE NO. ___________________
DATE ENTERED_____________
BY _________________________
DEPUTY CLERK

Counsel preferably will make the tag up in a color that will stand out (yet still allow for photocopying) but that is not essential. Place the tag on or near the lower right-hand corner or, if a photograph, on the back. Counsel should fill in the tag but leave the last two spaces blank. The parties must jointly prepare a *single* set of all trial exhibits that will be the official record set to be used with the witnesses and on appeal. Each exhibit must be tagged and in a separate folder (not in notebooks). Deposit the exhibits with the deputy clerk on the first day of trial. The tags can be adhesive or stapled on.

29. Counsel must consult with each other and with the deputy clerk at the end of each trial day and compare notes as to which exhibits are in evidence and any limitations thereon. If there are any differences, counsel should bring them promptly to the Court's attention.

30. In addition to the official record exhibits, two copies of the joint set of bench binders containing a copy of the exhibits must be provided to the Court on the first day of trial. Each exhibit must be separated with a label divider (an exhibit tag is unnecessary for the bench set). In large letters, the labels should identify the range of exhibit numbers contained in a binder.

31. Before the closing arguments, counsel must confer with the deputy clerk to make sure the exhibits in evidence are in good order. Before the case goes to the Court, counsel shall prepare an easy to read index of admitted exhibits, which should include all exhibits actually in evidence (and no others) stating the exhibit number and a brief, non-argumentative description (*e.g.*, letter from A. B. Case to D. E. Frank, dated August 17, 1999).

OBJECTIONS

32. Counsel shall stand when making objections and shall not make speaking objections.

33. There can only be one lawyer per witness per party for all purposes, including objections. Only one lawyer will be permitted to make the opening statement and closing argument unless the Court has given prior approval to more than one lawyer doing so.

TIME LIMITS

34. Ordinarily, the Court shall set fixed time limits at the final pretrial conference. All of your examination time (whether direct, cross, re-direct or re-cross) for all witnesses must fit within your time limit and you may allocate it as you wish. Opening and closing time limits shall be considered separately. Counsel must keep track of everyone's usage. At the end of each day, counsel must confer over the time used and the time remaining for all parties and advise the Court daily. The time taken on objections will still be charged to the examining party unless otherwise ordered.

SETTLEMENTS AND CONTINUANCES

35. Shortly before trial or the final pretrial conference, counsel occasionally wish jointly to advise the clerk that a settlement has been reached and seek to take the setting off calendar but it turns out later that there was only a settlement "in principle" and disputes remain. Cases, however, cannot be taken off calendar in this manner. Unless and until a stipulated dismissal or judgment is filed or placed on the record, all parties must be prepared to proceed with the final pretrial conference as scheduled and to proceed to trial on the trial date, or face dismissal of the case for lack of prosecution or entry of default judgment. Only an advance continuance expressly approved by the Court will release counsel and the parties from their obligation to proceed. If counsel expect that a settlement will be final by the time of trial or the final pretrial conference, they should notify the Court immediately in writing or, if it occurs over the weekend before the trial or conference, by voice mail to the deputy clerk. The Court will attempt to confer with counsel as promptly as circumstances permit to determine if a continuance will be in order. Pending such a conference, however, counsel must prepare and make all filings and be prepared to proceed with the trial.

IT IS SO ORDERED.

____

JEFFREY S. WHITE
United States District Judge

D. *Guidelines for Trial and Final Pretrial Conference in Civil Jury Cases*

GUIDELINES FOR TRIAL AND FINAL PRETRIAL CONFERENCE IN CIVIL JURY CASES BEFORE THE HONORABLE JEFFREY S. WHITE

FINAL PRETRIAL CONFERENCE AND REQUIRED FILINGS

Counsel shall not prepare a joint pretrial conference statement. Instead, please follow the following procedures:

1. In lieu of preparing a joint pretrial conference statement, the parties shall meet and confer in person and prepare a jointly signed proposed final pretrial order to be filed fourteen (14) calendar days in advance of the final pretrial conference. This joint pretrial conference order should contain: (i) a brief description of the substance of claims and defenses which remain to be decided; (ii) a statement of all relief sought; (iii) all stipulated facts; (iv) a list of all factual issues that remain to be tried, stating the issues with the same generality/specificity as any contested elements in the relevant jury instructions and organized by counts; (v) a joint exhibit list in numerical order, including a brief description of the exhibit and Bates numbers, a blank column for when it will be offered into evidence, a blank column for when it may be received into evidence, and a blank column for any limitations on its use; and (vi) each party's separate witness list for its case-in-chief witnesses (including those appearing by deposition) providing, for all such witnesses other than an individual plaintiff and an individual defendant, a short statement of the substance of his/her testimony and, separately, what, if any, noncumulative testimony the witness will offer. If non-cumulative testimony is not spelled out, the Court will presume the witness is cumulative. For each witness, state an hour/minute time estimate for both direct and cross examination. The Court uses this information to estimate the time limits to be allocated for trial. Items (v) and (vi) should be appendices to the proposed order. The proposed order should also state which issues, if any, are for the Court to decide, rather than the jury. The objective is to convert the proposed order to a final order with the benefit of any discussion at the final pretrial conference.

2. In addition to the joint pretrial order, fourteen (14) days in advance of the final pretrial conference, the parties also shall file the following materials:

(a) A joint set of proposed instructions on substantive issues of law arranged in a logical sequence. If undisputed, an instruction shall be identified as "Stipulated Instruction No. ____ Re ___________." The parties also must ensure that all modifications to form instructions are submitted to the Court, *i.e.*,if a model instruction includes bracketed language or blanks, the parties must provide the Court with the appropriate language from the brackets and the blanks shall be completed.

Even if stipulated, the instruction shall be supported by citation. If disputed, each version of the instruction shall be inserted together, back to back, in their logical place in the overall sequence. Each such disputed instruction shall be identified as, for example, "Disputed Instruction No. ____ Re ____________ Offered by ________________," with the blanks filled in as appropriate. All disputed versions of the same basic instruction shall bear the same number. Citations with pin cites are required. Any modifications to a form instruction must be clearly identified, *i.e.*, in bold or italics. If a party does not have a counter version and simply contends that no such instruction in any version should be given, then that party should so state (and explain why in the separate memoranda required by paragraph 2.b) on a separate page inserted in lieu of an alternate version. With respect to form preliminary instructions, general instructions, or concluding instructions, please simply cite to the numbers of the requested instructions in the current edition of the *Ninth Circuit Manual of Model Jury Instructions (Civil)*. Other than citing the numbers, the parties shall not include preliminary, general or concluding instructions in the packet, but shall include the full text of these instructions on the CDROM required by this Order. Again, if the form instructions contain bracketed language or blanks, the parties should provide the Court with the appropriate language from the brackets and all blanks should be completed.

(b) The parties are encouraged to keep disputed instructions to a minimum. To the extent they are unable to resolve their disputes, the court requires complete briefing on disputed instructions. Thus, a party supporting an instruction must submit a separate memorandum of law in support of its disputed instructions, organized by instruction number. Please quote exact, controlling passages from the authorities, without ellipses, and give pin cites. The party opposing a given instruction or instructions must include a responsive brief to the supporting party's memorandum, organized by instruction number and also shall quote exact, controlling passages from the authorities, without ellipses and with pin cites.

(c) A simplified statement of the case to be read to the jury during voir dire and as part of the proposed jury instructions. Unless the case is extremely complex, this statement should not exceed one page.

(d) A joint set of proposed voir dire questions supplemented as necessary by separate requests for good cause only. (Keep these to a minimum, please.)

(e) A trial brief not to exceed ten pages on any controlling issues of law.

(f) Excerpts of any deposition designations that are to be used in a parties' case in chief as to which there are objections. The parties should include with these excerpts the basis for the objection and the response thereto. If the parties do not have objections to deposition designations, they should follow the procedures set forth in paragraph 27.

(g) Excerpts of responses to interrogatories and requests for admissions that are to be used in a party's case-in-chief as to which there are objections. The parties should include with these excerpts the basis for the objection and the response thereto. If the parties do not have objections to responses to interrogatories or requests for admissions, they should follow the procedures set forth in paragraph 29.

(h) A list of objections to each exhibit, in tabular form. The first column should describe the exhibit, the second column should set briefly set forth the basis of the objection, and the third column should set forth a brief response thereto. The parties shall meet and confer, in person, in an attempt to resolve objections to the exhibits before this list is filed with the Court, to consider exhibit numbers, and to eliminate duplicate exhibits and confusion over the precise exhibit. Unless there is a genuine issue as to the authenticity of exhibits, a party that has produced documents should not object to the other party offering those documents as exhibits on the basis of authenticity or the best evidence rule. Finally, the Court normally will not entertain routine objections to exhibits on the basis of a lack of foundation.

(i) Any motions *in limine*, as to which the parties should follow the following procedure:

The motions *in limine* and all oppositions thereto must be filed no later than fourteen (14) calendar days prior to the Final Pretrial Conference, and shall be submitted to the Court collated and in a binder, as set forth below. Therefore, the parties must serve their motions *in limine* on the opposing party reasonably in advance of the pretrial to permit the opposing party to prepare and serve its opposition.[1] The Court does not permit reply briefs. Each motion should be presented in a separate memo and properly identified, for example, "Plaintiff's Motion *in Limine* No. 1 to Exclude . . . ."

Please limit motions *in limine* to circumstances that really need a ruling in advance. No more than five motions per side will be allowed. If a party seeks to file more than five motions *in limine*, they must file an administrative motion at least fourteen days before the motions *in limine* are due to be filed with the Court demonstrating extraordinarily good cause for allowing the excess motions. The administrative motion should summarize the subject matter of each proposed additional motion *in limine.*

Each motion *in limine* should address a single, separate topic, and contain no more than seven pages of briefing per side. Leave of Court will be required to exceed the page limitations. A binder containing all motions *in limine* should be submitted to the Clerk's office in an envelope clearly marked with the case number and "JSW chambers copy."

(j) If the parties intend to use special verdict forms, they should meet and confer in an effort to submit a joint proposed special verdict form. If the parties cannot agree on a proposed special verdict form, they may submit separate proposals.

3. The joint proposed final pretrial order, the jury instructions, proposed voir dire, the statement of the case required by Paragraph 2(c) of this Order, objections to exhibits required by paragraph 2(h) of this Order, and any proposed special verdict forms, shall be submitted in WordPerfect 10.0 format on a CD-ROM, as well as in hard copies. All hard-copy submissions should be submitted in a binder to the Clerk's office in an envelope clearly marked with the case number and "JSW chambers copies."

4. At the final pretrial conference, the above submissions shall be considered and argued.

PRETRIAL ARRANGEMENTS

5. Should a daily transcript and/or real-time reporting be desired, the parties shall make arrangements with the Supervisor of the Court Reporting Services, at (415) 522-2079, at least ten calendar days prior to the trial date.

6. During trial, counsel may wish to use overhead projectors, laser-disk/computer graphics, poster blow-ups, models or specimens of devices. The United States Marshal requires a court order to allow equipment into the courthouse.

If monitor screens are used, there should be a single large screen (not multiple small screens) viewable by the jury, the Court and the witness. It should be large and bright enough to be seen when placed on the opposite side of the courtroom from the jury. If counsel cannot conveniently see the screen, counsel may have a small monitor at counsel table. If both

1 The Court suggests, but does not require, that at least thirty (30) calendar days before the Final Pretrial Conference, the moving party serve, but not file, the opening brief and at least twenty (20) calendar days before the Final Pretrial Conference, the responding party serve the opposition.

overhead projector and video equipment are to be used, a single projection screen is best, thus requiring a projection-type video rather than a monitor. If video equipment is used, equipment capable of instantly accessing the relevant portions of transcripts and graphics should be used (rather than, for example, raw video tapes made at depositions which take time to forward or to rewind). Equipment should be shared by all counsel to the maximum extent possible. The Court provides no equipment other than an easel. For electronic equipment, parties should be prepared to maintain the equipment or have a technician handy at all times. For overhead projectors, the parties shall provide a spare bulb. The parties shall tape extension cords to the carpet for safety. The parties shall disassemble and store all equipment in the courtroom at the end of each court day. The parties may work with the deputy clerk, Jennifer Ottolini (415-522-4173), on all courtroom-layout issues.

SCHEDULING

7. Trial normally will be conducted from 8:00 a.m. to 1:30 p.m. (or slightly longer to finish a witness) with two fifteen-minute breaks, Monday through Thursday, excluding holidays. Counsel must arrive by 7:30 a.m., or earlier as needed for any matters to be heard out of the presence of the jury. The jury will be called at 8:00 a.m. This schedule may be modified at the discretion of the Court.

Subject to the Court's availability, the jury shall be chosen the Wednesday preceding the first day of trial at 8:30 a.m.

THE JURY

8. The Court will usually conduct the voir dire.

9. In civil cases, there are no alternate jurors and the jury is selected as follows:

The jurors will be given consecutive numbers and shall be seated by juror number. Jurors 1 through 18 are seated in the jury box. The remaining venire will be seated in the public benches. Hardship excuses will usually be considered at this point. The Court will then ask questions to the entire venire. The lawyers, at a side bar conference, will then advise if there are follow-up questions. For good cause, counsel may also ask questions of jurors at side bar. Challenges for cause will then be addressed. After a short recess, each side may exercise its allotment of peremptory challenges. Challenges must be made simultaneously in writing by each side (without knowing how the other side is exercising its challenges). The parties will write down the names and numbers of the candidates to be stricken. The eight (or other such size as will constitute the jury) surviving the challenge process with the lowest numbers become the final jury. For example, if the plaintiff strikes 1, 5 and 7 and the defendant strikes 2, 4 and 9, then 3, 6, 8, 10, 11, 12, 13 and 14 become the final jury. If both sides strike one or more of the same jurors, then the eight unstruck jurors with the lowest numbers will be seated. If more than eight jurors (or fewer) are to be seated, then the starting number will be adjusted. So too if more than a total of six peremptories is allowed. Once the jury selection is completed, the jurors' names will be read again and they will be seated in the jury box and sworn. The Court may alter the procedure in its discretion.

10. Jurors may take notes. Note pads will be distributed at the beginning of each trial. The note pads will be collected at the end of each day and locked in the jury room. Jurors will be instructed on the use of notes both in the preliminary and final jury instructions.

11. The Court may permit the jury to pose written questions to witnesses.

GENERAL DECORUM

12. A trial is a rational and civilized inquiry to seek a just result. Counsel are expected to conduct themselves with dignity and decorum at all times. Disruptive tactics or appeals to prejudice are not acceptable.

13. Colloquy between counsel on the record is not permitted – all remarks are to be addressed to the Court.

14. Vigorous advocacy does not preclude courtesy to opposing counsel and witnesses and respect for the Court. Addressing witnesses or parties by first names or the Court by "Judge" or "Sir" on the record is not appropriate.

15. Counsel shall not engage in activity at counsel table or move about the courtroom while opposing counsel is arguing or questioning witnesses, or in other ways cause distraction. Neither counsel nor client should indicate approval, disapproval or otherwise react to any testimony or argument.

OPENING STATEMENTS

16. Each side will have a predetermined time limit for its opening statement. Counsel must cooperate and meet and confer to exchange any visuals, graphics or exhibits to be used in the opening statements, allowing for time to work out objections and any reasonable revisions. Opening statements will commence as soon as the jury is sworn. Opening statements should be limited to an objective summary of what counsel expects the evidence to show; no argument or discussion of the law is permissible.

WITNESSES

17. At the close of each trial day, all counsel shall exchange a list of witnesses for the next two full court days and the exhibits that will be used during direct examination (other than for impeachment of an adverse witness). Within 24 hours of such notice, all other counsel shall provide any objections to such exhibits and shall provide a list of all exhibits to be used with the same witness on cross-examination (other than for impeachment). The first notice shall be exchanged prior to the first day of trial. All such notice should be provided in writing.

18. The parties shall have all upcoming witnesses on the same day available in the courthouse and ready to testify. Failure to have the next witness ready or to be prepared to proceed with the evidence will usually be deemed to constitute resting. If counsel plans to read in a transcript of a deposition, counsel must have a deposition prepared and vetted early on to read into the record.

19. A witness or exhibit not listed in the joint pretrial order may not be used without good cause. This rule does not apply to true rebuttal witnesses (other than rebuttal experts who must be listed). Defense witnesses are considered case-in-chief witnesses, not "rebuttal" witnesses.

20. When there are multiple parties, counsel are responsible for coordination of cross-examination to avoid duplication. If there are multiple parties on a side, counsel for only one party may cover a subject matter; reiteration of the examination, whether direct or cross, will not be permitted.

21. Counsel shall stand at or near the podium to ask questions, straying only to point out material on charts or overheads. Counsel should request permission from the Court to approach the witness or the bench.

22. Counsel shall treat witnesses with courtesy and respect, and not become familiar (*e.g.*, avoiding the use of first or nick-names).

23. Counsel shall pose brief, direct and simply stated questions, covering one point at a time. Leading questions may be used for background or routine matters.

24. Cross-examination similarly should consist of brief, simple questions. Cross-examination should not be a restatement of the direct examination and should not be used for discovery.

EXPERTS

25. At trial, direct testimony of experts will be limited to the matters disclosed in their reports. Omitted material may not ordinarily be added on direct examination. Illustrative animations, diagrams, charts and models may be used on direct examination only if they were part of the expert report, with the exception of simple drawings and tabulations that plainly illustrate the content of the report, which can be drawn by the witness at trial or otherwise shown to the jury. If cross-examination fairly opens the door, however, an expert may go beyond the written report on cross-examination and/or re-direct examination. By written stipulation, all parties may relax these requirements. The Court will not permit Federal Rule of Evidence 703 to be used to admit otherwise inadmissible evidence through the expert (*i.e.*, through the "back door"). At its discretion, the Court may require the parties' expert witnesses to testify immediately following one another, with appropriate explanatory instructions to the jury.

26. As to damages studies, the cut-off date for *past damages* will be as of the expert report (or such earlier date as the expert may select). In addition, the experts may try to project *future damages* (*i.e.*, after the cut-off date) if the substantive standards for future damages can be met. With timely leave of Court or by written stipulation, the experts may update their reports (with supplemental reports) to a date closer to the time of trial.

USE OF DEPOSITION DESIGNATIONS AND USE OF DEPOSITIONS FOR IMPEACHMENT OR SHORT READ-INS

27. Depositions can be used at trial to impeach a witness testifying at trial or, in the case of a party deponent, "for any purpose." For depositions to be used for impeachment purposes, the parties shall abide by the following procedure:

(a) On the first day of trial, counsel shall bring the original and clean copies of any deposition(s) intended to be used during the course of the trial. Any corrections must be readily available. If counsel need to use the deposition during a witness examination, they shall provide the Court with a copy and with any corrections at the outset of the examination. This will minimize delay between the original question and the read-ins of the impeaching material. Opposing counsel should have their copy immediately available.

(b) When counsel reads a passage into the record, counsel should seek permission from the Court. For example, counsel should state: "I wish to read in page 210, lines 1 to 10 from the witness' deposition." A brief pause will be allowed for any objection.

(c) The first time a deposition is read, counsel shall state the deponent's name, the date of the deposition, the name of the lawyer asking the question, and if it was a Federal Rule of Civil Procedure 30(b)(6) deposition. The first time a deposition is read, the Court will give an appropriate explanation to the jury about depositions. Do not embellish the deposition testimony with follow-on questions.

(d) When reading in the passage, counsel shall state "question" and then read the question exactly, followed by,"answer" and then read the answer exactly. Stating "question" and "answer" is necessary so the jury and the court reporter can follow who was talking at the deposition. Once the passage is on the record, move on. Opposing counsel may then immediately ask to read such additional testimony as is necessary to complete the context.

(e) To avoid mischaracterizing the record, counsel should not ask, "Didn't you say XYZ in your deposition?" It is unnecessary to ask a witness if he "recalls" the testimony or otherwise to lay a foundation.

(f) Subject to Federal Rule of Evidence 403, party depositions may be read into the record whether or not they contradict (and regardless of who the witness is on the stand). For example, a short party deposition excerpt may be used as foundation for questions for a different witness on the stand.

28. The following procedure applies to the manner in which deposition designations shall be presented to the jury. The parties shall have met in conferred sufficiently in advance of trial to ensure that they will be able to submit their objections to the Court at the pretrial conference pursuant to Paragraph 2(f) of this Order. In addition, the parties must have met and conferred regarding counter-designations, and shall submit any objections to counter-designations in accordance with Paragraph 2(f) of this Order. It does not apply to live witnesses whose depositions are read into the record while they are on the stand.

(a) To prepare designated deposition testimony to be read to the jury, counsel shall photocopy the cover page, the page where the witness is sworn, and then each page containing any testimony to be proffered, with lines through portions of such pages not proffered. In addition, counsel shall line through objections or colloquy unless they are needed to understand the question. Any corrections must be interlineated and references to exhibit numbers must conform to the trial numbers. Such interlineations should be done by hand. The finished packet should then be the actual script and should smoothly present the identification and swearing of the witness and testimony desired.

(b) When the packet is read to the jury, the examiner shall read the questions (and any relevant colloquy) from the lectern while a colleague sits in the witness stand and reads the answers. While reading the deposition the reader and "witness" shall refrain from undue emoting, emphasis or other dramatization. The same procedure shall be followed when a video-taped deposition is to be played instead, in order to facilitate rulings on objections. The video should omit any dead time, long pauses, and objections/colloquy not necessary to understand the answers.

REQUESTS FOR ADMISSIONS AND INTERROGATORIES

29. Please prepare responses to requests for admissions and interrogatory answers in the same manner for presentation to the jury in the same manner as deposition designations.

EXHIBITS

30. Use numbers only, not letters, for exhibits, preferably the same numbers as were used in depositions. Blocks of numbers should be assigned to fit the need of the case (*e.g.*, Plaintiff has 1 to 100, Defendant A has 101 to 200, Defendant B has 201 to 300, *etc.*). A single exhibit should be marked only once, just as it should have been marked only once in discovery

pursuant to this Court's discovery guidelines). If the plaintiff has marked an exhibit, then the defendant should not re-mark the exact document with another number. Different *versions* of the same document, *e.g.*, a copy with additional handwriting, must be treated as different exhibits with different numbers. To avoid any party claiming "ownership" of an exhibit, all exhibits shall be marked and referred to as "Trial Exhibit No. _____," not as "Plaintiff's Exhibit" or "Defendant's Exhibit." If an exhibit number differs from that used in a deposition transcript, then the latter transcript must be conformed to the new trial number if and when the deposition testimony is read to the jury (so as to avoid confusion over exhibit numbers). The jury should always hear any given exhibit referred to by its unique number. There should be no competing versions of the same exhibit number; any discrepancies must be brought to the Court's attention promptly.

31. The exhibit tag shall be in the following form:

UNITED STATES DISTRICT COURT
NORTHERN DISTRICT OF CALIFORNIA

TRIAL EXHIBIT 100

CASE NO. ____________________
DATE ENTERED________________
BY _________________________
DEPUTY CLERK

Counsel preferably will make the tag up in a color that will stand out (yet still allow for photocopying) but that is not essential. Place the tag on or near the lower right-hand corner or, if a photograph, on the back. Counsel should fill in the tag but leave the last two spaces blank. The parties must jointly prepare *single* a set of all trial exhibits that will be the official record set to be used with the witnesses and on appeal. Each exhibit must be tagged and in a separate folder (not in notebooks). Deposit the exhibits with the deputy clerk on the first day of trial. The tags can be adhesive or stapled on.

32. Counsel must consult with each other and with the deputy clerk at the end of each trial day and compare notes as to which exhibits are in evidence and any limitations thereon. If there are any differences, counsel should bring them promptly to the Court's attention.

33. In addition to the official record exhibits, two copies of the joint set of bench binders containing a copy of the exhibits must be provided to the Court on the first day of trial. Each exhibit must be separated with a label divider (an exhibit tag is unnecessary for the bench set). In large letters, the labels should identify the range of exhibit numbers contained in a binder.

34. Before the closing arguments, counsel must confer with the deputy clerk to make sure the exhibits in evidence are in good order. Before the case goes to the jury, counsel shall prepare an easy to read index of admitted exhibits, which should include all exhibits actually in evidence (and no others) stating the exhibit number and a brief, non-argumentative description (*e.g.*, letter from A. B. Case to D. E. Frank, dated August 17, 1999).

35. Exhibit notebooks for the jury will not be permitted. Publication must be by poster blow-up, overhead projection, or such other method as is allowed in the circumstances. Poster blow-ups should be about 4' x 6' to be seen by all jurors. Any overhead projector should have

a powerful light to help in jury viewing. Counsel must have a practical means for all important documents to be published to the jury. It is permissible to highlight, circle or underscore in the enlargements so long as it is clear that it was not on the original. The Court will not allow monitors and screens in the jury box — one large monitor or screen, if any, should be used.

OBJECTIONS

36. Counsel shall stand when making objections and shall not make speaking objections.

37. There can only be one lawyer per witness per party for all purposes, including objections. Only one lawyer will be permitted to make the opening statement and closing argument unless the Court has given prior approval to more than one lawyer doing so.

38. Side bar conferences are discouraged. The procedure described above should eliminate the need for most side bar conferences. If a lawyer requests and the Court agrees to a side bar, the side bar will be charged to that lawyer's time allotment.

39. To maximize jury time, counsel must alert the Court in advance of any problems that will require discussion outside the presence of the jury, so that the conference can be held before court begins or after the jury leaves for the day.

STIPULATIONS

40. You must read all stipulations to the jury (slowly) in order for them to become a part of the record.

TIME LIMITS

41. Ordinarily, the Court shall set fixed time limits at the final pretrial conference. All of your examination time (whether direct, cross, re-direct or re-cross) for all witnesses and side bar conference time (as specified above) must fit within your time limit and you may allocate it as you wish. Opening and closing time limits shall be considered separately. Counsel must keep track of everyone's usage. At the end of each day, counsel must confer over the time used and the time remaining for all parties and advise the Court daily. The time taken at a side bar or on objections will still be charged to the examining party unless otherwise ordered.

CHARGING CONFERENCE

42. As the trial progresses and the evidence is heard, the Court will fashion a comprehensive set of jury instructions to cover all issues actually being tried. Prior to the close of the evidence, the Court will provide a draft final charge to the parties. After a reasonable period for review, one or more charging conferences will be held at which each party may object to any passage, ask for modifications, or ask for additions. Any instruction request must be renewed specifically at the conference or it will be deemed waived, whether or not it was requested prior to trial. If, however, a party still wishes to request an omitted instruction after reviewing the Court's draft, then it must affirmatively re-request it at the charging conference in order to give the Court a fair opportunity to correct any error. Otherwise, as stated, the request will be deemed abandoned or waived.

SETTLEMENTS AND CONTINUANCES

43. Shortly before trial or the final pretrial conference, counsel occasionally wish jointly to advise the clerk that a settlement has been reached and seek to take the setting off calendar but it turns out later that there was only a settlement "in principle" and disputes remain. Cases, however, cannot be taken off calendar in this manner. Unless and until a stipulated dismissal or judgment is filed or placed on the record, all parties must be prepared to proceed with the

final pretrial conference as scheduled and to proceed to trial on the trial date, or face dismissal of the case for lack of prosecution or entry of default judgment. Only an advance continuance expressly approved by the Court will release counsel and the parties from their obligation to proceed. If counsel expect that a settlement will be final by the time of trial or the final pretrial conference, they should notify the Court immediately in writing or, if it occurs over the weekend before the trial or conference, by voice mail to the deputy clerk. The Court will attempt to confer with counsel as promptly as circumstances permit to determine if a continuance will be in order. Pending such a conference, however, counsel must prepare and make all filings and be prepared to proceed with the trial.

44. Local Rule 40-1 provides that jury costs may be assessed as sanctions for failure to provide the Court with timely written notice of a settlement. Please be aware that any settlement reached on the day of trial, during trial, or at any time after the jury or potential jurors have been summoned without sufficient time to cancel, will normally require the parties to pay juror costs.

IT IS SO ORDERED.

JEFFREY S. WHITE
United States District Judge

E. *Guidelines for Motions, Final Pretrial Conference, and Trial in Criminal Cases*

GUIDELINES FOR MOTIONS, FINAL PRETRIAL CONFERENCE, AND TRIAL IN CRIMINAL CASES BEFORE THE HONORABLE JEFFREY S. WHITE

MOTIONS

1. All motions, except those pertaining to sentencing, shall be filed at least thirty-five (35) calendar days in advance of the hearing date. Opposition briefs shall be filed at least twenty-one (21) calendar days in advance of the hearing date. Reply briefs shall be filed at least fourteen (14) calendar days in advance of the hearing date.

Motions for or relating to sentencing shall be filed at least seven (7) calendar days before the date on which Judgment and Sentencing is scheduled. Responses or objections to motions relating to sentencing shall be filed at least five (5) calendar days before the date on which Judgment and Sentencing is scheduled.

Although the parties are not required to file a Sentencing Memorandum, except as set forth in Criminal Local Rule 32-5(b), the Court encourages the parties to do so. If a party chooses to submit a Sentencing Memorandum to the Court, it must be filed at least seven (7) calendar days before the date on which Judgment and Sentencing is scheduled. Responses to Sentencing Memoranda shall be filed at least five (5) calendar days before the date on which Judgment and Sentencing is scheduled.

Courtesy copies of all briefs shall be delivered to the Clerk's Office in an envelope clearly marked with the case number, and "JSW Chamber's Copy."

2. Motions or Stipulations to Continue any proceeding on the Court's criminal calendar, except a trial, shall be submitted to the Court no later than 2:30 p.m. the day before the proceeding is to be heard. Motions to continue a trial date shall be filed no later than seven (7) calendar days prior to the trial date. Any opposition to a motion to continue trial shall be filed no later than (5) days prior to the trial date. Such motions will only be granted in extraordinary cases involving unforeseen circumstances and extremely good cause.

3. All motions and oppositions to motions shall comply with Criminal Local Rule 47-2(b), which requires that motions "presenting issues of fact ... be supported by affidavits or declarations which comply with the requirements of Civil Local Rule 7-5." Civil Local Rule 7-5, in turn, requires that "[f]actual contentions made in support of or in opposition to any motion must be supported by an affidavit or declaration and by appropriate references to the record." Moreover, other evidence in support of or in opposition to any motion "must be appropriately authenticated by an affidavit or declaration." That rule further requires that affidavits and declarations contain factual contentions only, avoiding conclusions and legal argument, and "conform as much as possible to the requirements of Federal Rule of Civil Procedure 56(e)." In accordance with Civil Local Rule 7-5, made applicable by Criminal Local Rule 47-2(b), any declaration or affidavit that does not comply with these requirements may be stricken.

4. *Ex Parte* Rule 17(c) Subpoena Requests: Before a defendant's *ex parte* application for document subpoena(s), made pursuant to Federal Rule of Criminal Procedure 17(c) may be granted, defendant is required to demonstrate that proceeding *ex parte* is "necessary to preserve the defendant's overriding constitutional rights" because to do otherwise would "reveal[ ] his trial strategy." *See United States v. Tomison*, 969 F. Supp. 587, 595 (E.D. Cal. 1997). In addition, defendant is required to show that the information sought is: (1) relevant; (2) admissible; and (3) specifically identified. *United States v. Nixon*, 418 U.S. 683, 700 (1974). If the defendant seeks production in advance of trial, he or she is required to demonstrate good cause for advance production. *See id.*

If the defendant is able to make the requisite showing above, Rule 17(c) requires production of the documents to the Court, not to the defendant. The Court will review the materials to determine whether they are responsive to the subpoena(s). Following the Court's determination, both parties will be entitled to inspect the responsive materials unless defendant is able to demonstrate an overriding need for confidentiality. *See Tomison*, 969 F. Supp. at 597. Applications which do not include the above showing will be denied.

FINAL PRETRIAL CONFERENCE

Counsel shall not prepare a joint pretrial conference statement. Instead please follow the following procedures:

5. In lieu of preparing a joint pretrial conference statement, the parties shall meet and confer in person and prepare a jointly signed proposed final pretrial order fourteen (14) days in advance of the Final Pretrial Conference. In addition to the matters set forth in Northern District Criminal Local Rule 17.1-1(b), this joint pretrial conference order should contain: (i) a brief description of the substance of the case; (ii) if appropriate, all stipulated facts; (iii) a joint exhibit list in numerical order, including a brief description of the exhibit and Bates numbers, a blank column for when it will be offered into evidence, a blank column for when it may be received into evidence, and a blank column for any limitations on its use; and (iv) each party's separate witness list for its case-in-chief witnesses (*see* N.D. Crim. L.R. 17.1-1(b)(9)); items (ii) and (iii) should be appendices to the proposed order. The proposed order should also state which issues, if any, are for the Court to decide, rather than the jury. The objective is to convert the proposed order to a final order with the benefit of any discussion at the final pretrial conference.

6. In addition to the joint pretrial conference order, the parties shall file the following:

(a) A joint set of proposed instructions on substantive issues of law arranged in a logical sequence. If undisputed, an instruction shall be identified as "Stipulated Instruction No. ____ Re ___________." The parties also must ensure that all modifications to form instructions are submitted to the Court, *i.e.*, if a model instruction includes bracketed language or blanks, the parties must provide the Court with the appropriate language from the brackets and the blanks shall be completed.

Even if stipulated, the instruction shall be supported by citation. If disputed, each version of the instruction shall be inserted together, back to back, in their logical place in the overall sequence. Each such disputed instruction shall be identified as, for example, "Disputed Instruction No. ____ Re ____________ Offered by _________________," with the blanks filled in as appropriate. All disputed versions of the same basic instruction shall bear the same number. Citations with pin cites are required. Any modifications to a form instruction must be clearly identified, *i.e.*, in bold or italics. If a party does not have a counter version and simply contends that no such instruction in any version should be given, then that party should so state (and explain why in the separate memoranda required by paragraph 2.b) on a separate page inserted in lieu of an alternate version. With respect to form preliminary instructions, general instructions, or concluding instructions, please simply cite to the numbers of the requested instructions in the current edition of the *Ninth Circuit Manual of Model Jury Instructions (Criminal)*.

Other than citing the numbers, the parties shall not include preliminary, general or concluding instructions in the packet, but shall include the full text of these instructions on the CD-ROM required by this Order. Again, if the form instructions contain bracketed language or blanks, the parties should provide the Court with the appropriate language from the brackets and all blanks should be completed.

(b) The parties are encouraged to keep disputed instructions to a minimum. To the extent they are unable to resolve their disputes, the court requires complete briefing on disputed instructions. Thus, a party supporting an instruction must submit a separate memorandum of law in support of its disputed instructions, organized by instruction number. Please quote exact, controlling passages from the authorities, without ellipses, and give pin cites. The party opposing a given instruction or instructions must include a responsive brief to the supporting party's memorandum, organized by instruction number and also shall quote exact, controlling passages from the authorities, without ellipses and with pin cites.

(c) A simplified statement of the case to be read to the jury during voir dire and as part of the proposed jury instructions. Unless the case is extremely complex, this statement should not exceed one page.

(d) A joint set of proposed voir dire questions supplemented as necessary by separate requests for good cause only. (Keep these to a minimum, please.)

(e) A trial brief not to exceed ten pages on any controlling issues of law.

(f) A list of objections to each exhibit, in tabular form. The first column should describe the exhibit, the second column should set briefly set forth the basis of the objection, and the third column should set forth a brief response thereto. The parties shall meet and confer, in person, in an attempt to resolve objections to the exhibits before this list is filed with the Court, to consider exhibit numbers, and to eliminate duplicate exhibits and confusion over the precise exhibit. Unless there is a genuine issue as to the authenticity of exhibits, a party that has produced documents should not object to the other party offering those documents as exhibits on the basis of authenticity or the best evidence rule. Finally, the Court normally will not entertain routine objections to exhibits on the basis of a lack of foundation.

(g) Any motions *in limine*, as to which the parties should follow the following procedure:

The motions *in limine* and all oppositions thereto must be filed no later than fourteen (14) calendar days prior to the Final Pretrial Conference, and shall be submitted to the Court collated and in a binder, as set forth below. Therefore, the parties must serve their motions *in limine* on the opposing party reasonably in advance of the pretrial to permit the opposing party to prepare and serve its opposition.[1] The Court does not permit reply briefs. Each motion should be presented in a separate memo and properly identified, for example, "Plaintiff's Motion *in Limine* No. 1 to Exclude . . . ."

Please limit motions *in limine* to circumstances that really need a ruling in advance. No more than five motions per side will be allowed. If a party seeks to file more than five motions *in limine*, they must file an administrative motion at least fourteen days before the motions *in limine* are due to be filed with the Court demonstrating extraordinarily good cause for allowing the excess motions. The administrative motion should summarize the subject matter of each proposed additional motion *in limine*.

Each motion *in limine* should address a single, separate topic, and contain no more than seven pages of briefing per side. Leave of Court will be required to exceed the page limitations. A binder containing all motions *in limine* should be submitted to the Clerk's office in an envelope clearly marked with the case number and "JSW chambers copy."

(h) If the parties intend to use special verdict forms, they should meet and confer in an effort to submit a joint proposed special verdict form. If the parties cannot agree on a proposed special verdict form, they may submit separate proposals.

7. The joint proposed final pretrial order, the jury instructions, proposed voir dire, the statement of the case, objections to exhibits, and any proposed special verdict forms, shall be submitted in WordPerfect format on a CD-ROM, as well as in hard copies. All hard-copy submissions should be submitted in a binder to the Clerk's office in an envelope clearly marked with the case number and "JSW chambers copies."

8. At the final pretrial conference, the above submissions shall be considered and argued.

PRETRIAL ARRANGEMENTS

9. Should a daily transcript and/or real-time reporting be desired, the parties shall make arrangements with the Supervisor of the Court Reporting Services, at (415) 522-2079, at least ten calendar days prior to the trial date.

10. During trial, counsel may wish to use overhead projectors, laser-disk/computer graphics, poster blow-ups, models or specimens of devices. If monitor screens are used, there should be a single large screen (not multiple small screens) viewable by the jury, the Court and the witness. It should be large and bright enough to be seen when placed on the opposite side of the courtroom from the jury. If counsel cannot conveniently see the screen, counsel may have a small monitor at counsel table. If both overhead projector and video equipment are to be used, a single projection screen is best, thus requiring a projection-type video rather than a monitor. If video equipment is used, equipment capable of instantly accessing the relevant portions of the video should be used (rather than, for example, raw video tapes which take time to forward or to rewind). Equipment should be shared by all counsel to the maximum extent possible. The Court provides no equipment other than an easel. The United States Marshal requires a court order to allow equipment into the courthouse. For electronic

[1] The Court suggests, but does not require, that at least thirty (30) calendar days before the Final Pretrial Conference, the moving party serve, but not file, the opening brief and at least twenty (20) calendar days before the Final Pretrial Conference, the responding party serve the opposition.

equipment, parties should be prepared to maintain the equipment or have a technician handy at all times. For overhead projectors, the parties shall provide a spare bulb. The parties shall tape extension cords to the carpet for safety. The parties shall disassemble and store all equipment in the courtroom at the end of each court day. The parties may work with the deputy clerk, Jennifer Ottolini (415-522-4173), on all courtroom-layout issues.

SCHEDULING

11. Trial normally will be conducted from 8:00 a.m. to 1:30 p.m. (or slightly longer to finish a witness) with two fifteen-minute breaks, Monday through Thursday, excluding holidays. Counsel must arrive by 7:30 a.m., or earlier as needed for any matters to be heard out of the presence of the jury. The jury will be called at 8:00 a.m. This schedule may be modified at the discretion of the Court.

Subject to the Court's availability, the jury shall be chosen the Wednesday preceding the first day of trial, at 8:30 a.m.

THE JURY

12. The Court will conduct the voir dire.

13. In criminal cases, there are two alternate jurors and the jury is selected as follows:

The jurors will be given consecutive numbers and shall be seated by juror number. Jurors 1 through 18 are seated in the jury box. The remaining venire will be seated in the public benches. Hardship excuses will usually be considered at this point. The Court will then ask questions to the entire venire. The lawyers, at a side bar conference, will then advise if there are follow-up questions. For good cause, counsel may also ask questions of jurors at side bar. Challenges for cause will then be addressed. After a short recess, each side may exercise its allotment of peremptory challenges. Challenges must be made simultaneously in writing by each side (without knowing how the other side is exercising its challenges). The parties will write down the names and numbers of the candidates to be stricken. The fourteen surviving the challenge process with the lowest numbers become the final jury. For example, if the Government strikes 1, 5 and 7 and the defendant strikes 2, 4 and 9, then 3, 6, 8, 10, 11, 12, 13, 14, 15, 16, 17, 18, 19, and 20 become the final jury, including the alternates. If both sides strike one or more of the same jurors, then the fourteen unstruck jurors with the lowest numbers will be seated. Once the jury selection is completed, the jurors' names will be read again and they will be seated in the jury box and sworn. The Court may alter the procedure in its discretion.

14. Jurors may take notes. Note pads will be distributed at the beginning of each trial. The note pads will be collected at the end of each day and locked in the jury room. Jurors will be instructed on the use of notes both in the preliminary and final jury instructions.

15. The Court may permit the jury to pose written questions to the witnesses.

GENERAL DECORUM

16. A trial is a rational and civilized inquiry to seek a just result. Counsel are expected to conduct themselves with dignity and decorum at all times. Disruptive tactics or appeals to

prejudice are not acceptable.

17. Colloquy between counsel on the record is not permitted – all remarks are to be addressed to the Court.

18. Vigorous advocacy does not preclude courtesy to opposing counsel and witnesses and respect for the Court. Addressing witnesses or parties by first names or the Court by "Judge" or "Sir" on the record is not appropriate.

19. Counsel shall not engage in activity at counsel table or move about the courtroom while opposing counsel is arguing or questioning witnesses, or in other ways cause distraction. Neither counsel nor client should indicate approval, disapproval or otherwise react to any testimony or argument.

OPENING STATEMENTS

20. Each side will have a predetermined time limit for its opening statement. Counsel must cooperate and meet and confer to exchange any visuals, graphics or exhibits to be used in the opening statements, allowing for time to work out objections and any reasonable revisions. Opening statements will commence as soon as the jury is sworn. Opening statements should be limited to an objective summary of what counsel expects the evidence to show; no argument or discussion of the law is permissible.

WITNESSES

21. At the close of each trial day, all counsel shall exchange a list of witnesses for the next two full court days and the exhibits that will be used during direct examination (other than for impeachment of an adverse witness). Within 24 hours of such notice, all other counsel shall provide any objections to such exhibits and shall provide a list of all exhibits to be used with the same witness on cross-examination (other than for impeachment). The first notice shall be exchanged prior to the first day of trial. All such notice should be provided in writing.

22. The parties shall have all upcoming witnesses on the same day available in the courthouse and ready to testify. Failure to have the next witness ready or to be prepared to proceed with the evidence will usually be deemed to constitute resting.

23. A witness or exhibit not listed in the joint pretrial statement may not be used without good cause. This rule does not apply to true rebuttal witnesses (other than rebuttal experts who must be listed). Defense witnesses are considered case-in-chief witnesses, not "rebuttal" witnesses.

24. Counsel shall stand at or near the podium to ask questions, straying only to point out material on charts or overheads. Counsel should request permission from the Court to approach the witness or the bench.

25. Counsel shall treat witnesses with courtesy and respect, and not become familiar (*e.g.*, avoiding the use of first or nick-names).

26. Counsel shall pose brief, direct and simply stated questions, covering one point at a

time. Leading questions may be used for background or routine matters.

27. Cross-examination similarly should consist of brief, simple questions. Cross-examination should not be a restatement of the direct examination and should not be used for discovery.

28. If the Court has made *in limine* rulings limiting testimony in a particular subject area, counsel are encouraged to request a sidebar in the event they believe a particular line of inquiry may implicate the Court's prior ruling. In the event this is necessary, counsel should request a sidebar and simply advise the Court that the request pertains to a pretrial ruling.

EXHIBITS

29. Prior to the Final Pretrial Conference, counsel must meet and confer in person to consider all exhibit numbers and objections and to eliminate duplicate exhibits and confusion over the precise exhibit.

30. Use numbers only, not letters, for exhibits. Blocks of numbers should be assigned to fit the need of the case (*e.g.*, Government has 1 to 100, Defendant A has 101 to 200, Defendant B has 201 to 300, etc.). A single exhibit should be marked only once. If one party has marked an exhibit, then another party should not re-mark the exact document with another number. Different *versions* of the same document, *e.g.*, a copy with additional handwriting, must be treated as different exhibits with different numbers. To avoid any party claiming "ownership" of an exhibit, all exhibits shall be marked and referred to as "Trial Exhibit No. _____," not as "Government's Exhibit" or "Defendant's Exhibit." The jury should always hear any given exhibit referred to by its unique number. There should be no competing versions of the same exhibit number; any discrepancies must be brought to the Court's attention promptly.

31. The exhibit tag shall be in the following form:

UNITED STATES DISTRICT COURT
NORTHERN DISTRICT OF CALIFORNIA

TRIAL EXHIBIT 100

CASE NO. ____________________
DATE ENTERED_______________
BY __________________________
DEPUTY CLERK

Counsel preferably will make the tag up in a color that will stand out (yet still allow for photocopying) but that is not essential. Place the tag on or near the lower right-hand corner or, if a photograph, on the back. Counsel should fill in the tag but leave the last two spaces blank. The parties must jointly prepare a *single* set of all trial exhibits that will be the official record set to be used with the witnesses and on appeal. Each exhibit must be tagged and in a separate folder (not in notebooks). Deposit the exhibits with the deputy clerk on the first day of trial. The tags can be adhesive or stapled on.

32. Counsel must consult with each other and with the deputy clerk at the end of each trial day and compare notes as to which exhibits are in evidence and any limitations thereon. If there are any differences, counsel should bring them promptly to the Court's attention.

33. In addition to the official record exhibits, two copies of the joint sent of bench binders containing a copy of the exhibits must be provided to the Court on the first day of trial. Each exhibit must be separated with a label divider (an exhibit tag is unnecessary for the bench set). In large letters, the labels should identify the range of exhibit numbers contained in a binder.

34. Before the closing arguments, counsel must confer with the deputy clerk to make sure the exhibits in evidence are in good order. Before the case goes to the jury, counsel shall prepare an easy to read index of admitted exhibits, which should include all exhibits actually in evidence (and no others) stating the exhibit number and a brief, non-argumentative description (*e.g.*, letter from A. B. Case to D. E. Frank, dated August 17, 1999).

35. Exhibit notebooks for the jury will not be permitted. Publication must be by poster blow-up, overhead projection, or such other method as is allowed in the circumstances. Poster blow-ups should be about 4' x 6' to be seen by all jurors. Any overhead projector should have a powerful light to help in jury viewing. Counsel must have a practical means for all important documents to be published to the jury. It is permissible to highlight, circle or underscore in the enlargements so long as it is clear that it was not on the original. The Court will not allow monitors and screens in the jury box — one large monitor or screen, if any, should be used.

OBJECTIONS

36. Counsel shall stand when making objections, briefly cite the ground of the objection and a citation (*e.g.*, hearsay, Federal Rule of Evidence 802), and shall not make speaking objections.

37. There can only be one lawyer per witness per party for all purposes, including objections. Only one lawyer will be permitted to make the opening statement and closing argument unless the Court has given prior approval to more than one lawyer doing so.
38. Side bar conferences are discouraged. The procedure described above should eliminate the need for most side bar conferences.

39. To maximize jury time, counsel must alert the Court in advance of any problems that will require discussion outside the presence of the jury, so that the conference can be held before court begins or after the jury leaves for the day.

STIPULATIONS

40. You must read all stipulations to the jury (slowly) in order for them to become a part of the record.

CHARGING CONFERENCE

41. As the trial progresses and the evidence is heard, the Court will fashion a comprehensive set of jury instructions to cover all issues actually being tried. Prior to the close of the evidence, the Court will provide a draft final charge to the parties. After a reasonable period for review, one or more charging conferences will be held at which each party may object to any passage, ask for modifications, or ask for additions. Any instruction request must be renewed specifically at the conference or it will be deemed waived, whether or not it was requested prior to trial. If, however, a party still wishes to request an omitted instruction after reviewing the Court's draft, then it must affirmatively re-request it at the charging conference in order to give the Court a fair opportunity to correct any error. Otherwise, as stated, the request will be deemed abandoned or waived.

IT IS SO ORDERED.

____

JEFFREY S. WHITE
United States District Judge

F. Standing Order for Civil Practice – Deposition Guidelines

STANDING ORDER FOR CIVIL PRACTICE DEPOSITION GUIDELINES

This Standing Order applies to all depositions in all matters assigned to Judge Jeffrey S. White and is intended to supplement the Civil Local Rules of this District regarding civil practice (Civil L.R. 30-1 and 30-2).

Depositions shall be conducted in accordance with the following rules:

1. **Conduct.** Counsel are expected to cooperate with and be courteous to each other and deponents. Each party should designate one attorney to conduct the principal examination of the deponent. Counsel should cooperate in the allocation of time to comply with any time set by the Court.

2. **Stipulations.** Unless contrary to an order of the Court, the parties may stipulate in writing to modify any practice relating to noticing or conducting a deposition. Stipulations for extension of discovery cut-offs set by the Court are not permitted, absent leave of Court. If counsel enter into stipulations at the beginning of the deposition, the terms of the stipulation should be fully stated on the record.

3. **Scheduling.** Absent extraordinary circumstances, before noticing a deposition, the noticing party must consult with opposing counsel and unrepresented proposed deponents to schedule depositions at mutually convenient times and places. Where an agreement cannot be reached and barring exigent circumstances, the party seeking the deposition may notice it at least twenty (20) days in advance. If the noticed date and place is unacceptable to the deponent or deponent's counsel, the deponent or deponent's counsel shall within ten (10) days of receipt of the notice, rely and counter-propose in writing with an alternative date and place falling within thirty (30) days of the date noticed by the party seeking the deposition.

4. **Objections and Instructions Not to Answer.** Counsel shall comply with Fed.R.Civ.P. 30(c)(2). Deposition objections may be made as to privilege or may be made in order to preserve the objection. Speaking objections or those calculated to coach the deponent are prohibited. A person may instruct a deponent not to answer a question only when necessary to preserve a privilege, to enforce a limitation directed by the Court, or to present a motion under Fed.R.Civ.P. 30(d)(3). When a privilege is claimed, the witness should nevertheless answer questions relevant to the existence, extent or waiver of the privilege, such as the date of the communication, who made the statement, to whom and in whose presence the statement was made, other persons to whom the contents of the statement have been disclosed, and the general subject matter of the statement, unless such information itself is privileged. Counsel may be subject to sanctions if they consistently impede, or otherwise unreasonably delay, the fair examination of the deponent.

5. **Private Consultation.** Private conferences between deponents and their attorneys in the course of deposition are improper and prohibited except for the sole purpose of

determining whether a privilege should be asserted.

6. Documents. Witnesses subpoenaed to produce documents should ordinarily be served at least 30 days before the scheduled deposition and arrangements should be made to permit inspection of the documents before the deposition commences. Extra copies of documents used during the deposition should ordinarily be provided to opposing counsel and the deponent. Deponents should be shown a document before being examined about it except when counsel seek to impeach or test the deponent's recollection.

7. Marking of Exhibits. Counsel shall comply strictly with Civil L.R. 30-2 and, at the outset of the case, shall meet and confer regarding the sequential numbering system that will be used for exhibits throughout the litigation and during trial. Documents shall be referred to by the Bates-stamp number assigned by the document repository.

8. Waiver of Transcription Filing. The parties and deponents are authorized and encouraged to waive transcription and filing of depositions that prove to be of little or no usefulness in the litigation or to agree to defer transcription and filing until the need for using the deposition arises.

9. Requests for Intervention by the Court. If a dispute arises during a deposition and involves a persistent obstruction of the deposition or a refusal to answer a material question on the basis of any ground other than privilege or the work product doctrine, counsel may arrange a telephonic conference with the Court through Chambers at (415) 522-4160. Any such conference shall be attended by the court reporter recording the deposition.

IT IS SO ORDERED.

JEFFREY S. WHITE
United States District Judge

G. *Standing Order for Patent Cases*

STANDING ORDER FOR PATENT CASES

The following instructions shall apply to all patent cases assigned to Judge Jeffrey S. White.

Joint Claim Construction Statement

1. The initial joint claim construction statement required by Patent Local Rule 4-3 shall be truly joint. Disputed terms, phrases, and clauses shall be designated as disputed. All other terms shall be presumed undisputed. For any term in dispute, the parties must agree on the identity of the term. With regard to disputed terms, phrases, or clauses, the joint statement shall list each disputed term, phrase, or clause (listed by claim); each party's proposed construction; and support for each party's proposed construction side by side. A model construction statement is attached to this Order.

2. Parties shall attach to the joint claim construction statement copies of all patents in dispute. Parties shall also make a complete prosecution history for each patent available to the Court upon request.

Claim Construction

3. As an initial matter, the Court will construe no more than ten terms. If more than ten terms are at issue, the parties shall meet and confer before the preparation of the joint claim construction statement on narrowing the selection of terms to be construed by the Court and shall jointly propose the ten terms requiring construction.

4. If a party genuinely believes that it will require that more than ten terms be construed, that party may request leave to designate additional terms for construction, pursuant to Civil Local Rule 7-11(b). The requesting party must demonstrate good cause and explain why other methods of limiting the claims at issue (such as the selection of representative claims or any grouping of claims by issues presented) would be ineffective. The request must be filed no later than two weeks before the deadline for filing the joint claim construction statement. If good cause is shown, the Court will either agree to construe all terms or schedule a second claim construction proceeding on the excess terms. If more than ten terms are submitted for construction without leave of court, the Court will construe the first ten terms listed in the joint claim construction statement and sanctions may be imposed.

5. Claim construction briefs shall address each disputed term, but only those that are truly disputed, following the order of the joint statement. The opening and opposition briefs shall not exceed 25 pages; the reply brief shall not exceed 15 pages. The Court anticipates that a meaningful meet and confer between the parties preceding the preparation of the joint claim construction statement will obviate the need for a party to propose in its briefs a claim construction that differs from that proposed in the statement. While the Court encourages the parties to negotiate mutually agreeable constructions, the Court discourages the parties from proposing new constructions for the first time in reply briefs or other filings which do not afford the opposing party an opportunity to respond. However, if it becomes necessary for a party to propose a different construction in its brief than that found in the joint claim construction statement, that party must clearly set forth the new construction and explain the basis for the change. Additionally, that party shall revise the joint claim construction

statement, so that the Court will have one document reflecting all current proposed constructions.

6. At the time of filing the reply briefs, the parties shall file an amended, final joint claim construction statement, including only the remaining disputed terms, phrases, and clauses.

Tutorial and Claim Construction Hearing

7. The Court will schedule a tutorial to occur one to two weeks prior to the claim construction hearing. Each side will be permitted 45-60 minutes to present a short summary and explanation of the technology at issue. The patent holder makes the first presentation. Visual aids are encouraged. The Court prefers that someone other than counsel make the presentation. Counsel will be permitted to make opening remarks and then a brief summation following the presentation. No argument will be permitted. The proceeding is not recorded and parties may not rely on statements made at the tutorial in other aspects of the litigation.

8. Prehearing conferences generally are not held. However, either party may request a telephone conference within two weeks prior to the hearing, or the parties may address any prehearing issues at the tutorial.

9. The patent holder will act as the moving party for the purposes of claim construction. Opening briefs in support of claim construction must be filed at least six weeks before the date of the claim construction hearing, and the briefing schedule set forth at Patent Local Rule 4-5 will apply.

10. The Court will not ordinarily hear extrinsic evidence at the claim construction hearing. Should it become apparent that testimony will be necessary, counsel may request a telephone conference with the Court within two weeks of the hearing to seek the Court's approval.

11. Demonstrative exhibits and visual aids are permissible at the hearing as long as they are based on information contained in the papers already filed. Counsel shall exchange copies of exhibits no later than forty-eight hours prior to the hearing.

12. The claim construction hearing generally will be scheduled for no longer than 3 hours on either Tuesday or Wednesday afternoon. The Court, however, will specially set the hearing on a different day and for a longer period of time if warranted. Counsel should request a telephone conference with the Court as soon as it is apparent that a special setting is necessary.

Subsequent Case Management Report

13. Upon issuance of the claim construction ruling, the Court will also set a date for the filing of a further joint case management status report. In that report, the parties must address the following topics:

a) whether either party wishes to certify the claim construction ruling for immediate appeal to the Federal Circuit;

b) the filing of dispositive motions, and timing of those motions;

c) if willful infringement has been asserted, whether the allegedly-infringing party wishes to rely on the advice of counsel defense. If so, the parties should be prepared to address proposals for resolving any attorney-client privilege issues that arise, and whether the parties believe bifurcation of the trial into liability and damages phases would be appropriate;

d) anticipated post-claim construction discovery;

e) any other pretrial matters; and

f) the progress of settlement discussions, if any.

The Court will review the reports and, if necessary, schedule a further case management conference and enter any appropriate orders.

Miscellaneous

14. All stipulated protective orders and filings shall comply with Civil Local Rule 79-5. Parties shall also submit a complete unredacted chambers copy of any brief or supporting papers lodged under seal with all confidential material highlighted.

IT IS SO ORDERED.

____

JEFFREY S. WHITE
United States District Judge

Sample Claim Chart

Claim Language (Disputed Terms in **Bold**) 'xxx Patent	Plaintiff's Proposed Construction and Evidence in Support	Defendant's Proposed Construction and Evidence in Support
1. A method for counting **ducks**, comprising the steps of: [or] **ducks** Found in claim numbers: 'xxx Patent: y, z 'yyy Patent: a, b	PROPOSED CONSTRUCTION: a bird that quacks. DICTIONARY/TREATISE DEFINITIONS: Webster's Dictionary ("duck: bird that quacks"); Field Guide ("bird call: quack"); INTRINSIC EVIDENCE: 'xxx Patent col. _:_ ("distinctive honking"); Prosecution History at __ ("This patent is distinguished from the prior art in that the quacking of the bird is featured"). EXTRINSIC EVIDENCE: McDonald Depo. at xx:xx ("I'd say the quacking makes it a duck"); '123 Patent at col _:__; Donald Decl. at ¶ __ .	PROPOSED CONSTRUCTION: a bird that swims DICTIONARY/TREATISE DEFINITIONS: Random House Dictionary ("an aquatic bird"); Field Guide (same) INTRINSIC EVIDENCE: 'xxx Patent col _:__ ("ducks may be found on or near bodies of water"); Prosecution History at __ ("water fowl are particularly amenable to being counted by this method"). EXTRINSIC EVIDENCE: G. Marx Depo at xx:xx ("like a duck to water"); '456 Patent at col _:__; Daffy Decl. at ¶ __.

(Or any other substantively similar format that permits the court to compare terms side by side)

H. Standing Order on Recusal

STANDING ORDER ON RECUSAL

The Court seeks the assistance of all parties in all actions before the Court to determine if there are any grounds for recusal under 28 U.S.C. § 455.

The Court particularly requests that all parties determine and advise whether the undersigned judge's former law firm, Orrick, Herrington & Sutcliffe, LLP, served as counsel concerning the matter-in-suit in this action prior to January 1, 2003, the date the undersigned withdrew as a member of the firm. Counsel and the parties should be aware that the undersigned would not ordinarily have been aware of all engagements undertaken by his former firm and must depend on the parties to bring any such circumstances to the Court's attention.

If any party believes, after inquiry, that any ground for recusal exists, please bring the facts and circumstances to the Court's attention by letter or notice served on all parties at the earliest possible date, but no later than five court days preceding the parties' first appearance before this Court.

IT IS SO ORDERED.

JEFFREY S. WHITE
United States District Judge

III. Judge White's Forms

A. *Application for Permission to Enter Plea of Guilty and Order Accepting Plea*

IN THE UNITED STATES DISTRICT COURT
FOR THE NORTHERN DISTRICT OF CALIFORNIA

Plaintiff,	No. CR________JSW
v.	**APPLICATION FOR PERMISSION TO ENTER PLEA OF GUILTY AND ORDER ACCEPTING PLEA**
Defendant.	(Fed. R. Crim. P., Rules 10 and 11)
________________________________/	

The defendant represents to the Court:

1. My full true name is ____________. I am years of age _____. I have gone to school up to and including _________________________. My most recent occupation has been . I request that all proceedings against me be in my true name.

2. I am represented by a lawyer; his/her name is ___________________.

3. I received a copy of the indictment/information (as used in the Application the term indictment includes information) before being called upon to plead. I have read the indictment or a translator who speaks _____________ read it to me, and I have discussed the indictment with my lawyer.

I fully understand every charge made against me. I understand these charges to be: _______.

4. I have told my lawyer all the facts and circumstances known to me about the charges made against me in the indictment. I believe that my lawyer is fully informed on all such matters.

5. I know that the Court must be satisfied that there is a factual basis for a plea of "GUILTY" before my plea can be accepted. I represent to the Court that I did the following acts in connection with the charges made against me in Counts____.
(In the above space defendant must set out in detail in his/her own handwriting what he/she did. If more space is needed, add a separate page.)

6. My lawyer has counseled and advised me on the nature of each charge, all lesser included charges, all penalties and consequences of each charge, all possible defenses that I may have in this case and the constitutional rights I am waiving.

7. I understand that my constitutional rights are as follows:

(a) the right to a speedy and public trial by jury;

(b) the right to see all of the evidence against me and to hear all witnesses called to testify against me and to have my attorney cross-examine them;

(c) the right to use the power and process of the court to compel the production of any evidence, including the attendance of any witnesses in my favor;

(d) the right to the assistance of a lawyer at all stages of the proceedings including trial and appeal and if I cannot afford one, to have the court appoint one to represent me without cost to me or based upon my ability to pay;

(e) the right to remain silent or to take the witness stand at my sole option and if I do not take the witness stand, no inference of guilt may be drawn from such failure and the jury must be so advised;

(f) the right against self-incrimination;

(g) the right to appeal from an adverse judgment;

(h) the right to appeal my sentence without any limitation contained in my plea agreement.

8. I know that I may plead "NOT GUILTY" to any offense charged against me and exercise all of my rights as listed above.

9. I know that if I plead "GUILTY" I am giving up all of the rights enumerated in paragraph 7 and that there will be no trial either before a court or jury.

10. I know that if I plead "GUILTY" the result of my plea is more than just an admission or confession of guilt and that it will result in my conviction, and that further, the court may impose the same punishment as if I had pleaded "NOT GUILTY," stood trial and been convicted by a jury.

11. My lawyer has discussed with me the maximum and minimum, if any, punishments which the law provides and the various provisions of the Sentencing Guidelines that may apply to me. I understand that the maximum punishment for the offense(s) charged in Count(s) ______________ of the indictment is ____________ years of imprisonment, a fine of $______________, and a period of ________years supervised release. I understand that there is a mandatory minimum punishment of _____________years imprisonment for the offense(s) charged in Count(s) ______________. I also understand that the minimum period of supervised release which the court may impose is ______________ (if applicable) and that if I violate any condition of supervised release the release may be revoked and I may be sentenced to all or a part of the term of supervised release imposed in addition to any other term of imprisonment which I have received.

I understand that I may be assessed the costs of confinement and/or supervision. I understand that I must pay a penalty assessment of $100.00 per count to which I plead (or $25.00 in the case of misdemeanor counts). I understand that I may be ordered to pay restitution in an amount determined by the court.

I know that the sentence I will receive is solely a matter within the control of the Judge. I understand that the Judge will make no decision regarding my sentence until the Judge has read and considered the pre-sentence investigation report prepared and submitted to the court by the Probation Department.

I also understand that the court and counsel cannot promise what sentence or sentencing range will be set and that these calculations will depend upon the Sentencing Guidelines as they apply to me. I have been advised that the court may sentence within the guideline range determined by the Probation Department or may depart upward or downward from the range. However, no promises have been made to me as to the range or departure.

12. If I am on probation, supervised release or parole in this or any other court, I know that by pleading guilty here my probation, release or parole may be revoked and I may be required to serve time in that case, which may be consecutive, that is, in addition to any sentence imposed upon me in this case.

13. I declare that no officer or agent of any branch of government (federal, state or local) has promised or suggested that I will receive a lighter sentence, or probation, or any other form of leniency, nor have any other promises been made if I plead "GUILTY," except as stated in the Plea Agreement I have signed, stated on the record in my entry of plea or as follows: ________________.
(In the space above insert any promises or concessions made to the defendant or to his/her attorney.)

If anyone else made such a promise or suggestion, except as noted in the previous sentence, I know that person had no authority to do it. No one has forced or coerced me into entering this plea. My willingness to plead guilty (does) (does not) result from prior discussions between my attorney and the government's attorney. (If it does, state any factors that influenced you that are not reflected in the plea agreement.) ________________.

14. I believe that my lawyer has done all that a lawyer could do to counsel and assist me, and I am satisfied with the advice and help he/she has given me.

15. I know that the court will not permit anyone to plead "GUILTY" who maintains he/she is innocent and, with that in mind and because I am "GUILTY," I respectfully request the court to accept my plea of "GUILTY" and to have the clerk enter my plea of "GUILTY" as follows: ____.

16. My mind is clear. I am not under the influence of alcohol or drugs and I am not under a doctor's care. The only drugs, medicines or pills that I took within the past seven days are:________________. (If none, so state.)

17. **I OFFER MY PLEA OF "GUILTY" FREELY AND VOLUNTARILY AND OF MY OWN ACCORD AND WITH FULL UNDERSTANDING OF ALL THE MATTERS SET FORTH IN THE INDICTMENT AND IN THIS APPLICATION AND IN THE CERTIFICATE OF MY LAWYER WHICH IS ATTACHED TO THIS APPLICATION. IN OFFERING MY PLEA OF "GUILTY" I FREELY AND VOLUNTARILY WAIVE (give up) THE CONSTITUTIONAL RIGHTS**

GUARANTEED TO ME AS STATED IN PARAGRAPH 7 ABOVE.

18. I waive the reading of the indictment in open court, and I request the court to enter my plea of "GUILTY" as set forth in Paragraph 15 of this application.

19. I understand that all of the above statements will be made in open court under oath and that any false statements may be used against me in a prosecution for perjury or false statement which is a felony.

20. ______I am proficient enough in English to read the above and have read and fully understand it.

______I am not proficient enough in English. I speak and understand______________ which is my native language. The above was read to me in____________________ and I fully understand it.

Signed by me in open court in the presence of my attorney this day of __________, 20___.

____
Defendant

INTERPRETER CERTIFICATION

I, ____________________, hereby certify that I am a duly ____________ interpreter in the English and ________________ languages and that I read all of the above to the defendant, that he/she stated he/she fully understood it, and I am satisfied that his/her answer is true and correct.

____
Date

____
Interpreter's signature

CERTIFICATE OF COUNSEL

The undersigned, as lawyer and counselor for the defendant ____________, hereby certifies:

1. I have read and fully explained to the defendant and believe he/she fully understands the allegations contained in the indictment of this case, the defenses he/she may have to each and every one of the allegations and the consequences of a plea of "GUILTY," including the pertinent Sentencing Guidelines provisions and maximum and minimum penalties.
2. I believe the defendant fully understands the constitutional rights he/she is waiving and that by entering a plea of "GUILTY" he/she is waiving each and every one of those rights.
3. Nothing has come to my attention which causes me to believe that the defendant lacks the ability to understand anything contained in the attached application or that at the

time of entering his/her plea he/she is under the influence of any drug or alcohol.

4. The plea of "GUILTY" offered by the defendant in Paragraph 15 accords with my understanding of the facts he/she related to me and is consistent with my advice to the defendant.

5. In my opinion the defendant's waiver of reading of the indictment in open court as provided by Rule 10 is voluntarily and understandingly made, and I recommend to the court that the waiver be accepted by the court.

6. Defendant has read the Plea Agreement she/he signed in the matter and I believe she/he fully understands it. I certify that no promises have been made to the defendant by the government or myself other than those contained in the Plea Agreement and if there are such other promises I must state them on the record before my client and the court.

7. In my opinion the plea of "GUILTY" offered by the defendant in Paragraph 15 of the application is voluntarily and understandingly made. I recommend that the court accept the plea of "GUILTY."

Signed by me in open court in the presence of the defendant above-named and after full discussion of the contents of this certificate with the defendant this day of ___________, 20 ___.

____

Attorney for the Defendant

ORDER

I find that:

1. The defendant enters this plea of guilty freely and voluntarily and not out of ignorance, inadvertence, fear or coercion.

2. The defendant understands and knowingly, freely and voluntarily waives his constitutional rights.

3. The defendant freely and voluntarily executed the within Application and understands its contents.

4. The defendant has admitted the essential elements of the crime charged.

IT IS THEREFORE ORDERED that the defendant's plea of "GUILTY" be accepted and entered as prayed for in the Application and as recommended in the certificate of his lawyer.

Done in open court this ____ day of ___________, 20___.

Dated: ____________________

____

JEFFREY S. WHITE
United States District Judge

Hon. Ronald M. Whyte

District Judge

Chambers Information

U.S. District Court, Northern District of California
Courtroom 6, 4th Floor
280 South First Street
San Jose, CA 95113

Scheduling Information

Courtroom Deputy: (408) 535-5375

Civil Law and Motion	Fridays at 9:00 a.m.
Criminal Law and Motion	Mondays at 9:00 a.m.
Case Management Conferences	Fridays at 10:30 a.m.
Pretrial Conferences	Thursdays at 2:00 p.m. (20 days before trial)
Trials	Mondays: 1:30 p.m.

Judge's Biography

Born 1942 in Pomona, CA

Federal Judicial Service:

-Judge, U. S. District Court, Northern District of California
-Nominated by George H.W. Bush on July 26, 1991, to a new seat created by 104 Stat. 5089; Confirmed by the Senate on February 6, 1992, and received commission on February 10, 1992. Assumed senior status on March 2, 2009.

Education:

-Wesleyan University, A.B., 1964
-University of Southern California Law School, J.D., 1967

Professional Career:

-Private Practice, Claremont, California, 1967-1968
-U.S. Navy, JAG Corps, 1968-1971
-Private Practice, San Jose, California, 1971-1989
-Judge, Santa Clara County Superior Court, 1989-1992

I. Judge Whyte's Procedures and Practices

A. *Standing Order Regarding Pretrial Preparation*

STANDING ORDER RE: PRETRIAL PREPARATION

IT IS HEREBY ORDERED that the following requirements and procedures shall apply in all civil cases scheduled for trial before the undersigned judge unless modified at least fifteen (15) days before the pretrial conference.

A. Not less than fifteen (15) days before the Pretrial Conference, lead counsel (and all parties appearing *pro se*) shall meet and confer in person with respect to accomplishing the requirements and procedures outlined below.

B. Not less than ten (10) court days before the Pretrial Conference, the parties shall serve and file (or lodge, as applicable):

1. **Trial Briefs (optional);**

2. **Motions *In Limine*;**

3. **Deposition and Discovery Responses.** One copy of any deposition transcript and any other discovery response any party intends to offer as evidence, other than solely for impeachment or rebuttal, shall be lodged with the court. The parties shall highlight the pertinent portions of the deposition transcripts and discovery responses;

4. **Proposed Voir Dire Questions (Jury Trials Only).** Proposed voir dire questions may be submitted to the court. The examination of trial jurors shall be conducted initially by the judge. The court will allow limited follow-up voir dire by attorneys (usually ten (10) minutes per side). Written juror questionnaires are permitted in limited situations. If the parties wish to submit juror questionnaires, they must contact the court to discuss procedures: (a) at least forty-five (45) days in advance of the pretrial conference if they wish to mail a questionnaire to prospective jurors or (b) at least fifteen (15) days before the pretrial conference if they wish the prospective jurors to come to the court before trial to fill out a questionnaire;

5. **Jury Instructions (Jury Trials Only).** The court has a basic set of preliminary instructions that will be given at the beginning of trial and a basic set of closing instructions that will be given before or after closing argument. These standard instructions are based upon the instructions in chapters 1, 3 and 4 of the Model Jury Instructions of the Ninth Circuit-Civil. The parties need not submit such standard instructions, unless they are dissatisfied with the model instructions.

The parties shall submit a **jointly prepared** proposed preliminary instruction that gives a neutral and concise summary of the positions of the parties, the elements of plaintiff's(s') claim(s) and the elements of any affirmative defense asserted by defendant(s).

The parties shall also submit a **joint** set of all proposed substantive closing instructions in a three-ring binder. The first section shall contain the instructions both sides agree should be given. The second section shall contain plaintiff's(s') proposed additional instructions with each proposed instruction immediately followed by defendant's(s') objection. The third section shall contain defendant's(s') proposed additional instructions with each proposed instruction immediately followed by plaintiff's(s') objection.

The court prefers parties use the Model Jury Instructions of the Ninth Circuit or California Jury Instructions Civil (BAJI), and, for patent cases, the Model Patent Jury Instructions for the Northern District. The court also frequently refers to Federal Jury Practice and Instructions, Fifth-Civil as a source for model instructions. All proposed instructions, however, must be **tailored, modified and supplemented** as necessary. Each proposed instruction shall be written in plain language, comprehensible to jurors, concise and free from argument, cover only one subject which shall be indicated in the caption, and be written out in full on a separate page. For each instruction, the parties must provide citation to the authority upon which the instruction is based.

If practical, the court requests that a copy of the instructions also be submitted on a disk in WordPerfect format;

6. **Form of Verdict (Jury Trials Only).** The parties shall serve and submit to the court a **jointly prepared** proposed form of verdict or, if the parties cannot agree, their respective proposals;

7. **Proposed Findings of Fact and Conclusions of Law (Non-Jury Trials Only).** In actions tried to the court without a jury, each party shall serve and file proposed Findings of Fact and Conclusions of Law. If practical, the court requests that a copy of the proposed findings and conclusions also be submitted on a disk in WordPerfect format; and

8. **Joint Pretrial Statement.** The Joint Pretrial Statement shall include the following:

a. Substance of the Action. A brief description of the general nature of the action;

b. Stipulations, Agreed Statement and Undisputed Facts. A statement of any stipulations requested or proposed for pretrial or trial purposes;

c. Disputed Factual Issues. A plain and concise statement of all disputed factual issues which remain to be decided;

d. Disputed Legal Issues. Without extended legal argument, a plain and concise statement of each disputed point of law concerning liability, relief, procedure or evidence. (When appropriate, full legal argument with citations to statutes and case law should be covered in a trial brief or motion *in limine*);

e. Deposition Excerpts and Discovery Responses. A list of any deposition testimony (by page and lines) or other discovery responses that each party may offer as evidence at trial, other than solely for impeachment or rebuttal;

f. Witnesses to be Called. A list of the name of each witness the parties may call at trial, other than solely for impeachment of rebuttal, together with a brief statement following each name describing the substance of the testimony to be given. Each party shall separately identify those witnesses the party presently intends to call and those the party may call if the need arises;

g. Exhibits, Schedules and Summaries. A list of all documents and other items to be offered as exhibits at trial, other than solely for impeachment or rebuttal. Each item on the list shall be identified by an exhibit number, followed by a brief statement describing its substance or purpose, and the identity of the sponsoring witness. The parties must have agreed on an allocation of exhibit numbers which will avoid duplicate numbers. The parties must limit the number of their exhibits to those essential to a fair representation of their cases. If possible, parties should stipulate to the authenticity and admissibility of exhibits prior to trial.

Any disputes regarding the authenticity or admissibility of any exhibits must be brought to the court's attention no later than the Pretrial Conference or the objections may be deemed waived;

h. Relief Prayed. A detailed statement of all the relief claimed, particularly itemizing all elements of damages claimed;

i. Estimate of Trial Time. A carefully reasoned estimate of the number of hours needed for the presentation of each party's case, including cross-examination of opposing witnesses and opening statement and closing arguments;

j. Amendments, Dismissal. A statement of any requested or proposed amendments to the pleadings or dismissals of parties, claims or defenses;

k. Settlement Discussion. The court requires the parties to have exhausted settlement possibilities **before** the pretrial conference. This requirement includes a settlement conference with the assigned magistrate judge or other settlement facilitator approved by the court; and

l. Miscellaneous. A statement describing any other subjects relevant to the trial of the action or material to its just, speedy and inexpensive determination.

C. **Not less than five (5) court days prior to the Pretrial Conference,** the parties shall serve and file (or lodge, as appropriate) the following:

1. **Oppositions to Motions *In Limine*;**

2. **Objections to the Use of Deposition Excerpts or other Discovery Responses.** Any objections to excerpts from depositions or other discovery responses designated in the Joint Pretrial Statement shall be filed in writing, along with a certification that counsel conferred with opposing counsel regarding any such objections;

3. **Counter-Designations.** In the event a party contends that a deposition excerpt or other discovery response is unacceptably incomplete, the party shall file a counter-designation listing any additional deposition testimony (by page and lines) or other discovery responses it contends are necessary for a complete and fair record. Any objections to the counter-designations shall be served (by fax and mail) and filed the day before the Pretrial Conference (the after-hours drop box may **not** be used for this filing); and

4. **Objections to Voir Dire, Proposed Findings, Verdict Forms, or to the Authenticity or Admissibility of any Trial Exhibits.** Any objections to the use of proposed voir dire, proposed verdict forms, or to the authenticity or admissibility of any trial

exhibits shall be filed in writing, along with a certification that counsel conferred with opposing counsel regarding such objections.

D. At the Pretrial Conference, lead counsel (and parties in *pro se*) will attend in person and be prepared to discuss all matters concerning Pretrial Preparation. The court will consider any trial management issue which is likely to promote a fair and efficient resolution of the case, including:

1. Entering a Pretrial Order, if needed;

2. Ruling, to the extent practicable, on motions *in limine* and on any objections to voir dire, exhibits, preliminary and, if practical, closing jury instructions and verdict form;

3. Allocating a fixed number of hours for each side for opening statements and the direct and cross-examination of witnesses;

4. Setting specific dates and times when trial will be in session; and

5. For jury trials, discussing the jury selection process. The court's usual practice is to have eight (8) person juries. The court will initially examine twenty (20) prospective jurors and then allow counsel for each side up to ten (10) minutes for follow-up questions. After the parties exercise any challenges for cause, the courtroom deputy will hand the parties a list with the prospective jurors numbered one (1) through the number of prospective jurors who remain after challenges for cause. The parties will then pass the list between themselves exercising their peremptory challenges (three (3) per side). A pass counts as a challenge. After the parties exercise their peremptory challenges, the examined jurors will be asked to return to the public seats in the courtroom and the eight (8) who will serve as the jury will be called back to the jury box by the courtroom deputy. The jurors will be the first eight (8) unchallenged prospective jurors on the list provided to counsel.

Questions concerning the provisions of this order should be directed to the courtroom deputy, Jackie Vierra, at (408) 535-5375.

Dated: February 24, 2003

RONALD M. WHYTE
United States District Judge

Hon. Claudia A. Wilken

District Judge

Chambers Information

U.S. District Court, Northern District of California
Courtroom 2, 4th Floor
1301 Clay Street
Oakland, CA 94612

Scheduling Information

Courtroom Deputy: (510) 637-3542

Civil Law and Motion	Thursdays at 2:00 p.m.
Criminal Law and Motion	Tuesdays at 2:00 p.m. (in custody) at 2:30 p.m. (not in custody)
Case Management Conferences and Pretrial Conferences	Wednesdays at 2:00 p.m.
Trials	Monday through Friday, 8:30 a.m – 1:30 p.m.

Judge's Biography

Born 1949 in Minneapolis, MN

Federal Judicial Service:

-Judge, U. S. District Court, Northern District of California
-Nominated by William J. Clinton on October 7, 1993, to a new seat created by 104 Stat. 5089; Confirmed by the Senate on November 20, 1993, and received commission on November 22, 1993.
-U.S. Magistrate, U.S. District Court for the Northern Dist. of California, 1983-1993

Education:

-Stanford University, B.A., 1971
-University of California, Berkeley, Boalt Hall School of Law, J.D., 1975

Professional Career:

-Staff Attorney, Federal Public Defender's Office, Northern District of California, 1975-1978
-Private Practice, Berkeley, California, 1978-1984
-Adjunct Professor, University of California, Boalt Hall School of Law, 1978-1984
-Professor, New College School of Law, 1980-1985

I. Judge Wilken's Procedures and Practices

A. *Notice Regarding Telephonic Appearance Procedures*

NOTICE RE TELEPHONIC APPEARANCE PROCEDURES FOR JUDGE CLAUDIA WILKEN

(Effective December 17, 2008)

I. POLICY GOVERNING TELEPHONIC APPEARANCES

Telephonic appearances are usually allowed for Case Management Conferences and Civil Motion hearings before Judge Claudia Wilken in Courtroom 2 for attorneys **located outside the Northern District of California**. Any request for a telephonic appearance must be Court approved in advance by contacting Judge Wilken's Courtroom Deputy, Nikki Riley, at (510) 637-3542. No telephonic appearance will be allowed unless it is made through **CourtCall**, an independent conference call company, pursuant to the procedures set forth in Section II. If an individual schedules a telephonic appearance and then fails to respond to the call of a matter on calendar, the Court may pass the matter or may treat the failure to respond as a failure to appear. Scheduling simultaneous telephonic appearances in multiple courts does not excuse a failure to appear. Individuals making use of the conference call service are cautioned that they do so at their own risk. Hearings generally will not be rescheduled due to missed connections.

II. SCHEDULING A TELEPHONIC APPEARANCE

By Telephone: Absent an emergency, telephone appearances may be arranged by calling **CourtCall at (866) 582-6878** not later than **3:00 p.m.** the court day prior to the hearing date.

III. PROCEDURE FOR TELEPHONIC APPEARANCE

Court Call will provide counsel with written confirmation of a telephonic appearance, and give counsel a number to call to make the telephonic appearance. It is counsel's responsibility to dial into the call not later than 10 minutes prior to the scheduled hearing.

CourtCall does not place a call to counsel.

The initial charge per participant for a CourtCall appearance is $30.00 for the first 45 minutes you are connected. For each additional 15 minute increment the charge is $7.00. If you do not timely call and connect with the Court Call operator, you will be billed for the call and the hearing may proceed in your absence.

Telephonic appearances are connected directly with the courtroom's public address system and electronic recording equipment so that a normal record is produced. To ensure the quality of the record, the use of car phones, cellular phones, speakerphones, public telephone booths, or phones in other public places is prohibited except in the most extreme emergencies. Participants should be able to hear all parties without difficulty or echo.

At the time of your hearing, you may initially be in the listening mode in which case you will be able to hear the case before yours just as if you were in the courtroom. After your call is connected to the courtroom, the Judge will call the case, request appearances, and direct the manner in which the hearing proceeds. Each time you speak, you should identify yourself for the record. The court's teleconferencing system allows more than one speaker to be heard, so the Judge can interrupt a speaker to ask a question or redirect the discussion. When the Judge informs the participants that the hearing is completed, you may disconnect and the next case will be called.

Telephonic appearances by multiple participants are only possible when there is compliance with every procedural requirement. Sanctions may be imposed when there is any deviation from the required procedures or the Court determines that a person's conduct makes telephonic appearances inappropriate. Sanctions may include dropping a matter from calendar, continuing the hearing, proceeding in the absence of an unavailable participant, a monetary sanction, and/or a permanent prohibition against a person appearing telephonically.

(3/5/2012)

B. Standing Order

STANDING ORDER
NOTICE

Case Management Conferences and Pretrial Conferences are conducted on **Tuesdays** at 2:00 p.m.

Criminal Law and Motion calendar is conducted on **Wednesdays** at 2:00 p.m. for defendants in custody and 2:30 p.m. for defendants not in custody.

Civil Law and Motion calendar is conducted on **Thursdays** at 2:00 p.m.

Effective January 3, 2012, Criminal Law and Motion calendar will be conducted on **Tuesdays** at 2:00 p.m. for defendants in custody and 2:30 p.m. for defendants not in custody.

Case Management Conferences and Pretrial Conferences will be conducted on **Wednesdays** at 2:00 p.m. Order of call is determined by the Court. Counsel need not reserve a hearing date for civil motions; however, counsel are advised to check the legal newspapers or the Court's website at www.cand.uscourts.gov for unavailable dates.

Motions for Summary Judgment: Any cross-motion for summary judgment shall be contained within the opposition to any motion for summary judgment, shall contain 25 pages or less, and shall be filed 14 days after the filing of the motion. The reply to a motion may contain up to 15 pages, shall include the opposition to any cross-motion, and shall be filed 7 days after the filing of the opposition. (See Civil Local Rule 7-3). The Court may, *sua sponte* or pursuant to a motion under Civil L.R. 6-3, reschedule the hearing so as to give a moving party time to file a reply to any cross-motion.

All discovery motions will be referred to a Magistrate Judge to be heard and considered at the convenience of his/her calendar. After a Magistrate Judge has been assigned, all discovery matters shall be noticed by the moving party for hearing on the assigned Magistrate Judge's regular law and motion calendar, or pursuant to that Judge's procedures.

(rev. 9/12/2011)

II. Judge Wilken's Case Management Orders

A. Minute Order and Case Management Order

IN THE UNITED STATES DISTRICT COURT
FOR THE NORTHERN DISTRICT OF CALIFORNIA

Plaintiff, No. C-_________ CW

v. **MINUTE ORDER AND CASE MANAGEMENT ORDER**

Defendant.
_________________________________/

Clerk: Nikki D. Riley Reporter:
Plaintiff Attorney:
Defendant Attorney:

A case management conference was held on:_____________ . The Case Management Statement and Proposed Order filed by the parties is hereby adopted by the Court as the Case Management Order for the case, except as may be noted below. The Court's standard Order for Pretrial Preparation also applies.

The case is hereby referred to the following ADR process:
Non-binding Arbitration: [ ] Early Neutral Evaluation: [ ]
Court-connected mediation: [ ] Private mediation: [ ]
Magistrate Judge settlement conference: [ ]
ADR session to be held by: ______________
(or as soon thereafter as is convenient to the mediator's schedule)

Deadline to add additional parties or claims: ______________
Date of next case management conference: ______________

Completion of Fact Discovery: ______________
Disclosure of identities and reports of expert witnesses: ______________
Completion of Expert Discovery: ______________

All case-dispositive motions to be heard at 2:00 P.M. on or before: ______________
Final Pretrial Conference at 2:00 P.M. on: ______________
A day Trial will begin at 8:30 A.M. on: ______________

Additional Matters: Copy of Court's Order for Pretrial Preparation given to attys in court. **A Further Case Management Conference will be held on ______________ whether or not dispositive motions are filed (or on whatever date dispositive motions are set).**

IT IS SO ORDERED.

Dated: __________________

____
CLAUDIA WILKEN
United States District Judge

Copies to: Chambers

B. *Order for Pretrial Preparation – Civil Trials*

IN THE UNITED STATES DISTRICT COURT
FOR THE NORTHERN DISTRICT OF CALIFORNIA

No. CR__________ CW

Plaintiff,

v.

Defendant.
____________________________________/

ORDER FOR PRETRIAL PREPARATION

PRETRIAL CONFERENCE

1. Not less than 28 days prior to the pretrial conference, counsel shall **exchange** (but not file or lodge) the papers described in Civil L.R. 16-10(b)(7),(8),(9), and (10), and their motions in limine.

2. At least 21 days before the final pretrial conference, lead counsel who will try the case shall meet and confer with respect to:

(a) Preparation and content of the joint pretrial conference statement;

(b) Resolution of any differences between the parties regarding the preparation and content of the joint pretrial conference statement and the preparation and exchange of pretrial materials to be served and lodged pursuant to this Order for Pretrial Preparation. To the extent such differences are not resolved, the parties will present the issues in the pretrial conference statement so that the judge may rule on the matter during the pretrial conference; and

(c) Settlement of the action.

3. Not less than 14 days prior to the pretrial conference, counsel shall submit the following.

(a) Pretrial Conference Statement. The parties shall file a joint pretrial conference statement containing the following information:

(1) The Action.

(A) Substance of the Action. A brief description of the substance of claims and defenses which remain to be decided.

(B) Relief Prayed. A detailed statement of all the relief claimed, particularly itemizing all elements of damages claimed.

(2) The Factual Basis of the Action.

(A) Undisputed Facts. A plain and concise statement of all relevant facts not reasonably disputed.

(B) Disputed Factual Issues. A plain and concise statement of all disputed factual issues which remain to be decided.

(C) Agreed Statement. A statement assessing whether all or part of the action may be presented upon an agreed statement of facts.

(D) Stipulations. A statement of stipulations requested or proposed for pretrial or trial purposes.

(3) Disputed Legal Issues. Without extended legal argument, a concise statement of each disputed point of law concerning liability or relief.

(4) Further Discovery or Motions. A statement of all remaining discovery or motions.

(5) Trial Alternatives and Options.

(A) Settlement Discussions. A statement summarizing the status of settlement negotiations and indicating whether further negotiations are likely to be productive.

(B) Consent to Trial Before a Magistrate Judge. A statement whether the parties consent to a court or jury trial before a magistrate judge, with appeal directly to the Ninth Circuit.

(C) Bifurcation, Separate Trial of Issues. A statement of whether bifurcation or a separate trial of specific issues is feasible and desired.

(6) Miscellaneous. Any other subjects relevant to the trial of the action, or material to its just, speedy and inexpensive determination.

(b) Exhibit List and Objections. The exhibit list shall list each proposed exhibit by its number (see Civil L.R. 30-2(b)), description, and sponsoring witness, followed by blanks to accommodate the date on which it is marked for identification and the date on which it is admitted into evidence. **No party shall be permitted to offer any exhibit in its case-in-chief that is not disclosed in its exhibit list without leave of the Court for good cause shown.** Parties shall also deliver a set of premarked exhibits to the Courtroom Deputy. The exhibit markers shall each contain the name and number of the case, the number of the exhibit, and blanks to accommodate the date admitted and the Deputy Clerk's initials. (Appropriate sample forms are available on the Court's website at www.cand.uscourts.gov). Any objections to exhibits which remain after the pretrial meeting shall be indicated in the pretrial statement.

(c) Witness List. In addition to the requirements of FRCivP 26(a)(3)(A), a brief statement describing the substance of the testimony to be given by each witness who may be called at trial. **No party shall be permitted to call any witness in its case-in-chief who is not disclosed in its pretrial statement without leave of Court for good cause shown.**

(d) Use of Discovery Responses. In addition to the requirements of FRCivP 26(a)(3)(B), a designation of any excerpts from interrogatory answers or from responses for admissions intended to be offered at trial. Counsel shall indicate any objections to use of these materials and that counsel have conferred respecting such objections.

(e) Trial briefs. Briefs on all significant disputed issues of law, including foreseeable procedural and evidentiary issues, which remain after the pretrial meeting.

(f) Motions in Limine. Any motions in limine that could not be settled at the pretrial meeting shall be filed with the pretrial statement. All motions in limine shall be contained within one document, limited to 25 pages pursuant to Civil L.R. 7-2(b), with each motion listed as a subheading. Opposition to the motions in limine shall be contained within one document, limited to 25 pages, with corresponding subheadings, and filed seven (7) days thereafter.

(g) Joint Proposed Voir Dire. The attached voir dire questionnaire will be given to the venire members, and copies of the responses will be made available to counsel at the beginning of voir dire. Counsel may submit a set of additional requested voir dire, to be posed by the Court, to which they have agreed at the pretrial meeting. Any voir dire questions on which counsel cannot agree shall be submitted separately. Counsel may be allowed brief follow-up voir dire after the Court's questioning.

(h) Joint Proposed Jury Instructions. As applicable, jury instructions §1.1A, §1.1C, §1.2 through §1.17, §1.19, §2.1 through §2.13, §3.1 through §3.3 from the Manual of Model Civil Jury Instructions for the Ninth Circuit (2007 Edition) will be given absent objection. Counsel shall jointly submit one set of additional proposed jury instructions, to which they have agreed at the pretrial meeting. The instructions shall be ordered in a logical sequence, together with a table of contents. Any instruction on which counsel cannot agree shall be marked as "disputed," and shall be included within the jointly submitted instructions and accompanying table of contents, in the place where the party proposing the instruction believes it should be given. Argument and authority for and against each disputed instruction shall be included as part of the joint submission, on separate pages directly following the disputed instruction. The parties shall email to cwpo@cand.uscourts.gov a copy of their proposed jury instructions in WordPerfect or Word format. The subject of the email should include the name of the parties, the case number and a description of the document.

(i) Proposed Verdict Forms, Joint or Separate.

(j) Proposed Findings of Fact and Conclusions of Law (Court Trial only). The parties shall email to cwpo@cand.uscourts.gov a copy of their proposed findings of fact and conclusions of law in WordPerfect or Word format. The subject of the email should include the name of the parties, the case number and a description of the document.

JURY SELECTION

The Jury Commissioner will summon 20 to 25 prospective jurors. The Courtroom Deputy will select their names at random and seat them in the courtroom in the order in which their names are called.

Voir dire will be asked of sufficient venire persons so that eight (or more for a lengthy trial) will remain after all peremptory challenges and an anticipated number of hardship dismissals and cause challenges have been made.

The Court will then take cause challenges, and discuss hardship claims from the individual jurors, outside the presence of the venire. The Court will inform the attorneys which hardship claims and cause challenges will be granted, but will not announce those dismissals until the process is completed. Each side may then list in writing up to three peremptory challenges. The attorneys will review each other's lists and then submit them to the Courtroom Deputy.

Then, from the list of jurors in numerical order, the Court will strike the persons with meritorious hardships, those excused for cause, and those challenged peremptorily, and call the first eight people in numerical sequence remaining. Those people will be the jury.

All jurors remaining at the close of the case will deliberate. There are no alternates.

SANCTIONS

Failure to comply with this Order is cause for sanctions under Federal Rule of Civil Procedure 16(f).

IT IS SO ORDERED.

Dated: ________________

____
CLAUDIA WILKEN
United States District Judge

C. Order for Pretrial Preparation for Criminal Jury Trial

IN THE UNITED STATES DISTRICT COURT
FOR THE NORTHERN DISTRICT OF CALIFORNIA

UNITED STATES OF AMERICA, Plaintiff, v. Defendant(s). ___________________________________/	No. CR_________ CW **ORDER FOR PRETRIAL PREPARATION FOR CRIMINAL JURY TRIAL**

Good cause appearing, it is hereby ordered that:

1. TRIAL DATE

a. Jury trial will begin on ____________________ at 8:30 A.M., in Courtroom 2, 4th Floor, 1301 Clay Street, Oakland, California.

b. The length of trial will be not more than _____ days.

2. DISCOVERY

Both sides will comply with the Federal Rules of Criminal Procedure, Crim. L.R. 16-1, and the United States will comply with Brady v. Maryland, 373 U.S. 83 (1963) and United States v. Agurs, 427 U.S. 97 (1976).

3. MOTIONS

Pretrial motions shall be noticed in accordance with Crim. L.R. 47-2 for any available Wednesday on or before ___________________________.

4. PRETRIAL CONFERENCE

a. A pretrial conference will be held on Wednesday, _________________ at 2:00 P.M. (in custody) or 2:30 P.M. (not in custody), in Courtroom 2. It shall be attended by the attorneys who will try the case.

b. **Not less than one week prior to the pretrial conference**, counsel shall comply with Crim. L.R. 17.1-1(b).

c. Jury instructions §1.1 through §1.12, §3.1 through §3.10 and §7.1 through §7.6 from the Manual of Model Jury Instructions for the Ninth Circuit (2003) will be given absent objection. Counsel shall jointly submit one set of additional proposed jury instructions, ordered in a logical sequence, together with a table of contents, using the Ninth Circuit Manual where possible, or Devitt and Blackmar or CALJIC, **not less than one week prior to the pretrial conference**. Any instructions on which counsel cannot agree shall be marked as "disputed," and shall be included within the jointly submitted instructions and accompanying table of contents, in the place where the party proposing the instruction believes it should be given. Argument and authority for and against each disputed instruction shall be included as part of the joint submission, on separate sheets directly following the disputed instruction. Counsel for the United States shall submit a verdict form. The attached voir dire will be given to the venire members. Counsel should submit an agreed upon set of additional requested voir dire questions to be posed by the Court. Any voir dire questions on which counsel cannot agree shall be submitted separately. Counsel will be allowed brief follow-up voir dire after the Court's questioning. Any motions *in limine* should be noticed for hearing at the pretrial conference in accordance with Criminal Local Rule 47-2.

5. JURY SELECTION

The Jury Commissioner will summon 35 to 40 prospective jurors. The Courtroom Deputy will select their names at random and seat them in the courtroom in the order in which their names

are called.

Voir dire will be asked of sufficient venire persons so that twelve (plus a sufficient number for alternates) will remain after all peremptory challenges and an anticipated number of hardship dismissals and cause challenges have been made.

The Court will then take cause challenges, and discuss hardship claims from the individual jurors, outside the presence of the venire. The Court will inform the attorneys which hardship claims and cause challenges will be granted, but will not announce those dismissals until the process is completed. Peremptory challenges will be made in writing and passed between counsel in accordance with Crim. L.R. 24-2 and 24-3. The Court will strike the persons with meritorious hardships, those excused for cause, and those challenged peremptorily, and call the first twelve people (plus alternates) in numerical sequence remaining. Those people will be the jury.

Dated: ____________________

____
CLAUDIA WILKEN
United States District Judge

III. Judge's Wilken's Forms

A. Exhibit List

IN THE UNITED STATES DISTRICT COURT
FOR THE NORTHERN DISTRICT OF CALIFORNIA

Case No.____________________________ Date______________________

________________________________ vs. ________________________________

EXHIBIT LIST				
□ Plaintiff			□ Defendant	
EXHIBIT NUMBER	DESCRIPTION	SPONSORING WITNESS	DATE	
			Marked for Identification	Admitted in Evidence

B. *Exhibit Markers*

Plaintiff's Exhibit Markers

π PLAINTIFF π

United States District Court
Northern District of California

Case No.________________________
Case Title ________________________
Exhibit No.________________________
Date Entered________________________

Richard W. Wieking, Clerk
By: __________________, Deputy Clerk

Defendant's Exhibit Markers

Δ DEFENDANT Δ

United States District Court
Northern District of California

Case No.________________________
Case Title ________________________
Exhibit No.________________________
Date Entered________________________

Richard W. Wieking, Clerk
By: __________________, Deputy Clerk

Counsel shall meet and confer pursuant to Civil L.R. 30-2(b) and assign blocks of numbers to the exhibits (i.e., Plaintiff 1 - 199; Defendant 200 – 400.)

Exhibit markers should be placed on the lower right-hand corner of the exhibit. Exhibits should be contained within a binder with each exhibit separated by a tabbed page denoting the exhibit number.

C. *Juror Questionnaire*

JUROR QUESTIONNAIRE

Please fill out this form as completely as possible and print clearly. Since we want to make copies for the attorneys and the Court, do not write on the back of any page. If you need more room, continue at the bottom of the page. Thank you for your cooperation.

1. Your name:____

2. Your age:____

3. The city where you live:______________________________
How long have you lived there:___________________________

4. Your place of birth:__________________________________

5. Do you rent or own your own home?_____________________

6. Your marital status: (circle one)
single married live with partner separated divorced widowed

7. What is your occupation, and how long have you worked in it? (If you are retired, please describe your main occupation when you were working).__________________________

8. Who is (or was) your employer?____

9. How long have you worked for this employer? ______________

10. Please list the occupations of any adults with whom you live. ___________________

11. If you have children, please list their ages and sex and, if they are employed, please give their occupations.____

12. Please describe your educational background:
Highest grade completed: _________________________________
College and/or vocational schools you have attended:___________________________
Major areas of study:_____________________________________

13. Have you ever served on a jury before? ________ How many times?________
If yes: State/County Court _______ Federal Court _______
When? ____
Was it a civil or criminal case? _________________________
Did the jury(ies) reach a verdict? _______________________

14. Attached is a list of the parties in this case, the law firms representing the parties, attorneys in this case, and persons who are potential witnesses in this case. Do you know, or think you know, any of the persons listed?
Yes:_____ No:_____
If so, make a check next to their name.

This page intentionally left blank.

This page intentionally left blank.

MAGISTRATE JUDGES

Hon. Laurel Beeler

Magistrate Judge

Chambers Information

U.S. District Court, Northern District of California
Courtroom C, 15th Floor
450 Golden Gate Avenue
San Francisco, CA 94102

Scheduling Information

Courtroom Deputy: (415) 522-3140

Civil Law and Motion	First and Third Thursdays at 11:00 a.m.
Criminal Law and Motion	First and Third Thursdays at 9:30 a.m.
Criminal Duty Matters	9:30 a.m.
Case Management Conferences	Thursdays at 10:30 a.m.

Judge's Biography

Federal Judicial Service:

Magistrate Judge, U. S. District Court, Northern District of California, appointed in 2010.

Education:

-Bowdoin College, A.B.
-University of Washington School of Law, J.D.

Professional Career:

-Assistant United States Attorney, Northern District of California
-Law Clerk, Honorable Cecil F. Poole, United States Court of Appeals for the Ninth Circuit
Civil Appeals Division Chief, United States Court of Appeals for the Ninth Circuit, Office of Staff Attorneys

I. Judge Beeler's Procedures and Practices

A. *Standing Order*

STANDING ORDER FOR UNITED STATES MAGISTRATE JUDGE LAUREL BEELER

(Effective March 20, 2012)

Parties shall comply with the procedures in the Federal Rules of Civil or Criminal Procedure, the local rules, the general orders, this standing order, and the Northern District's general standing order for civil cases titled "Contents of Joint Case Management Statement." Local rules, general orders, general standing orders, and a summary of the general orders' electronic filing requirements (including the procedures for emailing proposed orders to chambers) are available at http://www.cand.uscourts.gov (click "Rules" or "ECF-PACER"). The parties' failure to comply with any of the rules and orders may be a ground for monetary sanctions, dismissal, entry of judgment, or other appropriate sanctions.

A. CALENDAR DATES AND SCHEDULING

1. The criminal motions calendar is on the first and third Thursdays of the month at 9:30 a.m. The civil motions calendar is on the first and third Thursdays of the month at 11 a.m. Civil case management conferences are Thursdays at 10:30 a.m. and are not recorded unless a party is pro se or unless counsel requests recording.
2. Parties who notice motions under the local rules need not reserve a hearing date in advance if the date is available on the Court's on-line calendar (click "Calendars" at http://www.cand.uscourts.gov). Depending on its schedule, the Court may reset or vacate hearings.
3. For scheduling questions, please call Judge Beeler's courtroom deputy, Lashanda Scott, at (415) 522-3140.

B. CHAMBERS COPIES

4. Under Civil Local Rule 5-1(b), parties must lodge an extra paper copy of any filing and mark it as a copy for "Chambers." Please three-hole punch the chambers copy.

C. CIVIL DISCOVERY

5. **Evidence Preservation.** After a party has notice of this order, it shall take the steps needed to preserve information relevant to the issues in this action, including suspending any document destruction programs (including destruction programs for electronically-maintained material).
6. **Production of Documents In Original Form.** When searching for documents and material under Federal Rule of Civil Procedure 26(a)(1) or after a Federal Rule of Civil Procedure 34(a) request, parties (a) should search all locations – electronic and otherwise – where responsive materials might plausibly exist, and (b) to the maximum extent feasible, produce or make available for copying and/or inspection the materials in their original form, sequence, and organization (including, for example, file folders).

7. **Privilege Logs.** If a party withholds material as privileged, see Fed. R. Civ. P. 26(b)(5) and 45(d)(2)(A), it must produce a privilege log as quickly as possible, but no later than fourteen days after its disclosures or discovery responses are due, unless the parties stipulate to or the Court sets another date. Privilege logs must contain the following: (a) the subject matter or general nature of the document (without disclosing its contents); (b) the identity and position of its author; (c) the date it was communicated; (d) the identity and position of all addressees and recipients of the communication; (e) the document's present location; (f) the specific privilege and a brief summary of any supporting facts; and (g) the steps taken to ensure the confidentiality of the communication, including an affirmation that no unauthorized persons received the communication.

8. **Expedited Procedures for Discovery Disputes.** The parties shall not file formal discovery motions. Instead, and as required by the federal rules and local rules, the parties shall meet and confer to try to resolve their disagreements. *See* Fed. R. Civ. P. 37(a)(1); Civil L. R. 37-1. After attempting other means of conferring such as letters, phone calls, or emails, lead counsel for the parties must meet and confer **in person**. (If counsel are located outside of the Bay Area and cannot confer in person, lead counsel may meet and confer by telephone.) Either party may demand such a meeting with ten days' notice. If the parties cannot agree on the location, the location for meetings shall alternate. Plaintiff's counsel shall select the first location, defense counsel shall select the second location, and so forth. If the parties do not resolve their disagreements through this procedure, the parties shall file a joint letter brief **of no more than five pages** instead of a formal motion five days after lead counsels' in-person meet-and-confer. The letter brief must be filed under the Civil Events category of "Motions and Related Filings > Motions – General > Discovery Letter Brief." Lead counsel for both parties must sign the letter and attest that they met and conferred in person. The joint letter shall set out each issue in a separate section and include in that section each parties' position (with appropriate legal authority) and proposed compromise. (This process allows a side-by-side analysis of each disputed issue.) If the disagreement concerns specific discovery that a party has propounded, such as interrogatories, requests for production of documents, or answers or objections to such discovery, the parties shall reproduce the question/request and the response in its entirety in the letter. The Court then will review the letter and determine whether future proceedings are necessary. In emergencies during discovery events such as depositions, the parties may contact the Court pursuant to Civil Local Rule 37-1(b).

D. CONSENT CASES

9. In cases that are randomly assigned to Judge Beeler for all purposes, the parties should file their written consent to the assignment of a United States Magistrate Judge for all purposes, or their written declination of consent, as soon as possible. If a party files a dispositive motion (such as a motion to dismiss or a motion for remand), the moving party must file the consent or declination simultaneously with the motion. Similarly, the party opposing the motion must file the consent or declination simultaneously with the opposition.

10. The first joint case management conference statement in a case must contain all of the information in the Northern District's standing order titled "Contents of Joint Case Management Statement." Subsequent statements for further case management conferences should not repeat information contained in an earlier statement and instead should report only progress or changes since the last case management conference and any new recommendations for case management.

E. SUMMARY JUDGMENT MOTIONS

11. Motions for summary judgment shall be accompanied by a joint statement of the material facts that the parties agree are not in dispute. The joint statement shall include – for each undisputed fact – citations to admissible evidence. The parties shall comply with the procedures set forth in Civil Local Rule 56-1(b). The parties may not file – and the Court will not consider – separate statements of undisputed facts. Failure to stipulate to an undisputed fact without a reasonable basis for doing so may result in sanctions. *See* Civil L. R. 56-1(b).

IT IS SO ORDERED.

LAUREL BEELER
United States Magistrate Judge

II. Judge Beeler's Forms

A. Exhibit List

EXHIBIT LIST

__________ v. __________, C _____ LB

EXHIBIT NUMBER	Date Offered into Evidence	Date Admitted into Evidence	Sponsoring Witness	Limits on Use	Description and Bates Range

Hon. Jacqueline S. Corley

Magistrate Judge

Chambers Information

U.S. District Court, Northern District of California
Courtroom F, 15th Floor
450 Golden Gate Avenue
San Francisco, California 94102

Scheduling Information

Courtroom Deputy: (415) 522-2015

Civil Law and Motion	Thursdays at 9:00 a.m.
Criminal Law and Motion	Thursdays at 11:00 a.m.
Case Management Conferences	Thursdays at 1:30 p.m.
Pretrial Conferences	Thursdays at 1:30 p.m.
Trial	8:30 a.m. – 2:00 p.m.

Judge's Biography

Federal Judicial Service:

Magistrate Judge, U. S. District Court, Northern District of California, appointed in 2011.

Education:

-University of California at Berkeley, B.A.
-Harvard Law School, J.D.

Professional Career:

-Private Practice, San Francisco, California
-Law Clerk, Honorable Charles R. Breyer, U.S. District Court, Northern District of California
-Private Practice, San Francisco, California
-Private Practice, Boston, Massachusetts
-Law Clerk, Honorable Robert Keeton, U.S. District Court, District of Massachusetts

I. Judge Corley's Procedures and Practices

A. Civil Standing Order

CIVIL STANDING ORDER FOR MAGISTRATE JUDGE JACQUELINE SCOTT CORLEY

(Revised January 13, 2012)

Parties shall comply with the procedures in the Federal Rules of Civil or Criminal Procedure, the Northern District of California's Local Rules and General Orders, and this standing order, all of which are available at http://www.cand.uscourts.gov. The parties' failure to comply with any of the rules or orders may be grounds for monetary sanctions, dismissal, entry of judgment, or other appropriate sanctions.

CALENDAR DATES

- Civil motions are heard on Thursday at 9:00 a.m. During the months when Judge Corley is on criminal duty, the Court may move any Thursday 9:00 a.m. motions to Thursday afternoon.
- Civil case management, status, and pretrial conferences are heard on Thursdays at 1:30 p.m.

SCHEDULING

- Parties should notice motions (other than discovery motions) pursuant to the local rules. Parties need not reserve a hearing date, but should confirm the Court's availability at http://www.cand.uscourts.gov. For scheduling questions, please call Judge Corley's courtroom deputy, Ada Means at (415) 522-2015.

CONSENT CASES

- In civil cases that are randomly assigned to Judge Corley for all purposes, the parties should file their written consent to the assignment of a United States Magistrate Judge for all purposes, or their written declination of consent, as soon as possible.
- In no event shall the consent or declination be filed later than the deadlines specified in Civil Local Rule 73-1(a)(1) and (2).

CHAMBERS COPIES AND PROPOSED ORDERS

- Under Civil Local Rule 5-1(b) parties must lodge an extra paper copy of any filing and mark it as a copy for "Chambers." Please three-hole punch the chambers copy and submit it to the San Francisco Clerk's Office. All exhibits shall be clearly delineated with labels. If the filing includes exhibits over two-inches thick, the parties shall place the chambers copy in a binder. In a case subject to electronic filing, chambers copies must be submitted by the close of the next court day following the day the papers are filed electronically. The parties do not need to submit chambers copies for stipulations, pro hac vice applications and similar non-motion filings.
- Any stipulation or proposed order in a case subject to e-filing should, in addition to being e-filed, be submitted by email to jscpo@cand.uscourts.gov as a word processing attachment on the same day the document is e-filed. This address should only be used

for this stated purpose unless otherwise directed by the Court.

CIVIL CASE MANAGEMENT

- No later than seven (7) days before the initial case management or status conference, the parties shall file a Joint Case Management Statement in full compliance with the Northern District of California's general standing order for civil cases entitled "Contents of Joint Case Management Statement," a copy of which is attached hereto.
- Parties may not continue a case management, status, or pretrial conference without Court approval. Each party shall be represented in person at the Case Management Conference by counsel (or a party if in pro se), who shall be (1) prepared to address all of the matters referred to in the Northern District of California's general standing order on Joint Case Management Statements; and (2) have full authority to enter stipulations and make admissions pursuant to that order. Permission for a party to attend by telephone may be granted, in the Court's discretion, upon written request made in advance of the hearing if the Court determines that good cause exists to excuse personal attendance, and that personal attendance is not needed in order to have an effective conference. The facts establishing good cause must be set forth in the request.
- All case management, status and pretrial conferences are audio recorded. They are not reported by a court reporter unless counsel requests a court reporter in advance.

CIVIL DISCOVERY

Discovery disputes referred from a district court judge

- Discovery disputes in cases referred by a district court judge to this Magistrate Judge must follow either procedure no. 1 or procedure no. 2, set forth below, depending on the status of the dispute at the time of the referral by the district court.

Procedure No. 1: Motions noticed for hearing before the district court and subsequently referred to this magistrate judge shall maintain the original district court briefing schedule. Judge Corley will reschedule a hearing on the motion to a date on Judge Corley's civil law and motion calendar.

Procedure No. 2: Discovery disputes which arise after the case has been referred to this Magistrate Judge, or before a formal motion has been filed before the district court, shall follow the procedure below:

- The parties shall meet and confer in person, or, if counsel are located outside the Bay Area, by telephone, to attempt to resolve their dispute informally. A mere exchange of letters, e-mails, telephone calls or facsimile transmissions does not satisfy the meet and confer requirement.
- If the parties are unable to resolve their dispute informally after a good faith effort, they shall prepare a joint statement of not more than eight pages stating the nature and status of the dispute. Issue-by-issue, the joint

letter shall describe each unresolved issue, summarize each party's position with appropriate legal authority, and provide each party's final proposed compromise before addressing the next issue. The parties are strongly encouraged to submit a joint statement, but in the rare instances when a joint statement is not possible, each side may submit a statement of not more than two pages. The joint statement or individual statements shall be e-filed (unless the case is exempt from e-filing requirements) and courtesy copies submitted as required by the Civil Local Rules.

- Upon review of the parties' submission[s], the Court will advise the parties of how the Court intends to proceed. The Court may issue a ruling or schedule a telephone conference or in person conference with the parties, and at such conference may issue rulings, order more formal briefing, or set further hearing dates. The Court may also order the parties to come to the courthouse to meet and confer in good faith.

Discovery disputes in cases which are assigned to Judge Corley for all purposes through consent of the parties.

- The parties shall follow procedure no. 2 above for all discovery disputes in cases assigned to Judge Corley for all purposes.

UNREPRESENTED (PRO SE) PARTIES

- Parties representing themselves should visit the link titled "Representing Yourself" on the Court's homepage, www.cand.uscourts.gov. The link discusses the Court's "Legal Help Center" for unrepresented parties which is located on the 15th floor, room 2796, of the courthouse, 450 Golden Gate Avenue, San Francisco.

IT IS SO ORDERED.

JACQUELINE SCOTT CORLEY
United States Magistrate Judge

B. *Settlement Conference Standing Order*

SETTLEMENT CONFERENCE STANDING ORDER FOR MAGISTRATE JUDGE JACQUELINE SCOTT CORLEY

1. Counsel shall ensure that whatever discovery is needed for all sides to evaluate the case for settlement purposes is completed by the date of the Settlement Conference. Counsel shall cooperate in providing discovery informally and expeditiously.

2. Lead trial counsel shall appear at the Settlement Conference with the parties. Any party who is not a natural person shall be represented by the person(s) with **unlimited** authority to negotiate a settlement. An insured party shall appear with a representative of the carrier with full authority to negotiate up to the limits of coverage. A person who needs to call another person not present before agreeing to any settlement does not have full authority.

3. Personal attendance of a party representative will rarely be excused by the Court. To nonetheless seek to excuse a party from personally attending a settlement conference, counsel for that party shall meet and confer with counsel for all other parties to determine if there are any objections to the moving party's absence. Counsel must then lodge a letter with the Court, with copies to all parties, seeking to excuse the party's participation. The letter shall recite the reasons for seeking the party's absence, as well as whether the other parties agree or object to the request and the reasons for any objection. The application to excuse a party must be lodged no later than the lodging of the Settlement Conference Statement.

4. Each party shall prepare a Settlement Conference Statement, which must be LODGED with the undersigned's Chambers (NOT electronically filed) no later than seven (7) calendar days prior to the conference. Please 3-hole punch the document at the left side. Each party shall also submit their Settlement Conference Statement in .pdf format and email their statement to JSCPO@cand.uscourts.gov.

5. The Settlement Conference Statement shall be served on opposing counsel. Any party may submit an additional confidential statement to the Court. The contents of this confidential statement will not be disclosed to the other parties.

6. The Settlement Conference Statement shall include at least the following:

- **a.** a. A brief statement of the facts of the case.
- **b.** A brief statement of the claims and defenses including, but not limited to, statutory or other grounds upon which the claims are founded, and a candid evaluation of the parties' likelihood of prevailing on the claims and defenses; and a description of the major issues in dispute.
- **c.** A summary of the proceedings to date and any pending motions.
- **d.** The relief sought.
- **e.** Any discrete issue that, if resolved, would facilitate the resolution of the case.
- **f.** The party's position on settlement, including present demands and offers and a history of past settlement discussions.

7. The parties shall notify Chambers immediately at (415) 522-2172 if a case settles prior to the date set for the Settlement Conference.

Hon. Nathanael M. Cousins

Magistrate Judge

Chambers Information

U.S. District Court, Northern District of California
Courtroom A, 15th Floor
450 Golden Gate Avenue
San Francisco, CA 94102

Scheduling Information

Courtroom Deputy: (415) 522-2039

Civil Law and Motion	Wednesdays at 9:00 a.m.
Criminal Law and Motion	Wednesdays at 11:00 a.m.
Pretrial Conferences	Wednesdays at 2:00 p.m.
Trials	Mondays, Tuesdays, Thursdays, and Fridays from 9:00 a.m. to 4:00 p.m.
Case Management Conferences	Wednesdays at 10:00 a.m.

Judge's Biography

Federal Judicial Service:

Magistrate Judge, U. S. District Court, Northern District of California, appointed in 2011.

Education:

-Stanford University, B.A.
-University of California, Hastings College of Law, J.D.

Professional Career:

-Adjunct Professor, University of California, Hastings College of Law
-Federal Prosecutor, U.S. Attorney's Office, Northern District of California
-Attorney, Antitrust Division of the U.S. Department of Justice
-Private Practice, Chicago, Illinois
-Law Clerk, Honorable F.A. Little, Jr., Chief Judge of the U.S. District Court, Western District of Louisiana

I. Judge Cousins' Procedures and Practices

A. *Civil Standing Order*

CIVIL STANDING ORDER
Magistrate Judge Nathanael M. Cousins

SCHEDULING

Civil motions are heard on Wednesdays at 9:00 a.m.

Civil case management conferences are held on Wednesdays at 10:00 a.m.

Civil pretrial conferences are held on Wednesdays at 2:00 p.m.

Parties are not required to reserve a hearing date but should confirm the Court's availability at http://www.cand.uscourts.gov. For questions regarding scheduling, please contact courtroom deputy Lili Harrell at 415.522.2039 or Lili_Harrell@cand.uscourts.gov.

CASES INITIALLY ASSIGNED TO JUDGE COUSINS

In civil cases initially assigned to this Court for all purposes, each party must file written consent to the jurisdiction of a magistrate judge or a written request for reassignment to a district judge as soon as possible but no later than the deadlines specified in Civil Local Rule 73-1(a).

COURTESY COPIES

For motion-related filings only, the parties must lodge an extra paper copy and mark it as a copy for "NC Chambers."

PROPOSED ORDERS

In all cases subject to e-filing, the parties must send via email all stipulations and proposed orders in WordPerfect format to ncpo@cand.uscourts.gov on the same day they e-file these documents.

DISCOVERY

Discovery motions referred to this Court and noticed for a hearing by a district judge will follow the briefing schedule set by the district judge, but the hearing will be rescheduled in accordance with this Court's civil motion calendar.

For all other discovery disputes in cases that have been referred to this Court, the parties must meet and confer to attempt to resolve their dispute as described below. If the parties are unable to reach a resolution through this process, they must file a joint statement of five pages or less that: (1) explains the nature and status of the dispute; (2) describes each unresolved issue; (3) summarizes each party's position with respect to each unresolved issue; and (4) states each party's proposed compromise with respect to each unresolved issue. The parties must not attach any declarations, affidavits, or exhibits to the statement. In the rare event that the parties are unable to file a joint statement, each party may file a statement of two pages or less. The statement(s) must be filed in ECF under the Civil Events category of Motions and Related Filings > Motions: General > Discovery Letter Brief. Upon review of the statement(s), the Court will advise the parties regarding the need, if any, for more briefing, a hearing, or a telephonic conference.

MEET AND CONFER REQUIREMENT

The parties must attempt to resolve their disputes informally by meeting and conferring in person. If counsel are located outside of the Bay Area, the parties must confer by telephone. A mere exchange of letters, emails, telephone calls, or facsimile transmissions does not satisfy the requirement to meet and confer.

IT IS SO ORDERED.

February 10, 2012

NATHANAEL M. COUSINS
United States Magistrate Judge

B. Settlement Conference Standing Order

SETTLEMENT CONFERENCE STANDING ORDER
MAGISTRATE JUDGE NATHANAEL M. COUSINS

SCHEDULING

To coordinate scheduling, please contact courtroom deputy Lili Harrell at Lili_Harrell@cand.uscourts.gov or 415.522.2039. Settlement conferences typically are held on Tuesdays and Thursdays at 9:30 a.m or 1:00 p.m.

A party seeking to continue a settlement conference must file a request in ECF as soon as possible after meeting and conferring with opposing counsel. The request must demonstrate a compelling reason for the continuance and state whether the opposing parties object to the continuance. Any party that objects to the continuance must file an opposition in ECF within two days of the filing date of the request for the continuance.

The parties must contact courtroom deputy Lili Harrell immediately if the case settles before the settlement conference takes place.

PERSONS REQUIRED TO ATTEND SETTLEMENT CONFERENCE

All parties and their counsel are required to attend the settlement conference. Non-natural persons must be represented by a person with unlimited authority to negotiate a settlement. An insured party must appear with a representative of the carrier with full authority to negotiate up to the limits of coverage. A person who must call another person not present at the conference before agreeing to a settlement does not have unlimited authority.

SETTLEMENT CONFERENCE STATEMENT

No later than seven days prior to the conference, each party must send a settlement conference statement to Judge Cousins' Chambers at 450 Golden Gate Avenue, 15th Floor, San Francisco, California 94102. Additionally, each party must serve its statement on opposing counsel and send it via email in PDF format to ncpo@cand.uscourts.gov. The statement must not be filed in ECF.

The settlement conference statement must include:

- **(a)** a brief statement of the facts of the case;
- **(b)** a brief statement of the claims and defenses raised, including statutory or other grounds upon which the claims are founded;
- **(c)** a candid evaluation of the parties' likelihood of prevailing on the claims and defenses;
- **(d)** a description of the major issues in dispute and any discrete issue that, if resolved, would facilitate the resolution of the case;
- **(e)** a summary of the proceedings to date;
- **(f)** a listing of all pending motions;
- **(g)** the relief sought;

(h) the party's position on settlement, including present demands, offers, and a history of past settlement discussions.

Any party may submit an additional confidential statement to the Court, the contents of which will not be disclosed to any other party.

DAY OF SETTLEMENT CONFERENCE

On the day of the conference, each party must check in with courtroom deputy Lili Harrell in Courtroom A, 15th Floor, 450 Golden Gate Avenue, San Francisco, California.

IT IS SO ORDERED.

December 1, 2011

____

NATHANAEL M. COUSINS
United States Magistrate Judge

Hon. Paul Singh Grewal

Magistrate Judge

Chambers Information

U.S. District Court, Northern District of California
Courtroom 5, 4th Floor
280 South First Street
San Jose, California 95113

Scheduling Information

Courtroom Deputy: (408) 535-5378

Civil Law and Motion	Tuesdays at 10:00 a.m.
Criminal Law and Motion	Thursdays at 10:30 a.m. and 1:30 p.m.
Pretrial Conferences	Tuesdays at 2:00 p.m.
Trials	Mondays at 9:30 a.m.
Status Conferences and Case Management Conferences	Tuesdays at 2:00 p.m.

Judge's Biography

Federal Judicial Service:
Magistrate Judge, U. S. District Court, Northern District of California, appointed in 2010.

Education:
-Massachusetts Institute of Technology, B.S.
-University of Chicago, J.D.

Professional Career:
-Private Practice, San Francisco, California
-Law Clerk, Honorable Arthur J. Gajarsa, U.S. Court of Appeals, Federal Circuit
-Private Practice, San Francisco, California
-Law Clerk, Honorable Sam H. Bell, U.S. District Court, Northern District of Ohio

I. Judge Grewal's Procedures and Practices

A. Settlement Conference Procedures

SETTLEMENT CONFERENCE PROCEDURES

TO PLAINTIFF(S):

The Magistrate Judge requires that plaintiff serve copies of these procedures on all parties and file a certificate of service with the Court. If, for any reason your case should settle before the scheduled conference please notify the Magistrate Judge's staff immediately.

TO ALL PARTIES AND COUNSEL OF RECORD:

Unless otherwise permitted in advance by the Court, counsel shall appear at the Settlement Conference with the parties or with the person or persons having full authority to settle the case. Only in rare exceptional situations will the persons with full authority to settle be allowed to be on the telephone standby and then only with the permission of the Court.

At least five (5) court days before the Settlement Conference the parties shall lodge a Settlement Conference Statement with the Clerk's Office (Room 2112) where it will be forwarded to the Magistrate Judge.

Copies of the Settlement Conference Statements shall not be served upon the other parties or counsel. The Court and its personnel will not permit other parties or counsel to have access to these statements.

The Settlement Conference Statement shall include the following:

1. A brief statement of the facts of the case.
2. A brief statement of the claims and defenses including statutory or other grounds upon which the claims and defenses are founded; a forthright evaluation of the parties' likelihood of prevailing on the claims and defenses; and a description of the major issues in dispute.
3. A summary of the proceedings to date including rulings on motions and motions outstanding.
4. An estimate of the cost and time to be expended for further discovery, pretrial and trial.
5. A brief statement of the parties' undisputed facts and issues.
6. Any discrete issues that, if resolved, would aid in the disposition of the case.
7. The relief sought.
8. The party's position on settlement, including present demands and offers and any history of past settlement discussion, offers and demands.

Dated: December 2, 2010

PAUL S. GREWAL
United States Magistrate Judge

B. Standing Order for Civil Practice

STANDING ORDER FOR CIVIL PRACTICE IN CASES ASSIGNED FOR ALL PURPOSES TO MAGISTRATE JUDGE PAUL S. GREWAL

(December 2010)

The parties shall follow the General Orders of the Court for the Northern District of California, the Local Rules, and the Federal Rules of Civil Procedure, except as expressly modified herein. Failure to comply with any of the rules and orders may be deemed sufficient grounds for monetary sanctions, dismissal, entry of default judgment, or other appropriate sanctions. The rules and the court's general orders are supplemented and modified as follows:

I. CASE MANAGEMENT CONFERENCE

A Case Management Conference will be held 2:00 p.m. on the date set forth in the "Order Setting Initial Case Management Conference and ADR Deadlines" that is issued when the case is filed. The Case Management Conference will be held in Courtroom 5, United States Courthouse, 280 South First Street, San Jose, CA 95113. This conference may be continued only on order of the Court; parties may not stipulate to continue a case management conference without leave from the Court.

II. MOTION PRACTICE

A. **Discovery Motions.** All parties who want their discovery motions before Magistrate Judge Grewal to be heard on shortened time may serve and file along with their discovery motion, either: (1) a stipulation of the parties pursuant to Local Rule 6-2; or (2) a motion to shorten time under Civil Local Rule 6-3. Otherwise, all discovery matters shall be noticed in accordance with Civil Local Rule 7-2. Upon receipt of the moving papers, this court may in its discretion modify the briefing and hearing schedule.

B. **Law and Motion Calendar.** Magistrate Judge Grewal's Civil Law and Motion calendar is heard every Tuesday at 10:00 a.m.

C. **Dispositive Motions.** If, before the Case Management Conference, any party files a motion that cannot be heard by the magistrate judge without the consent of the parties (see 28 U.S.C. section 636(c)), then within five (5) court days all parties who have not yet done so shall file either a "Consent to Proceed Before a United States Magistrate Judge," or else a "Declination to Proceed Before a United States Magistrate Judge and Request for Reassignment." Both forms are available from the clerk of the court, or from the Forms (Civil) section of the court's website at www.cand.uscourts.gov. **Magistrate Judge Grewal will not hear argument on dispositive motions without affirmative, written consents.**

III. EFFECT OF REASSIGNMENT TO A DISTRICT COURT JUDGE

In the event a case that is originally assigned to Magistrate Judge Grewal is later reassigned to a District Court Judge in the San Jose Division, and unless otherwise ordered by the court, the case will remain assigned to Magistrate Judge Grewal for all discovery matters.

IV. TRIAL PRACTICE (FOR COURT OR JURY TRIAL AS APPLICABLE)

A. **Ten (10) Court Days Prior to the Pretrial Conference.** Unless otherwise ordered, if the trial will be a jury trial, the parties shall exchange (but not file) their respective proposed jury instructions in order to begin preparing the joint set of jury instructions required by section IV.B.5., below. Unless otherwise ordered, the parties shall serve and file (or lodge, if so specified) the following documents:

1. **Trial Briefs.**

2. **Motions *In Limine*.**

3. **Depositions and Discovery Responses.** One copy of any deposition transcripts and any other discovery responses either party intends to offer as evidence, other than solely for impeachment or rebuttal, shall be lodged (not filed) with the court. The parties shall highlight the pertinent portions of the deposition transcripts and discovery responses.

4. **Proposed Voir Dire Questions (Jury Trials Only).** Proposed voir dire questions shall be filed with the court. The examination of trial jurors shall be conducted by the Magistrate Judge. The court will also allow limited follow up voir dire by attorneys. Juror questionnaires are permitted in limited situations. If the parties wish to submit juror questionnaires, the parties must contact the court well in advance of the pretrial conference to discuss procedures.

5. **Form of Verdict (Jury Trials Only).** In addition to the paper copy, each party shall also file a proposed form of verdict.

6. **Proposed Findings of Fact and Conclusions of Law (for Non-Jury Trials Only).** In addition to the paper copy, each party shall also file Proposed Findings of Fact and Conclusions of Law.

7. **Joint Pretrial Statement.** The Joint Pretrial Statement shall include the following:

   a. **Substance of the Action.** A brief description of the general nature of the action.

   b. **Stipulations, Agreed Statement and Undisputed Facts.** A statement of: (I) any stipulations requested or proposed for pretrial or trial purposes; (ii) whether all or part of the action may be presented upon an agreed statement of facts; and (iii) all relevant facts not reasonably in dispute, as well as any facts to which the parties will stipulate for the trial record without the necessity of supporting testimony or exhibits.

   c. **Disputed Factual Issues.** A plain and concise statement of all disputed factual issues which remain to be decided.

   d. **Disputed Legal Issues.** Without extended legal argument, a plain and concise statement of each disputed point of law concerning liability, relief, procedure and/or evidence. (When appropriate, full legal argument with citations to statutes and case law should be submitted by way of a

Trial Brief.)

e. **Deposition Excerpts and Discovery Responses.** Pursuant to Fed.R.Civ.P. 26(a)(3), a list of any deposition testimony (by page and lines) or other discovery responses that each party may offer as evidence at trial, other than solely for impeachment or rebuttal.

f. **Witnesses to be Called.** Pursuant to Fed.R.Civ.P. 26(a)(3), a list of the name of each witness each party expects to call at trial, other than solely for impeachment or rebuttal, together with a brief statement following each name describing the substance of the testimony to be given. Each party shall separately identify those witnesses whom the party expects to call and those witnesses whom the party may call if the need arises.

g. **Exhibits, Schedules and Summaries.** Pursuant to Fed.R.Civ.P. 26(a)(3), a list of all documents and other items to be offered as exhibits at the trial, other than solely for impeachment or rebuttal. Each item on the list shall be identified by an exhibit number, followed by a brief statement describing its substance or purpose, and the identity of the sponsoring witness. The parties must meet and confer on a division of exhibit numbers which will avoid duplication of numbering. If possible, parties should stipulate to the authenticity and admissibility of exhibits prior to trial. **Any disputes regarding the authenticity and/or admissibility of any exhibits must be brought to the court's attention no later than the Pretrial Conference, or the objections will be deemed waived.**

h. **Relief Prayed.** A detailed statement of all the relief claimed, particularly itemizing all elements of damages claimed as well as witnesses, documents or other evidentiary material to be presented concerning the amount of those damages.

i. **Estimate of Trial Time.** An estimate of the number of court days needed for the presentation of each party's case, indicating any possible reductions in time through proposed stipulations, agreed statements of facts, or expedited means of presenting testimony and exhibits.

j. **Amendments, Dismissals.** A statement of any requested or proposed amendments to pleadings or dismissals of parties, claims or defenses.

k. **Settlement Discussion.** A statement indicating whether further settlement negotiations would likely be productive.

l. **Miscellaneous.** A statement describing any other subjects relevant to the trial of the action or material to its just, speedy, and inexpensive determination.

B. Five (5) Court Days Prior to the Pretrial Conference.

Unless otherwise ordered, the parties shall serve and file the following not less than five (5) court days prior to the pretrial conference.

1. **Oppositions to Motions *In Limine*.**

2. **Objections to the use of Deposition Excerpts or other Discovery Responses.** Unless otherwise ordered, any objections to excerpts from depositions, or other discovery responses, designated in the Joint Pretrial Statement shall be filed in writing, along with a certification that counsel conferred with opposing counsel regarding any such objections.

3. **Counter-Designations.** In the event a party contends that a deposition excerpt or other discovery response is incomplete without inclusion of addition deposition excerpts or other discovery responses, the party shall file a counter-designation listing any additional deposition testimony (by page and lines) or other discovery responses it contends are necessary for a complete and fair record. Any objections to the counter-designations shall be served (by mail and electronically, such as by email attachment or fax) and filed the day before the Pretrial Conference (the after – hours drop box may ***not*** be used for this filing).

4. **Objections to Voir Dire and Verdict Forms.** Unless otherwise ordered, any objections to use of proposed voir dire or verdict forms shall be filed in writing, along with a certification that counsel conferred with opposing counsel regarding such objections.

5. **Jury Instructions (Jury Trials Only).** The court has a standard set of preliminary instructions which will be given at the beginning of trial and standard closing instructions which will be given prior to closing argument based upon the MODEL JURY INSTRUCTIONS OF THE NINTH CIRCUIT. The parties should *not* submit preliminary or closing instructions.

   The parties shall file a **joint** set of all proposed substantive instructions, unless specific leave to the contrary is granted by the Court. The Court prefers parties to use the MODEL JURY INSTRUCTIONS OF THE NINTH CIRCUIT or CALIFORNIA JURY INSTRUCTIONS, modified and supplemented as necessary. The parties shall also submit to the court: 1) an electronic copy of all proposed instructions, either on fixed media such as a CD Rom disk, and 2) an additional copy of the proposed jury instructions in a three-ring binder for the court's use.

   In the event parties are unable to agree on the language of a particular instruction, the objecting party shall submit an alternative instruction, placed immediately following the instruction to which an objection is being made, and a brief statement of the ground for the objection. **Challenged instructions must be clearly marked and identified.**

   Each proposed instruction shall be written in plain language, comprehensible to jurors, concise and free from argument, cover only one subject which shall be indicated in the caption, and be written out in full on a separate page. On a separate page following each instruction, the parties must provide citation to the authority upon which each instruction is based.

PAUL S. GREWAL
United States Magistrate Judge

Hon. Maria-Elena James
Chief Magistrate Judge

Chambers Information
U.S. District Court, Northern District of California
Courtroom B, 15th Floor
450 Golden Gate Avenue
San Francisco, CA 94102

Scheduling Information
Courtroom Deputy: (415) 522-4708

Civil Law and Motion	Thursdays at 10:00 a.m.
Criminal Law and Motion	Thursdays at 10:00 a.m.

Judge's Biography

Federal Judicial Service:
-Magistrate Judge, U. S. District Court, Northern District of California, appointed in 1994.

Education:
-University of San Francisco School Law School, J.D.

Professional Career:
-Commissioner, Superior Court of San Francisco
-Supervising Attorney, San Francisco
-Deputy City Attorney, San Francisco
-Staff Attorney, National Labor Relations Board
-Deputy Public Defender, San Francisco
-Director, Small Claims Court Education Project, Consumer Fraud Unit of the San Francisco
-District Attorney's Office

I. Judge James' Procedures and Practices

A. Case Management Standing Order

CASE MANAGEMENT STANDING ORDER
Magistrate Judge Maria-Elena James

1. Civil Law & Motion is heard on Thursdays at 10:00 a.m. Parties need not reserve a hearing date for civil matters; instead, they should confirm Magistrate Judge James' availability on the district court web site, www.cand.uscourts.gov. Motions are governed by the Civil Local Rules and the Federal Rules of Civil Procedure. Motions for summary judgment shall be accompanied by a joint statement of undisputed facts in compliance with Civil L. R. 56-2(b).

2. Criminal motions are scheduled with the courtroom deputy, Rose Maher, at (415) 522-4708, for any Thursday at 10:00 a.m. when the judge is available, or during the regular criminal calendar while Judge James is on criminal duty. Motions are governed by the Federal Rules of Criminal Procedure and the Criminal Local Rules.

3. Discovery disputes are governed by Magistrate Judge James' Discovery Standing Order, enclosed herewith and available on the Court's website.

4. Counsel shall meet and confer prior to the Case Management Conference and file a Joint Case Management Conference Statement no later than seven days prior to the c.m.c. The statement shall address the information contained in the Joint Case Management Statement and [proposed] Case Management Order form, enclosed herewith and available on the Court's website.

5. At least seven days prior to the c.m.c., each party shall file the magistrate jurisdiction consent/declination form, enclosed herewith and available on the Court's website. In the event that any defendant(s) files a motion to dismiss, defendant(s) shall file the consent/request form at the time the motion is filed and plaintiff(s) shall file the consent/declination form fourteen days thereafter, at the time the opposition is due.

6. In all "E-Filing" cases, in addition to filing papers electronically, the parties shall lodge with chambers a printed copy of the papers by noon of the next court day following the day the papers are filed electronically. These printed copies shall be marked "Chambers Copy" and shall be submitted to the Clerk's Office in an envelope clearly marked "Magistrate Judge Maria-Elena James" and include the case number. **ALL CHAMBERS COPIES OF ELECTRONICALLY FILED DOCUMENTS MUST INCLUDE ON EACH PAGE THE RUNNING HEADER CREATED BY THE ECF SYSTEM. ELECTRONICALLY FILED DOCUMENTS MUST BE CITED IN ALL OTHER DOCUMENTS AS FOLLOWS: DKT#__ AT __.**

Dated: March 29, 2012

MARIA-ELENA JAMES
United States Magistrate Judge

B. Standing Order for Discovery and Dispute Procedures

STANDING ORDER
DISCOVERY & DISPUTE PROCEDURES

This standing order informs all parties of the procedures for cases assigned to Magistrate Judge Maria-Elena James for trial or referred for purposes of discovery. This Order is intended to address all case-related discovery, including that which involves non-parties, and therefore applies whether or not an individual or entity is named in the complaint. Failure to abide by this Standing Order may result in the imposition of sanctions pursuant to Federal Rule of Civil Procedure 16(f) and Civil Local Rule 37-3.

1. Parties shall propound disclosures and discovery in accordance with Federal Rules of Civil Procedure 26 through 37 and the corresponding Civil Local Rules for the Northern District of California. A copy of the Local Rules is available at the Clerk's Office and at the Court's Web site - www.cand.uscourts.gov. No exceptions to the limitations established in the Federal and Local Rules shall be permitted except pursuant to stipulation of the parties or order of the Court.

2. No motions to compel shall be considered. Instead, the parties must meet and confer in person for the purpose of resolving all disputes. If unable to resolve any disputes through this procedure, the parties shall draft and file a jointly-signed letter that contains the following:

(a) A cover page with the case caption and an attestation that the parties met and conferred in person prior to filing the letter, as well as the signature of both parties or counsel;

(b) A section which sets forth the unresolved dispute and any pertinent factual background; and

(c) Each party's position, including relevant legal authority.

The joint letter shall be limited to five pages, excluding the cover page, and may not be accompanied by exhibits or affidavits other than exact copies of interrogatories, requests for production of documents and/or responses, privilege logs, and relevant deposition testimony. The parties need not state all disputes in one letter; rather, it is preferable that the parties file a separate letter for each dispute.

3. In the event that the parties are unable to meet and confer as directed above, or a moving party is unable to obtain the opposing party's portion of a joint letter after the meet and confer session, the moving party shall file a written request for a telephonic conference for the purpose of enforcing the Court's meet and confer requirement, or for the Court to fashion an alternative procedure. The written request shall include a declaration which states any attempt to meet and confer and/or obtain the joint letter, the reasons for the inability to comply with the standing order, and (if possible) three dates and times at which all parties are available for a telephonic conference. The moving party may attach exhibits to the declaration, but the declaration and exhibits combined may not exceed seven pages. The Court will not excuse a party from the requisite in-person meeting unless good cause is shown.

4. In the event that the parties are participating in a deposition or a site inspection and a dispute arises, the parties may contact the courtroom deputy, Rose Maher, to inquire whether Magistrate Judge James is available to address the dispute telephonically. In the event that Magistrate Judge James is unavailable, the parties shall follow the procedures for requesting a telephonic conference as set forth in paragraph 3 above. In such a case, the deposition or site inspection shall proceed with objections noted for the record.

5. No motion for sanctions may be filed until after the moving party has complied with the requirements of paragraphs 2 and 3 above. Motions for sanctions shall be filed separately, pursuant to Federal Rule 37 and Civil Local Rules 7 and 37-3.

6. The parties shall comply with Civil Local Rule 6 regarding any requests to change time.

7. Pursuant to Civil Local Rule 11-4(c), with the exception of communication with the courtroom deputy regarding scheduling, no party may contact the Court ex parte without prior notice to the opposing party. All communications or questions to the Court shall be presented in writing, properly filed, and include a certification that all parties were served a copy of the written communication.

8. In all "E-Filing" cases, in addition to filing papers electronically, the parties shall lodge with chambers a printed copy of the papers by noon of the next court day after filing. These printed copies shall be marked "Chambers Copy" and shall be submitted to the Clerk's Office in an envelope marked with "Magistrate Judge Maria-Elena James - Chambers Copy" and the case name and number.

IT IS SO ORDERED.

Dated: March 29, 2012

MARIA-ELENA JAMES
United States Magistrate Judge

Hon. Elizabeth D. Laporte

Magistrate Judge

Chambers Information

U.S. District Court, Northern District of California
Courtroom E, 15th Floor
450 Golden Gate Avenue
San Francisco, CA 94102

Scheduling Information

Courtroom Deputy: (415) 522-3694

Civil Law and Motion	Tuesdays at 9:00 a.m.
Criminal Law and Motion	Tuesdays at 11:00 a.m.
Case Management Conferences	Tuesdays at 10:00 a.m.

Judge's Biography

Federal Judicial Service:

-U.S. District Court Magistrate Judge, Northern District of California Nominated by William J. Clinton on April 4, 1998, to a seat vacated by Joan Brennan.

Education:

-Princeton University, B.A., 1975
-Oxford University-St. Anne's College, M.A., 1977
-Yale Law School, J.D., 1982

Professional Career:

-Law Clerk to the Honorable Marilyn Hall Patel, 1982-1983
-Private Practice, 1983-1991
-Administrative Law Judge, California Department of Insurance, 1991-1996
-Chief of Special Litigation, San Francisco City Attorney's Office, 1996-1998

I. Judge Laporte's Procedures and Practices

A. Standing Order

STANDING ORDER
Magistrate Judge Elizabeth D. Laporte

1) Civil law and motion is heard on Tuesdays at 9:00 a.m. Criminal law and motion is heard on Tuesdays at 1:15 p.m. Counsel need not reserve a hearing date in advance. However, noticed dates may be reset as the court's calendar requires.

2) Case Management Conferences are held on Tuesdays at 10:00 a.m. Pretrial Conferences are held on Tuesdays at 2:00 p.m.

3) Discovery motions may be addressed to the Court in three ways. A motion may be noticed on not less than 35 days pursuant to Civil L.R. 7-2. Alternatively, any party may seek an order to shorten or enlarge time under Civil L.R. 6-3 if the circumstances justify that relief. In emergencies during discovery events, the Court is available pursuant to Civil L.R. 37-1(b).

In the event a discovery dispute arises, counsel (or if *pro se*, the party) seeking discovery or a protective order shall confer in good faith with opposing counsel (or *pro se* party) in an effort to resolve the dispute without court action, as required by Fed. R. Civ. P. 37 and Civil L.R. 37-1(a).

The Court will not consider discovery motions unless the moving party has complied with Fed. R. Civ. P. 37 and Civil L.R. 37-1(a).

4) The Court strives to set matters and render decisions in a timely manner. The Court encourages parties to advise the Court by letter to chambers of any matter that appears to have been unduly delayed.

IT IS SO ORDERED.

Dated: July 26, 2005

ELIZABETH D. LAPORTE
United States Magistrate Judge

B. Standing Order on Confidential and Sealed Documents

STANDING ORDER ON CONFIDENTIAL AND SEALED DOCUMENTS
Magistrate Judge Elizabeth D. Laporte

IT IS HEREBY ORDERED as follows:

DESIGNATION OF DOCUMENTS

Before designating any specific information "Confidential" or "Confidential - Attorneys' Eyes Only," the designating party's counsel shall make a good faith determination that the information warrants protection under Rule 26(c) of the Federal Rules of Civil Procedure. The burden of establishing confidentiality shall be on the designating party.

Counsel are cautioned that over-designation of documents may result in sanctions. The filing of documents designated "Confidential" or "Confidential - Attorneys' Eyes Only" puts an additional burden on the Court. Often the party filing the document is not the designating party. In that situation the party does not have the option to unilaterally de-designate documents before submitting them to the Court, and therefore may have no choice but to request that they be filed under seal. Over-designating documents can thus result in unnecessary work for the Court in sorting out the documents that deserve sealing from those that do not, as well as additional work for the parties who must then re-file public versions of the non-confidential documents. The best way to avoid this result is for counsel to use best efforts to make appropriate designations at the outset, and to promptly de-designate a document when it comes to counsel's attention that the document is over-designated.

Before seeking to file under seal a document that another party has designated as Confidential or Confidential - Attorneys Eyes Only, Counsel shall review the document. If in Counsel's good faith judgment portions or all of the document have been unnecessarily designated as Confidential or Confidential - Attorneys Eyes Only, Counsel shall meet and confer with counsel for the designating party to attempt to resolve the issue.

REQUESTS TO FILE DOCUMENTS UNDER SEAL PURSUANT TO CIVIL LOCAL RULE 79-5

Any party wishing to file with the court any document(s) designated "Confidential" or "Confidential - Attorneys' Eyes Only" shall lodge the document(s) along with a Request for Sealing pursuant to Civil Local Rule 79-5, and any proposal to seal documents must be narrowly tailored to seal only that material for which good cause to seal has been established. All requests to seal must comply with Civil Local Rule 79-5. The parties are cautioned that "[b]road allegations of harm, unsubstantiated by specific examples or articulated reasoning, do not satisfy the Rule 26(c) test." Beckman Indus. Inc. v. International Ins. Co., 966 F.2d 470, 476 (9th Cir. 1992). Counsel may wish to put material which counsel seeks to seal in an appendix or an exhibit.

Dated: September 12, 2003

ELIZABETH D. LAPORTE
United States Magistrate Judge

II. Judge Laporte's Case Management Orders

A. *Case Management and Pretrial Order for Court Trial*

**IN THE UNITED STATES DISTRICT COURT
FOR THE NORTHERN DISTRICT OF CALIFORNIA**

Plaintiff,

v.

Defendant.
_______________________________/

No. C _________ EDL

CASE MANAGEMENT AND PRETRIAL ORDER FOR COURT TRIAL

Following the Case Management Conference held on _______________, IT IS HEREBY ORDERED THAT:

A further case management conference is set for _______________ before Magistrate Judge Laporte in Courtroom E, 15th Floor, U.S. District Court, 450 Golden Gate Avenue, San Francisco, California. An updated joint case management conference statement shall be filed no later than _______________.

Pursuant to Fed. R. Civ. P. 16, IT IS FURTHER ORDERED THAT the following case
management and pretrial order is entered:

1. TRIAL DATE

a. Court trial shall begin on ______________ at ______ in Courtroom E, 15th Floor, U.S. District Court, 450 Golden Gate Avenue, San Francisco, California. Any party who wants to order a daily transcript must notify the Court Reporter Supervisor at least two weeks before trial.

b. The length of the trial will be not more than ________ days.

2. DISCOVERY

a. All non-expert discovery shall be completed no later than ____________. There will be no further non-expert discovery after that date except by order of the Court for good cause shown. Motions to compel non-expert discovery must be filed within the time limits contained in Civil Local Rule 26-2.

b. Each side shall be limited to ___ depositions. Each party may propound ___ requests for documents, ___ interrogatories and ____ requests for admission on each opposing party.

c. Initial expert disclosures shall be made no later than __________. Rebuttal expert disclosures shall be made no later than __________. All treating physicians who will provide opinion testimony beyond that which can be provided by a lay person must be disclosed as expert witnesses, but they need not prepare expert reports unless ordered to do so by the Court.

d. All expert discovery shall be completed no later than _________. There will be no further expert discovery after that date except by order of the Court for good cause shown. Motions to compel expert discovery must be filed within the time limits contained in Civil Local Rule 26-2.

e. Rule 26(e)(1) of the Federal Rules of Civil Procedure requires all parties to supplement or correct their initial disclosures, expert disclosures, pretrial disclosures, and responses to discovery requests under the circumstances itemized in that Rule, and when ordered by the Court. The

Court expects that the parties will supplement and/or correct their disclosures promptly when required under that Rule, without the need for a request from opposing counsel. **In addition to the general requirements of Rule 26(e)(1), the parties will supplement and/or correct all previously made disclosures and discovery responses 28 days before the fact discovery cutoff date.**

f. Pursuant to Civil L.R. 37-1(b), telephone conferences are available to resolve disputes during a discovery event, such as a deposition, where the resolution during the event likely would result in substantial savings of expense or time.

g. **Privilege logs.** If a party withholds information that is responsive to a discovery request, and is otherwise discoverable under the Federal Rules of Civil Procedure, by claiming that it is privileged, or protected from discovery under the attorney work product doctrine or any other protective doctrine (including, but not limited to, privacy rights), that party shall prepare a "privilege log" (Fed. R. Civ. P. 26(b)(5)) setting forth the privilege relied upon and specifying separately for each document or for each category of similarly situated documents:

1. The name, job title, or capacity of the author;
2. The name, job title, or capacity of each recipient;
3. The date the document was prepared and, if different, the date(s) on which it was sent to or shared with persons other than its author(s);
4. The title and description of the document;
5. The subject matter addressed in the document;
6. The purpose(s) for which it was prepared or communicated; and
7. The specific basis for the claim that it is privileged.

The privilege log will be produced as quickly as possible, but no later than 14 days after the discovery responses are due (in a rolling production, 14 days after each set of documents is produced),

unless the parties stipulate or the Court orders otherwise in a particular case.

h. In responding to requests for documents and materials under Rule 34 of the Federal Rules of Civil Procedure, all parties shall affirmatively state in a written response served on all other parties the full extent to which they will produce materials and shall, promptly after the production, confirm in writing that they have produced all such materials so described that are locatable after a diligent search of <u>all</u> locations at which such materials might plausibly exist.

3. MOTIONS

The last day to file a motion, or stipulation and proposed order, to join other parties shall be ________.

The last day to file a motion, or stipulation and proposed order, to amend the pleadings shall

be ___________.

The last day for hearing dispositive motions shall be _________. Dispositive motions shall be served and filed no later than **thirty-five (35) days** prior to the scheduled hearing date. Any opposition shall be served and filed no later than **twenty-one (21) days** prior to the hearing date. Any reply to the opposition shall be served and filed no later than **fourteen (14) days** prior to the date of the hearing.

4. ALTERNATIVE DISPUTE RESOLUTION/SETTLEMENT CONFERENCE

A settlement conference shall be scheduled before another Magistrate Judge of this court. Counsel will be contacted by that judge's chambers with a date and time for the conference during ________, or as soon thereafter as is convenient to the judge's calendar.

5. PRETRIAL CONFERENCE

a. A pretrial conference shall be held on ____________ at ______ in Courtroom E, 15th Floor. **Each party shall attend personally or by lead counsel who will try the case.** The timing of disclosures required by Federal Rule of Civil Procedure 26(a)(3) and other pretrial disclosures shall be governed by this order.

b. **At least thirty (30) days** prior to the date of the pretrial conference, lead counsel shall meet and confer regarding:

(1) Preparation and content of the joint pretrial conference statement;

(2) Preparation and exchange of pretrial materials to be served and lodged pursuant to paragraph 5(c) below; and

(3) Settlement of the action.

c. **At least twenty (20) days** prior to the pretrial conference, counsel and/or parties shall:

(1) Serve and file a joint pretrial statement that includes the pretrial disclosures required by Federal Rule of Civil Procedure 26(a)(3) as well as the following supplemental information:

(a) *The Action.*

(i) Substance of the Action. A brief description of the substance of claims and defenses which remain to be decided.

(ii) Relief Prayed. A detailed statement of all the relief claimed, particularly itemizing all elements of damages claimed as well as witnesses, documents or other evidentiary

material to be presented concerning the amount of those damages.

(b) *The Factual Basis of the Action.*

(i) Undisputed Facts. A plain and concise statement of all relevant facts not reasonably disputable, as well as which facts parties will stipulate for incorporation into the trial record without the necessity of supporting testimony or exhibits.

(ii) Disputed Factual Issues. A plain and concise statement of all disputed factual issues which remain to be decided.

(iii) Agreed Statement. A statement assessing whether all or part of the action may be presented upon an agreed statement of facts.

(iv) Stipulations. A statement of stipulations requested or proposed for pretrial or trial purposes.

(c) *Disputed Legal Issues.*

Without extended legal argument, a concise statement of each disputed point of law concerning liability or relief, citing supporting statutes and decisions, and any procedural or evidentiary issues.

(d) *Trial Preparation.*

(i) Witnesses to Be Called. With regard to witnesses disclosed pursuant to Federal Rule of Civil Procedure 26(a)(3)(A), a brief statement describing the substance of the testimony to be given.

(ii) Estimate of Trial Time. An estimate of the number of hours needed for the presentation of each party's case, indicating possible reductions in time through proposed stipulations, agreed statements of facts, or expedited means of presenting testimony and exhibits.

(iii) Use of Discovery Responses. Designate excerpts from discovery that the parties intend to present at trial, other than solely for impeachment or rebuttal, from depositions specifying the witness page and line references, from interrogatory answers, or from responses to requests for admission.

(e) *Trial Alternatives and Options.*

(i) Settlement Discussion. A statement summarizing the status of settlement negotiations and indicating whether further negotiations are likely to be productive.

(ii) Amendments, Dismissals. A statement of requested or

proposed amendments to pleadings or dismissals of parties, claims or defenses.

(iii) Bifurcation, Separate Trial of Issues. A statement of whether bifurcation or a separate trial of specific issues is feasible and desired.

(f) *Miscellaneous.*

Any other subjects relevant to the trial of the action or material to its just, speedy and inexpensive determination.

(2) Serve and file trial briefs, motions *in limine* (including any motion regarding the qualifications or testimony of any expert witness), excerpts from discovery that will be offered at trial (including a copy of the deposition testimony or admission), and **joint** proposed findings of fact and conclusions of law. The findings of fact shall set forth in simple, declarative sentences, separately numbered, all factual contentions relied upon by the party in support of its claims for relief and shall be free of pejorative language and argument. Counsel shall submit separately their disputed findings of fact and conclusions of law. Counsel shall deliver to chambers a copy of their proposed findings of fact and conclusions of law on a computer diskette compatible with WordPerfect 6.1, 7, 8, 9 or 10 or 8.0 for Windows.

(3) Serve and file an exhibit setting forth the qualifications and experience for each expert witness;

(4) Serve and file a list of each party's exhibits by number (plaintiff) or letter (defendant), including a brief statement describing the substance and purpose of each exhibit and the name of the sponsoring witness;

(5) Exchange exhibits which shall be prepared (plaintiff shall use numbers; defendant shall use letters) and tabbed. Exhibits shall be three-hole punched and shall be submitted in binders. Each exhibit shall be marked on the front page or on the back of the last page with the information contained in Exhibit A to this Order; and

(6) Deliver two sets of all prepared exhibits to chambers (exhibits are not to be filed).

No party shall be permitted to call any witness or offer any exhibit in its case in chief that is not disclosed in its pretrial statement, exchanged with opposing counsel, and delivered to the Court, by the above deadline, without leave of the Court and for good cause.

d. **At least ten (10) days** prior to the pretrial conference, after meeting and conferring in a good faith attempt to resolve any objections, counsel and/or parties shall serve and file: (1) any objections to exhibits or to use of deposition excerpts or other discovery; (2) any objections to nonexpert witnesses; (3) any opposition to a motion *in limine*. No replies shall be filed.

e. All motions *in limine* and objections shall be heard at the pretrial conference.

6. All documents filed with the Clerk of the Court shall list the civil case number followed only by the initials **"EDL."** One copy must be clearly marked as a **chambers** copy.

Chambers' copies shall be three-hole punched at the left side, suitable for insertion into standard binders. In addition, all motions *in limine*, trial briefs, and findings of fact and conclusions of law shall be accompanied by a diskette containing a copy of the document formatted in WordPerfect 6.1, 7, 8, 9 or 10 (Windows) or 8.0 (Windows).

Dated: ____________________

____
ELIZABETH D. LAPORTE
United States Magistrate Judge

EXHIBIT A

[Form of Exhibit Tags]

UNITED STATES DISTRICT COURT NORTHERN DISTRICT OF CALIFORNIA Case Number: PLTF / DEFT EXHIBIT NO.______________ Date Admitted:________________________ By:_______________________________ Lili M. Harrell, Deputy Clerk	UNITED STATES DISTRICT COURT NORTHERN DISTRICT OF CALIFORNIA Case Number: PLTF / DEFT EXHIBIT NO.______________ Date Admitted:________________________ By:_______________________________ Lili M. Harrell, Deputy Clerk

B. Case Management and Pretrial Order for Jury Trial

IN THE UNITED STATES DISTRICT COURT
FOR THE NORTHERN DISTRICT OF CALIFORNIA

Plaintiff,

v.

Defendant.
____________________________/

No. C ________ EDL

CASE MANAGEMENT AND PRETRIAL ORDER FOR JURY TRIAL

Following the Case Management Conference held on ______________, IT IS HEREBY ORDERED THAT:

A further case management conference is set for ______________ before Magistrate Judge Laporte in Courtroom E, 15th Floor, U.S. District Court, 450 Golden Gate Avenue, San Francisco, California. An updated joint case management conference statement shall be filed no later than ______________.

Pursuant to Fed. R. Civ. P. 16, IT IS FURTHER ORDERED THAT the following case
management and pretrial order is entered:

1. TRIAL DATE

a. Jury trial shall begin on ____________ at _____ in Courtroom E, 15th Floor, U.S. District Court, 450 Golden Gate Avenue, San Francisco, California. Any party who wants to order a daily transcript must notify the Court Reporter Supervisor at least two weeks before trial.

b. The length of the trial will be not more than _______ days.

2. DISCOVERY

a. All non-expert discovery shall be completed no later than __________. There will be no further non-expert discovery after that date except by order of the Court for good cause shown. Motions to compel non-expert discovery must be filed within the time limits contained in Civil Local Rule 26-2.

b. Each side shall be limited to ___ depositions. Each party may propound ___ requests for documents, ___ interrogatories and ____ requests for admission on each opposing party.

c. Initial expert disclosures shall be made no later than _________. Rebuttal expert disclosures shall be made no later than _________. All treating physicians who will provide opinion testimony beyond that which can be provided by a lay person must be disclosed as expert witnesses, but they need not prepare expert reports unless ordered to do so by the Court.

d. All expert discovery shall be completed no later than ________. There will be no further expert discovery after that date except by order of the Court for good cause shown. Motions to compel expert discovery must be filed within the time limits contained in Civil Local Rule 26-2.

e. Rule 26(e)(1) of the Federal Rules of Civil Procedure requires all parties to supplement or correct their initial disclosures, expert disclosures, pretrial disclosures, and responses to discovery requests under the circumstances itemized in that Rule, and when ordered by the Court. The

Court expects that the parties will supplement and/or correct their disclosures promptly when required under that Rule, without the need for a request from opposing counsel. **In addition to the general requirements of Rule 26(e)(1), the parties will supplement and/or correct all previously made disclosures and discovery responses 28 days before the fact discovery cutoff date.**

f. Pursuant to Civil L.R. 37-1(b), telephone conferences are available to resolve disputes during a discovery event, such as a deposition, where the resolution during the event likely would result in substantial savings of expense or time.

g. **Privilege logs.** If a party withholds information that is responsive to a discovery request, and is otherwise discoverable under the Federal Rules of Civil Procedure, by claiming that it is privileged, or protected from discovery under the attorney work product doctrine or any other protective doctrine (including, but not limited to, privacy rights), that party shall prepare a "privilege log" (Fed. R. Civ. P. 26(b)(5)) setting forth the privilege relied upon and specifying separately for each document or for each category of similarly situated documents:

1. The name, job title, or capacity of the author;
2. The name, job title, or capacity of each recipient;
3. The date the document was prepared and, if different, the date(s) on which it was sent to or shared with persons other than its author(s);
4. The title and description of the document;
5. The subject matter addressed in the document;
6. The purpose(s) for which it was prepared or communicated; and
7. The specific basis for the claim that it is privileged.

The privilege log will be produced as quickly as possible, but no later than 14 days after the discovery responses are due (in a rolling production, 14 days after each set of documents is produced),

unless the parties stipulate or the Court orders otherwise in a particular case.

h. In responding to requests for documents and materials under Rule 34 of the Federal Rules of Civil Procedure, all parties shall affirmatively state in a written response served on all other parties the full extent to which they will produce materials and shall, promptly after the production, confirm in writing that they have produced all such materials so described that are locatable after a diligent search of <u>all</u> locations at which such materials might plausibly exist.

3. MOTIONS

The last day to file a motion, or stipulation and proposed order, to join other parties shall be ________.

The last day to file a motion, or stipulation and proposed order, to amend the pleadings shall

be ___________.

The last day for hearing dispositive motions shall be __________. Dispositive motions shall be served and filed no later than **thirty-five (35) days** prior to the scheduled hearing date. Any opposition shall be served and filed no later than **twenty-one (21) days** prior to the hearing date. Any reply to the opposition shall be served and filed no later than **fourteen (14) days** prior to the date of the hearing.

4. ALTERNATIVE DISPUTE RESOLUTION/SETTLEMENT CONFERENCE

A settlement conference shall be scheduled before another Magistrate Judge of this court. Counsel will be contacted by that judge's chambers with a date and time for the conference during ________, or as soon thereafter as is convenient to the judge's calendar.

5. PRETRIAL CONFERENCE

a. A pretrial conference shall be held on _____________ at ______ in Courtroom E, 15th Floor. **Each party shall attend personally or by lead counsel who will try the case.** The timing of disclosures required by Federal Rule of Civil Procedure 26(a)(3) and other pretrial disclosures shall be governed by this order.

b. **At least thirty (30) days** prior to the date of the pretrial conference, lead counsel shall meet and confer regarding:

(1) Preparation and content of the joint pretrial conference statement;

(2) Preparation and exchange of pretrial materials to be served and lodged pursuant to paragraph 5(c) below; and

(3) Settlement of the action.

c. **At least twenty (20) days** prior to the pretrial conference, counsel and/or parties shall:

(1) Serve and file a joint pretrial statement that includes the pretrial disclosures required by Federal Rule of Civil Procedure 26(a)(3) as well as the following supplemental information:

(a) *The Action.*

(i) Substance of the Action. A brief description of the substance of claims and defenses which remain to be decided.

(ii) Relief Prayed. A detailed statement of all the relief claimed, particularly itemizing all elements of damages claimed as well as witnesses, documents or other evidentiary

material to be presented concerning the amount of those damages.

(b) *The Factual Basis of the Action.*

(i) Undisputed Facts. A plain and concise statement of all relevant facts not reasonably disputable, as well as which facts parties will stipulate for incorporation into the trial record without the necessity of supporting testimony or exhibits.

(ii) Disputed Factual Issues. A plain and concise statement of all disputed factual issues which remain to be decided.

(iii) Agreed Statement. A statement assessing whether all or part of the action may be presented upon an agreed statement of facts.

(iv) Stipulations. A statement of stipulations requested or proposed for pretrial or trial purposes.

(c) *Disputed Legal Issues.*

Without extended legal argument, a concise statement of each disputed point of law concerning liability or relief, citing supporting statutes and decisions, and any procedural or evidentiary issues.

(d) *Trial Preparation.*

(i) Witnesses to Be Called. With regard to witnesses disclosed pursuant to Federal Rule of Civil Procedure 26(a)(3)(A), a brief statement describing the substance of the testimony to be given.

(ii) Estimate of Trial Time. An estimate of the number of hours needed for the presentation of each party's case, indicating possible reductions in time through proposed stipulations, agreed statements of facts, or expedited means of presenting testimony and exhibits.

(iii) Use of Discovery Responses. Designate excerpts from discovery that the parties intend to present at trial, other than solely for impeachment or rebuttal, from depositions specifying the witness page and line references, from interrogatory answers, or from responses to requests for admission.

(e) *Trial Alternatives and Options.*

(i) Settlement Discussion. A statement summarizing the status of settlement negotiations and indicating whether further negotiations are likely to be productive.

(ii) Amendments, Dismissals. A statement of requested or

proposed amendments to pleadings or dismissals of parties, claims or defenses.

(iii) Bifurcation, Separate Trial of Issues. A statement of whether bifurcation or a separate trial of specific issues is feasible and desired.

(f) *Miscellaneous.*

Any other subjects relevant to the trial of the action or material to its just, speedy and inexpensive determination.

(2) Serve and file trial briefs, motions *in limine* (including any motion regarding the qualifications or testimony of any expert witness), proposed voir dire questions, jury instructions, verdict forms and excerpts from discovery that will be offered at trial (include a copy of the deposition testimony or admission). The parties shall submit proposed jury instructions **jointly**. If there are any instructions on which the parties cannot agree, those instructions may be submitted separately;

(3) Serve and file an exhibit setting forth the qualifications and experience for each expert witness;

(4) Serve and file a list of each party's exhibits by number (plaintiff) or letter (defendant), including a brief statement describing the substance and purpose of each exhibit and the name of the sponsoring witness;

(5) Exchange exhibits which shall be premarked (plaintiff shall use numbers; defendant shall use letters) and tabbed. Exhibits shall be three-hole punched and shall be submitted in binders. Each exhibit shall be marked on the front page or on the back of the last page with the information contained in Exhibit A to this Order; and

No party shall be permitted to call any witness or offer any exhibit in its case in chief that is not disclosed in its pretrial statement, exchanged with opposing counsel, and delivered to the Court, by the above deadline, without leave of the Court and for good cause.

d. **At least ten (10) days** prior to the pretrial conference, after meeting and conferring in a good faith attempt to resolve any objections, counsel and/or parties shall serve and file: (1) any objections to exhibits or to use of deposition excerpts or other discovery; (2) any objections to non-expert witnesses; (3) any objection to proposed voir dire questions, jury instructions and verdict forms that the parties have been unable in good faith to resolve; (4) any opposition to a motion *in limine*. No replies shall be filed.

e. All motions *in limine* and objections shall be heard at the pretrial conference.

6. JURY TRIAL

a. Counsel shall submit an agreed upon set of voir dire questions to be posed by the Court. Any voir dire questions on which counsel cannot agree may be submitted separately. Counsel shall be allowed brief follow-up voir dire after the Court's questioning.

b. The following jury instructions from the Manual of Model Civil Jury Instructions for the Ninth Circuit (2007 Edition) shall be given absent objection: 1.1-1.2, 1.6-

1.14, 1.18, 2.11. Counsel shall submit **jointly** an agreed upon set of case specific instructions, using the Ninth Circuit Manual where appropriate. Do not submit duplicates of those listed above. Any instructions on which counsel cannot agree may be submitted separately. Each requested instruction shall be typed in full on a separate page with citations to the authority upon which it is based <u>and</u> a reference to the party submitting. A **second blind copy** of each instruction and verdict form shall also be submitted, omitting the citation to authority and the reference to the submitting party.

7. All documents filed with the Clerk of the Court shall list the civil case number followed only by the initials **"EDL."** One copy must be clearly marked as a **chambers** copy. Chambers copies shall be three-hole punched at the left side, suitable for insertion into standard binders. In addition, all proposed jury instructions, motions *in limine*, form of verdict and trial briefs shall be accompanied by a diskette containing a copy of the document formatted in WordPerfect 6.1, 7, 8, 9 or 10 (Windows) or 8.0 (Windows).

Dated: ____________________

____
ELIZABETH D. LAPORTE
United States Magistrate Judge

<u>EXHIBIT A</u>

[Form of Exhibit Tags]

UNITED STATES DISTRICT COURT NORTHERN DISTRICT OF CALIFORNIA Case Number: PLTF / DEFT EXHIBIT NO.____________ Date Admitted:____________________ By:______________________________ Lili M. Harrell, Deputy Clerk	UNITED STATES DISTRICT COURT NORTHERN DISTRICT OF CALIFORNIA Case Number: PLTF / DEFT EXHIBIT NO.____________ Date Admitted:____________________ By:______________________________ Lili M. Harrell, Deputy Clerk

C. *Notice of Settlement Conference and Settlement Conference Order*

IN THE UNITED STATES DISTRICT COURT
FOR THE NORTHERN DISTRICT OF CALIFORNIA

Plaintiff,

v.

Defendant.

_______________________________________/

No. C __________ EDL

NOTICE OF SETTLEMENT CONFERENCE AND SETTLEMENT CONFERENCE ORDER

TO ALL PARTIES AND COUNSEL OF RECORD:

The above matter was referred to Magistrate Judge Elizabeth D. Laporte for Settlement Conference. You are hereby notified that the conference is scheduled for _______________ at _____, Courtroom E, 15th Floor, Federal Building, 450 Golden Gate Avenue, San Francisco, California 94102. If the above date is not possible for the parties and counsel, or if the parties believe that settlement discussions would be more productive at a different time, counsel shall confer with each other and then contact Magistrate Judge Laporte's Courtroom Deputy **within a week** at (415) 522-3694 to determine whether it is possible and appropriate to reschedule the conference.

Lead trial counsel shall appear at the Settlement Conference with the parties and with the person or persons having **full authority** to negotiate and to settle the case. In all cases in which a party is insured, the carrier's claims representative and attorney, if any, with **full authority** to negotiate up to the limits of coverage shall also attend the Settlement Conference. In cases where settlement authority rests with a governing body, counsel shall advise the Court and opposing counsel by letter at least 72 hours prior to the conference, of the manner in which the governing body will appear.

Personal attendance by counsel will not be excused under any circumstances and personal attendance by a party will rarely be excused. Permission for a party to attend by telephone may be granted, in the Court's discretion, upon written request made at least two weeks in advance of the conference, **if** the party lives and works outside of the Northern District of California **and** the Court determines that personal attendance would constitute a hardship and is not needed in order to have an effective settlement conference. The nature of the hardship must be explained. A copy of the written request must be served on all other parties. Any objection to the request must be submitted within forty-eight (48) hours of receipt. Both the request and objection may be submitted in letter form either by mail or facsimile to (415) 522-2002. If telephone attendance is allowed, the party must be available throughout the entire conference.

On or before ___________, the parties shall deliver directly to the Magistrate Judge a Confidential Settlement Conference Statement which should not be filed with the Clerk of the Court or served upon other parties.

The Confidential Settlement Conference Statement shall not exceed twenty-five (25) pages of text exclusive of exhibits. (Parties are encouraged to include as exhibits any key documents and deposition excerpts). The Confidential Settlement Conference Statement shall include the following:

1. A brief statement of the facts of the case.

2. A brief statement of the claims and defenses including, but not limited to, statutory or other grounds upon which the claims are founded, a candid, forthright evaluation of the parties' likelihood of prevailing on the claims and defenses and a description of the major issues in dispute.

3. A list of the key facts in dispute and a brief statement of the specific evidence relevant to those facts.

4. A summary of the proceedings to date and any pending motions.

5. An estimate of the out of pocket expenses, attorney's fees and time to be expended for further discovery, pretrial and trial.

6. The relief sought, including an itemization of damages.

7. The party's position on settlement, including present demands and offers and a history of past settlement discussions.

8. If there have been no prior settlement discussions, plaintiff must serve a demand letter outlining its theories for recovery, supporting facts and damages in writing **at least 7 business days before** the conference, and defendant must respond in writing **at least 3 business days before** the conference.

It is not unusual for conferences to last several hours or at times, all day. No participant in the settlement conference will be permitted to leave the settlement conference before it is concluded without the permission of the settlement conference judge.

Parties are encouraged to participate and frankly discuss their case. Statements they make during the conference will not be admissible at trial to prove or disprove liability in the event the case does not settle. The parties should be prepared to discuss such items as their settlement objectives, any impediments to settlement that they perceive, whether they have enough information to discuss settlement and, if not, what additional information is needed and the possibility of a creative resolution of the dispute.

Any request to continue the settlement conference shall be submitted in writing as soon as possible after consultation with the opposing party. **The request must demonstrate a compelling reason for a continuance**, and state whether the opposing party(ies) agree or oppose the request. Any party who objects to the continuance should submit a written response within 2 business days. Submission by facsimile is acceptable at facsimile number (415) 522-2002. **A paper copy of all electronically filed documents must be delivered to chambers no later than 12:00 noon on the day after the document is electronically filed.**

The parties shall notify Magistrate Judge Laporte's Courtroom Deputy **immediately** at (415) 522-3694 if this case settles prior to the date set for settlement conference.

Dated: ___________________

ELIZABETH D. LAPORTE
United States Magistrate Judge

D. Order Regarding Case Management Conference

IN THE UNITED STATES DISTRICT COURT
FOR THE NORTHERN DISTRICT OF CALIFORNIA

Plaintiff,

v.

Defendant.
______________________________/

No. C ________ EDL

ORDER RE CASE MANAGEMENT CONFERENCE

Lead trial counsel who will try this case are directed to confer in advance of the Case Management Conference with respect to all matters contained in the March 1, 2007 Standing Order for all Judges of the Northern District of California regarding Contents of Joint Case Management Conference, including **a discovery plan and discovery limits** and all other matters described in Federal Rules of Civil Procedure 16(a), 16(b) and 26(f) and Civil Local Rule 16-10. Pursuant to Civil L.R. 16-10(a), **lead trial counsel shall attend the Case Management Conference** and be prepared to discuss all matters referred to in this order. Counsel shall have the authority to enter stipulations and make admissions regarding all matters described herein.

PLAINTIFF IS DIRECTED TO SERVE COPIES OF THIS ORDER AT ONCE UPON ALL PARTIES IN THIS ACTION AND UPON THOSE SUBSEQUENTLY JOINED IN ACCORDANCE WITH THE PROVISIONS OF FEDERAL RULES OF CIVIL PROCEDURE 4 AND 5 AND CIVIL LOCAL RULES 4 AND 5, and to file with the Clerk of the Court a Certificate reflecting such service.

Failure to comply with this order, the provisions of Federal Rule of Civil Procedure 16 and 26(f) or the provisions of Civil L.R. 16-10 may be grounds for sanctions. (See Fed. R. Civ. P. 16(f)).

Dated: ________________

____
ELIZABETH D. LAPORTE
United States Magistrate Judge

E. Order Regarding Discovery Procedures

IN THE UNITED STATES DISTRICT COURT
FOR THE NORTHERN DISTRICT OF CALIFORNIA

Plaintiff,

v.

Defendant.
______________________________/

No. C ________ EDL

ORDER RE DISCOVERY PROCEDURES

TO ALL PARTIES AND COUNSEL OF RECORD:

The above matter has been referred to Magistrate Judge Elizabeth D. Laporte. All hearing dates are subject to the availability of Judge Laporte's calendar. You may review Judge Laporte's calendar and scheduling information on the District Court's website, http://www.cand.uscourts.gov/.

The ____________ will be heard on ____________ at _______ in Courtroom E, 15th Floor, United States District Court, 450 Golden Gate Avenue, San Francisco, California, 94102. Opposition briefs are due __________, and reply briefs are due ___________.

DISCOVERY MOTIONS

Discovery motions are heard on Judge Laporte's civil law and motion calendar and are to be set on Tuesday mornings at 9:00 a.m., Courtroom E, 15th Floor, United States District Court, 450 Golden Gate Avenue, San Francisco, California, 94102.

1. Discovery motions may be addressed to the Court in three ways. A motion may be noticed on not less than 35 days pursuant to Civil L.R. 7-2. Alternatively, any party may seek an order to shorten or enlarge time under Civil L.R. 6-3 if the circumstances justify that relief. In emergencies during discovery events, the Court is available pursuant to Civil L.R. 37-1(b).

In the event a discovery dispute arises, counsel (or if *pro se*, the party) seeking discovery or a protective order shall confer in good faith with opposing counsel (or *pro se* party) in an effort to resolve the dispute without court action, as required by Fed. R. Civ. P. 37 and Civil L.R. 37-1(a). A declaration setting forth these meet and confer efforts and the final positions of each party shall be included in the moving papers. The Court will not consider discovery motions unless the moving party has complied with Fed. R. Civ. P. 37 and Civil L.R. 37-1(a).

Motions to compel fact discovery must be filed within the time limits contained in Civil Local Rule 26-2. Motions to compel expert discovery must be filed within the time limits contained in Civil Local Rule 26-2.

2. Motions for sanctions shall be filed by separate motion in accordance with the Federal Rule of Civil Procedure 37 and Civil L.R. 37-3. The parties shall comply with their meet and confer obligations pursuant to Civil L.R. 37-1(a). Parties who refuse to meet and confer will be subject to sanctions pursuant to Civil L.R. 37-3.

3. All filings of documents relating to motions referred to Magistrate Judge

Laporte shall list the civil case number and the District Court Judge's initials followed by the designation "(EDL)." At the time of filing of original papers with the clerk's office, the parties are required to submit two conformed copies of each document, one of which shall be designated **"EDL Chambers Copy."** If documents are filed electronically, a paper chambers copy of each electronically filed document must be delivered to the Court no later than 12:00 noon on the day after the filing. The paper chambers copy must be marked "Chambers Copy" and must be lodged with the Clerk's Office, in an envelope clearly marked with the judge's name, case number, and "Chambers Copy." Parties must not <u>file</u> a paper copy of any document with the Clerk's Office that has already been filed electronically.

4. Rule 26(e)(1) of the Federal Rules of Civil Procedure requires all parties to supplement or correct their initial disclosures, expert disclosures, pretrial disclosures, and responses to discovery requests under the circumstances itemized in that Rule, and when ordered by the Court. The Court expects that the parties will supplement and/or correct their disclosures promptly when required under that Rule, without the need for a request from opposing counsel. **In addition to the general requirements of Rule 26(e)(1), the parties will supplement and/or correct all previously made disclosures and discovery responses 28 days before the fact discovery cutoff date.**

5. **Privilege logs.** If a party withholds information that is responsive to a discovery request, and is otherwise discoverable under the Federal Rules of Civil Procedure, by claiming that it is privileged, or protected from discovery under the attorney work product doctrine or any other protective doctrine (including, but not limited to, privacy rights), that party shall prepare a "privilege log" (Fed. R. Civ. P. 26(b)(5)) setting forth the privilege relied upon and specifying separately for each document or for each category of similarly situated documents:

a. The name and job title or capacity of the author;

b. The name and job title or capacity of each recipient;

c. The date the document was prepared and, if different, the date(s) on which it was sent to or shared with persons other than its author(s);

d. The title and description of the document;

e. The subject matter addressed in the document;

f. The purpose(s) for which it was prepared or communicated; and

g. The specific basis for the claim that it is privileged.

The privilege log will be produced as quickly as possible, but no later than 14 days after the discovery responses are due, unless the parties stipulate or the Court orders otherwise in a particular case.

6. In responding to requests for documents and materials under Rule 34 of the Federal Rules of Civil Procedure, all parties shall affirmatively state in a written response served on all other parties the full extent to which they will produce materials and shall, promptly after the production, confirm in writing that they have produced <u>all</u> such materials so described that are locatable after a diligent search of <u>all</u> locations at which such materials might plausibly exist.

7. All documents shall be filed at the Clerk's Office in compliance with the Civil

Local Rules. Documents not filed in compliance with those rules will not be considered by the Court.

8. Discovery motions may be submitted without argument upon stipulation of the parties and order of the Court no later than two (2) court days before the hearing.

9. The Court strives to set matters and render decisions in a timely manner. The Court encourages parties to advise the Court by letter to chambers of any matter that appears to have been unduly delayed.

The failure of counsel or a party to abide by this Order may result in sanctions pursuant to Federal Rule of Civil Procedure 16(f). A party or counsel has a continuing duty to supplement the initial disclosure when required under Federal Rule of Civil Procedure 26(e)(1).

Dated: ___________________

____
ELIZABETH D. LAPORTE
United States Magistrate Judge

Hon. Howard R. Lloyd

Magistrate Judge

Chambers Information

U.S. District Court, Northern District of California
Courtroom 2, 5th Floor
280 South First Street
San Jose, CA 95113

Scheduling Information

Courtroom Deputy: (408) 535-5365

Civil Law and Motion	Tuesdays at 10:00 a.m.
Criminal Law and Motion	Thursdays at 1:30 p.m.
Pretrial and Case Management Conferences	Tuesdays at 1:30 p.m.

Judge's Biography

Federal Judicial Service:

-Magistrate Judge, U.S. District Court, Northern District of California, appointed in 2002.

Education:

-College of William and Mary, B.A.
-University of Michigan Law School, J.D.

Professional Career:

-Independent Arbitrator and Mediator
-Private Practice, San Jose, California

I. Judge Lloyd's Procedures and Practices

A. Standing Order Regarding Civil Discovery Disputes

STANDING ORDER RE: CIVIL DISCOVERY DISPUTES

1. Effect of Delay on Discovery Disputes.

The parties and counsel are cautioned not to allow discovery disagreements to drag on unresolved until some important looming deadline forces them into action. Because of the press of its other business, the court may not be able to give the dispute its attention with the same celerity that some or all of the parties think is necessary.

2. Resolving Discovery Disputes

In order for this court to efficiently and flexibly respond to discovery disputes, and accounting both for (1) parties' and counsels' obligation to diligently strive to resolve such disputes without court involvement and (2) the limitations on available judicial resources: effective immediately this court adopts a new procedure for resolving discovery disputes.

A. Absent leave of court, formal noticed discovery motions may no longer be filed and, if filed contrary to this order, will not be heard.

B. Instead, parties (and non-parties involved in a discovery dispute) will first use the customary convenient means of communication - telephone, e-mail, correspondence, person to person talks between members of opposing litigation teams - to try to reach agreement.

C. If that fails to lead to complete agreement, then LEAD COUNSEL (and any unrepresented person), accompanied by anyone else whose presence is needed to fully explore resolution, shall meet IN PERSON for as long as and as often as is needed to reach full agreement.

i. Unjustified delay in arranging the meeting, especially where the dispute is time sensitive, or refusal to attend or to participate meaningfully will be grounds for sanctions and/or for entry of an order in favor of the other side. Except in extreme circumstances, excuses such as press of business, inconvenience, or cost will not suffice.

ii. Hopefully, the parties can agree on a site for the in-person meeting of lead counsel. The most sensible way would probably be for the party advancing the dispute to pick the place for the first meeting, the other party pick the site for the second, and alternating thereafter. If the parties cannot agree, then the court requires lead counsel meet at a location approximately half way between their offices.

D. If the meeting(s) between lead counsel do not resolve the dispute, then within 5 business days after conclusion of the session(s) (or, 5 days after reaching impasse as to a particular issue) the parties shall file on pleading paper a "Discovery Dispute Joint Report #___" ("Joint Report"). In no event may a Joint Report be filed later than 7 days after the discovery cut-off date(s), as prescribed in Civil L.R. 37-3. As usual, a chambers copy should also be submitted.

i. The Joint Report's cover page will contain: the case caption; a one sentence identification of the issue it covers; the date, place, and length of time of the joint meeting; the close of discovery and any other date that is relevant; and the attestations of lead counsel that they complied with this Standing Order.

ii. To avoid needless complexity and unwieldiness, the Joint Report should deal with only one issue (or, at most, a few inextricably related issues).

iii. The Joint Report, including the cover page, shall not exceed 11 pages. It should describe the dispute and the facts essential to understanding it. Then, in a format that allows ready comparison, it should give each party's position (with brief citation to important authority), and - finally - each party's final and "most reasonable" proposal for how the court should decide.

iv. The only exhibit permitted to the Joint Report is an exact copy of the discovery request(s) in issue and the response(s) (if any) to it (i.e.,: requests for documents, interrogatories, privilege log, non-party subpoena, etc.) If it consists of more than just a few pages, the exhibit shall be indexed.

v. A single lead-counsel-in-person session may produce more than one Joint Report, but the court would look with disfavor on any attempt to use multiple Joint Reports to skirt the page limitation.

vi. Unjustified delay or refusal to participate meaningfully in the preparation of the Joint Report is grounds for imposition of sanctions or entry of an order sought by the other side.

E. Upon receipt of the Joint Report, the court will decide what further proceedings, if any, are appropriate. If the issue is clearly presented and ripe for decision, it may simply issue a ruling. Alternatively, other options include: scheduling a telephone conference, calling for further briefing, or, rarely, holding a hearing.

F. Any party seeking an award of attorney fees or other expenses in connection with a discovery dispute shall file a noticed motion pursuant to the Northern District Local Rules. It would ordinarily be presumptuous to file such a motion before the court has ruled on the dispute.

G. When the parties have become, or expect to become, engaged in a succession of discovery disputes or otherwise require the ongoing assistance of a neutral decision maker, the court recommends they consider appointment of a Special Master.

IT IS SO ORDERED.

Dated: June 3, 2011

HOWARD R. LLOYD
United States Magistrate Judge

B. Standing Order Regarding Initial Case Management

STANDING ORDER RE: INITIAL CASE MANAGEMENT

1. In cases that are randomly assigned to Judge Lloyd for all purposes, the parties are requested to file their written consent to the assignment of a U.S. Magistrate Judge for all purposes, or their written declination of consent, as soon as possible.

2. The civil motion calendar is heard on Tuesdays at 10:00 a.m. The criminal motion calendar is heard on Thursdays at 9:30 a.m. Motions may be noticed for hearing pursuant to Civil L.R. 7. Counsel need not reserve a hearing date in advance for civil motions, although noticed dates may be reset as the Court's calendar requires. HOWEVER, do not notice a motion over a civil discovery dispute. Instead, follow this court's "Standing Order re: Civil Disputes."

3. Parties with questions regarding scheduling (excluding settlement conferences) should contact Judge Lloyd's Administrative Law Clerk at (408) 535-5411.

4. A Case Management Conference will be held on the date and time specified in the Order Setting Initial Case Management Conference in Courtroom 2, United States Courthouse, 280 South First Street, San Jose, California. This conference may be continued only by Court Order pursuant to Civil L.R. 16-2(e). Parties may not stipulate to continue a Case Management Conference without Court approval.

5. Pursuant to Civil L.R. 16-9, no later than seven (7) days before the Case Management Conference, the parties shall file a Joint Case Management Statement. For the required format and contents of this filing, follow the "Standing Order for All Judges of the Northern District of California: Contents of Joint Case Management Statement." If preparation of a joint statement would cause undue hardship, the parties may serve and file separate statements, which shall include a description of the undue hardship.

6. Plaintiff or removing Defendant shall serve a copy of this Standing Order on all parties to this action and on all parties subsequently joined, in accordance with Fed.R.Civ.P 4 and 5. Following service, Plaintiff shall file a certificate of service, in accordance with Civil L.R. 5-6.

IT IS SO ORDERED.

Dated: August 22, 2002
Amended February 26, 2007
Amended June 3, 2011

HOWARD R. LLOYD
United States Magistrate Judge

C. Standing Order Regarding Pretrial Preparation

STANDING ORDER RE: PRETRIAL PREPARATION

Good cause appearing, IT IS HEREBY ORDERED that the following requirements and procedures shall apply in all cases scheduled for trial before the undersigned judge.

A. **Not less than fifteen (15) days prior to the Pretrial Conference**, lead counsel (and all parties appearing *pro se*) shall meet and confer in person with respect to accomplishing the requirements and procedures outlined below.

B. **Not less than ten (10) court days prior to the Pretrial Conference**, the parties shall serve and file (or lodge, as applicable):

1. **Trial Briefs (optional);**

2. **Motions *In Limine*;**

3. **Deposition and Discovery Responses.** One copy of any deposition transcript and any other discovery response either party intends to offer as evidence, other than solely for impeachment or rebuttal, shall be lodged with the court. The parties shall highlight the pertinent portions of the deposition transcripts and discovery responses;

4. **Proposed Voir Dire Questions (Jury Trials Only).** Proposed voir dire questions shall be submitted to the court. The examination of trial jurors shall be conducted by the Judge. The court will also allow limited follow up voir dire by attorneys. Juror questionnaires are permitted in limited situations. If the parties wish to submit juror questionnaires, the parties must contact the court well in advance of the pretrial conference to discuss procedures;

5. **Jury Instructions (Jury Trials Only).** The court has a standard set of preliminary instructions which will be given at the beginning of trial and standard closing instructions which will be given prior to closing argument based upon the MODEL JURY INSTRUCTIONS OF THE NINTH CIRCUIT. The parties should not submit preliminary or closing instructions.

The parties shall file a **joint** set of all proposed substantive instructions, unless specific leave to the contrary is granted by the Court.

The Court prefers parties to use the MODEL JURY INSTRUCTIONS OF THE NINTH CIRCUIT OR CALIFORNIA JURY INSTRUCTIONS, modified and supplemented as necessary.

In the event parties are unable to agree on the language of a particular instruction, the objecting party shall submit an alternative instruction, placed immediately following the instruction to which an objection is being made, and a brief statement of the ground for the objection. Challenged instructions must be clearly marked and identified.

Each proposed instruction shall be written in plain language, comprehensible to jurors, concise and free from argument, cover only one subject which shall be indicated in the caption, and be written out in full on a separate page. On a separate page following each instruction, the parties must provide citation to the authority upon which each instruction is based;

6. **Form of Verdict (Jury Trials Only).** Each party shall serve and submit to the court its proposed form of verdict;

7. **Proposed Findings of Fact and Conclusions of Law (for Non-Jury Trials Only).** In actions tried to the court without a jury, each party shall file Proposed Findings of Facts and Conclusions of Law; and

8. **Joint Pretrial Statement.** The Joint Pretrial Statement shall include the following:

a. Substance of the Action. A brief description of the general nature of the action;

b. Stipulations, Agreed Statement and Undisputed Facts. A statement of: (i) any stipulations requested or proposed for pretrial or trial purposes; (ii) whether all or part of the action may be presented upon an agreed statement of facts; and (iii) all relevant facts not reasonably in dispute, as well as any facts to which the parties will stipulate for the trial record without the necessity of supporting testimony or exhibits;

c. Disputed Factual Issues. A plain and concise statement of all disputed factual issues which remain to be decided;

d. Disputed Legal Issues. Without extended legal argument, a plain and concise statement of each disputed point of law concerning liability, relief, procedure and/or evidence. (When appropriate, full legal argument with citations to statutes and case law should be covered in a Trial Brief.);

e. Deposition Excerpts and Discovery Responses. Pursuant to Fed. R. Civ. P. 26(a)(3), a list of any deposition testimony (by page and lines) or other discovery responses that each party may offer as evidence as trial, other than solely for impeachment or rebuttal;

f. Witnesses to be Called. Pursuant to Fed. R. Civ. P. 26(a)(3), a list of the name of every witness each party expects to call at trial, other than solely for impeachment or rebuttal, together with a brief statement following each name describing the substance of the testimony to be given. Each party shall separately identify those witnesses the party intends to call and those the party may call if the need arises;

g. Exhibits, Schedules and Summaries. Pursuant to Fed. R. Civ. P. 26(a)(3), a list of all documents and other items to be offered as exhibits at trial, other than solely for impeachment or rebuttal. Each item on the list shall be identified by an exhibit number, followed by a brief statement describing its substance or purpose, and the identity of the sponsoring witness. The parties must have agreed on an allocation of exhibit numbers which will avoid duplicate numbers. If possible, parties should stipulate to the authenticity and admissibility of exhibits prior to trial. **Any disputes regarding the authenticity and/or admissibility of any exhibits must be brought to the court's attention no later than the Pretrial Conference, or the objections will be deemed waived;**

h. Relief Prayed. A detailed statement of all the relief claimed, particularly itemizing all elements of damages claimed as well as witnesses, documents or other evidentiary material to be presented concerning the amount of those damages;

i. Estimate of Trial Time. A carefully reasoned estimate of the number of hours needed for the presentation of each party's case, including cross-examination of opposing witnesses;

j. Amendments, Dismissals. A statement of any requested or proposed amendments to the pleadings or dismissals of parties, claims or defenses.

k. Settlement Discussion. A statement indicating whether further settlement negotiations would likely be productive; and

l. Miscellaneous. A statement describing any other subjects relevant to the trial of the action or material to its just, speedy, and inexpensive determination.

C. **Not less than five (5) court days prior to the Pretrial Conference**, unless otherwise ordered, the parties shall serve and file (or lodge, as appropriate) the following:

1. **Oppositions to Motions *In Limine*;**

2. **Objections to the use of Deposition Excerpts or other Discovery Responses.** Unless otherwise ordered, any objections to excerpts from depositions or other discovery responses designated in the Joint Pretrial Statement shall be filed in writing, along with a certification that counsel conferred with opposing counsel regarding any such objections;

3. **Counter-Designations.** In the event a party contends that a deposition excerpt or other discovery response is unacceptably incomplete, the party shall file a counter-designation listing any additional deposition testimony (by page and lines) or other discovery responses it contends are necessary for a complete and fair record. Any objections to the counter-designations shall be served (by fax and mail) and filed the day before the Pretrial Conference (the after-hours drop box may not be used for this filing); and

4. **Objections to Voir Dire, Proposed Findings, Verdict Forms, or to the Authenticity or Admissibility of any Trial Exhibits.** Unless otherwise ordered, any objections to the use of proposed voir dire, proposed findings, verdict forms, or to the authenticity or admissibility of any trial exhibits shall be filed in writing, along with a certification that counsel conferred with opposing counsel regarding such objections.

D. **At the Pretrial Conference**, lead counsel (and parties in *pro se*) will attend in person and be prepared to discuss all matters concerning Pretrial Preparation. The court will consider any trial management issue which is likely to promote a fair and efficient resolution of the case, including:

1. Entering the Pretrial Order;

2. Ruling, to the extent practicable, on Motions *in Limine* and on any objections to voir dire, findings, verdict forms, jury instructions, and exhibits;

3. Allocating a fixed number of hours for each side for the direct and cross-examination of witnesses;

4. Setting specific dates and times when trial will be in session; and

5. For jury trials, discussing the jury selection process.

Questions concerning the provisions of this order should be directed to the Administrative Law Clerk at (408) 535-5411.

Dated: July 8, 2002

HOWARD R. LLOYD
United States Magistrate Judge

D. *Standing Order Regarding Settlement Conference and Procedures*

STANDING ORDER RE: SETTLEMENT CONFERENCE PROCEDURES

Lead trial counsel shall appear at the Settlement Conference with the parties and with the person or persons having full authority to negotiate and to settle the case. In all cases in which a party is insured, the carrier's claims representative (and attorney, if any) with full authority to negotiate up to the limits of coverage shall also attend the Settlement Conference.

Personal attendance by counsel will not be excused under any circumstances and personal attendance by a party will rarely be excused. Permission for a party to attend by telephone may be granted upon written request made at least ten (10) calendar days in advance of the conference, **if** the party lives and works outside of the Northern District of California **and** attendance would constitute a severe, demonstrable hardship. The nature of the hardship must be explained. A copy of the written request must be served on all other parties. Any objection to the request must be submitted within forty-eight (48) hours of receipt. Both the request and objection may be submitted in letter form either by mail or facsimile to (408) 535-5410. If telephone attendance is allowed, the party must be available throughout the entire conference.

Not later than seven (7) calendar days before the Settlement Conference, each party shall submit to Judge Lloyd a:

- **Settlement Conference Statement, and a**
- **Confidential Settlement Letter.**

Both shall be placed in a sealed envelope marked "Settlement Conference Documents, Attn: Magistrate Judge Lloyd" and lodged with the Clerk's office, Room 2112, at the Courthouse in SanJose. The Clerk will forward the envelope to Judge Lloyd's chambers. These papers will not be filed with the Court.

At the same time, a copy of the Settlement Conference Statement SHALL be served on all counsel and parties in *pro se*.

A copy of the Confidential Settlement Letter SHALL NOT be served on other counsel or *pro se* parties.

The form and content of the Settlement Conference Statement may vary depending upon the nature of the case, the stage of the proceedings, and economic considerations. Generally, it should include the following information:

1. Statement of Facts. A brief description of the substance of the claims and defenses presented.

2. Summary of Proceedings. A brief list of previous motions and their disposition, plus pending motions.

3. Undisputed Matters. A plain and concise statement of all material facts not reasonably disputable.

4. Issues of Fact. A plain and concise statement of the major factual issues in dispute.

5. Issues of Law. Including references to statutes and case law, a brief statement

of the disputed points of law with respect to liability and damages. Extended legal argument is not necessary.

6. Relief Sought. A statement of the relief claimed, including a particularized itemization of all elements of damages.

7. Prior Settlement Discussions. A summary of prior settlement activity between the parties, including demands and offers.

The **Confidential Settlement Letter** shall include the following:

1. Party Representative. If the party is not a natural person, the name, title, and level of responsibility of the person(s) attending the Settlement Conference on behalf of the party.

2. Litigation Costs. A brief statement of the approximate litigation costs to date and the estimated cost and time projected for further discovery, pretrial proceedings and trial.

3. Settlement Analysis. A brief and forthright evaluation of the strengths and weaknesses of the case and the probabilities of prevailing on the major issues in dispute.

4. Discrete Issues. Are there any discrete issues affecting the parties which, if resolved, would aid in the disposition of the case?

5. Current Settlement Position. Set forth a reasonable proposal of settlement.

6. Other. Any other pertinent information which counsel or a *pro se* party wishes to share with the court in confidence.

Because the settlement conference will likely involve some assessment by Judge Lloyd of the claims, defenses, and relief sought in the case, parties should bring with them documents, deposition testimony, and any other materials which support their positions.

It is not unusual for conferences to last two, three, or more hours. Parties are encouraged to participate and frankly discuss their case. Statements they make during the conference will not be admissible at trial to prove or disprove liability in the event the case does not settle. The parties should be prepared to explore such topics as their settlement objectives, perceived impediments to settlement, and possible creative avenues of resolution that would not be possible except through a negotiated settlement.

Any request to continue the Settlement Conference shall be submitted in writing promptly after consultation with the opposing party. Submission by facsimile is acceptable (408) 535-5410.

The parties shall notify Magistrate Judge Lloyd's Courtroom Deputy **immediately** at (408) 535-5365 if this case settles prior to the date set for Settlement Conference.

IT IS SO ORDERED.

Dated: May 14, 2003

HOWARD R. LLOYD
United States Magistrate Judge

Hon. Donna M. Ryu

Magistrate Judge

Chambers Information

U.S. District Court, Northern District of California
Courtroom 4, 3rd Floor
1301 Clay Street
Oakland, California 94612

Scheduling Information

Courtroom Deputy: (510) 637-3639

Civil Law and Motion	Second and Fourth Thursdays at 11:00 a.m.
Criminal Law and Motion	Second and Fourth Thursdays at 11:00 a.m. (or during the regular criminal calendar when Magistrate Judge Ryu is on criminal calendar duty)
Criminal Duty Matters	Daily on Duty Months at 9:30 a.m.
Case Management Conferences	Wednesdays at 1:30 p.m.

Judge's Biography

Federal Judicial Service:

-Magistrate Judge, U.S. District Court, Northern District of California, appointed in 2010.

Education:

-Yale University, B.A.
-University of California at Berkeley Law School, J.D.

Professional Career:

-Clinical Professor of Law, University of California Hastings College of the Law,
-Associate Professor and Associate Director, Women's Employment Rights Clinic of Golden Gate University Law School
-Private Practice, San Francisco, California

I. Judge Ryu's Procedures and Practices

A. Standing Order

STANDING ORDER
FOR MAGISTRATE JUDGE DONNA M. RYU
(Revised February 22, 2011)

Parties shall comply with the procedures in the Federal Rules of Civil or Criminal Procedure, the Northern District of California's Local Rules and General Orders, and this standing order, all of which are available at http://www.cand.uscourts.gov. The parties' failure to comply with any of the rules or orders may be grounds for monetary sanctions, dismissal, entry of judgment, or other appropriate sanctions.

CALENDAR DATES AND SCHEDULING

1. Criminal motions are heard on the second and fourth Thursdays of the month at 11:00 a.m., or during the regular criminal calendar when Judge Ryu is on criminal calendar duty. Civil motions are also heard on the second and fourth Thursdays of the month at 11:00 a.m. Civil case management and status conferences are heard on Wednesdays at 1:30 p.m. Civil pretrial conferences are heard on Wednesdays at 3:00 p.m.

2. Parties should notice motions (other than discovery motions) pursuant to the local rules. Parties need not reserve a hearing date, but should confirm the Court's availability at http://www.cand.uscourts.gov. The Court may reset hearing dates as the Court's calendar requires.

3. For scheduling questions, please call Judge Ryu's courtroom deputy, Ivy Garcia at (510) 637-3639.

CONSENT CASES

4. In civil cases that are randomly assigned to Judge Ryu for all purposes, the parties should file their written consent to the assignment of a United States Magistrate Judge for all purposes or their written declination of consent ***as soon as possible***, and in no event later than the deadlines specified in Civil L.R. 73-1(a)(1) and (2).

CHAMBERS COPIES AND PROPOSED ORDERS

5. Under Civil L.R. 5-1(b), parties must lodge an extra paper copy of any filing and mark it as a copy for "Chambers." Please three-hole punch the chambers copy and submit it to the Oakland Clerk's Office. In a case subject to electronic filing, chambers copies must be submitted by the close of the next court day following the day the papers are filed electronically.

6. Any stipulation or proposed order in a case subject to e-filing should be submitted by email to dmrpo@cand.uscourts.gov as a word processing attachment on the same day the document is e-filed. This address should only be used for this stated purpose unless otherwise directed by the Court.

CIVIL CASE MANAGEMENT

7. No later than seven (7) days before the initial case management or status conference, the parties shall file a Joint Case Management Statement in full compliance with the Northern District of California's general standing order for civil cases entitled "Contents of Joint Case Management Statement," a copy of which is attached hereto.

8. Parties may not stipulate to continue a case management, status, or pretrial conference without Court approval. Each party shall be represented **in person** at the Case Management Conference by lead trial counsel (or a party if *in pro se*), who shall be (1) prepared to address all of the matters referred to in the Northern District of California's general standing order on Joint Case Management Statements; and (2) have full authority to enter stipulations and make admissions pursuant to that order. Permission for a party to attend by telephone may be granted, in the Court's discretion, upon written request made at least two weeks in advance of the hearing if the Court determines that good cause exists to excuse personal attendance, and that personal attendance is not needed in order to have an effective conference. The facts establishing good cause must be set forth in the request.

9. All case management, status and pretrial conferences are audio recorded. They are not reported by a court reporter unless counsel requests a court reporter in advance.

CIVIL DISCOVERY

Discovery Disputes

10. In order to respond to discovery disputes in a flexible, cost-effective and efficient manner, the Court uses the following procedure. The parties shall not file formal discovery motions. Instead, as required by the federal and local rules, the parties shall first meet and confer to try to resolve their disagreements. The meet and confer session must be ***in person or by telephone***, and may not be conducted by letter, e-mail, or fax. If disagreements remain, the parties shall file a joint letter no later than five (5) business days after the meet and confer session. **Lead trial counsel for both parties must sign the letter**, which shall include an attestation that the parties met and conferred in person or by telephone regarding all issues prior to filing the letter. Going issue-by-issue, the joint letter shall describe each unresolved issue, summarize each party's position with appropriate legal authority; and provide each party's final proposed compromise before moving to the next issue. The joint letter shall not exceed ten (10) pages without leave of Court. In the rare instance that a joint letter is not possible, each side may submit a letter not to exceed four (4) pages, which shall include an explanation of why a joint letter was not possible. When appropriate, the parties may submit one exhibit to the letter that sets forth each discovery request at issue in full, followed immediately by the objections and/or responses thereto. No other information shall be included in any such exhibit. No other exhibits shall be submitted without prior approval by the Court. The Court will review the submission(s) and determine whether formal briefing or proceedings are necessary.

11. In emergencies during discovery events (such as depositions), any party may, after exhausting good faith attempts to resolve disputed issues, seek judicial intervention pursuant to Civil L.R. 37-1(b) by contacting the Court through the courtroom deputy. If the Court is unavailable, the discovery event shall proceed with objections noted for the record.

12. In the event that a discovery hearing is ordered, the Court has found that it is often

efficient and beneficial for the parties if counsel appear ***in person***. This provides the opportunity, where appropriate, to engage counsel in resolving aspects of the discovery dispute while remaining available to rule on any disputes that counsel are not able to resolve. For this reason, the Court expects counsel to appear in person. Permission for a party to attend by telephone may be granted, in the Court's discretion, upon written request made at least two weeks in advance of the hearing if the Court determines that good cause exists to excuse personal attendance, and that personal attendance is not needed in order to have an effective discovery hearing. The facts establishing good cause must be set forth in the request.

Privilege Logs

13. If a party withholds information that is responsive to a discovery request by claiming that it is privileged or otherwise protected from discovery, that party shall ***promptly*** prepare and provide a privilege log that is sufficiently detailed and informative for the opposing party to assess whether a document's designation as privileged is justified. *See* Fed.R.Civ.P. 26(b)(5). The privilege log shall set forth the privilege relied upon and specify separately for each document or for each category of similarly situated documents:

(a) the title and description of the document, including number of pages or Bates-number range;
(b) the subject matter addressed in the document;
(c) the identity and position of its author(s);
(d) the identity and position of all addressees and recipients;
(e) the date the document was prepared and, if different, the date(s) on which it was sent to or shared with persons other than its author(s); and
(f) the specific basis for the claim that the document is privileged or protected.

Failure to furnish this information promptly may be deemed a waiver of the privilege or protection.

IT IS SO ORDERED.

____

DONNA M. RYU
United States Magistrate Judge

II. Judge Ryu's Case Management Orders

A. Notice of Settlement Conference and Settlement Conference Order

IN THE UNITED STATES DISTRICT COURT
FOR THE NORTHERN DISTRICT OF CALIFORNIA

Plaintiff(s), v. Defendant(s). _______________________________/	No. C-xx-xxxxx (DMR) **NOTICE OF SETTLEMENT CONFERENCE AND SETTLEMENT CONFERENCE ORDER**

TO ALL PARTIES AND COUNSEL OF RECORD:

The above matter was referred to Magistrate Judge Donna M. Ryu for settlement purposes.

You are hereby notified that a settlement conference is scheduled for ______________, **at ____p.m.**, at the U.S. District Court, 1301 Clay Street, Oakland, California 94612. For courtroom number and floor information, please check the Court's on-line calendar at http://www.cand.uscourts.gov (click "Calendars" link on left side, click link to Judge Ryu's calendar) or call Judge Ryu's Courtroom Deputy, Ivy Garcia, at (510) 637-3639, one week prior to the scheduled settlement conference.

It is the responsibility of counsel to ensure that whatever discovery is needed for all sides to evaluate the case for settlement purposes is completed by the date of the settlement conference. Counsel shall cooperate in providing discovery informally and expeditiously.

A. Meet and Confer Requirement.

No later than **fourteen (14) calendar days** before the settlement conference and prior to the preparation of their Exchanged Settlement Conference Statements and Confidential Settlement Letters, counsel for the parties must meet and confer (in person or by phone) to discuss matters pertinent to improving the prospects that the settlement negotiations will be productive. During the meet and confer, counsel may address any subjects they feel are appropriate, but they **must** discuss the following:

1. Who will attend the conference on behalf of each party, including counsel and identification of the person(s) with full authority to make the final decision as to whether any settlement offer is made, accepted, or rejected (e.g., either the party or another person(s) if full authority does not rest with the party). 2. Which persons or entities must approve a proposed settlement agreement before it can be executed, as well as the nature and duration of any such approval process.

3. Whether insurance is available to cover all or part of the claimed losses or to fund all or part of any party's defense; whether tenders have been made to any insurance companies; and if insurance is available, the name of and position held by each claims representative who will be attending the settlement conference. 4. Whether it would

be useful for settlement demands and/or offers to be made before the settlement conference is convened.

5. Whether there are particular documents or other tangible things that should be brought to the conference (e.g., to educate the settlement judge or to support or explain significant contentions).

6. Any unusual issues or factors that could come into play in the settlement negotiations or any especially sensitive matters that other counsel should be alerted to before the conference.

B. Lodged Settlement Conference Documents.

No later than ten (10) calendar days prior to the settlement conference, each party shall submit the following:

(1) an **Exchanged Settlement Conference Statement**; and
(2) a **Confidential Settlement Letter**.

Two copies of **each** document shall be **LODGED (not filed)** with the U.S. District Court Clerk's Office in **Oakland**, located at 1301 Clay Street, Suite 400S, 4th Floor, Oakland, California 94612. The documents shall be submitted in a sealed envelope addressed to Magistrate Judge Ryu and prominently marked **"SETTLEMENT CONFERENCE DOCUMENTS - DO NOT FILE."**

1. **Exchanged Settlement Conference Statements.** Counsel **shall serve** a copy of the Settlement Conference Statement on all parties. Furthermore, counsel are **strongly encouraged** prior to the settlement conference to share with their clients the contents of the Settlement Conference Statement(s) received from opposing counsel.

The Settlement Conference Statement shall not exceed ten (10) pages of text. Parties are encouraged to include as exhibits any key documents and deposition excerpts up to twenty (20) pages. The Settlement Conference Statement **shall include** the following:

a. A brief statement of the facts of the case.

b. A brief statement of the **principal** claims and defenses.

c. A description of the **key** factual and legal issues that are in dispute and a plain and concise statement of the **specific** evidence relevant to their determination. Portions of any exhibits relied upon by the parties shall be referenced and highlighted.

d. A summary of the proceedings to date and a description of any pending motions.

e. The bases for any damages calculations and a description of any nonmonetary relief sought or non-monetary components of settlement offers or demands.

f. A description of each component of each party's most recently communicated settlement demand or offer (describing specifically any non-monetary terms that were demanded or offered).

g. For each party, a list of the names, titles, and positions of all persons who will be attending the conference.

h. Where the party is a governmental entity, a description of which persons or entities must approve a proposed settlement agreement before it can be executed, as well as the nature and duration of that approval process.

2. **Confidential Settlement Letters.** The Confidential Settlement Letter **shall not be served** upon other parties. The Confidential Settlement Letter shall not exceed five (5) pages of text and **shall include** the following:

a. Separately for each principal claim and defense, a forthright evaluation of the strengths and weaknesses and likelihood that the party submitting the Confidential Letter will prevail. Citations to any key legal authorities relied upon by the parties as part of this evaluation shall be provided.

b. An estimate of the out-of-pocket expenses, attorneys' fees, and time: (a) **spent to date** and (b) **to be expended** for further discovery, pretrial, and trial. If plaintiff seeks attorneys' fees and costs, plaintiff's counsel shall be prepared at the conference to provide sufficient information to enable the fee claim to be evaluated for purposes of settlement.

c. A history of past settlement discussions (without revealing communications whose disclosure to a settlement judge is prohibited), a description of the principal obstacles (factual, legal, or other) to reaching agreement, and the reason the parties' assessments of the settlement value of the case differ.

d. A realistic settlement figure or terms (including any non-monetary terms) that, given all the circumstances, the party submitting the Confidential Letter would consider seriously.

e. Where the party is insured or is a governmental entity, any foreseeable barriers to insurance coverage or approval of a proposed settlement, or special concerns that the insurer or governmental entity might want addressed.

f. A brief discussion of any of the subjects identified in Section A of this Order that might be significant in the settlement dynamic.

C. **Mandatory Personal Attendance.**

Lead trial counsel shall appear at the settlement conference with the **parties and with the person(s) having full authority** to make the final decision as to whether any settlement offer is made, accepted, or rejected (if full authority does not rest with the party). A person who needs to call another person not present before making, accepting, or rejecting any settlement offer does **not** have such full authority. If a party is a **governmental entity**, its governing body shall designate one of its members or a senior executive to appear at the settlement conference with authority to participate in the settlement conference and, if a tentative settlement agreement is reached, to recommend the agreement to the governmental entity for its approval. An **insured party** shall appear with a representative of the carrier with **full authority to negotiate up to the limits of coverage**.

Personal attendance is mandatory and will rarely be excused by the Court, and then only upon a written request that is timely under the circumstances and that demonstrates extraordinary hardship. Personal attendance may be excused only upon written authorization from the Court. If the Court permits attendance by telephone, the person who is excused from personally appearing must be available to participate by telephone throughout the entire conference.

D. Duration and Content of Settlement Conference.

It is not unusual for settlement conferences to last three (3) or more hours. Parties and their representatives should be prepared to devote the entire day to the conference if necessary. Parties are encouraged to participate in the settlement conference and frankly discuss their case. Statements they make during the conference will not be admissible at trial in the event the case does not settle. The parties and their representatives should be prepared to discuss such issues as their settlement objectives; any impediments to settlement they perceive; whether they have enough information to discuss settlement and if not, what additional information is needed; and the possibility of a creative resolution of the dispute.

E. Continuances.

Any request to continue the settlement conference shall state the reason therefor and be submitted in writing as soon as possible after consultation with the opposing party but well in advance of the scheduled conference date. The request must demonstrate **a compelling reason for a continuance and shall state whether it is joined or opposed by the other party(ies)**. Submission of such request shall be **filed** with the Court; a courtesy copy must be provided no later than 12:00 noon on the day after the document is filed and may be submitted by facsimile (510-637-1014). **Parties must appear on the calendared date unless the Court issues an Order continuing the matter.**

If the date to which a continuance is sought would be past a deadline for holding the settlement conference that was set by the judge to whom the case is assigned for trial, the party seeking the continuance must secure permission from the trial judge to hold the settlement conference during the proposed new time frame **before seeking the continuance from Judge Ryu**. A writing evidencing the trial judge's extension of the deadline must accompany the party's request to Judge Ryu for the continuance.

The parties shall immediately notify Judge Ryu's Courtroom Deputy, Ivy Garcia, at (510) 637-3639, if this case settles prior to the date set for the settlement conference.

Any failure to comply with the requirements of this Order may subject the parties and/or counsel to sanctions.

IT IS SO ORDERED.

Dated: ____________________

____
DONNA M. RYU
United States Magistrate Judge

Hon. Joseph C. Spero

Magistrate Judge

Chambers Information

U.S. District Court, Northern District of California
Courtroom G, 15th Floor
450 Golden Gate Avenue
San Francisco, CA 94102

Scheduling Information

Courtroom Deputy: (415) 522-2035

Civil Law and Motion	Fridays at 9:30 a.m.
Criminal Law and Motion	Fridays at 10:30 a.m.
Case Management Conferences	Fridays at 1:30 p.m.

Judge's Biography

Federal Judicial Service:

-Magistrate Judge, U.S. District Court, Northern District of California, appointed in 1999.

Education:

-Columbia University School of Law, J.D., 1981

Professional Career:

-Private Practice, San Francisco, California
-Law Clerk, U.S. Ninth Circuit Court of Appeals

I. Judge Spero's Procedures and Practices

A. Civil Standing Orders

CIVIL STANDING ORDERS FOR MAGISTRATE JUDGE JOSEPH C. SPERO

(Revised November 15, 2010)

The parties shall follow the General Orders of the Court for the Northern District of California, the Local Rules, and the Federal Rules of Civil Procedure, except as expressly modified herein. Failure to comply with any of the rules and orders may be deemed sufficient grounds for monetary sanctions, dismissal, entry of default judgment, or other appropriate sanctions.

A. STANDING ORDER RE CALENDAR AND CONFERENCES

1. Civil Law and Motion is heard on Fridays at 9:30 a.m. Counsel need not reserve a hearing date in advance for civil motions. However, noticed dates may be reset as the Court's calendar requires.

2. Criminal Law and Motion is heard on Fridays at 10:30 a.m.

3. Case Management Conferences and Pretrial Conference are heard on Fridays at 1:30 p.m. Case Management Conferences are no longer recorded unless requested by counsel or in cases where at least one party appears pro se. Requests to appear telephonically at case management conferences must be filed and served one (1) week before the conference in accordance with Civil L.R. 16-10(a).

4. In cases that are randomly assigned to Judge Spero for all purposes, a Consent to Proceed before a U.S. Magistrate Judge and a Declination to Proceed before a U.S. Magistrate Judge and a Request for Reassignment to a United States District Judge forms will be mailed to all parties. The parties are requested, within two (2) weeks from receipt of the form, to complete and file the form indicating their consent or request for reassignment to a District Judge.

5. Parties with questions regarding all scheduling should be addressed to Judge Spero's courtroom deputy, Karen Hom at (415) 522-2035.

6. In all "E-Filing" cases, when filing papers that require the Court to take any action (i.e., motions, meet and confer letters, administrative requests), the parties shall, in addition to filing papers electronically, lodge with chambers a printed copy of the papers on three-hold punch paper (including all exhibits) by the close of the next court day following the day the papers are filed electronically. **These printed copies shall be marked "JCS Chambers Copy" and shall be submitted to the Clerk's Office in an envelope clearly marked with the case number, "Magistrate Judge Joseph C. Spero," and "E-filing Chambers Copy." Parties shall not file a paper copy of any document with the Clerk's office that has already been filed electronically.**

7. Any proposed stipulation or proposed order in a case subject to electronic filing shall be sent by mail to jcspo@cand.uscourts.gov. This address is to be used only for proposed orders unless otherwise directed by the Court.

B. STANDING ORDER ON DISCOVERY DISPUTES

8. In lieu of filing formal discovery motions, lead trial counsel for Plaintiff(s) and lead trial counsel for Defendant(s) shall meet and confer **in person** regarding the subject matter of the Motion(s) in an effort to resolve these matters. After attempting other means to confer on the issue (i.e., letter, phone call, e-mail) any party may demand such a meeting on ten (10) business days' notice. The location of the meeting will alternate with the first location selected by counsel for Plaintiff, the second by counsel for Defendant, etc. Within five (5) business days of the lead trial counsels' meet-and-confer session, the parties shall provide a detailed Joint Letter to the Court, not to exceed ten (10) pages without leave of Court. This Joint Letter shall include a description of every issue in dispute and, with respect to each such issue, a detailed summary of each party's final substantive position and their final proposed compromise on each issue. Upon receipt of the Joint Letter the Court will determine what future proceedings are necessary.

9. As soon as a party has notice of this order, the party shall take such affirmative steps as are necessary to preserve evidence related to the issues presented by the action, including, without limitation, interdiction of any document destruction programs and any ongoing erasures of emails, voice mails, and other electronically recorded material to the extent necessary to preserve information relevant to the issues presented by this action.

10. In responding to requests for documents and materials under Fed. R. Civ. P. 34, all parties shall affirmatively state in a written response served on all other parties the full extent to which they will produce materials and shall, promptly after the production, confirm in writing that they have produced *all* such materials so described that are locatable after a diligent search of *all* locations at which such materials might plausibly exist. It shall not be sufficient to object and/or to state that "responsive" materials will be or have been produced.

11. In searching for responsive materials in connection with Fed. R. Civ. P. 34 requests or for materials required to be disclosed under Fed. R. Civ. P. 26(a)(1), parties must search computerized files, emails, voice mails, work files, desk files, calendars and diaries, and any other locations and sources if materials of the type to be produced might plausibly be expected to be found there.

12. To the maximum extent feasible, all party files and record should be retained and produced in their original form and sequence, including file folders, and the originals should remain available for inspection by any counsel on reasonable notice.

13. Except for good cause, no item will be received in evidence if the proponent failed to produce it in the face of a reasonable and proper discovery request covering the item, regardless of whether a motion to overrule any objection thereto was made.

14. Privilege logs shall be promptly provided and must be sufficiently detailed and informative to justify the privilege. *See* Fed. R. Civl P. 26(b)(5). No generalized claims of privilege or work product protection shall be permitted. With respect to each communication for which a claim of privilege or work product is made, the asserting party must at the time of its assertion identify: (a) all persons making and receiving the privileged or protected communication, (b) the steps taken to ensure the confidentiality of the communication, including affirmation that no unauthorized persons have received the communication, (c) the date of the communication, and (d) the subject matter of the communication. Failure to furnish this information at the time of the assertion will be deemed a waiver of the privilege

or protection.

DEPOSITIONS

15. Absent extraordinary circumstances, counsel shall consult in advance with opposing counsel and unrepresented proposed deponents to schedule depositions at mutually convenient times and places. Where an agreement cannot be reached as to any party deponent or a deponent represented by counsel of record, the following procedure may be invoked by the party seeking any such deposition. The party seeking such a deposition may notice it at least thirty (30) days in advance. If the noticed date and place is unacceptable to the deponent or the deponent's counsel, then within ten (10) days or receipt of the notice, the deponent or counsel form the deponent must reply and counter-propose in writing an alternative date and place falling within thirty (30) days of the date noticed by the party seeking the deposition.

16. Counsel and parties shall comply with Fed. R. Civ. P. 30(d)(1). Deposition objections must be as to privilege or form only. Speaking objections are prohibited. When a privilege is claimed, the witness should nevertheless answer questions relevant to the existence, extent or waiver of the privilege, such as the date of a communication, who made the statement, to whom and in whose presence the statement was made, other persons to whom the contents of the statement have been disclosed, and the general subject matter of the statement, unless such information is itself privileged. Private conferences between deponents and attorneys in the course of interrogation, including a line of related questions, are improper and prohibited except for the sole purpose of determining whether a privilege should be asserted.

C. STANDING ORDER ON MOTIONS FOR SUMMARY JUDGMENT

17. Motions for summary judgment shall be accompanied by a joint statement of the material facts not in dispute by citations to admissible evidence. The parties shall file a joint statement of undisputed facts. If the parties are unable to reach complete agreement after meeting and conferring, they shall file a joint statement of the undisputed facts about which they do agree. Separate statements of undisputed facts shall not be filed and will not be considered by the Court.

D. SANCTIONS

18. Failure to comply with this Order of the Local Rules of this Court may result in sanctions. *See* Fed. R. Civ. P. 16(f), Civil L.R. 1-4.

Dated: November 15, 2010

JOSEPH C. SPERO
United States Magistrate Judge

B. Notice of Rule Discontinuing Service by Mail

NOTICE OF RULE DISCONTINUING SERVICE BY MAIL

This is an E-filing case. Pursuant to Local Rule, the Court will no longer serve any counsel by mail. If counsel wish to be served with documents generated by the Court, they must register for E-filing pursuant to Local Rule 5-4 and General Order 45.

IT IS SO ORDERED.

Dated: May 30, 2003

JOSEPH C. SPERO
United States Magistrate Judge

II. Judge Spero's Case Management Orders

A. *Standing Order Regarding Case Management Conference*

**IN THE UNITED STATES DISTRICT COURT
FOR THE NORTHERN DISTRICT OF CALIFORNIA**

No. C__________ JCS

Plaintiff,

v.

Defendant.
________________________________/

STANDING ORDER RE: CASE MANAGEMENT CONFERENCE

Lead trial counsel who will try this case are directed to confer in advance of the Case Management Conference with respect to all matters contained in the **March 1, 2007 Standing Order for all Judges of the Northern District of California** regarding Contents of the Joint Case Management Conference, including a **discovery plan and discovery limits** and all other matters described in Fed. R. Civ. P. 16(c), and 26(f) and Civil L.R. 16-10. Not less than seven (7) days before the conference, counsel shall file a Joint Case Management Conference Statement in compliance with Local Rule 16-9. If one or more of the parties is not represented by counsel (*a party appearing pro se*), the parties may file separate case management conference statements. Pursuant to Civil L.R. 16-10(a) each party shall be represented at the Case Management Conference by lead trial counsel (or a party if *in pro se*) prepared to address all of the matters referred to in this Order, and with authority to enter stipulations and make admissions pursuant to this Order.

Plaintiff(s) shall serve copies of this Order and the Court's Standing Orders at once on all parties to this action, and on any parties subsequently joined, in accordance with the provisions of Fed. R. Civ. P. 4 and 5. Following service, plaintiff(s) shall file a certificate of service with the Clerk of this Court.

Failure to comply with this Order, the provisions of the Federal Rules of Civil Procedure 16 and 26(f) or the provisions of Civil L.R. 16-10 may be grounds for sanctions. (*See* Fed. R. Civ. P. 16(f), Civil L.R. 1-4.

Dated: April 21, 2008

____
JOSEPH C. SPERO
United States Magistrate Judge

III. Judge Spero's Forms

A. Exhibit Tag

COURT'S exhibit tag shall be in the following form:

UNITED STATES DISTRICT COURT
NORTHERN DISTRICT OF
CALIFORNIA

TRIAL EXHIBIT 100

Case No. ________________
Date Entered ______________
By________________________
Deputy Clerk

Hon. Nandor J. Vadas

Magistrate Judge

Chambers Information

U.S. District Court, Northern District of California
Courtroom 205A, 2nd Floor
514 H Street
Eureka, CA 95501

> **Note:** Although Judge Vadas' chambers is located in Eureka, he regularly presides over cases in both Eureka and the Bay Area.

Scheduling Information

Courtroom Deputy: (707) 445-3612

Civil Law and Motion	Tuesdays at 10:00 a.m.
Criminal Law and Motion	Mondays at 1:00 p.m.
Civil Status and Case Management Conferences	Tuesdays at 2:00 p.m.
Civil Pretrial Conferences	Tuesdays at 2:30 p.m.

Judge's Biography

Federal Judicial Service:

-Magistrate Judge, U.S. District Court, Northern District of California, appointed in 2004.

Education:

-University of California at Santa Cruz
-University of California Hastings College of the Law, J.D.

Professional Career:

-Deputy District Attorney, Humboldt County
-Special Assistant United States Attorney, Northern District of California
-Deputy District Attorney, City and County of San Francisco

I. Judge Vadas' Procedures and Practices

A. *Standing Orders*

NOTICE: Plaintiff is directed to serve a copy of these Standing Orders at once upon all parties to this action and upon those subsequently joined, and to file with the Clerk of Court a certificate of service reflecting such service.

STANDING ORDERS OF MAGISTRATE JUDGE NANDOR J. VADAS

(Revised April 7, 2011)

1. **Compliance With Federal Rules, General Orders and Local Rules.** All parties shall consult and comply with all applicable Federal Rules, as well as the General Orders and Local Rules of the U.S. District Court for the Northern District of California ("Court"), except as expressly modified herein. Failure to comply with any applicable rule or order may be deemed sufficient grounds for monetary sanctions, dismissal, entry of default judgment, or other appropriate sanctions. The aforementioned rules and orders are supplemented and modified as follows.

2. **Consent/Declination to Proceed Before a Magistrate Judge.** In cases that are randomly assigned to Judge Vadas for all purposes, a "Consent to Proceed before a U.S. Magistrate Judge" and a "Declination to Proceed before a U.S. Magistrate Judge and Request for Reassignment to a United States District Judge" will be provided to all parties. The parties are requested, within two (2) weeks of the receipt of these forms, to complete and file the form reflecting their consent or declination as to Judge Vadas' jurisdiction as presiding judge. All pleadings filed in cases in which Judge Vadas is the presiding judge shall bear the designation "EUREKA DIVISION." **In the event that a case that is originally assigned to Judge Vadas as the presiding judge and is later reassigned to a District Court Judge, unless otherwise ordered by the Court, the case will remain assigned to Judge Vadas for all discovery matters.**

3. **Filing and Lodging Pleadings and Documents.** Unless expressly requested by the Court, documents should **not** be faxed to chambers, but should be filed and lodged in accordance with the Court's Local Rules. The Court should **not** be routinely copied on correspondence between counsel. Pro se litigants should review the Court's Handbook for Litigants Without a Lawyer, which is also available on the Court's website (www.cand.uscourts.gov/prosehandbk), for further instruction on filing and lodging procedures. Pro se litigants are reminded to deliver in person or mail their filings to the Clerk's Office in San Francisco at Clerk's Office, U.S. District Court, 450 Golden Gate Avenue, 16th Floor, San Francisco, CA 94102. All litigants, including pro se litigants, should deliver or mail their chambers copies of filings as provided in Paragraph 13 below.

4. **Motion Practice.** All motions to be heard by Judge Vadas shall be filed, served and noticed in accordance with the applicable Local Rules. Pursuant to Civil Local Rule 5-1(a), any papers filed in connection with any motion referred to Judge Vadas must be filed in the Clerk's Office at the division where the chambers of the referring judge are located. Pursuant to Civil Local Rule 5-1(b), the chambers copies of papers filed in connection with any motion pending before Magistrate Judge Vadas must either be delivered to Magistrate

Judge Vadas' chambers at 514 H Street, 2nd Floor, Eureka, CA 95501, or mailed to Magistrate Judge Nandor J. Vadas, P.O. Box 1306, Eureka, CA 95502.

5. Criminal Law and Motion. Judge Vadas' criminal law and motion calendar takes place on Mondays at 1:00 p.m. at the Eureka Federal Courthouse. Hearings on criminal motions pending before Judge Vadas must be scheduled with the Judge's courtroom deputy, Gloria Masterson.

6. Civil Law and Motion. Judge Vadas' civil law and motion calendar takes place on Tuesdays at 10:00 a.m. in Courtroom 205A on the 2nd floor of the U.S. Post Office and Courthouse, 514 H Street, Eureka, CA 95501-1038 ("Eureka Federal Courthouse"). **Hearings on civil motions pending before Judge Vadas must be scheduled with the Judge's courtroom deputy, Gloria Masterson** (Gloria_Masterson@cand.uscourts.gov or 707-445-3612).

7. Status and Case Management Conferences. Status and case management conferences are generally held on Tuesdays at 2:00 p.m. at the Eureka Federal Courthouse.

8. Pre-Trial Conferences. Pre-trial conferences are generally held on Tuesdays at 2:30 p.m. at the Eureka Federal Courthouse.

9. Requests for Continuances/Status Conferences. Parties wanting to continue hearings, request special status conferences, or make other procedural changes shall do so either by a signed stipulation and proposed order or, if a stipulation is not possible, by a written ex parte application and order. Briefing schedules may not be changed by stipulation. Any change in the hearing date does not alter the original briefing schedule unless otherwise ordered by the Court. Any request to reschedule a case management conference shall be made in writing, and by stipulation if possible, at least ten calendar days prior to the scheduled case management conference date.

10. Telephonic Appearance Requirements and Procedures. Any party requesting to appear telephonically for a proceeding before Judge Vadas must obtain advance permission to do so by contacting the Judge's courtroom deputy, Gloria Masterson, **at least four business days prior to the proceeding**. If multiple parties wish to appear telephonically, it is the responsibility of the parties to make arrangements to conference all telephonic participants together and to provide Ms. Masterson, **at least two business days prior to the proceeding**, with **a single number** to contact all parties when the Court is ready to proceed. For matters scheduled during a law and motion or other rolling calendar, **all** parties appearing telephonically must be available (at the number provided to Ms. Masterson) from the scheduled start of the calendar until their matter is called.

Unless specified otherwise by the court, **the court does not permit the use of payphones, cellular phones or speakerphones of any kind when participating in any court proceeding telephonically**. All telephone equipment used for teleconferencing must be fully capable of duplex operation. Duplex (also known as "full-duplex") communication mode provides transmission and reception (in both directions) simultaneously. This means that all parties can talk and hear at the same time.[1] A handset or headset is almost always duplex, but you must check the device's documentation or test it to be sure (if you and the

---

1 Half-duplex communication (in contrast to duplex) transmits and receives in only one direction at a time. This means that if you are talking, you cannot hear anyone else on the line, and if they are talking, they cannot hear anyone else. Half-duplex telephone communications are unacceptable for all calls.

party on the other end can talk and hear at the exact same time - the device is duplex).

11. Settlement Conferences. All parties appearing before Judge Vadas for a settlement conference shall comply with Judge Vadas' Settlement Conference Standing Order, which is available on the Court's website (www.cand.uscourts.gov > Judges > Nandor J. Vadas > Standing Orders).

12. Discovery Disputes. All parties with a discovery dispute in a case pending before, or referred to, Judge Vadas shall comply with the following:

a. Discovery motions may be addressed to the Court in three ways. A motion may be noticed on not less than thirty-five (35) days notice pursuant to Civil L.R. 7-2. Alternatively, a party may seek an order shortening time under Civil L.R. 6-3 if the circumstances justify that relief. In emergencies during discovery events (e.g., depositions), the Court is available pursuant to Civil L.R. 37-1(b).

b. In the event a discovery dispute arises, counsel for the party seeking discovery shall in good faith confer in person with counsel for the party failing to make that discovery in an attempt to resolve the dispute without the Court's involvement, as required by Federal Rule of Civil Procedure 37 and Civil L.R. 37-1(a). The meeting must be **in person**, except where good cause is shown why a telephone conference is adequate. A declaration setting forth these meet and confer efforts, and the final positions of each party, shall be included in the moving papers. **The Court will not consider discovery motions unless the moving party has complied with Fed. R. Civ. P. 37 and Civil L.R. 37-1.**

c. Any party seeking Court intervention during a discovery event, or filing an emergency or ex parte application relating to a discovery dispute, **must** contact Judge Vadas' courtroom deputy, Gloria Masterson at 707-445-3612 prior to filing any documents.

d. Any party seeking an award of attorney fees or other expenses as sanctions in connection with a discovery dispute shall file a separate motion as required by Civil Local Rule 37-3.

e. In cases referred to Judge Vadas for discovery, if a party wishes to file a document under seal, that party shall first file a written request for a sealing order setting forth the good cause and accompanied by a proposed order, as provided by Civil Local Rule 79-5.

13. Lodging of Chambers Copies. In all "E-Filing" cases when filing papers in connection with any motion for determination by the Judge, the parties shall, in addition to filing papers electronically, lodge with chambers two (2) printed copies of the papers by the close of the next court day following the day the papers are filed electronically. These printed copies shall be marked "Chambers Copy" and shall be delivered to Magistrate Judge Vadas' chambers at 514 H Street, 2nd Floor, Eureka, CA 95501, or mailed to Magistrate Judge Nandor J. Vadas, P.O. Box 1306, Eureka, CA 95502. Parties shall not file a paper copy of any document with the Clerk's Office that has already been filed electronically. All chambers copies of filings containing exhibits must contain exhibit tabs. Chambers copies of filings in excess of 50 pages must be submitted in binders.

14. Electronic Submission of Proposed Orders. Any proposed order in a case subject to electronic filing shall be e-filed (in .pdf format) and emailed (in Word or Word Perfect format) to njvpo@cand.uscourts.gov.

15. Motions for Summary Judgment. Motions for summary judgment in cases assigned to Magistrate Judge Vadas for trial shall be accompanied by a statement of the material facts not in dispute supported by citation to admissible evidence. The parties shall file a joint statement of undisputed facts wherever possible. If the parties are unable to reach complete agreement after meeting and conferring, they shall file a joint statement of the undisputed facts about which they do agree. Any party may then file a separate statement of the additional facts which the party contends are undisputed.

16. Court Reporters and Electronic Recording of Proceedings. Unless specifically requested, the Court does not provide a court reporter for most pre-trial proceedings. The court records such proceedings electronically, a copy of which may be obtained by submitting a request to Judge Vadas' courtroom deputy, Gloria Masterson. Such requests must be accompanied by a check for twenty-six dollars made payable to the Clerk of Court for the Northern District of California and **mailed directly to the San Francisco Clerk's Office at 450 Golden Gate Ave., 16th Floor, San Francisco, CA 94102**. Each such request must include the case name and number, as well as the date and time of the proceeding for which a copy of the recording is requested. **A party who wishes to have a court reporter present for a pretrial proceeding in a civil matter must notify Judge Vadas' courtroom deputy at least two weeks in advance of the date set for the proceeding.**

17. Questions. Parties are reminded that most procedural questions are answered in the Federal Rules, the Local Rules, and/or these Standing Orders. Parties should **not** contact chambers for answers to procedural questions without first carefully examining the **current** provisions of these authorities. Current versions of the Local Rules and these Standing Orders can be found on the Court's website at www.cand.uscourts.gov. Questions regarding scheduling and case management should be directed to Judge Vadas' courtroom deputy, Gloria Masterson.

18. Pro Se Assistance. Parties representing themselves should consult the Court's Pro Se Handbook and/or Legal Help Center. The Pro Se Handbook and the contact information for the Legal Help Center can be found on the Court's website at www.cand.uscourts.gov.

19. Timeliness; Feedback. The Court strives to set matters and render decisions in a timely manner. The Court encourages parties to advise the Court by letter to chambers of any matter that appears to have been unduly delayed.

IT IS SO ORDERED.

____

NANDOR J. VADAS
United States Magistrate Judge

II. Judge Vadas' Case Management Orders

A. *Case Management and Pretrial Order*

IN THE UNITED STATES DISTRICT COURT
FOR THE NORTHERN DISTRICT OF CALIFORNIA

Plaintiff(s), v. Defendant(s). _______________________________/	No. C __ -______ NJV **CASE MANAGEMENT AND PRETRIAL ORDER**

Pursuant to Federal Rule of Civil Procedure 16 and Civil Local Rule 16-10(b), the following case management and pretrial order is entered:

1. **TRIAL DATE**

a. [Court/Jury] trial will begin on [DATE] at 9:30 a.m. in Courtroom 205A, 2nd Floor, 514 H Street, Eureka, CA 95501 ("Eureka Federal Courthouse").

b. The length of the trial will be no more than [___] days.

2. **DISCOVERY**

a. All non-expert discovery shall be completed by [DATE].

b. Experts shall be disclosed by [DATE].

c. All discovery from experts shall be completed by [DATE].

d. In the event of a discovery dispute the parties shall use the procedure outlined in the court's standing orders. The court's standing orders are available on the website for the U.S. District Court for the Northern District of California at www.cand.uscourts.gov. Click on "Judges" on the left side of the District Court's home page and select Magistrate Judge Vadas. On the Judge Information page, click on the link for Judge Vadas' standing orders on the lower left.

3. **MOTIONS**

All dispositive motions shall be served and filed not less than **thirty-five (35)** days prior to the scheduled hearing date. Any opposition shall be served and filed no later than **twenty-one (21)** days prior to the hearing date. Any reply to the opposition shall be served and filed no later than **fourteen (14) days** prior to the hearing. Prior to a dispositive motion, the parties shall meet and confer and, at the time the motion is filed, submit a **joint** statement of undisputed facts.

a. The last day for filing a dispositive motion will be [DATE].

b. The last day for a hearing on a dispositive motion will be [DATE], which is thirty-five (35) days after the last day for filing a dispositive motion.

4. ALTERNATIVE DISPUTE RESOLUTION (ADR)

The court hereby refers this case for **one** of the following:

a. A settlement conference to be scheduled before another Magistrate Judge of this court. Counsel will be contacted by that judge's chambers with a date and time for the conference as soon as it is convenient to the judge's calendar.

b. Referral to ADR for purpose of scheduling [mediation, arbitration, or ENE] to be completed within [30] days.

5. FURTHER CASE MANAGEMENT CONFERENCE

A further Case Management Conference will be held within thirty (30) days of unsuccessful settlement conference or ADR proceedings. Parties shall jointly propose a date on a Tuesday at 2:00 p.m. Pursuant to L.R. 16-10(d), at least seven (7) days before a further Case Management Conference, the parties must file a **Joint** Case Management Conference Statement.

6. PRETRIAL CONFERENCE

a. A final pretrial conference shall be held at least thirty (30) days before the date set for trial. The pretrial conference shall be held on Tuesday, [DATE] at 2:30 p.m. in the Eureka Federal Courthouse. Each party shall attend personally or by counsel who will try the case.

b. **Not less than thirty (30) days** prior to the date of the pretrial conference, all counsel or parties shall meet and fulfill the requirements of L.R. 16-10(b).

7. PRETRIAL FILINGS

a. **Not less than twenty (20) days** prior to the pretrial conference, counsel or parties shall:

(i) serve and file a **joint** pretrial statement pursuant to L.R. 16-10(b). The joint final pretrial conference statement shall include the disclosures required by Fed. R. Civ. P. 26(a)(3) as well as the following:

THE ACTION
- Substance of the Action
- Relief Prayed

FACTUAL BASIS FOR THE ACTION
- Undisputed Facts
- Disputed Factual Issues
- Agreed Statement
- Stipulations

DISPUTED LEGAL ISSUES

(List)

TRIAL PREPARATION

Witnesses to be Called

Exhibits, Schedules and Summaries

Trial

Estimate of Trial Time

Use of Discovery Responses at Trial

Further Discovery or Motions

TRIAL ALTERNATIVES AND OPTIONS

Settlement Discussions

Amendments - Dismissals

Bifurcation, Separate Trial of Issues

MISCELLANEOUS

Any other concerns of the parties

(ii) Serve and file **trial briefs**, which shall specify each cause of action and defense remaining to be tried along with a statement of the applicable legal standard (no opposition shall be filed);

(iii) Serve and file **motions in limine** which shall be contained in one document. Two (2) courtesy copies of motions in limine shall be provided. Motions in limine will be decided at the Pretrial Conference.

(iv) Serve and file a list of **discovery excerpts** from depositions (specifying the witness, page and line references), interrogatory answers, and requests for admission that will be offered at trial, and whether the excerpt is to be offered in lieu of testimony or for impeachment or rebuttal purposes.

(v) Serve and file a list of **witnesses** likely to be called at trial, in person or by deposition, other than solely for impeachment or rebuttal, with a brief statement describing the substance of the testimony to be given.

(vi) Serve and file a numerical **list of exhibits** (including demonstrative exhibits that may be admitted into evidence but not those that are purely illustrative), with a brief statement describing the substance and purpose of each exhibit and the name of the sponsoring witness.

(vii) For cases to be tried by jury, serve and file proposed **joint voir dire questions** and **joint jury instructions** (further instructions regarding jury instructions are below).

(viii) For cases to be tried by the court, serve and file **proposed findings of fact and conclusions of law**.

(ix) Serve and file a proposed **verdict form** which contains no reference to the submitting party.

b. No party shall be permitted to call any witness or offer any exhibit in its case in chief that is not disclosed in these pretrial filings without leave of court and for good cause.

c. **Not less than ten (10) days** prior to the final pretrial conference, counsel or parties shall serve and file any **opposition or objection** to those items required by paragraph 7(a) of this order. Additionally, counsel or parties shall file any objections to the qualifications of expert **witnesses** contained in the opposing party's witness list. Objections not filed as required will be deemed waived. No replies shall be filed. All motions and objections shall be heard at the pretrial conference unless otherwise ordered.

d. At least **two (2) week before trial**, the parties shall:

(i) **exchange exhibits** which shall be premarked (see label below), tabbed and in binders; and

(ii) deliver to chambers the original and two duplicate sets of all exhibits premarked, tabbed and in binders. Exhibits are not to be filed.

For numbering exhibits, the plaintiff shall use numbers and the defendant shall use letters.

Exhibit Label:

UNITED STATES DISTRICT COURT
NORTHERN DISTRICT OF
CALIFORNIA

Case No. ________________
Exhibit No. _______________
Date entered: _____________

RICHARD W. WIEKING, Clerk
By: ______________________
Deputy Clerk

8. JURY TRIAL

a. Counsel shall submit an **agreed upon set** of additional **voir dire** questions to be posed by the court. Any voir dire questions on which counsel cannot agree may be submitted separately. Counsel will be allowed brief follow-up voir dire after the court's questioning.

b. **Jury Instructions**. The following jury instructions from the Manual of Model Civil Jury Instructions for the Ninth Circuit will be given absent objection: 1.1-1.14, 1.18, 1.19, and 3.1-3.5. The Ninth Circuit Manual of Model Jury Instructions is available on the Ninth Circuit website at www.ca9.uscourts.gov (library tab > jury instructions > civil).

Counsel shall submit an agreed upon set of proposed case specific instructions, using the Ninth Circuit Manual where appropriate. The proposed joint instructions should include the Ninth Circuit model jury instructions listed above. Any instructions on which counsel cannot agree may be submitted separately. Counsel shall submit a table of contents with their jury instructions. Each requested instruction shall be typed in full on a separate page with citations to the authority upon which it is based; a title at the top of the page; check boxes next to given, modified, and withdrawn at the bottom of the page, as shown below; and a reference to the party submitting it. When a Ninth Circuit model jury instruction is used, the Ninth Circuit model jury instruction number and title shall be listed at the top of the page. In addition to the chambers copies, counsel shall email a Word or Word Perfect version of their jury instructions to the njvpo@cand.uscourts.gov.

[ ] Given
[ ] Modified
[ ] Withdrawn

9. All documents filed with the Clerk of the Court shall list the civil case number followed by the initials "NJV." One copy shall be clearly marked **chambers** copy.

DATED: ____________________

NANDOR J. VADAS
United States Magistrate Judge

B. Notice of Settlement Conference and Settlement Conference Order

IN THE UNITED STATES DISTRICT COURT
FOR THE NORTHERN DISTRICT OF CALIFORNIA

Plaintiff(s),	No. C ________ NJV
v.	**NOTICE OF SETTLEMENT CONFERENCE AND SETTLEMENT CONFERENCE ORDER**
Defendant(s). ________________________/	

TO ALL PARTIES AND COUNSEL OF RECORD:

The above matter was referred to Magistrate Judge Nandor J. Vadas for settlement purposes. You are hereby notified that a Settlement Conference is scheduled for **Date, at 10:00 a.m.**, in Courtroom 205 A, 2nd Floor, 514 H Street, Eureka, California.

It is the responsibility of counsel to ensure that whatever discovery is needed for all sides to evaluate the case for settlement purposes is completed by the date of the Settlement Conference. Counsel shall cooperate in providing discovery informally and expeditiously.

Lead trial counsel shall appear at the Settlement Conference with the parties. Any party who is not a natural person shall be represented by the person(s) with **unlimited** authority to negotiate a settlement. A person who needs to call another person not present before agreeing to any settlement does not have full authority. If a party is a governmental entity, its governing body shall designate one of its members or a senior executive to appear at the Settlement Conference with authority to participate in the Settlement Conference and, if a tentative settlement agreement is reached, to recommend the agreement to the governmental entity for its approval. An insured party shall appear with a representative of the carrier with full authority to negotiate up to the limits of coverage. Personal attendance of a party representative will rarely be excused by the Court, and then only upon separate written application demonstrating substantial hardship served on opposing counsel and lodged as early as the basis for the hardship is known but no later than the Settlement Conference Statement.

Each party shall prepare a Settlement Conference Statement, which must be LODGED with the undersigned's Chambers (NOT electronically filed) no later than fourteen (14) calendar days prior to the conference.

Each party shall also submit their Settlement Conference Statement in .pdf format to NJVPO@cand.uscourts.gov.

The Settlement Conference Statement need not be served on opposing counsel. The parties are encouraged, however, to exchange Settlement Conference Statements. If Settlement Conference Statements are exchanged, any party may submit an additional confidential settlement letter to the Court not to exceed three (3) pages. The contents of this confidential settlement letter will not be disclosed to the other parties.

The Settlement Conference Statement shall not exceed ten (10) pages of text and twenty (20) pages of exhibits and shall include the following:

1. A brief statement of the facts of the case.
2. A brief statement of the claims and defenses including, but not limited to, statutory or other grounds upon which the claims are founded, and a **candid** evaluation of the parties' likelihood of prevailing on the claims and defenses. The more candid the parties are, the more productive the conference will be.
3. A list of the key facts in dispute and a brief statement of the specific evidence relevant to a determination of those facts.
4. A summary of the proceedings to date and any pending motions.
5. An estimate of the cost and time to be expended for further discovery, pretrial and trial.
6. The relief sought, including an itemization of damages.
7. The party's position on settlement, including present demands and offers and a history of past settlement discussions. The Court's time can best be used to assist the parties in completing their negotiations, not in starting them. Accordingly, Plaintiff(s) must serve a demand in writing no later than fourteen (14) days before the conference and Defendant(s) must respond in writing no later than eight (8) days before the conference. The parties are urged to carefully evaluate their case before taking a settlement position since extreme positions hinder the settlement process.

It is not unusual for the conference to last three (3) or more hours. Parties are encouraged to participate and frankly discuss their case. Statements they make during the conference will not be admissible at trial in the event the case does not settle. The parties should be prepared to discuss such issues as:

1. Their settlement objectives.
2. Any impediments to settlement they perceive.
3. Whether they have enough information to discuss settlement. If not, what additional information is needed?
4. The possibility of a creative resolution of the dispute.

The parties shall notify Chambers immediately at (707) 445-3612 if this case settles prior to the date set for Settlement Conference. Counsel shall provide a copy of this order to each party who will participate in the conference.

IT IS SO ORDERED.

Date: ________________

____
NANDOR J. VADAS
United States Magistrate Judge

C. Order for Criminal Pretrial Preparation

IN THE UNITED STATES DISTRICT COURT
FOR THE NORTHERN DISTRICT OF CALIFORNIA

No. CR ________ NJV

Plaintiff,

ORDER FOR CRIMINAL PRETRIAL PREPARATION

v.

Defendant.
_______________________________/

Good cause appearing, IT IS HEREBY ORDERED that:

A. TRIAL DATE. Trial before the COURT/JURY shall be on DAY, DATE at TIME in Courtroom 205A.

B. TRIAL LENGTH. The estimated length of trial is _________.

C. MOTIONS. All motions shall comply with Criminal Local Rule 47-2 and shall be heard on DAY, DATE at TIME in Courtroom 205A. All motions shall be filed and served by _________. Any opposition shall be filed and served by ________. Before filing any motion, counsel for each party shall confer concerning any matter covered by Criminal Local Rule 16-1 relevant to the case, in particular subparagraphs (a),(b) and (c).

D. PRETRIAL CONFERENCE. A Pretrial Conference shall be held on ________ at _____, in Courtroom 205A. Not less than four days before the Pretrial Conference, counsel for the Government shall:

(1) Serve and file a trial memorandum briefly stating the legal basis for the charges and the anticipated evidence, and addressing any evidentiary, procedural or other anticipated legal issues, including but not limited to the matters listed in Criminal Local Rule 17.1-1(b)(1) - (15);

(2) Serve and file a list of all witnesses who may be called, together with a brief summary of the testimony of each;

(3) Serve and file proposed jury instructions on all substantive issues and on any procedural issue not adequately covered by the court's standard instructions (which are published in the Ninth Circuit Manual of Model Jury Instructions);

(a) any instruction contained in the Ninth Circuit Model Instructions Manual may be requested by designation of its number;

(b) each other instruction shall be requested by setting forth the instruction in full test on a separate sheet with reference to supporting legal authority;

(4) Serve and lodge a proposed form of verdict and proposed questions for jury voir dire; and

(5) Serve and lodge three sets of all exhibits to be offered at trial, together with a complete list of those exhibits. Each item shall be premarked using the form attached; generally, the government shall use numbers and the defendant shall use letters. (See attachment).

Not less than four days before the Pretrial Conference, defense counsel shall comply with subparagraphs (3) and (4) above, and, to the extent consistent with the defendant's right to an effective defense, with subparagraphs (1),(2) and (5) above.

In particular, counsel shall confer in advance and be prepared to discuss with the court any anticipated evidentiary objections or motions *in limine* and any means for shortening and simplifying the trial (*e.g.*, by stipulating to such matters as chain of custody, nature of substances, use of the mails, admissibility of copies, etc.)

E. CHALLENGES. The procedure for exercising peremptory challenges in Criminal Local Rules 24-2 and 24-3 will be observed absent objection by the parties.

F. COPIES. Each document filed or lodged with the court must be accompanied by a copy for use in the Judge's chambers.

G. TRANSCRIPTS. If transcripts will be requested during or immediately after trial, arrangements must be made with the Court Reporter at least one week before trial commences. Call (707) 445 3612.

H. CHANGE OF PLEA. Counsel shall give prompt notice to the United States Attorney and to the court of any intention to change a previously entered not guilty plea. A written plea agreement must be submitted at least one day in advance of the plea.

DATED: ____________________

____
NANDOR J. VADAS
United States Magistrate Judge

ATTACHMENT 5, EXHIBIT FORM

UNITED STATES DISTRICT COURT
NORTHERN DISTRICT OF
CALIFORNIA

Case No. ________________
Exhibit No. ______________
Date entered: _____________

RICHARD W. WIEKING, Clerk
By: ______________________
Deputy Clerk

Hon. Bernard Zimmerman
Magistrate Judge

Chambers Information
U.S. District Court, Northern District of California
Courtroom D, 15th Floor
450 Golden Gate Avenue
San Francisco, CA 94102

Scheduling Information
Judicial Assistant: (415) 522-2067

Civil Law and Motion	First and third Wednesdays at 10:00 a.m.
Criminal Law and Motion	Second and fourth Wednesdays at 1:30 p.m.
Case Management Conferences	Mondays at 4:00 p.m.

Judge's Biography
Federal Judicial Service:
-Magistrate Judge, U.S. District Court, Northern District of California, appointed in 1995.

Education:
-University of Chicago Law School, J.D., 1970

Professional Career:
-Legal Consultant, Third Constitutional Convention of the Commonwealth of the Northern Mariana Islands
-Private Practice, San Francisco, California
-Law Clerk, Honorable Frederick J.R. Heebe, U.S. District Court, Eastern District of Louisiana

I. Judge Zimmerman's Procedures and Practices

A. *Initial Discovery Order*

INITIAL DISCOVERY ORDER

All discovery in this matter has been referred to United States Magistrate Judge Bernard Zimmerman.

In the event a discovery dispute arises, the parties shall meet in person or, if counsel are outside the Bay Area, by telephone and make a good faith effort to resolve their dispute. Exchanging letters or telephone messages about the dispute is insufficient. The Court will not read subsequent positioning letters; parties shall instead make a contemporaneous record of their meeting using a tape recorder or a court reporter.

In the event they cannot resolve their dispute, the parties must participate in a telephone conference with the Court **before** filing any discovery motions or other papers. The party seeking discovery shall request a conference in a letter **filed electronically** not exceeding two pages (with no attachments) which briefly explains the nature of the action and the issues in dispute. Other parties **shall reply** in similar fashion within **two days** of receiving the letter requesting the conference. The Court will contact the parties to schedule the conference.

After the conference with the Court, if filing papers is deemed necessary, they should be filed electronically with the Clerk's Office, with one hard copy delivered directly to Magistrate Judge Zimmerman's Chambers (Room 15-6688). A chambers copy of all briefs shall be submitted on a diskette formatted in WordPerfect or e-mailed to the following address: **bzpo@cand.uscourts.gov.**

Dated: ________________

____
BERNARD ZIMMERMAN
United States Magistrate Judge

B. Standing Order

STANDING ORDER
FOR MAGISTRATE JUDGE BERNARD ZIMMERMAN

1. Parties shall consult and comply with all provisions of the Local Rules relating to continuance, motions, briefs, and all other matters, unless superseded by these Standing Orders.

2. Within 30 days of filing a complaint, plaintiff shall serve and file either a written consent to Judge Zimmerman's jurisdiction or a written request for reassignment to a district judge. Within 30 days of being served with a complaint or third party complaint, a defendant or third party defendant shall serve and file either a written consent to Judge Zimmerman's jurisdiction or a written request for reassignment to a district judge.

3. Civil law and motion is heard on the first and third Wednesdays of every month at 10:00 a.m. Criminal law and motion is heard on the second and fourth Wednesdays of every month at 1:30 p.m.

4. A copy of any brief or other document containing a legal citation **shall** be submitted to chambers on a diskette formatted preferably in WordPerfect 5, 6, 8, 9, X3 or sent by e-mail to: bzpo@cand.uscourts.gov. A chambers copy of any document **may** be submitted on CD-ROM with hypertext links to exhibits.

5. Any proposed order in a case subject to electronic filing shall be sent by email to: bzpo@cand.uscourts.gov. This address is to be used only for proposed orders unless otherwise directed by the court.

6. Unless expressly requested by the Court, documents should **not be faxed** to chambers but should be filed or lodged in accordance with the Local Rules of Court. The Court should not be routinely copied on correspondence between counsel.

7. Parties are reminded that most procedural questions are answered in the Local Rules or these Standing Orders. See especially Civil Local Rule 7-11. Parties should not contact Chambers for answers to procedural questions. The Local Rules are available for public viewing at the Court's internet site: http://www.cand.uscourts.gov.

8. Parties representing themselves should consult the *Pro Se* Handbook for District Courts, which is available for public viewing at the Court's internet site: http://www.cand.uscourts.gov.

9. Plaintiff is directed to serve a copy of these Standing Orders at once upon all parties to this action and upon those subsequently joined in accordance with provisions of Rules 4 and 5, Federal Rules of Civil Procedure, and to file with the Clerk of Court a certificate reflecting such service.

IT IS SO ORDERED.

Dated: January 13, 2009

BERNARD ZIMMERMAN
United States Magistrate Judge

II. Judge Zimmerman's Case Management Orders

A. Settlement Conference Order – Patent Case

IN THE UNITED STATES DISTRICT COURT
FOR THE NORTHERN DISTRICT OF CALIFORNIA

Plaintiff, v. Defendant. ________________________________/	No. C_________ ZM **SETTLEMENT CONFERENCE ORDER – PATENT CASE**

The above matter was referred to me for settlement purposes.

On _________, I conducted a telephonic hearing at which both sides were represented by counsel. With the consent of the parties and good cause appearing, **IT IS HEREBY ORDERED** that no later than _________, ______________________________, shall meet in person, preferably outside the presence of counsel, to discuss a resolution of this dispute. They shall meet in or in any other place to which they both agree. The principals are urged to explore a creative, business resolution of their dispute. If the case settles, the parties are to notify the Court immediately.

Each party shall provide the other informally, expeditiously and pursuant to Federal Rule of Evidence 408 with all information reasonably needed to further the progress of the settlement negotiations. Confidential information may be provided subject to a protective order.

If there is no settlement, it is **ORDERED** that a telephonic conference is scheduled for _________________, to discuss the status of the negotiations. Counsel for plaintiff shall get counsel for defendant on the line and call chambers at 522-4093. The principals need not participate.

It is further **ORDERED** that a Settlement Conference is scheduled for _______________________, in Courtroom G, 15th Floor, Federal Building, 450 Golden Gate Avenue, San Francisco, California 94102. Counsel who will try the case shall appear at the Settlement Conference with the party principals who met earlier. The negotiations will be principally among the party principals in my presence.

Each party shall prepare a Settlement Conference Statement, which must be served on opposing counsel and lodged (not faxed) with my chambers no later than seven calendar days prior to the conference. The Statement shall not be filed with the Clerk of the Court. The Statement **may** be submitted on CD-ROM with hypertext links to exhibits. Otherwise, the portion of exhibits on which the party relies **shall** be highlighted. The Settlement Conference Statement shall not exceed ten pages of text and twenty pages of exhibits and shall include the following:

1. A brief statement of the facts of the case.

2. A brief statement of the claims and defenses including, but not limited to, statutory or other grounds upon which the claims are founded.

3. A summary of any related litigation.

4. A summary of the proceedings to date and any pending motions.

5. An estimate of the cost and time to be expended for further discovery, pretrial and trial.

6. The relief sought, including an itemization of damages.

7. The parties' position on settlement, including present demands and offers and a history of past settlement discussions. The Court's time can best be used to assist the parties in completing their negotiations, not in starting them. So there is no confusion about the parties' settlement position, plaintiff must serve a demand in writing no later than fourteen days before the conference and defendant must respond in writing no later than eight days before the conference. The parties are urged to carefully evaluate their case before taking a settlement position since extreme positions hinder the settlement process.

Along with the Statement each party shall lodge with the court a document of no more than three pages containing a **candid** evaluation of the parties' likelihood of prevailing on the claims and defenses, and any other information that party wishes not to share with opposing counsel. The more candid the parties are, the more productive the conference will be. This document shall not be served on opposing counsel.

It is not unusual for conferences to last three or more hours. Parties are encouraged to participate and frankly discuss their case. Statements they make during the conference will not be admissible at trial in the event the case does not settle. The parties should be prepared to discuss such issues as:

1. Their settlement objectives.

2. Any impediments to settlement they perceive.

3. Whether they have enough information to discuss settlement. If not, what additional information is needed.

4. The possibility of a creative resolution of the dispute.

The parties shall notify chambers immediately if this case settles prior to the date set for settlement conference. Counsel shall provide a copy of this order to each party who will participate in the conference.

Dated: August 28, 2001

BERNARD ZIMMERMAN
United States Magistrate Judge

www.ingramcontent.com/pod-product-compliance
Lightning Source LLC
LaVergne TN
LVHW080007210926
848481LV00011B/2967
* 9 7 8 0 9 8 3 8 3 0 2 3 8 *